JOHN WESLEY
and
THE ANGLICAN EVANGELICALS
of the
EIGHTEENTH CENTURY

Previous work by the Author:

John Wesley and The Christian Ministry;
The Sources and Development of his Opinions
and Practice.
S.P.C.K. London, 1963.

JOHN WESLEY
and
THE ANGLICAN EVANGELICALS
of the
EIGHTEENTH CENTURY

A Study in Cooperation and Separation
With
Special reference to The
Calvinistic Controversies

* * *

ALBERT BROWN-LAWSON

The Pentland Press
Edinburgh • Cambridge • Durham

First published in 1994 by
The Pentland Press Ltd.
1 Hutton Close
South Church
Bishop Auckland
Durham

ISBN 1 85821 095 X

Typeset by CBS, Felixstowe, Suffolk
Printed and bound by Antony Rowe Ltd., Chippenham

ACKNOWLEDGMENTS

In a work of this kind, the author cannot claim sole credit but rather express his gratitude to many whose help and advice have proved so valuable.

My great indebtedness is to Professor (now Emeritus) K.H.D. Haley, F.B.A., of the Department of Mediaeval and Modern History in the University of Sheffield. For twelve years, with infinite patience, he supervised this study, giving unstinting advice and suggestions. I would also like to add the name of Professor (Now Emeritus) W.R. Ward, of the Department of History in the University of Durham who was my external examiner for his honest and constructive criticism in the final stage.

As on other occasions, I must mention the late Dr. E. Gordon Rupp, F.B.A., Dixie Professor of Ecclesiastical History in the University of Cambridge for his initial encouragement. As my former tutor at London, he it was, who first inspired my interest in Church History and never failed to be of great assistance in my subsequent studies.

The help, so readily given in respect of the final chapter, by the late Mr. Geoffrey Williams of the Evangelical Library, London; and of Mr. M.J. Micklewright for information, already acknowledged in the script; is gladly acknowledged as is the encouragement and interest afforded by the late Miss Stephanie Wright of the same library. To the Evangelical Library and all others whose services have been used, I offer my best thanks.

Finally, and by no means least, my thanks to the Pentland Press for attending so efficiently to each stage of the publication.

Other acknowledgements will be found in the script, often by way of footnotes.

This book was originally a thesis accepted by the University of Sheffield in the Faculty of Arts, for the degree of Doctor of Philosophy.

Albert Brown-Lawson
November, 1993.

TABLE OF CONTENTS

PREFACE

The purpose of this study, as the title and subtitle indicate, is to review the extent to which the evangelical clergy were prepared to cast in their lot with Wesley and his movement. Most of these evangelical clerics were of the Calvinistic persuasion, theologically. The term 'evangelical' was not used among them. Rather it was a nineteenth-century term for an eighteenth-century group. They would rather have regarded themselves simply as 'church-men' or 'gospel-men'. The term 'Methodist', however, soon became almost exclusively used for Wesley's movement together with any clergy who agreed both in respect of Church Order and theology, whether their ministry was regular or otherwise, e.g. Vincent Perronet of Shoreham who did not itinerate, or John P Dickinson who, as a clergyman, was also Wesley's assistant at his new chapel in City Road, London.

Conversely, the study also reveals the reasons why, before very long, most of the evangelical clergy declined to cooperate with Wesley.[1]

The subject seems naturally to fall into two major parts, namely: The difficulties created by the subject of Church Order and, secondly, theological differences. Each aspect of both these subjects will be dealt with fully in its turn. It is indeed, a study in cooperation *and* separation.

It will become increasingly clear that the instigator of irregular forms of ministry, namely George Whitefield, was also the one responsible for great and undue emphasis on the theological differences between the Evangelicals and the Methodists. The mutual influence of Whitefield and Selina, Countess of Huntingdon, can be seen to be the cause of the greater part of the dissensions of this period. Whitefield was the theological influence over Lady Huntingdon which together with her own authority and financial influence, she, in turn, exercised over the evangelical clergy. Whitefield, it will be noticed, kept in close touch with all these

---

1. William Grimshaw of Haworth, whilst not agreeing theologically with Wesley, remained loyal to him to the end of his life (d.1763). Furthermore he itinerated over a wide area to the end of his ministry.

men, many of whom from time to time quarrelled with Wesley either about Church Order or doctrine, much as, in respect of the latter subject, they would mostly describe themselves as 'moderate Calvinists'. Both Wesley and the Countess exercised almost a papal authority over their respective subjects with one major exception. Wesley was indisputably irregular in his ministry. For many years, the Countess cleverly contrived to exercise what was, in fact, an irregular ministry within the terms of the law, by using her supposed privilege of erecting 'propriety' chapels where she felt an evangelical ministry was required and then appointing to them her clerical friends as chaplains. Unfortunately, after a disastrous Ecclesiastical Court case, this system came to grief in 1783. By this time, there had taken place a prolonged controversy between Wesley and the Countess and her circle. Most of her clerical coadjutors left her to return to their regular ministries and her movement became another brand of Dissenters. The groups, both of the Countess and Wesley, remained completely aloof. Wesley, who was still technically within the Established Church in spite of the fact that he had broken so many of her cherished rules in respect of Church Order, vowed he would never leave her.

Of the two principal reasons for the divisions between Wesley and the Evangelicals, the theological one was the more predominant. The initial difference between the Wesleys and Whitefield set the tone for further and deeper quarrels which occurred long after reconciliation between them had been effected. The regrettable affair between John Wesley and James Hervey reveals clearly the almost unbelievable intrigue which existed in the midst of a mighty revival of religion. Hardly had this died away when the final outburst of controversy took place over a purely misunderstood minute of Wesley's 1770 Conference.

Over and above these two main reasons for the decline in cooperation between the two groups of Christians engaged in the same endeavour, namely reviving the Church and vital religion, there is demonstrated yet again the divisive nature of revival. The Reformation reformed but it also divided; the laudable work of William Booth had to launch out away from Methodism in which it was born as Methodism itself had done once Wesley had been placed in his grave. The same can be said of the

Pentecostal Revival in America and England in the early 1920s. Perhaps, for the most part, new wine cannot be contained in old bottles, but to give credit where it is due, the Calvinistic Evangelicals who remained faithful to the Established Church certainly were not altogether failures in making the old bottles reasonably fit to contain the new wine!

The second part of the study is really a record of the conflict of Calvinistic and Arminian views in their various facets. They seemed to be irreconcilable and they are still there today. Whether there could ever be a compromise worked out between them, will have to be left for the reader to judge for himself.

After more than two centuries, it will still make one marvel how, in the midst of revival in which the Love of God was preached to, and accepted by, others, there could coexist between the exponents so much acrimony, bitterness and vindictiveness. Also it is perturbing that when so much valuable work was being done, any time at all could be found to expend on such unedifying pursuits, as debating endlessly on the finer points of doctrine and in such a self-opinionated manner, the effects of which hindered the church, even to the present time.

The two views both had their firm basis in God's redeeming love for mankind. One was arrived at through cool, relentless logic; the other sprang from a very human view which saw God as Love and Mercy. The first by that very same logic limited the proffered salvation; the other opened the gates to all.

This study, then, retails the growth of a great revival of religion but because of the various events which marred it, also provides one of the saddest success stories in the history of the Christian Church.

PART ONE

CHURCH ORDER

CHAPTER ONE

THE EIGHTEENTH-CENTURY BACKGROUND

The Evangelical struck a characteristic note when he emphasized the necessity of personal religion. He insisted on the total depravity of human nature. The Image of God was not only defaced but effaced by the Fall. The only way of salvation for a man's soul was faith, and faith alone, in the atoning work of Christ which was a vicarious sacrifice, not only on behalf of, but instead of, man. It was God's grace, or undeserved mercy which effected man's salvation. Once saved, man was further justified by his faith; he was, he believed, regarded then by God as if he had never sinned. The work of the Holy Spirit was most important in conversion. Without His aid, man could not turn to God. With it, he proceeded from the time of conversion to sanctification, or the making 'holy' of man. It is this Spirit which 'witnessed', i.e. whereby man had an inner consciousness that he was in a state of grace. The Evangelical also believed in the plenary inspiration of all the canonical books of Holy Scripture.[1] These principles, then, were the burden or 'evangel' of the Evangelical, and, to him, there was but one way of discharging it, hence the characteristic emphasis on preaching. The Evangelical was primarily a preacher of good news, but often too, a pastor of those who, by heeding his message, had experienced this 'New Birth'.

---

1. Modern Evangelicals would also add the teaching of the immediacy of the Second Advent of Our Lord.

Broadly speaking, all Evangelicals were agreed on these basic ideas, but the interpretation of them was quite another matter and it will readily be seen that in this era, acrimonious dispute arose which later will require detailed investigation.

The main point of difference was the conception of man's salvation and the two conflicting schools of thought which found their respective champions in the Evangelicals on one hand, and the Wesleys on the other, were those of Calvin (or more correctly, Calvinism) and Arminius. These opposing views had been the ground of controversy in past generations.

To Calvin, salvation was of God and God only. This was a logical consequence of his major tenet: the Sovereignty of God. The whole system of Calvinism was developed in his *Institutes* from this one idea. No limits can be set on the Omnipotence of God,[2] for to do so would be to deny His freedom. There could be no place for any real choice on the part of a created being, and the place of man in the universe was necessarily decided by *divine* decree. This is explicit in Holy Scripture, which contains all that is necessary to know God and one's duty to one's neighbour.

In the conditions of innocence, man could attain blessedness through his own efforts, but the Fall was permitted by God and human nature became utterly depraved. All man desired and all that he did was sin. Even his good works, if he was outside the Christian Faith, were sins. The Christian's good works were not regarded as sin because of the imputation of the merits of Christ.[3]

So rigidly did Calvin hold the idea of God's sovereignty, that he seemed to overlook the divine attributes of justice and mercy. It did not occur to Calvin that God could be wholly love. Thus he went on quite logically to teach the doctrine of absolute predestination whereby God willed some to be saved and the rest to be damned. This implied not only

---

2.   Cf. *Institutes of the Christian Religion* (London, 1949, Book 1, ch.1): '...men are never duly touched and impressed with a conviction of their insignificance until they have contrasted themselves with the majesty of God.'

3.   Calvin J. *Institutes of the Christian Religion* (London, 1949, Book 3, ch. 14.)

that God willed the reprobation of those who were damned but also the sin which led to it.[4]

He who was elected to be saved was therefore subject to the irresistible grace of God, i.e. not a grace which man could resist, but rather a grace which *renews* the will, a process which could not fail to succeed. The very righteousness of Christ was *imputed* to him. This does not mean it was *imparted* to him, but that it was substituted for any pretence of righteousness a man may have thought he had. Furthermore, he was bound, come what may, to persevere to eternal life. He could never fall away.[5]

It was on the subject of predestination or election that Evangelicals became divided. It was also here where Calvinism differed from Calvin's own views. There were two views of election or predestination, namely sublapsarianism which was a doctrine of moderate Calvinism which taught that God permitted the fall of Adam without preordaining it. This is sometimes called infralapsarianism. The other view was that of supralapsarianism which taught that God willed the fall of Adam and the introduction of sin into the world. Election and predestination therefore preceded the Fall. These distinctions are interpretations of Calvin's successors. Furthermore, it is not fair to Calvin to identify his teaching purely with predestination and election as many have done. His five main emphases, namely predestination, irresistible grace, original sin, particular redemption and perseverance of the saints, were not peculiar to Calvin. Other reformers, such as Luther and Zwingli had stated them even less

---

4. *Ibid.* (Book 3, ch. 21, p.206): 'The predestination by which God adopts some to the hope of life, and adjudges others to eternal death, no man who would be thought pious, ventures simply to deny... By predestination we mean the eternal decree of God, by which he determined with Himself whatever he wished to happen with regard to every man. All are not created on equal terms, but some are preordained to eternal life, others to eternal damnation; and accordingly, as each has been created for one or the other of these ends, we say that he has been predestined to life or death...'

5. Augustine, on whom Calvin depended for many of his views, had previously taught that the elect had not only the gift of salvation, but also of final perseverance.

guardedly than Calvin, whilst Augustine had also held these views.

However, the Calvinistic system will be seen to be the result of stark and relentless logic, allowing no exceptions to any finding. Its weakness lay in the fact that it gave an inadequate conception of God who saved and Man whom he wished to save. SG Dimond makes the point here that Calvinism, like Deism, '...exalts the transcendence of God at the expense of His immanence, and reduces finite will to an illusion, making men even in his acceptance of Divine Grace, the passive creature instead of the consenting child of God.[6] There is too little place given to His love and compassion.

A further objection to the system is the tendency to antinomianism. If the elected saved was bound to persevere to the end, knowing that he would achieve his goal in due course, he could well set aside the obligations to the moral law. This, as will be seen, was one of the perils uppermost in the mind of Wesley in his subsequent controversies with the Calvinists.

Arminius, on the other hand, was strongly opposed to the deterministic logic of Calvin. To him, the sovereignty of God was not incompatible with free will in man. Christ died for all; the onus was upon man. He could accept or reject the offer of salvation. Both the sublapsarian and supralapsarian views of predestination, he regarded as unscriptural. Irresistible grace and the necessary perseverance of the elect were both denied. Prevenient grace, he emphatically asserted. This grace, a gift of God, was the illumination or inspiration of the Holy Spirit which precedes the free determination of man's will. It was man who made the choice. When received, it was the beginning of the process which led to his justification. He was justified by faith which in itself had merit.[7]

Arminianism, however, was not without its weaknesses. Critics of the system have seen in it tendencies both to Pelagianism, i.e. the view that

6. *Psychology of The Methodist Revival.* (Oxford, 1926, p.239.)
7. The term neonomianism can be applied to this idea, i.e. it introduces a new law - the law of grace whereby man who finds a legal righteousness as impossible, has a substitute in an evangelical righteousness accepted by God, though imperfect, for Christ's sake.

man took the initial and fundamental step by his own efforts towards salvation, apart from the assistance of God's grace, and also to Socinianism which taught that all Christian doctrines which could not be based on human reason, must be rejected.

* * *

Returning to the general ideas of the Evangelical's doctrines, none of them could rightly be described as a departure from the teaching of the Established Church. True, most of them appeared new to the greater part of the Church, for the simple reason that they had failed to be stressed from the majority of Anglican pulpits. John Wesley mentioned in his *Journal* for 13 September, 1739:

> 'A serious clergyman desired to know in what points we differed from the Church of England. I answered "To the best of my knowledge in none." He asked, "In what points then, do you differ from other clergy of the Church of England?" I answered, "In none from that part of the clergy who adhere to the doctrine of the Church."'[8]

And again, on 15 October, 1739:

> 'From Acts xxviii,22, I simply described the plain old religion of the Church of England, which is now almost everywhere spoken against under the new name of Methodism.'[9]

To what kind of Church did this visitation of evangelical revival come? First of all, it was an unspiritual church. Sufficient has already been written about the moral and spiritual standards of the nation in the early part of the eighteenth century and the inability of the Church to deal

---

8.   J.W.J. (Vol. 2, pp.274-5).
9.   *ibid.* (Vol. 2, p.293).

with the situation. Much also has been said about the absentee parsons whose interest in the accumulation of rich livings[10] took precedence over any interest in their flocks, and whose knowledge of the art of gambling exceeded that of the Scriptures. There were members of the episcopal bench who were rarely, if ever, to be seen in their dioceses.[11] When the clergy failed to fulfil their ordination vows, it was hardly to be expected that the people would take the initiative in setting standards of conduct. One notable Evangelical is credited with saying that a converted minister in the Establishment was 'as rare as a comet'.[12]

Secondly, it was an impoverished Church. The fourth Act of Uniformity of 1662 which insisted on the use of a revised liturgy in every church and chapel and also upon regular ordination of all clergy according to the Anglican rite before St Bartholomew's Day following, together with a formal declaration of their entire acceptance of the service book, resulted in the ejectment of 1,200 incumbents. In 1689, the Non-Juror controversy took place, which concerned some 400 clergy and a number of laymen. The clergy were ejected from their livings because they refused to take the oath of allegiance to William and Mary, contending that they had already taken the oath to James II and could not transfer their allegiance to another sovereign at the bidding of Parliament. Thus the Church was denied the services of the statesmen Sancroft, Archbishop of Canterbury; the saintly hymnwriter, Bishop Ken; Scholars like William Sherlock and Jeremy Collier. Equally grievous was the loss of able layman like Henry Dodwell and Henry Hyde, Earl of Clarendon. It was some time later that they were joined by William Law, scholar and mystic who was to exert a profound influence over the Wesleys and many of the Evangelicals.

---

10. e.g. Richard Watson, Bishop of Llandaff, who was also Professor of Divinity at Cambridge, Rector of Somersham and Archdeacon of Ely. On his promotion to Llandaff, he had to relinquish the archdeaconry and voluntarily gave up the living of Northwold. However, he was presented, in addition to those he retained, with the lucrative living of Knaptoft in Leicestershire.

11. Benjamin Hoadly, successively Bishop of Bangor, Hereford and Winchester, is a typical example.

12. i.e. Augustus Montague Toplady.

These Non-Jurors held services of their own and maintained an episcopal succession, but eventually the group died out.

Yet there were still good and conscientious clergy, many of them in poor country livings like the one immortalized in Goldsmith's *Deserted Village*, passing rich on forty pounds per annum. There was also the occasional bishop whose life and work stood out as a rebuke to his brethren.[13]

Another factor which must not be overlooked was that there had been in the early part of the century a shift of population coupled with the neglect of the State Church to re-church the people in new parishes.

Contemporary dissent showed no more a promising picture than did the Established Church. The great leaders such as Baxter, Owen and Howe were gone. Philip Doddridge and Isaac Watts were principal figures but their influence was exerted in purely local spheres. Moreover it must be remembered that dissenters still laboured under penal laws which operated to their disadvantage. The Toleration Act of 1689 had granted freedom of worship to dissenters on certain prescribed conditions. It also exempted them from the penalties of existing statutes, e.g. against 'conventicles' but they were still debarred from civil office until 1828 and also from attending the universities. Provided they accepted the doctrine of the Trinity and were willing to take the oaths of allegiance and supremacy, they were able to hold religious services without molestation, provided this was done with open doors. The Act had done little more than repeal the Conventicle Act of 1664 which had forbidden meetings to take place in private houses which were attended by more than five persons for the purpose of worship other than that prescribed by the Book of Common Prayer. They had won the freedom to worship as they pleased and register both their meeting houses and ministers with the

---

13. Such were Gilbert Burnet, Bishop of Salisbury, who alone spoke out against pluralities; Thomas Wilson, Bishop of Sodor and Man, a stern but pious prelate; Edmund Gibson, Bishop of London, who carried out a number of reforms in his diocese and had some sympathy with the Wesleys. In 1724 he had urged the clergy in his diocese to preach the doctrines peculiar to Christianity as 'a new way of obtaining forgiveness of sin and reconciliation with God'.

authorities, thus gaining recognition. They were quite content to live and worship quietly rather than proselytize and possibly come into conflict with authority.

It is not true to say that in the early eighteenth century, religious interest was completely dead. In fact, in the intellectual circles, it was very much alive as it had always been. Healthy opposition rarely fails to arouse any organization to rise to its own defence, that is, if it has any belief at all in its existence. A spirit of rationalism, or 'Deism' as it came to be known, arose both outside and within the Church. Natural religion, whilst advocating virtue and morality, found no place for revelation. The Divinity of Christ, The Scriptures and the fact of the Resurrection were among the targets for attack. All forms of evangelical Christianity were opposed. Religion was to be expressed in reason. Emotion could be dispensed with. Beginning with such writers as Hobbes and Locke, various aspects of Deistical thought found champions in able exponents like Nicholas Tindal, John Toland and Charles Blount. The Church, fortunately was not slow to defend itself and could produce equally able writers in Dr Richard Bentley, Dr Samuel Clarke and Bishop Warburton. A most popular apologist of orthodox thought was Thomas Sherlock, Bishop of Bangor, though the only writer who produced lasting works was Joseph Butler, successively Bishop of Bristol and Durham.

There can be no doubt who won this battle of intellect. The Church emerged victoriously, for Deism was never widely accepted in this country, as for example it was in France. The depicting of God as absentee landlord of the universe; the abandonment of belief in rewards and punishments and the doubting of a Divine Providence, failed. The battle, however, had been fought on reason alone. This meant that the emotional and practical side of religion was completely overlooked in the controversy.[14] There was, therefore, an element of defeat even in the

---

14. Gragg, C.E. *The Church and the Age of Reason* (London, 1960, Chapter 10, p.141) says 'The Hanoverian Church of England, despite its redeeming qualities, stood sorely in need of reform. The age of reason had forgotten certain fundamental human needs; natural religion might satisfy the minds of some, but the hearts of multitudes were hungry.'

victory.

The outcome of this was the repercussions on the life of the nation. Morals were sadly abandoned and the vicious felt free to follow their own desires and every man did that which was right in his own eyes.

Furthermore, religious earnestness was branded as fanaticism or 'enthusiasm' as it was termed. Hence the brutal opposition to the Methodists and other Evangelicals during the middle part of the century. After the defeat of 'Deism', peace was desired - peace from controversy and peace from 'enthusiasm'.

If the intellectual strata of the Church had made their contribution by rational defence, another group endeavoured to promote a serious interest in religion by fellowship. One cannot overstress the importance of the religious societies not only on account of the good that they did, but because they were the model on which were based the later weekly societies of the Methodists and the monthly and quarterly meetings of the Calvinistic Methodists. Dr Woodward in his *Account of The Religious Societies in the City of London* tells of the various groups associated with such names as Dr Horneck; Revd Thomas Tenison, Vicar of St Martin-in-the-Fields and the Revd William Beveridge, Vicar of St Peter's Cornhill. By the beginning of the eighteenth century, similar societies were to be found in many parts of the country. 8 March 1698 saw the founding of the Society for Promoting Christian Knowledge by Dr Thomas Bray,[15] to disperse Bibles and religious literature both at home and abroad. Both the SPCK and its offshoot, the Society for the Propagation of the Gospel, are still prominent societies within the Church of England at the present time. A society with a somewhat different purpose came into being in 1691. Named the Society for the Reformation of Manners, it undertook to suppress vice and immorality. Lawyers, magistrates, MPs and tradesmen, whether Anglicans or Dissenters united to root out wickedness in the community. Their methods included

---

15. Both John Wesley and his father, Samuel Wesley were members of the SPCK.

employing informers and instituting prosecutions under existing laws.[16] One of the London groups in 1736 claimed that 100,650 persons had been proceeded against in the 42 years of its existence. By 1740, however, most of these societies had become extinct. Whatever their temporary success may have been, their ultimate failure was inevitable. If the dull moralistic preaching (if any at all) from the average contemporary pulpit was not heeded, the application of force was not likely to have any lasting effect. The religious societies themselves were good and laudable enterprises but they catered for only a select group of people, as the arguments of the intellectual defenders interested only a minority. The masses were left untouched and revival (in the evangelical sense) seemed as far away as ever.

Turning from speaking of religious societies in general, it is now time to make reference to one in particular, namely the 'Holy Club' at Oxford. John Wesley gave his own account of its formation:

'In November, 1729, four young gentleman of Oxford, Mr John Wesley, Fellow of Lincoln College; Mr Charles Wesley, student of Christ Church; Mr Morgan, Commoner of Christ Church; and Mr Kirkham of Merton College; began to spend some evenings in a week together, in reading chiefly the Greek Testament. The next year, two or three of Mr John Wesley's pupils desired the liberty of meeting with them, and afterwards one of Mr Charles Wesley's pupils. It was in 1732 that Mr Ingham of Queen's College, and Mr Broughton of Exeter, were added to their number. To these, in April, was joined Mr Clayton of Brazen-Nose, with two or three of his pupils.

---

16. John Wesley preached a sermon in aid of the Society for the Reformation of Manners in 1763 at West Street Chapel, Seven Dials. Wesley and the Methodists had revived the society and it numbered 160 members, half of them Methodists. The text was the same as his father had used when he preached for them 65 years before: 'Who will rise up with me against the wicked?'

About the same time, Mr James Hervey was permitted to meet with them, and afterward, Mr Whitefield.'[17]

Three stages of its existence are clearly traceable. Firstly, up to 1730, the salvation of their own souls was their sole object. Besides the reading of the Greek Testament and group prayers, the university rule, now almost totally neglected, of attending the Holy Communion weekly, was faithfully kept. It was natural that this regular habit would cause some surprise to other students and earned for the Club the lasting nickname of 'Methodist'.[18]

Secondly, in 1730, a philanthropic outlook developed among the members due to William Morgan's visit to the castle gaol to see a man condemned for the killing of his wife and to speak to the debtors imprisoned there. At his suggestion, the other members[19] took up this work and also regularly visited and relieved the sick and poor of the district, providing a school for the education of underprivileged children.

The third stage began in 1732 when John Clayton joined them. Clayton was a native of Manchester and was close friend of Thomas Deacon, physician and Non-Juror who had founded the 'True British Catholic Church', publishing his own prayer-book. The latter was the result of a thorough research into the worship and practices of the early church and he was an authority on the apostolic constitutions and ecclesiastical canons. The influence of Deacon, through Clayton, on the group was clearly to be seen. The ministry of the Wesley brothers in America was coloured throughout by a desire to imitate the primitive church, which, at this time, had been the object of the group as a whole.

---

17. J.W. *Works* (Vol. 6, p.402) Wesley should have added the names of John Gambold and John Whitelamb.
18. This name had been given to an ancient sect of physicians because of their methodical treatment of their patients.
19. Samuel Wesley advised his sons to seek first the permission of the Prison Chaplain and the Bishop, which they did, and consent was readily given. Samuel was glad to hear of this work as he had visited the prison himself when a student at Oxford.

Through Clayton's encouragement, John Wesley published a discourse entitled *The Duty of Constant Communion* which later appeared as a sermon in 1788,[20] from which one may learn his views on that sacrament. Assisted by Clayton, he also published a collection of forms of prayer for every day of the week.[21] Wesley recorded in the *Journal* the effects of Clayton's joining of the group:

> 'The two points whereunto by the blessing of God, we had before attained, we endeavoured to hold fast: I mean the doing what good we can; and in order thereto, communicating as often as we have opportunity. To these, by the advice of Mr Clayton, we added a third - the observing the fasts of the Church, the general neglect of which we can by no means apprehend to be a lawful excuse for neglecting them.[22]

Many writers, including Wesley himself, referred to the Holy Club as Oxford Methodism. Some difficulty arises here as to how to relate the works of the Club to the evangelical activities of the Methodist people after 1738. Only one member of the Oxford Club could be correctly described as 'evangelical' during his Oxford days, in the light of the defining paragraphs which began this chapter. This was George Whitefield.[23] Son of a Gloucester innkeeper, he entered Pembroke College as a servitor in 1732 when eighteen years of age. Before coming up to the University, he had met with William Law's *Serious Call to a Devout and*

20. J.W. *Works* (Vol.10, pp.280-292.) In a footnote, he says: 'The following discourse was written above five and fifty years ago, for the use of my pupils at Oxford. I have added very little, but retrenched much; as I then used more words than I do now. But I thank God, I have not yet cause to alter my sentiments, in any point which is therein.'
21. Simon, J.S. *Studies of John Wesley* (Vol.1): *John Wesley and The Religious Societies* (London, 1921, pp.104-5) thinks that in the original edition there would be contained a series of questions for self-examination.
22. J.W.J. (Vol.1, p.101.)
23. Loane, Marcus L. *Oxford and the Evangelical Succession* (London, 1950, p.22) describes him as the Holy Club's most famous recruit.

Holy Life, but as soon as he was at Oxford, procured a copy for himself. 'God worked powerfully upon my soul, as He has since upon many others,' he said. 'By that and his other excellent treatise upon *Christian Perfection*.'[24] Whitefield was at the University a year before he joined with the members of the Holy Club. Particularly helpful to him was Charles Wesley who, he recorded, loaned him Franke's treatise *Against the Fear of Man: The Country Parson's Advice to His Parishioners* ('which was wonderfully blessed to me') and Scrougall's *Life of God in the Soul of Man* ('and though I had fasted, watched and prayed, and received the Sacrament so long, yet I never knew what true religion was, till God sent me that excellent treatise by the hands of my never-to-be-forgotten friend.') He continued:

> 'At my first reading it, I wondered what the author meant by saying, "That some falsely placed religion in going to church, doing hurt to no one, being constant in the duties of the closet, and now and then reaching out their hands to give alms to their poor neighbours." "Alas," thought I, "if this be not true religion, what is?" God showed me, for in reading a few lines further, that "true religion was union of the soul with God, and Christ formed within us" a ray of Divine light was instantaneously darted in upon my soul, and from that moment, but not till then, did I know that I must be a new creature...'[25]

This was in every sense an evangelical conversion. Of the other members of the Club, the same cannot be said at this stage. Striving to save their own souls, indeed they were, but not by faith, rather it was by good works and religious exercises. The subsequent ministry of the Wesley brothers until 1738 is proof sufficient in their case. A look at the careers of the other members is revealing.

---

24. It will be seen later how important was the influence of William Law on the Evangelicals.
25. G.W.J. (pp.46-47.)

James Hervey, a pupil of Wesley, did become a convinced Evangelical, but not for some considerable time. Take, for example, this letter from Hervey to his sister; from Lincoln College, 16 September, 1733:

> 'The seeds of piety, if implanted in our tender breasts, duly cherished and constantly cultivated, will bud and blossom even in the winter of our days... To walk humbly with our God, dutifully with our parents, and charitably with all, will be an inexhaustible source of never-ceasing comforts... it is now, dear sister, it is now in our power to make such happy provision as even then, in those forlorn circumstances, may charm our memories with ravishing recollections, and regale all our faculties with the continual feat of applauding conscience. What sweet complacency, what unspeakable satisfaction shall we reap from the contemplation of an uninterrupted series of spotless actions! No present uneasiness will prompt us impatiently to wish for our dissolution, nor anxious fear for futurity make us immoderately dread the impending stroke. All will be calm, easy and serene. All will be soothed by this precious, this invaluable thought, that by reason of the meekness, the innocence, purity, and other Christian graces which adorned the several stages of our progress through the world, our names and our ashes will be embalmed; the chambers of our tomb consecrated into a paradise of rest; and our souls white as our looks, by an easy transition, become angels of light...'[26]

A further letter to his sister written on 28 March 1734[26] encouraged her to continue reading 'holy and edifying books' and also to bear

---

25. Tyerman, Luke *The Oxford Methodists* (London, 1873, pp.204-5.) Also Hervey, James, *Works* (London, 1787, vol.5, pp.3 - 4.)
26. Hervey, James *Works* (London, 1787, Vol.5, p.5.)

obediently and humbly the chastisements of God by way of infirmities and they would '...bring forth in you the peaceable fruits of righteousness.' The following year,[27] in a letter to George Whitefield, he wrote in a different vein of the meritorious passion of Christ dying for mankind, but implied that the benefits could be obtained only through Holy Communion and in this letter he now deprecated salvation through good works. Whilst progressing in his soteriological views, he did not embrace the full evangelical faith until 1739.[28]

Charles Kinchin became Rector of Dummer and had successively employed Whitefield and Hervey as his curates and, after his Oxford days, embraced evangelical teaching in 1739. Had he lived, he might well have become an outstanding Evangelical, but he died in 1742, being in his latter years one of only eight Anglican incumbents who allowed Wesley the use of his pulpit.

Two Holy Club members, Benjamin Ingham, who accompanied the Wesleys on their American voyage, and John Gambold, became Moravians, the former finally starting a religious connexion of his own[29] and the latter resigning an Anglican living to become a Moravian bishop.

Thomas Broughton is worthy of special mention, but whether or not he could ever be regarded as belonging to the Evangelical fraternity, is debatable. Leaving Oxford, he officiated at Cowley, near Uxbridge and then become curate at the Tower of London. Due to Whitefield's influence, he had presented to him the lectureship of St Helen's, Bishopsgate Street. Feeling under an obligation to allow his friend the use of his pulpit, he soon lost his lectureship. After the conversion of the Wesleys, they soon found opposition in Broughton. Charles entered into numerous arguments with him between 1738 and 1742. Broughton strenuously denied that justification was by faith, and maintained it was by man's works. As late as 1743, Charles Wesley recorded that, as a result of a visit to Newgate

---

27. Tyerman L. *The Oxford Methodists* (pp.205-6) Also Hervey James Works (*op.cit.*) (Vol. 5, p.5.)
28. Tyerman (*op.cit.*) (pp.223-4.) See also *Evangelical Magazine* (1794, p.503.)
29. 'Inghamite' chapels are still in existence, mostly in the North of England, e.g. in Ossett, Yorkshire (Ingham's birthplace).

Prison:

> 'I found the poor souls turned out of the way by Mr Broughton. He told them, "There is no knowing our sins forgiven," and, if they could expect it, not such wretches as they, but the good people, who had done so and so. As for his part, he had it not himself; it was plain they could not receive it.'[30]

It is interesting to note that Henry Venn, who was a most prominent Evangelical in the church, was offered the living of Wotton, but an 'anonymous' letter to the patron, Sir John Evelyn, recommended that Broughton was more worthy of preferment. Broughton was instituted, and, as Tyerman argues,[31] if Broughton had still persisted in his opposition to evangelicalism, Venn would definitely not have taken such an action. Broughton's most useful work, however, was that of secretary to the SPCK, a post which he held until his death in 1777.

As for Clayton, he never changed his views and remained a ritualistic High-Churchman. Once the Wesleys had relinquished the notion of salvation by works, the friendship ceased. In 1755, John visited Manchester and mentioned that he heard, with appreciation, Clayton's reading of the service, but there was no indication of any friendly intercourse. A year later, Charles's words are significant:

> '1756. Tuesday, 26 October. My *former* friend, Mr Clayton, read prayers at the Old Church, with great solemnity.'
> 'Saturday, 30 October. I dined with my candid friend and censor, Dr Byrom. I stood close to Mr Clayton in church (as all the week past), but not a look would be cast towards me; so stiff was his parochial pride.'[32]

---

30. Tyerman, Luke *The Oxford Methodists* (London, 1873, pp.346-7.)
31. *ibid.* (p.348.) The letter was, of course, written by Venn. See also Venn, J. *Life of Henry Venn* (London, 1837, pp. 18-9.)
32. Jackson, Thomas *Life of the Revd Charles Wesley, MA* (London, 1839, Vol. 2, p.124 and p.128.)

Little need be said of the remainder of the Oxford Methodists, for they soon faded into obscurity. John Hutchins became a Moravian; John Whitelamb, who married a sister of the Wesleys, became Rector of Wroote, which was part of their father's old living. Christopher Atkinson became incumbent of Thorpe Arch, near Wetherby in Yorkshire and nothing more was heard of him. The briefest word will suffice about the unfortunate Westley Hall. It would appear, that on the surface, he feigned evangelical fervour, but, as Tyerman describes him,[33] he proved to be 'a hawk among the doves of the Wesley family'. Having married a sister of the Wesleys, his subsequent immoral conduct was a perpetual embarrassment to all concerned.

It must, however, be mentioned at this juncture that a revival of religion had already been taking place some years before the members of the Holy Club had been enlightened, or even before the society was formed. It was to be seen in America, Wales and Scotland. As early as 1730-32, it was witnessed in the Presbyterian Church in Freehold, New Jersey under the ministry of the Revd John Tennant. In 1734, Jonathan Edwards became instrumental in a similar revival in Northampton, New England, which was, in due course, to have its effects in England.

Nearly twenty years before the conversion of the Wesleys, a Welsh clergyman, Griffith Jones, preached with great success in his parish at Llandowror in Carmarthenshire. Subsequently he influenced another clergyman, Daniel Rowlands,[34] curate of Llangeitho where his brother was vicar. Equally important was the conversion in a different part of the principality, of a young schoolmaster, Howell Harris, at Talgarth. A layman he remained, but devoted himself to itinerant preaching and by 1736 had both achieved outstanding success with the masses and the hostility of the authorities, ecclesiastical and secular. Another Welsh preacher, a clergyman and convert of Griffith Jones, was Howell Davies. Because of his evangelicalism, he was relieved of his curacy at Llysyfran in Pembrokeshire. Henceforth he became an itinerant preacher, officiating

---

33. His conversion was in 1733, the same year as Whitefield's.
34. The revival in Wales will be dealt with more fully in chapter 3.

wherever he was invited, confining his labours mostly to that same county.

This beginning of revival was confined to Wales, furthered by these four principal Evangelicals who preached in their own tongue to their own people. Possibly this is the reason that the revival spread no further than the land of their fathers. England was as yet untouched.[35]

The awakening in Scotland was contemporary with that of the work of the Wesleys and Whitefield but there was no connection between the two. The Scottish revival began with the preaching of a certain James Robe at Kilsyth. Another beginning took place at Cambuslang and the movement quickly spread to the larger towns and cities. An atmosphere was thus engendered into which Whitefield was later to enter so successfully. It was also one in which Wesley was to make such small progress.

Nevertheless, it is important to note that apart from the revivals in Wales, Scotland and America, light was dawning on a number of men who were to feature so prominently in evangelicalism of this period. Moreover, their own conversion was in no wise connected with these revivals or with the Oxford Holy Club, or even later Methodism. In any case, as has already been pointed out, the Holy Club cannot correctly be regarded as evangelical. Two common factors emerged from this - the literary influence (as in the case of Whitefield) and the personal contact.

Of many who could be mentioned here, a word about the more prominent ones must suffice. One of the most famous was William Grimshaw who, after ordination, was made curate of Todmorden in West Yorkshire. Later, he became Vicar of Haworth of Brontë fame. Spiritual guides he had none. In 1734, he became more serious about religion. It was not, however, until 1745, when he had read Brook's *Precious Remedies against Satan's Devices* and, more importantly, Owen *On*

---

35. Binns, L. Elliott *The Early Evangelicals: A Religious and Social Study* (London, 1953, pp.13ff) had an interesting note furnished by a parishioner of Dr Martin's at St Breward whose father recalled that when he was young, one could have walked a mile to church on the heads of the people in the lanes who were going to worship. Whether this could be regarded as a revival of religion in Cornwall or simply tradition, one cannot say.

Justification that he fully embraced the evangelical position.

Descended from a line of clergymen, Henry Venn[36] had been in the church's ministry for about five years until he possessed that satisfaction of soul characteristic of the Evangelicals. Personal influence was absent, but basic in his reading was the independent study of the Bible and Law's *Serious Call*.

Personal influence is undisputed in the case of Augustus Montague Toplady, a student at Trinity College, Dublin. He was the only instance of those listed here, whose conversion was due to direct preaching. The preacher concerned was James Morris. The only information available about this Evangelist is that he lacked refinement! His labours in 1755, however, brought about the transformation of one whose short life was to feature greatly, even if notably in controversy, in the English revival of religion.

A totally different Evangelical to whom reference must also be made, is John Berridge. He became serious in his religious thoughts early in life through contact with another boy. He lapsed, but again became serious in 1749 and adopted the evangelical faith in 1757, a fact attributable, it appears, purely to prayer and reading.

Rowland Hill, a clergyman who received no higher orders in the church other than deacon, experienced conversion when but a boy, the sole means being his brother Richard. Both brothers feature prominently in the final Calvinistic controversy.[37]

One Evangelical, the circumstances of whose conversion cannot be traced, is William Romaine. It appears that from the earliest days, having been brought up in a godly home, he could be said to have been of the evangelical persuasion.

There is no evidence of any radical change in views or the undergoing

---

36. Born 2 March 1724 at Barnes, Surrey. Educated Jesus and St John's College Cambridge and later Fellow of Queen's.
37. Richard was educated at Westminster School and Magdalen College Oxford (MA 1754). He attacked the University for expelling evangelical undergraduates in 1768. Rowland was educated at Shrewsbury, Eton and St John's College, Oxford (BA 1769).

of any noticeable emotional experience. His life and ministry are a classic example that such an experience is not *always* essential. A stranger fact about Romaine is that he was at Oxford precisely at the same time as the Wesleys and other members of the Holy Club. There is no evidence that he had any contact with them, due no doubt, as Ryle suggests, to his preoccupation with his literary pursuits, outstanding scholar as he was.[38]

The most remarkable conversion of all is that of John Newton,[39] occurring after an adventurous and profligate life at sea, first of all as seaman and then master, of slave ships. He came under the influence of the Methodist preaching and later that of Whitefield, in Liverpool, where he was subsequently employed as a tide surveyor, 1755-1760. After ordination (which he procured with difficulty) he was successively curate at Olney where he was a good friend of William Cowper, the poet, and later became Rector of St Mary Woolnoth, London.

There were many other Evangelicals[40] all of whom arrived at their theological position in similar ways and whose names will appear in conjunction with those of the Wesleys in the following pages.

Before concluding this chapter, one last point of interest is a common literary influence shared by many of these men, namely that of William Law. Law (1686-1761) was a prolific writer, and his writings fell into three sections, namely controversial, devotional and mystical. His *Serious Call to a Devout and Holy Life. Adapted to the State and Condition of all Orders of Christians*, first published in 1728, is an appeal for Christian holiness and contains such characters as the 'men of affairs' and the 'women of fashion'. Samuel Johnson claimed that his own attention to religion was first drawn by the reading of this book. Wesley said it could hardly be excelled, if it be equalled, in the English tongue,

---

38. Born at West Hartlepool, 25 September 1714, of French Protestant stock. Educated, Houghton-Le-Spring Grammar School, Hertford College, Oxford and Christ Church, Oxford. (MA October 1737.)
39. Born 1725. Converted 10 March 1748.
40. See Chapter Four for Samuel Walker of Truro. He was converted through the influence of a schoolmaster belonging to his church.

either for beauty of expression or for justice and depth of thought. Law's *Treatise on Christian Perfection* is a work on practical morality, possessing both charm and beauty, calling for a change in man's nature, a renunciation of the world and self-denial, and the necessity of Divine grace. It was first published in 1726. These two works were far-reaching in their influence on the Wesleys and the Evangelicals. The *Serious Call* was used as a text book for devotional exercises by members of the Holy Club. The *Treatise on Christian Perfection* aroused Wesley's interest in the doctrine of Christian Perfection which was to become one of their major emphases.[41] Besides the Wesleys and the other Oxford Methodists, including Whitefield and Hervey, the *Serious Call* had a profound effect, in particular, on Venn, Newton, Thomas Scott, Thomas Adam and others.

However, Law's later views were to separate him from Wesley and the Evangelicals. Whilst Wesley continued to respect Law, he differed from him when the latter adopted mysticism. Maybe this was due to a misunderstanding by Wesley, or to the fact that his association previously with Moravian mysticism had prejudiced him. Wesley felt that Law attached no importance to the Atonement or to justification by faith. Henry Venn[42] had early awaited Law's two works: *The Spirit of Love* and *The Spirit of Prayer* (2 Vols) but 'he read till he came to the passage wherein Mr Law seemed to represent the blood of Christ as of no more avail in procuring our salvation, than the excellence of his moral character. "What," he exclaimed, "does Mr Law thus degrade the death of Christ, which the Apostles represent as a sacrifice for sins, and to which *they* ascribe the highest efficiency in procuring our salvation! Then farewell such a guide! Henceforth I will call no man master."'

Hervey, too, expressed later dissatisfaction with Law's outlook. Writing to Lady Shirley, he said:

'Mr Law's last book I have not seen; neither indeed do I desire

---

41. See Chapter Ten.
42. Venn, John L. *Life of Henry Venn*, MA (London, 1837, pp.19-20.)

to see it; especially if it be written in the same strain as one of his letters upon Divine Love, which happened to fall in my way. *Fall in my way!* No, truly. It did not *fall*, but soared. Soared in mystical flights and metaphysical subtilties, far too high for my grovelling apprehension to follow. And not *in my way*, but as far remote from my trite and vulgar way of thinking, as Britain is from Japan...'[43]

Nevertheless, Law, by the appeal of the two works first mentioned, was a forerunner of the Revival - but never an actor in it. He stood aloof from its subsequent course and disassociated himself from it.[44]

43. Hervey, James *Works* (London, 1787, Vol. 6, pp.377-8.)
44. For the Wesleys' relationships with Law, see: Baker, Eric W. *A Herald of The Evangelical Revival: A Critical Enquiry into the Relation of William Law to John Wesley and the Beginnings of Methodism* (London, 1948.) Also Green, J. Brazier *John Wesley and William Law* (London, 1946.)

CHAPTER TWO

THE WORLD PARISH (I)

It seems a strange coincidence that the ship which was carrying Whitefield to his new appointment in America should pass within sight of the one which was bearing John Wesley from the same continent, and neither knew of it until John landed at Deal in January, 1738. Charles Wesley had already arrived at Deal on 2 December 1736 with the intention of 'procuring more labourers for America', but he did not return. Still sore about the treatment he had received in Georgia, and learning that Whitefield was beginning his voyage there, John decided by 'lot'[1] to write to him dissuading him from his American ministry. Whitefield gave his answer thus:

Downs, 1 February 1738

'I received the news of your arrival (blessed be God!) with the utmost composure, and sent a servant immediately on shore to wait on you, but found that you were gone. Since that, your kind letter has reached me. But I think many reasons may be

---

1.   Wesley had learnt the principle of sortilege from the Moravians. See his *Principles of a Methodist Further explained* (London, 1746.) for his justification of this practice. The writing of his letter to Whitefield as a result of casting lots was to be brought up by the latter during a later disagreement over doctrine.

urged against my coming to London. For, first, I cannot be hid
if I come there; and the enemies of the Lord will think I am
turning back, and so blaspheme that holy name wherewith I
am called. Secondly I cannot leave the flock committed to my
care on shipboard, and, perhaps while I am at London the ship
may sail. Thirdly, I see no cause for not going forwards to
Georgia. Your coming rather confirms (as far as I can see)
than disannuls my call. It is not fit that the colony should be
left without a shepherd. And though they are a stiffnecked and
rebellious people, yet as God hath given me the affections of
all where I have been, why should I despair of finding His
presence in a foreign land?'[2]

Had Whitefield yielded to the suggestion of Wesley, it is hard to
conceive the difference this would have made to the religious development
in that continent.

What is difficult to understand about Wesley's discouraging of
Whitefield is that in the first instance, Whitefield was going to America
as a result of John's own challenge. He had written to Whitefield and the
other Methodists who remained at Oxford, on 10 September 1736 stating
the need for assistance in the work at Savannah:

'Here is none to search out and lay hold on the *mollia
tempora fandi,*[3] and to persuade him to save his soul alive...
Does any err from the right way? Here is none to recall him...
Is any wavering? Here is none to confirm him. Is any falling?
There is none to lift him up. Who will rise up with me against
the wicked? Who will take God's part against the evil-doers...
Does your heart burn within you to turn many others to
righteousness? Behold the whole land, thousands of thousands
are before you! I will resign to any of you, all or any part of

---

2.   Tyerman, Luke *The Life of George Whitefield* (Vol. I, London, 1890, p.115.)
3.   i.e. 'Apt times for speech'.

my charge. Choose what seemeth good in your own eyes...'[4]

Whitefield mentions in his Journals that he had received a personal letter from John sometime in December, 1736[5] which said:

'Only Mr Delamotte is with me, till God shall stir up the hearts of some of His servants, who, putting their lives in His hands, shall come over and help us, where the harvest is so great, and the labourers so few. What if thou art the man, Mr Whitefield?'

George had been considering going to Georgia for some time and now he had decided to go. He was convinced that his decision was the right one, for, according to the *Journals,*[6] this very letter seems to have constituted the call. What was more, he argued, his friend Kinchin had been appointed Dean of Corpus Christi College and would therefore reside at Oxford and could continue the prison work. Hervey was ready to serve the cure of Dummer. By going to America, he could be under the tuition of Wesley. There was also the opportunity of missionary work amongst the Indians. There would also be the chance of 'retirement and privacy' in which he delighted. In any case, to say the least, a sea voyage would do him no harm!

He had just completed a six weeks' supply at Dummer in Hampshire for Kinchin. By way of temptation, '...a very profitable curacy in London' had been offered to him, but he had declined. Until the time of his embarkation, he preached in churches up and down the country with great acceptance - at least with the laity. There were growing objections by the clergy - the main point being that he preached regeneration. For a short time he assisted as locum at Stonehouse in Gloucestershire. A

---

4. J.W.L. (Vol.1, p.205.) Whitefield had already written to Wesley reporting on the Oxford Methodists and the fact that he himself was supplying for Broughton as curate of the Tower.
5. G.W.J. (p.79.) There is no mention of this in Wesley's *Letters*.
6. G.W.J. (p.80.)

number of his sermons were now published by popular request, and, as a preacher, it seems he could have had no equal. It is all the more amazing when one realizes that, at the time, he was only twenty-two years of age.[7]

Whitefield's first ministry in Georgia was brief but apparently very successful. That he fully appreciated the work of John and Charles Wesley is abundantly clear from his *Journals*:

> 'Surely, I must labour most heartily, since I come after such worthy predecessors. The good, Mr John Wesley has done in America, under God, is inexpressible. His name is very precious among the people: and he has laid such a foundation, that I hope neither men nor devils will ever be able to shake. Oh, that I may follow him, as he has Christ.'[8]

By November, 1738, he was in England, having travelled via Ireland where he was received by the Church authorities. The main reasons for his early return were to obtain Priest's Orders and to raise money for a projected Orphan House in America.

He returned to find the Wesley brothers had undergone a spiritual experience which was to change their whole lives and work - 21 May at , appropriately enough, Whitsunday, in the case of Charles, and 24 May in respect of John. After the awakening, or so more popularly known, 'conversion', the brothers preached everywhere a pulpit was offered them. At this time, there was no hint whatever of any irregularity on their part. All the preaching was done in churches only. From the decisive 24 May to the end of that year, John preached (according to the *Journal*) a total of twenty-eight times. It must, of course, be pointed out that from

---

7.   Bishop Benson of Gloucester, as an act of kindness and encouragement, had ordained Whitefield into Deacon's orders when he was under age (i.e., when he was twenty-one). It was during the good bishop's last illness that Lady Huntingdon assured him that of all his ordinations, he would regret that of Whitefield's the least.

8.   G.W.J. (p.157.)

June until September of this period, he was visiting the Moravian settlement at Herrnhut in Germany.

Charles, on the other hand, became temporary and unofficial curate of the Revd George Stonehouse, Vicar of Islington in July, 1738.[9] He also officiated in other London churches, including St Margaret's Westminster, St John's Clerkenwell, St Botolph's, St George's, St Clement's and St Helen's, Bishopgate. Also, on one occasion, he preached in Westminster Abbey and afterwards assisted at Holy Communion. Perhaps his most praiseworthy ministry during this period was exercised among the condemned felons in Newgate Gaol.

However, this usefulness in orthodox circles was not to continue for long. Complaints had been made against the Wesleys to the Bishop of London, Dr Gibson, before whom they duly appeared to give an account of themselves. The complaints were (a) that they preached an absolute assurance of salvation and on this point the Bishop agreed with them, though it is doubtful whether his notion of assurance was theirs; (b) That they were Antinomian because they preached justification by faith alone; (c) That they rebaptized those who had received only Dissenter's baptism. (In this, of course, they were definitely in error. His Lordship was certainly not very pleased about this practice); (d) That their religious societies were conventicles. The Bishop did not think they were but admitted he could not speak authoritatively and bade them read the law concerning this for themselves.

Charles was soon in trouble at Islington, namely with the churchwardens, on account of his preaching. Stonehouse, weak man as he was, obligingly gave way and dismissed his new 'curate'. George Stonehouse was an interesting figure. He could rightly be called one of the early Evangelicals of the century, but on 1 July, 1740, sold his living of which his family were the impropriators and joined the Moravians,

9.   According to Crawshaw, Article *Was Charles Wesley ever Curate of Islington?* it has been proved that there was nothing official about this appointment. In any case, Charles was later in trouble with the churchwardens for not having a local licence. (W.H.S. Proc. Vol V. pp 238-9.)

whom afterwards he left. He told John Wesley on 5 June 1740,[10] according to the *Journal* that he was selling his living because no honest man could officiate in the Church of England and that no man with a good conscience could join in the prayers of the Church because they were full of 'horrid lies'. It is a pity that Stonehouse took this course for had he continued at Islington and possessed a stronger character, his church would have been a great centre for evangelical endeavour in London. It is a strange turn of history that later, this very church has become a centre for modern evangelicalism of the Anglican church.

Early in 1739, John found himself excluded from almost all Anglican pulpits in London. In that year he preached only thirteen times in Anglican churches and assisted on one occasion only, according to the *Journal*. He was refused the use of a pulpit on six occasions. Most of the services at which he preached were held in churches in Bristol or in the South-West. Tyerman[11] is surely wrong when he gives only eight churches in which he was allowed to preach. The reference is more likely to be to London churches only for he never mentions the Bristol churches.

Whitefield, who had returned to London by 8 December 1738, was received favourably by both the Archbishop of Canterbury and the Bishop of London.[12] A few churches welcomed him as preacher, but he complained on Sunday, 10 December that '...five churches had already denied me, and some of the clergy, if possible, would oblige me to deport out of their coasts.'[13] Tyerman[14] thinks the reason for this attitude was the result of Whitefield's publishing his *Journals of a Voyage from London to Gibraltar, and from Gibraltar to Savannah*, which, '...whilst full of devotion, faith and godly zeal...yet contained words, phrases and

---

10. Stonehouse later earned a reputation as a skilful inventor.
11. Tyerman, Luke *The Life and Times of John Wesley* (London, 1871, Vol.1, p.224.)
12. The Bishop of London was also responsible for the work in the American colonies.
13. G.W.J. (p.193.) He found himself excluded from all the London churches except St Helen's Bishopgate, Christ Church, Spitalfields, Wapping Chapel and Islington Parish Church. He was soon to be excluded from the latter for the same reason as Charles Wesley, namely for not having a diocesan licence.
14. Tyerman, Luke *The Life of George Whitefield* (London, 1890, Vol.1, p.180.)

sentences which it was unwise to print...there was a modicum of pious egotism, and there were rapturous expressions unfamiliar to Pharisaic ears...' Another reason, Tyerman thinks, may well have been that the Wesleys were faithful and ardent friends. The latter had by now been in full and open fellowship with the Moravians, who, after all, had been instrumental in their spiritual awakening. It was, however, a fellowship which was not to last. Furthermore, the Wesleys' doctrine of justification by faith appeared, curiously enough, to have given offence to many members of the Established Church.

A letter sent by Wesley to the Moravians in Germany, entitled *To the Church at Herrnhut*, reveals that Whitefield, Charles and himself were by no means alone in their evangelistic endeavours and doctrines, not even in the Church of England:

> 'Nor hath He left Himself without other witnesses of His grace and truth. Ten ministers I know now in England who lay the right foundation - 'The blood of Christ cleanseth us from all sin'. Over and above whom I have found one Anabaptist, and one, if not two, of the teachers among the Presbyterians here, who, I hope, love the Lord Jesus Christ in sincerity, and teach the way of God in truth.'[15]

Opposition and persecution were now common to both Whitefield and the Wesleys. As J.C. Ryle points out,[16] 'Churchwardens who had no eye for drunkenness and impurity, were filled with intense indignation about what they called "breaches of order",' and 'even Bishops who could tolerate Arianism, Socinianism and Deism, were filled with indignation

---

15. J.W.L. (Vol.1, p.261.) Note that Wesley does not refer to Presbyterian *ministers* but *teachers*. See also Gillies, John *Memoirs of the Life of the Reverend George Whitefield, MA* (London, 1772, p.44.) He mentions others who are 'labouring', especially Benjamin Ingham in the North.

16. Ryle, J.C. *Select Sermons of George Whitefield* (London, 1954 edition.) Preface on *George Whitefield and His Ministry* (p.18.) Dr Ryle was the first bishop of Liverpool and an avowed Evangelical.

at a man who fully declared the atonement of Christ and the work of the Holy Ghost.'

Hostility to both then began to take written forms. Against Whitefield's insistence on the New Birth, in particular, a Revd Tipping Silvester published a sermon which he had preached entitled: *Sermon Recommended to the Religious Societies* (Oxon. 1738). His main point was that men are born again at their baptism. According to the title-page, this was intended to be read by the Religious Societies with which, as the author would know, the Wesleys and Whitefield were closely connected and for whom they had often preached. Intended also for the Societies was another literary assault against Whitefield, namely *Remarks on the Reverend Mr Whitefield's Journal.*[17] Among other accusations was the significant one of '...placing religion in perturbation of mind, possessions of God, ecstatic flights, and supernatural impulses...' and of '...insinuating that he was a peculiar favourite of heaven.'[18]

The writers would have in mind the newly formed society in Fetter Lane. The Editor of Whitefield's *Journals* is not quite correct when he declares[19] that John Wesley founded it. It was a joint foundation on 1 May 1738 by John and Charles Wesley, Henry Piers, (Vicar of Bexley and a clergyman whose conversion was due to Charles Wesley's influence) and James Hutton, who published many of Wesley's works.[20] The meetings were first held at Hutton's house in Little Wild Street and then in an old Nonconformist meeting house together with the house adjoining at No 32 Fetter Lane. Rules for the society were drawn up on the advice of Peter Boehler, the Moravian. The Wesleys, Whitefield, Piers and

---

17. The full title was *Remarks on the Reverend Mr Whitefield's Journal. Wherein his main Inconsistencies are pointed out and his Tenets considered. The whole shewing the dangerous tendency of his Doctrine. Addressed to the Religious Societies. Ex tuo ipsius ore te damnebo.* (London, 1738.)
18. The Journals of Whitefield had certainly contributed much to the opposition to the Wesleys and himself. This particular quotation was obviously one of the first published statements indicating his Calvinistic position.
19. G.W.J. (p.196.)
20. Tyerman, Luke *The Life and Times of John Wesley* (London, 1871, Vol.1, p.301.)

Hutton later left the society when Philip Molther, another Moravian infected it with his weird notions of 'stillness', i.e. that until a man has faith, he should leave off all the means of grace, such as praying, Bible study and partaking of the Holy Communion.

In respect of Wesley's doctrine of assurance, i.e. that true faith was always followed by the assurance of the forgiveness of sins, the Revd Arthur Bedford, Chaplain to His Royal Highness, Frederick, Prince of Wales, printed a sermon which he had preached in St Lawrence Jewry, London.[21] In it he claimed that to have received his 'assurance' would inevitably lead to spiritual pride which, in turn, would have bad results. Instead of bringing a man nearer heaven, it drove him further away. If he were to have this assurance, he prayed that he might always be able to conceal it from others and would feel obliged to thank God for it in private only!

Whitefield describes in his *Journals*[22] a conference which he held at Islington:

'...concerning several things of very great importance, with seven true ministers of Jesus Christ, despised Methodists, whom God has brought together from the East and the West, the North and the South. What we were in doubt about, after prayer, we determined by lot, and everything else was carried on with great love, meekness, and devotion. We continued in fasting and prayer till three o'clock, and then parted with a full conviction that God was going to do great things among us. Oh that we may be in any way instrumental to His glory! That He would make us vessels pure and holy, meet for our Master's use!'

He made no mention of the names of these true ministers, but Wesley

21. J.W.J. (Vol.2, p.82.) See also article on this in the *Arminian Magazine* for 1782, p.429.
22. G.W.J. (p.196.)

in his Journal (Diary only) stated that at 8.30 a.m. on the same day he was at Islington with 'G Whitefield, Hut(chings),[23] Hall, Ingham, Kinchin and Charles (Wesley).' There was prayer followed by conversation and singing; At 2.30, '...tea, conversed'. J.S. Simon[24] says that Dr Whitehead, one of Wesley's biographers, quoting from an original manuscript, told of John's having met John Gambold, one of the original Oxford Methodists and later a Moravian, and another clergyman named Robson, in High Wycombe about 12 November. After prayer and consultation they agreed:

1. To meet yearly at London, if God permit, on the eve of Ascension Day.
2. To fix then the business to be done the ensuing year; where, when and by whom.
3. To meet quarterly there, as many as can; namely on the second Tuesday in July, October, and January.
4. To send a monthly account to one another of what God hath done in each of our stations.
5. To inquire whether Mr Hall, Sympson,[25] Rogers, Ingham, Hutchins, Kinchin, Stonehouse, Cennick, Oxlee[26] and Brown will join us herein.
6. To consider whether there be any others of our spiritual friends who are able and willing so to do.

This conference, however, never materialized but it was not proposed in vain. The discerning eye can see in it some of the later types of meeting adopted by the Methodist movement. On the other hand, this unsuccessful

23. John Hutchings (or Hutchins) was another Oxford Methodist who later turned Moravian.
24. Simon, J.S. *Studies of John Wesley* (London, 1921, Vol.1: *John Wesley and the Religious Societies* pp.327-9.)
25. Sometimes spelt 'Simpson'. He is not to be confused with Rev David Simpson, evangelical Vicar of Christ Church, Macclesfield, with whom Wesley was friendly.
26. Wesley sometimes spells his name as 'Oxley' (See J.W.J. Vol.2, p.131.) He was a Moravian.

attempt to draw these evangelically minded friends[27] into a properly organized group marked the end of the sincere attempt to keep the growing revival channelled through orthodox methods.

Neither Whitefield nor the Wesleys desired to do anything which could be interpreted as disloyalty to the Church of England. J.C. Ryle is quite right when he says that Whitefield '...loved the Church in which he had been ordained; he gloried in her Articles; he used her Prayer Book with pleasure.'[28]

Similar words were uttered on numerous occasions by the Wesleys themselves, though George appeared to be somewhat less scrupulous about doing what the Church forbad when circumstances necessitated it, than were John and Charles, the latter in particular. Their desire was to preach in consecrated buildings at the invitation of the incumbent, though by 1739 this had become almost impossible. The biblical necessity of preaching the Gospel, they felt, was now laid upon them, whether on orthodox lines or otherwise. It was a necessity which became the mother of invention in respect of what they did by way of the unusual and the irregular.

Firstly, parish church doors were closed, but those of the Religious Societies were still open. Many of these were operating with episcopal sanction but the one in Fetter Lane,[29] closely associated with Wesley and his friends was not. It was not, for example, restricted to Anglicans, being a joint Anglican-Methodist-Moravian foundation. In any case, for clergymen like Whitefield and the Wesleys to go from society to another, preaching, would be to transgress the rule of not '...lifting up one's voice in another's parish' (without the incumbent's permission). Furthermore, they were often meeting in private houses and there was a definite rule

---

27. A number of these friends were destined, in any case, to go their separate ways ere long.
28. Ryle, J.C. *George Whitefield and His Ministry*, article in *Select Sermons of George Whitefield* (London, 1964, p.21.)
29. The Wesleys and Whitefield, as has already been mentioned, were soon to leave the Fetter Lane society over the teaching on 'stillness' introduced by Philip Molther, a Moravian.

about this.[30]

Secondly the practice of praying and preaching extempore offended against no known law.[31] It had, of course been a common Puritan practice, but by now was regarded as unusual. It was on Monday 25 December[32] that Whitefield declared that this was the first time he had prayed extempore '...before such a number in public'. One can assume from this that he must have already done so in smaller companies. Whitefield's remarks referred to his conducting worship and expounding to a society in Redcross Street at which two- to three-hundred people were present.[33]

He says: 'God grant I may pursue the method of expounding and praying extempore. I find God blesses it more and more.'[34] His *Journals* for Friday, 26 January[35] mentioned that he discussed with a clergyman for two hours, the subject of private societies such as those of the Methodists, and also the matter of extempore prayer. The clergyman objected on the authority of the Canons and the Act of Uniformity of Charles II, 1662. Whitefield said that the Act was against seditions and schismatical meetings and theirs was not, neither were they for *public* worship. There is no record of when Charles Wesley began praying extempore, though by a perusal of his *Journal*,[36] it is fairly certain that

---

30. The *Clergyman's Assistant dc* (London, 1808.) the section on 'The Constitutions and Canons of the Church of England'. (No.71, p.55.) 'Ministers not to preach, or administer the Communion in private houses... No Minister shall preach, or administer the Holy Communion in any private house, except it be in times of necessity, when any being so impotent as he cannot go to church, or very dangerously sick...'
31. *ibid*. Eliz.Cap.ii (p.161.) There does not appear to be any prohibition of this providing that the set forms of prayers have been used at the prescribed times. Any further devotions by way of set prayers or otherwise would be optional.
32. G.W.J. (p.194.)
33. G.W.J. (p.197.)
34. G.W.J. (p.197.)
35. *ibid* (p.202.)
36. See G.W.J. (1736-39 p.150) 'I was often since assisted to pray readily and earnestly, without a form.'

this would be soon after his conversion. John, however, met with the practice when in Georgia, at Darien, for he recorded in the Journal for Sunday, 2 January 1737[37] that he '...was surprised to hear an extempore prayer before a written sermon. Are not then the words we speak to God to be set in order at least as carefully as those we speak to our fellow-worms? One consequence of this manner of praying is, that they have public service only once a week. Alas, my brethren! I bear you record ye have a zeal for God, but not according to knowledge.'

Yet, in the *Diary* for the same day there is the short, significant sentence: 'I prayed extempore!' The exclamation mark speaks for itself.[38] He would, of course, have later seen instances of extempore prayer among the Moravians. One of the questions he addressed to them in August, 1737 was: 'Do you prefer extempore to set forms of prayer in public?' The answer was: 'Our hymns are forms of prayer. For the rest, every one speaks as he is moved by the Holy Ghost.'[39] By 1 April 1738 (Saturday) he was convinced about the rightness of this method. 'Being at Mr Fox's society, my heart was so full I could not confine myself to the forms of prayer which we were accustomed to use there. Neither do I purpose to be confined to them any more; but to pray indifferently, with a form, or without, as I may find suitable to particular occasions.'[40] He went on to say that a certain Mr Allen came to him full of goodwill, to exhort him not to leave the church; or (which was the same thing in his account) to use extemporary prayer; which he said '...I will prove to be a demonstration to be no·prayer at all. For you cannot do two things at once. But thinking how to pray, and praying, are two things. *Ergo*, you cannot both think and pray at once.' Wesley replied by asking whether it may not be proved by the self-same demonstration, that praying by a form is no prayer at all? E.g. 'You cannot do two things at once. But reading and praying are two things. *Ergo*, you cannot both read and pray

---

37. J.W.J. (Vol.1, p.309.)
38. J.W.J. (Vol.1, p.309.)
39. *ibid.* (Vol.1, p.374.)
40. *ibid.* (Vol.1, p.449.) See also Vol.2, p.404.

at once. QED.'

Extempore preaching was no breach of any law, but again it was indeed unusual in an age of polite and polished literary discourses in Anglican circles. J.C. Ryle can hardly be correct when he says[41] Whitefield was an extempore preacher immediately after ordination, '...preaching the pure gospel with uncommon gifts of voice and manner'. Whitefield in his *Journals* mentioned the notes he used for his sermons, so he cannot have been an extempore preacher early in his ministry. See also *Journals* for January, 1737[42] when he was asked to preach at St John's church in Bristol. He said, that, having his notes about him, he complied. Admittedly, by early 1738 he could write[43]: 'I...preached extempore (as I constantly do morning and evening).' Ryle, of course, is right when he asserts that such a preacher as George would be at that time '...an entire novelty in London.'

Charles Wesley's first attempt at extempore preaching is clear from his *Journal* for 20 October 1738: 'Seeing so few present at St Antholin's, I thought of preaching extempore; afraid, yet ventured on the promise, "Lo, I am with you always"; and spake on Justification from Romans iii for three-quarters of an hour, without hesitation. Glory be to God, who keepeth His promise for ever.'[44]

John admitted preaching thus: 'Above forty years ago' on Sunday January, 1776. According to a note by the Editor of the Standard Edition of the *Journal*, this occasion would have been in August 1735. 'This is the first time,' he said, 'that, having no notes about me, I preached extempore.'[45]

Thirdly, two more serious irregularities were to be adopted in the near future, one of which will be the subject of the next section of this chapter and the chapter following, namely that of open-air preaching. Again, it

---

41. Ryle J.C. *George Whitefield and His Ministry,* article in *Select Sermons of George Whitefield* (London, 1964, p.17.)
42. G.W.J. (p.81.)
43. *ibid.* (p.101.)
44. C.W.J. [1736-9] (pp.207-8.)
45. J.W.J. (Vol.6, p.96.)

cannot be said of itself to be illegal provided it was confined to one's own parish. Unfortunately in the case of the Wesleys and Whitefield it was not so. Whitefield had been appointed to Savannah whilst the Wesleys were unbeneficed clergy. Whitefield was more quickly reconciled to this practice than were the Wesley brothers. In fact it was George who took the initiative. It is also to him that the expression 'world parish' can be ascribed and *not* to John Wesley.

Whitefield set out for Bristol on 7 February 1739 and travelled via Windsor and Basingstoke where he met his old friends Kinchin and Hutchings. Thence he visited Salisbury where he called on Susannah Wesley, the mother of John and Charles. She informed him that she did not like the way they were living and wished they had some place where they could '...regularly preach'. Neither did she care for the innovations they were making in the Church. Bath was the next place of call and at each town he took the opportunity of preaching. His companion was a William Seward. Through the ministry of Charles Wesley and the Methodists, Seward had been converted. William accompanied Whitefield to America in August 1739. Seward returned from America to attend to business both public and private.[46] He met Charles Wesley in Bristol and, whilst the meeting was cordial, the Baptists to whom his brother belonged influenced him against Charles. Seward later joined Howell Harris, the Welsh Evangelist. Seward was so badly treated by the opponents of Methodism whilst at Hay, that he received injuries on 22 October 1740 which proved fatal. He thus became Methodism's first martyr.

Whitefield found many friends awaiting him at Bristol, but also many enemies. News had travelled to Bristol about the trouble which took place when George had been asked to preach at St Margaret's, Westminster; an invitation which occasioned a great cry of opposition. He found the pulpit of St Mary, Redcliffe at Bristol closed to him. Soon he was in trouble with the Chancellor of the Diocese for preaching, and attempting to preach, without a Diocesan licence. Apparently another

46. Tyerman, Luke *The Life and Times of the Rev John Wesley* (London, 1871-2, Vol.1, pp.165ff.)

objection levelled against him was that he preached false doctrine. He had to content himself with preaching to Religious Societies and to condemned felons in Bristol's Newgate Gaol! It was at this point that he began to wonder if he really needed to go to America to preach to the 'Indians' or any other kind of heathen. He found at Kingswood, according to his *Journals*[47] many colliers who appeared to be in a sort of ecclesiastical no man's land and he was concerned about them. On Saturday, 17 February, he went with Seward and another friend, and Whitefield can best be left to describe the scene himself:

> 'My bowels have long since yearned toward the poor colliers, who are very numerous, and as sheep having no shepherd. After dinner, therefore, I went upon a mount, and spake to as many people as came unto me. There were upwards of two hundred. Blessed be God that I have now broken the ice! I believe I was never more acceptable to my Master than when I was standing to teach those hearers in the open fields. Some may censure me: but if I thus pleased men, I should not be the servant of Christ.'[48]

There were about twenty more preaching excursions to the Kingswood neighbourhood and also itineraries which included Bath, Cardiff and parts of Wales. The Bath visit was important for it was here that he first met the Revd Griffith Jones of Llandowror, one of the greatest leaders of the Welsh revival. Also he met Paul Orchard at whose home, Stoke Abbey, in North Devon, James Hervey, one of the Oxford Methodists was recuperating after a serious illness. Hervey had requested Orchard to see if the rumours about Whitefield and his irregular habits of preaching were correct and let him know his judgement. A third friend he met at Bath was the Revd George Thompson, Evangelical vicar of St Gennys in

47. G.W.J. (pp.215-6.)
48. *ibid.* (p.216.)

Cornwall, who will feature later in this study.[49]

Before he set off for Wales, and realizing that the time for his return to America was approaching, he began to think of a suitable successor for his irregular, yet most successful, ministry in Bristol. Not only was he anxious for the continuance of the open-air preaching, but also for the organization of the resultant societies into which the new converts could be drafted.

Mainly through three letters,[50] he had received from John, Whitefield had learnt of the useful evangelical labours of the Wesleys in London and wrote to John, urging him to come to Bristol as quickly as possible, indicating the opportunities there:

> Bristol, 22 March 1739
>
> Reverend Sir,
>   I rejoice at the success which God has given you at Oxford and elsewhere. I immediately kneeled down and prayed that you may go on from conquering to conquer.
>   I thank you most heartily for your kind rebuke.[51] I can only say it was too tender. I beseech you, whenever you see me do wrong, rebuke me sharply. I have still a word or two to offer in defence of my behaviour, but shall defer it till I come to town. If I have offended, I humbly ask pardon, and desire the brethren to pray that I may be such as God would have me be.
>   If the brethren, after prayer for direction, think proper, I

---

49. See Chapter Three, Section (i).
50. J.W.L. (Vol.1, pp.280-1 for 26 February 1739; Vol.1, pp.281-4 for 16 March 1739; Vol.1, pp.287-8 for 20 March 1739.) In the letter of 16 March he mentions his meeting John Cennick at Reading where the latter had founded a society.
51. The rebuke referred to was given by Wesley to Whitefield in respect of what he had done in Bristol. Good though it may have been, it had been done without consultation with the society at Fetter Lane of which he was a member. It had been agreed by the members there that they should not undertake anything, not even a journey, without bringing the matter before the society.

wish you would be here the latter end of next week.'

Here follow directions for travel. Then:

> 'Come, I beseech you; come quickly. I have promised not to
> leave this people till you or somebody come to supply my
> place...'

After a few more paragraphs, a PS dated 23 March is added containing
the following:

> 'I beseech you to come next week; it is advertised in this day's journal.
> I pray for a blessing on your journey, and in our meetings. The people
> expect you much. Though you come *after*, I heartily wish you may be
> preferred *before* me...'[52]

John's reaction can be gleaned from his *Journal* for March[53] where he
mentioned that he was fully employed between the Fetter Lane society
and many others so that there was no thought of leaving London.
However, letters arrived from both Whitefield and Seward but Wesley
was disinclined to leave the capital. A search of the Scriptures was made,
and, fortunately they were apparently in harmony with the proposed
move.

On Wednesday 28 March he recorded that his proposed journey was
brought before the society. Charles at first objected but they all betook
themselves to the Scriptures and then decided to settle the matter by lot
and the result was that Wesley should respond to his Bristol invitation.[54]

Accordingly, Wesley left London and was greeted by Whitefield on
Saturday 31. On the first of April, Whitefield introduced him to the
practice of field-preaching before leaving the district. Wesley commented

52. Tyerman, Luke *The Life of George Whitefield* (London, 1890, Vol.1, p.193.)
53. No day is given.
54. J.W.J. (Vol.2, pp.157-8.)

apprehensively on his new task the previous day:

> 'In the evening, I reached Bristol and met Mr Whitefield there. I could scarce reconcile myself at first to this strange way of preaching in the fields, of which he set me an example on Sunday; having been all my life (till very lately) so tenacious of every point relating to decency and order, that I should have thought the saving of souls almost a sin if it had not been done in a church.'[55]

On the first of April:

> 'In the evening, Mr Whitefield being gone,[56] I began expounding Our Lord's Sermon on the Mount (one pretty remarkable precedent for field-preaching, though I suppose there were churches at that time also) to a little society which as accustomed to meet once or twice a week in Nicholas Street.'[57]

It must be argued here that the comparison with Our Lord's teaching in the open-air is hardly a fair one. Jesus was not an official teacher of the Jewish Church and although synagogues were closed to him, he broke no church rule in expounding out of doors. Neither was he to be regarded as a preacher, lay or ordained. He did not belong to the Church, nor was he a priest of it - He *was* the Church; He *was* the ministry and a man's ministry stemmed from him!

A further quotation must be given from Wesley's *Journal*:

55. J.W.J. (Vol.2, p.167.) Could this truthfully be said to be the first time he had preached in the open-air? When his brother Charles had ministered to felons from Newgate Gaol, about to be executed, he often spoke to the waiting crowds and on at least one occasion, it was John who spoke to them.
56. Whitefield left Bristol for South Wales on Monday 2 April.
57. J.W.J. (Vol.2, p.168.)

John Wesley

'At four in the afternoon, I submitted to be more vile,[58] and proclaimed in the highways the glad tidings of salvation, speaking from a little eminence in a ground adjoining the city to about three thousand people...'[59]

According to his *Journal*,[60] Wesley seems to have enjoyed a similar success to that of his colleague Whitefield. Nevertheless it must be borne in mind that Wesley, even more than Whitefield, was apt to exaggerate the numbers of the crowds, the estimating of which with any degree of accuracy would be impracticable. The population of Bristol at this time would be about 35,000. Between his first attempt at open-air preaching in Bristol and Tuesday 17 April, Wesley had spoken seven times in that city and once in Bath. In addition he had addressed various already existing religious societies in Bristol. There had been such societies here for fifty years, as there were in other places and these were based on the rules of those of Dr Horneck. Wesley, however was now founding his own societies as well. One of the purposes for which Whitefield had urged him to come to Bristol was to organize these as the people, he said, '...were ripe for bands'. One quite regular ministry of John's must be mentioned. During this period, he officiated a number of times in Clifton Church for the vicar, a Mr Hodges, who was a dying man.[61]

Whilst in Bristol, regular visits were paid to Newgate Gaol, and no doubt this ministry was made possible by the fact that the keeper, Abel Dagge, was one of the converts of Whitefield. However, Wesley was later to suffer the same fate as that of Whitefield, in that official permission was withheld.

Charles Wesley also came into the picture at this point. The unpleasant

---

58. Compare G.W.J. for 13 May 1739, p.265: 'But if this is to be vile, Lord grant that I may be more vile...'
59. J.W.J. (Vol.2, pp.172-3.) The text was Isaiah Ch.1xi.vs.1&2.
60. J.W.J. (Vol.2, pp.173-177.)
61. This Mr Hodges is not to be confused with John Hodges, Vicar of Wenvoe in Wales - an Evangelical who loaned Wesley his church on a number of occasions.

experiences leading up to his exclusion at St Mary's, Islington, seem to be the first cause of his taking to outdoor preaching, but not without much inner conflict. Towards the end of April 1739, a number of entries in his *Journal* reveal his admiration for Whitefield's novel method of expounding. The first occasion for Charles to follow suit appeared to be 27 May:[62]

> 'Franklyn, a farmer, invited me to preach in his field. I did so, to about five hundred on "Repent, for the kingdom of heaven is at hand". I returned to the house rejoicing.'

Scruples about preaching either out of doors or in a non-Anglican building still remained. On Thursday 31 May,[63] a Quaker sent him a pressing invitation to preach at Thackstead (Thaxted). 'I still scrupled about preaching in another's parish,' he confessed, 'till I had been refused the church.' However, he consented and preached on 'The Scripture hath concluded all under sin' to many Quakers and about 700 others.[64]

Again, there was some trepidation present on Saturday 23 June:

> 'My inward conflict continued. I perceived it was the fear of man; and, that, by preaching in the field next Sunday, as George Whitefield urges me, I shall break down the bridge, and become desperate.'[65]

The next day he preached to '...near ten thousand helpless sinners

---

62. C.W.J. (1736-9, p.233.)

63. *ibid.* (p.234.)

64. *ibid.* (p.235.) By 4 June he was still attending Whitefield's field-preaching. 'What?' he asks, 'has Satan gained by turning me out of the churches?' By this time, John was also preaching out of doors in the capital.

65. C.W.J. (1736-9, p.240.)

waiting for the Word, in Moorfields.'[66]

Of course, Charles too, was not to indulge in this novelty without courting opposition. Later the same week[67] he seemed to be shocked by hearing the Dean of Christ Church, Oxford speaking with '...unusual severity against field-preaching and Mr Whitefield'. He was to hear similar criticisms against field-preaching from the Vice-Chancellor, who, whilst not objecting to the Methodists as such, took exception to the 'irregularity of doing good in other men's parishes'.[68] The next day, the Dean continued, said Charles, 'to bring me off from preaching abroad, from expounding in houses, from singing psalms; denied justification by faith alone and all vital religion; promised me, however, to read Law and Pascal.'[69]

William Law, who had previously been such a friend and source of spiritual inspiration to the Wesley brothers and other evangelicals, now looked askance at the Methodists declaring to Charles[70] that he '...had great hopes that (they) would have been dispersed by little and little into livings, and have leavened the whole lump.'

After many experiences of field-preaching, Charles, by 25 August, was still not completely happy about it.

In a letter dated that day, he said:

---

66. *ibid.* (p.240.) It must also be noted that later the same day, by invitation of the Rector, he officiated at Newington, but as soon as this service was finished, he was on the common 'crying to the multitudes'.
67. C.W.J. (1736-39, p.241.) Saturday 30 June. The Dean of Christ Church apparently had spoken privately to Charles as he also did the following day.
68. *ibid.* (p.242.) Monday 2 July. The previous day he had preached at St Mary's before the University.
69. On Sunday 8 July he was threatened by a man for trespass as he walked over an open field to Kennington Common, see C.W.J. (1736-9, p.242.) On Wednesday 25, he was sued.
70. *ibid.* (p.246.)

Gloucester, 25 August.

'Before I went forth into the street and highways, I sent, after my custom, to borrow the church. The minister (one of the better disposed) sent back a civil message, that he would be glad to drink a glass of wine with me, but durst not lend me his pulpit for fifty guineas... Mr Whitefield durst lend me his field, which did just as well...'[71]

The preference is obvious. Field-preaching was imperative, but he never was fully reconciled to it. One must pause here and take a critical look at the beginnings of this unusual and illegal method of expounding the Gospel. Whitefield was the instigator and this may well have been due to his deepening friendship with the two brothers, Ralph and Ebenezer Erskine of Scotland, who no doubt helped to establish him firmer in his Calvinistic views.[72] They had become irregular in Scotland where, in the State Church there, the parish system existed and they appeared to have had no scruples in violating other men's parishes. In England, by 1739, most Anglican churches were closed to Whitefield and the Wesley brothers. The former had little conscience about invading the parishes of others whereas the Wesleys, especially Charles, were not happy about the practice. But it was, on the whole, a dead church whose rules they had to keep. Upon their hearts lay the burden of the necessity of communicating the Gospel in all its fullness to many in need of it. What other course could have been taken? It is a singular fact, but where there has been a revival there has often also been a division within the churches, usually due to the differing attitudes to it. The same applied in the eighteenth century. New methods have had to be applied. There is no confining the Holy Spirit's activities to man-created rules and laws. So where there is a lack of spirituality in high places, there is also misunderstanding and

---

71. C.W.J. (1736-9, p.255.) The same day he wrote of a Presbyterian minister as a 'teacher' as his brother had already done. See page 31.
72. Tyerman, Luke *The Life of George Whitefield* (London, 1890, Vol.1, pp.267-270.)

opposition. Our Lord's words were seen to be strikingly relevant in respect of new wine in old bottles. The old bottles were indeed tried but it was the new ones which held the new movement. The old bottles, however, certainly remained intact, retaining as they did, the old - in fact, the very old wine.[73]

---

73. Mention might be made of the unusual phenomena which occurred during these occasions of preaching. Men, women, and sometimes children would fall down in fits and remain for some time in a cataleptic condition. In some cases, there were sudden deaths. Most of these incidents took place during John's preaching. As far as it can be traced, they never took place during Whitefield's preaching though he saw these happenings during John's ministry. John believed these phenomena to be the result of the Holy Spirit's work, though he felt that in some instances there was devil possession. Whitefield too, ascribed the happenings to the work of the Holy Spirit. He would know of similar occurrences during the ministry in Scotland of the Erskines and also during that of Jonathan Edwards in America. Charles, however, was very sceptical and believed that much of this type of incident was feigned and was the work of Satan doing more harm than good to the evangelical movement. Similar outbreaks of this kind of phenomenon were also witnessed during the Everton Revival (see Chapter Three, Section iv) at Haworth and Newcastle. These incidents were indeed similar to those recorded in the Acts of the Apostles and also those which took place during the Pentecostal Revival in the early 1920s.

CHAPTER THREE

THE WORLD PARISH (II)

It is time now to turn from the initial partnership of the Wesleys and Whitefield and assess to what extent there were others of evangelical inclinations with whom they agreed on the idea of the world parish and who, to a certain degree, emulated their roving ministry.

It must be said at the outset that the numbers of such clergy were few and represented an odd assortment of places. Inevitably there were the Welsh Evangelicals who deserve special mention, for, as has already been stated, the revival in the Principality was well developed by the time of the Wesleys' conversion. But, in England, apart from two ministers in Cornwall, the main Evangelicals were Baddiley in Derbyshire (of whom, unfortunately, not much is known) Grimshaw of Haworth, and Berridge of Everton, who, with his neighbour, Hicks of Wrestlingworth, was responsible for the notable revival in that part of Bedfordshire. Finally, it is incumbent to make a note of the opposition to itinerant preaching by Evangelicals, especially that of James Hervey of Weston Favell who wrote at great length against it. It is significant that his attitude was strongest prior to his own evangelical awakening, not that there is any evidence that he altered his views afterwards. There were far more serious subjects for correspondence with Wesley within a very short time of his conversion, as later chapters of this study will reveal.[1]

---

1.   See Chapters Eight and Nine.

As with Wales, Evangelicalism was already established in Cornwall prior to the Wesleys' own phenomenal success in that county. The leading light was Samuel Walker,[2] Rector of Truro, who was converted through his friendship with George Conon, headmaster of Truro Grammar School. His admiration of the early Methodists was beyond doubt whilst he disapproved of their irregularities. Of the itinerancy he had little to say to the Wesleys, but as the next chapter will show, his main objection was to the employment of lay-preachers. About 1750, he founded for his fellow Cornish Evangelicals, a Clerical or 'Parsons' Club. Most of the members of the Club must either have been known to John Wesley or else he had heard of them, for in the *Journal* for Monday 8 September 1760,[3] he declared, after hearing an account of two young clergymen, a Mr C—— and Mr Phelps:

> 'Surely God has a favour for the people in these parts! He gives them so serious, zealous, lively preachers. By these and the Methodists together, the line is now laid, with no considerable interruption, all along the North Sea, from the eastern point of Cornwall to the Land's End. In a while, I trust there will be no more cause on these coasts to accuse *Britannos hospitibus feros*.[4]

Mr 'C' was Samuel Cooper, Curate of Cubert. G.C.B. Davies[5] says his name appeared in the marriage registers at Truro as officiating minister in February 1760, and also on several occasions after Walker's departure. It is strange that on Wesley's numerous visits to Cubert, Cooper was never mentioned. In the *Journal* for 10 September 1760,

---

2.   See J.W.L. (Vol.4, p.407.) Letter to Thomas Adam 31 October 1755 in which he declared that Walker was the only minister who had refused to become irregular, whose ministry had been at all effective in converting souls.
3.   J.W.J. (Vol.4, pp.406-7.)
4.   i.e. 'Britons as inhospitable, or cruel, to strangers.' J.W.J. (Vol.4, p.407.)
5.   Davies, C.C.B. *The Early Cornish Evangelicals. 1735-1760.* (London, 1951, pp.85-6.)

Phelps was referred to as a 'man of humble, loving, tender spirit. Between him on the one hand, and the Methodists on the other, most in his parish are now awakened. Let but our brethren have zeal according to knowledge, and few will escape them both.'[6] Wesley mentioned him on one further occasion only – Saturday, 18 September 1762.[7]

Of the other members of the Club, Wesley made no mention. There was Henry Phillips, incumbent at Gwennap, six miles from Truro, of whose ministry Walker spoke very highly, mentioning especially his large congregations. Phillips, however, according to Davies,[8] regarded the Methodists as Dissenters, mentioning on one occasion that there were about forty or fifty of them in his parish.

Thomas Mitchell, who was admitted to the benefice of Veryon on 1 October 1743 and remained there until his death in 1773 was another member of the Club. On one occasion he preached at the Bishop's visitation and called upon the clergy to preach Christ and study the Gospel. His Lordship took occasion afterwards to say that the clergy already did this and a controversy resulted.[9]

Another member was John Penrose who was a schoolfellow of Walker's and incumbent of St Gluvias near Penryn until he died in 1776.[10]

Mydhope Wallis was also a member about whom Wesley seemed to know nothing. He was incumbent of St Endellion. It was to him in a letter dated 10 September 1754 that Walker denied being a Methodist, though he admitted they were a 'sincere people'.[11]

James Vowler, Curate of St Agnes and predecessor there of Phelps, was definitely known to Wesley for on Saturday 3 September 1757 he described Vowler in the *Journal* as one '...who rejoices in the love of God, and both preaches and lives the Gospel'. The following day he recorded that he heard the Curate preach '...two such thundering sermons

---

6.   J.W.J. (Vol.4, p.407.) Phelps was Curate of St Agnes.
7.   J.W.J. (Vol.4, p.529.)
8.   Davies *op.cit.* (p.26.)
9.   Davies *op.cit.* (p.77.)
10. Davies *op.cit.* (p.78.)
11. Davies *op.cit.* (p.83.)

at church as I have scarce heard these twenty years. Oh how gracious is God to the poor sinners of St Agnes!'[12] These statements, however, require comparing with that written in a letter to Walker dated 19 September 1757 in which Wesley said that Vowler '...preaches the *true* Gospel but not the *whole* Gospel.'[13]

Only two of the Cornish evangelical clergy joined Wesley in his itinerant labours as well as offering him their pulpits, though there were others who merely did the latter. The first of these was John Bennet. He had been admitted to a sizership at Queen's College, Cambridge on 7 September 1693, matriculating two years later. He took his BA in 1696/7 and his MA in 1726. He was a contemporary of Samuel Wesley, father of John. He was ordained deacon at Exeter, 19 September 1697 and priest on 15 March 1700. Five years later he was licensed to the perpetual curacy of North Tamerton, staying there for fifteen years. Here he was known as a sporting person, being especially interested in hunting. On 29 September 1720 he was licensed to the curacy of Tresmere. In 1731 he was then licensed to Laneast. Bennet's meeting with Wesley was probably due to the fact that he had been a friend of Wesley's father. His conversion would possibly take place after his going to Laneast.[14]

The other Evangelical was George Thompson, Vicar of St Gennys. Thompson matriculated at Exeter College, Oxford on 17 February 1716 and graduated Ll.B on 17 December 1719. He was ordained deacon on 1 July 1722 and next day licensed to the curacy of Jacobstowe in North Cornwall. He was priested in London in 1726. He was the author of *Original Hymns*. In September 1732, he was given the living of St Gennys where, within a few years, he was converted due to dreams. He became a recluse for a month until he found peace. At his death he was chaplain to the Fortieth Regiment of Foot.[15]

Both Bennet and Thompson appeared on two occasions before the

12. J.W.J. (Vol.4, p.234.)
13. J.W.L. (Vol.3, p.222.)
14. Davies *op.cit.* (pp.34ff.)
15. Davies *op.cit.* (pp.50-1.)

successive Bishops of Exeter – the second being Dr Lavington, the great antagonist of early Methodism, to account for their irregular ministries. Of the two, Bennet appeared to have been the closer friend of Wesley's because Thompson became an extreme Calvinist, a fact which was indicated in his hymns. Nevertheless, it was at Thompson's request that Wesley was sent for to minister to him in the closing days of his life.[16]

One only of the Cornish evangelical clergy admitted to having been indebted to the Methodism of the Wesleys. This was Thomas Vivian, Vicar of Cornwood, who, in 1748, informed Wesley that he owed a debt of gratitude to him for the blessing which came upon his soul through reading his writings. Later, however, Wesley declared that Vivian had fallen into 'the pit of the Decrees'[17] and 'knows him no more!' The lack of full cooperation between the Cornish Evangelicals and the Wesleys had the same two basic reasons (as elsewhere), namely, either the subject of Church Order or doctrine.

The Wesleys' work in the Principality of Wales inevitably brought them into contact with the Welsh Evangelicals, pride of place amongst whom must be afforded Howell Harris. It was Howell's suggestion which first brought John to Wales. His friendship with the Wesleys lasted a lifetime but on many occasions it was in danger of foundering owing to doctrinal differences of which more will be said later.

Born at Trevecca in Brecknockshire on 23 January 1714, he was for a time a schoolteacher, and after a short and apparently unprofitable single term at Oxford University he returned to his home district, devoting his time to his profession and building chapels. The Trevecca community was founded by him and included the Countess of Huntingdon's college for the training of both Anglican and Dissenting ministers. For a time, he accepted a commission in the Brecknockshire militia on the understanding that he would be permitted to preach wherever he went.

---

16. See J.W.J. (Vol.3, pp.132;181;184;196.) Davies *op.cit.* (p.30.) mentions that in the parish registers of St Gennys, Thompson's name is sometimes spelt without the 'p'. Wesley's last ministry is mentioned in J.W.J. (Vol.6, p.360.)
17. i.e. Calvinism.

Attempts were made, but in vain, to procure ordination for him. Although he became founder of Welsh Calvinistic Methodism, he never left the Anglican Church in which he remained a layman. He was no opponent of Church Order and discipline. His concern was for a church which was spiritually unproductive. Nevertheless his itinerant preaching naturally brought him into conflict with the Church authorities, but there were many clergy and laymen who were in sympathy with him. By doctrine, at first a keen Arminian, he was won over to a moderate Calvinism and this was no doubt due to his close association with the local Dissenters, especially the Baptist community. He died on 21 July 1773 and was buried near the altar in the parish church of Talgarth[18] near Brecon, before which, on Whitsunday, 1735 he had experienced conversion.

His first encounter with John Wesley was in Bristol on 1 June 1739 and it is worth noting that this was three months after his introduction to George Whitefield. Harris confessed that he had been tempted not to meet Wesley because he had heard that he was an 'Arminian and a Freewiller'.[19] Wesley undoubtedly had a high regard for Harris for he praised him in a letter to James Hutton.[20] On Monday 7 April 1740, John received a pressing invitation from Howell to preach in Wales, the letter revealing that others had attempted to prejudice him against Wesley, but unsuccessfully.[21]

In the Spring of 1740, Harris, who had already had some association with the Fetter Lane Society, left it to join the new Foundry society begun by the Wesleys. For a month, May-June, he assisted Charles Wesley there despite the fact that their doctrinal differences were known to both. They agreed, after discussing their respective views, that they had more

---

18. I have noticed when visiting the church, that a suitable memorial inscribed in the Welsh language has been placed on the south wall of the chancel commemorating his life and work.
19. J.W.J. (Vol.2, pp.223-5.)
20. J.W.L. (Vol.1, p.342.) Dated 12 April 1740.
21. J.W.J. (Vol.2, p.341.) Wesley visited Wales again on 1-6 October 1740 but without association with Harris.

in common than that which would separate them.

In June, however, there arose a precarious situation as a result of Charles Wesley's expulsion of a Mr Acourt from the society in London.[23] Harris remonstrated with Wesley about this and assumed that it was because Acourt held the view of 'election'. No, said Wesley, it was not because he held this view, but that by his insisting on preaching it, he had caused a division there. It is difficult to decide whether Harris's preaching had aggravated the situation or whether the influence of other people was to blame.[24]

November, 1740, saw Charles' first visit to Wales where he received a kindly welcome from some evangelical clergy, including John Hodges, Vicar of Wenvoe who was to be a friend to the Wesleys for many years. He was also to find that the more extreme Calvinists had also prepared for his visit by attempting to undermine the friendship between himself and Howell Harris. A letter from Charles to Howell quickly brought the former to Cardiff[25] and '...all misunderstandings vanished at sight of each other, and our hearts were knit together as at the beginning...'

Further theological difficulties arose at Bristol when, on 9 October 1741, John Wesley received a request to call on Harris and found him in the company of Joseph Humphreys and Mr Simpson. Wesley recorded[26] that they '...immediately fell on their favourite subject...' – and one can well imagine that this would be some tenet of Calvinism. However, they accepted John's suggestion that controversy should give way to prayer and all ended well. Harris again saw Wesley at the New Room, Bristol the following day, declaring that he had renounced and utterly abandoned the doctrine of reprobation. As for not falling from grace, he believed that it ought not to be mentioned to the unjustified, or to any that were slack

---

23. J.W.J. (Vol.2, pp.353-5.)
24. J.W.L. (Vol.1, pp.342-3.) Jackson, Thomas *Life of the Revd Charles Wesley*, MA (London, 1841, Vol.1, pp.238-9.) blames John Cennick who had by now become a Calvinist, for causing this estrangement.
25. Two letters were sent by Charles to Harris warning him of the dangers of the Quietist principles to which Harris was quickly becoming attached.
26. J.W.J. (Vol.2, p.507.)

and careless, much less to those who lived in sin, but only to the earnest and disconsolate mourners. He did himself believe it was possible for one to fall away who had been 'enlightened' with some knowledge of God, who had tasted of the heavenly gift, and been made partaker of the Holy Ghost. This fact certainly ranked him as a very moderate Calvinist. He wished they could all agree to keep 'close' in the controversial points, to the 'very words of Holy Writ'. He accounted no man so justified as not to fall till he had a thorough abiding hatred to all sin and a continual hunger and thirst after all righteousness.

The friendship and harmony was further cemented on Thursday the 15th by a request from Harris to Wesley to meet him at the New Passage.[27] There followed a preaching tour, but, at St Brides-in-the-Moors, Joseph Humphreys reappeared, and began a dispute. Howell Harris and Daniel Rowlands, an evangelical clergyman to whom further reference will be made, successfully opposed him, a task which Harris himself had to perform again only two days later.

It was inevitable that this friendship should from time to time be coloured by doctrinal differences. A letter from Wesley dated 6 August 1742[28] showed that Harris must have just made a contentious reference to Christian Perfection, but attempts to overcome this were successful by agreeing that '...no man can merit anything but hell, seeing that all other merit is in the blood of the Lamb.' If they could agree on this they could be using their energies '...rising up against evil-doers'.

No further contact was recorded until Wednesday 29 May 1745 when they had a lengthy discussion on Antinomianism and Wesley noted with relief that Harris was not yet carried away by it. But, he queried: 'How long will he be able to stand? Only till he consents to stand neuter. When he is brought not to oppose, he will quickly yield.[29]

One most important conviction which he shared was the desire that the Methodists would not leave the Church and, in a letter dated 28 February

---

27. J.W.J. (Vol.2, pp.508-9.)
28. J.W.L. (Vol.2, p.8.)
29. J.W.J. (Vol.3, p.178.)

1748, Wesley passed on to Harris a commendation of him by a clergyman (Revd T. Ellis) for his efforts to that end.[30]

John noted in March 1756 that Harris's health had broken down but that he had built a house complete with chapel which he later visited in 1763. In August 1769 the cooperation continued. Wesley preached at Trevecca at Lady Huntingdon's School which had now been open just one year, and afterwards gave an exhortation to Howell's family at the latter's request. On Friday 14 August 1772 at Harris's invitation he again preached at Trevecca and seemed pleased to hear his host complain that he could no longer bear with the students there as they preached '...bare-faced reprobation' and '...so broad Antinomianism' and has had to oppose them publicly.[31]

The last reference to Harris was on 17 August 1775 when once more he preached at Trevecca. Howell had died since the last visit and Wesley's words about him on that occasion revealed the warmest regard and the 'happiest thoughts'.[32]

However, this was another side to the Harris-Wesley relationship. According to G.T. Roberts,[33] it appears that the friendship was similar to that of the Wesleys with Whitefield. These men were big enough to rise above their differences in doctrine but their respective followers were not and one is left in no doubt that the continuous role of Harris was that of peacemaker. On more than one occasion he was tempted to break with the Wesleys for good. 'Harris loved to love,' declares Roberts[34] 'but we suspect that some Methodists in London and Bristol were finding hatred a not unpleasant sensation.'

---

30. J.W.L. (Vol.2, pp.128-9.) Ellis had suggested to Wesley that he should write 'some little thing' advising the Methodists not to leave the Church and not to rail at their ministers. Wesley immediately wrote *A Word to a Methodist*.
31. J.W.J. (Vol.5, p.482.)
32. J.W.J. (Vol.5, p.482.)
33. Roberts G.T. *Howell Harris* (London, 1951, p.39.)
34. Robert G.T. *op.cit.* (p.39.) Harris, when defending Wesley to the Countess of Huntingdon could say of him that he was the greatest man who could first 'bow and love'.

Nevertheless Harris attended at least five of Wesley's Conferences: 1747; 1748; 1749; 1763 and 1767. It was at the penultimate one that he declared he could never call himself a preacher but an exhorter – '...his gifts being so...' However, his greater loyalty and his deeper affection were to Whitefield and it was he, not Wesley, who proved to be the inspirer, adviser and leader of the Welsh Methodists.

It is noteworthy that with the other prominent Welsh Evangelicals, the Wesleys had very little contact. Griffith Jones of Llandowror could justifiably be said to have been the Father of the Welsh Revival. He instituted the circulating Welsh Schools, the object of which was to teach the poor to read the Welsh language, and to receive religious instruction. Yet Wesley's introduction to him took place in Bath on Tuesday 9 April 1739 and his sole comment on Jones is that he was refreshed by his company for an hour or so.[35] On Thursday 12 April he says Jones called on him at Bristol on his return to his native land, and went with him to the society at Castle Street. There was also a casual mention of Jones in a letter to John Glass of 1 November 1757 as a 'popular preacher'.[36] Jones, however, was no itinerant preacher. On the contrary, one of his converts, Daniel Rowlands (1713-1790) successively curate to his elder brother and then to his son (both of whom held the living of Llangeitho) became, out of a sense of local need, an itinerant preacher during the week, returning to his church on Sundays. For his irregular labours, his curate's licence was withdrawn by the bishop. Whilst he continued to reside at the Rectory with his son, a chapel was erected for him at Llangeitho. His expulsion gave a great impulse to Welsh Calvinistic Methodism. His meetings with Wesley were rare and the only one which has already been noted in connection with Howell Harris was on Thursday 8 May 1740 at Bristol.

Of Howell Davies, the 'Apostle of Pembrokeshire', and another convert of Griffith Jones, a little more is recorded. Wesley appreciated at Bath on Monday 17 September 1764 that the fact Davies had preached there on

---

35.   J.W.L. (Vol.pp.297-300.) Letter to James Hutton.
36.   J.W.L. (Vol.3, p.232.)

the previous day had resulted in a larger congregation for himself,[37] than he had known before. Wesley was somewhat less appreciative on Wednesday 2 September 1769,[38] when he declared that the work of God had been hindered in Pembrokeshire by Davies' lay-preachers who opposed his own. To avoid damage and lack of harmony, Wesley drew up rules for his own preachers for their relationship with those of Davies.[39]

On Tuesday 22 August, Wesley preached in Caerphilly Church where Davies, then Rector of Prendergast, read the prayers.[40] Davies was a keen Calvinist and, like Harris and Rowlands was another great promoter of the Methodist Revival in Wales. Like the latter, but unlike the former, he was ejected from the Anglican Church, but in common with both, he adopted the practice of itinerant preaching.

No reference was made to Thomas Jones, the curate of Cwm Isu[41] for fifty years, whom Howell Harris mentioned many times in his *Diary* and who was also a friend of Griffith Jones. No doubt this was because of his isolated position in the Black Mountains. Whilst his labours were more restricted than other Evangelicals of the period, his influence on Harris was incalculable.

Finally, one or two comments need to be made on the Wesleys' association with the Welsh Evangelicals. It is significant that the contacts were rare, when, basically, their work was the same. From 1742, however, Calvinistic Methodism was firmly established,[42] emphasising the doctrinal differences between them. A number of clergy, according to Wesley, were friendly and loaned him their churches, but these appear to have been men who were not committed to either side. John Hodges of Wenvoe remained the most loyal friend, but even he decreased in Wesley's

---

37. J.W.J. (Vol.5, p.94.) Richard Bateman, one of Wesley's college friends, and later Rector of St Bartholomew's, London, was converted under Davies.
38. J.W.J. (Vol.5, pp.229-230.)
39. See Chapter Four.
40. J.W.J. (Vol. 3, p. 333.)
41. Or Cwmoe.
42. The year of the first meeting of the Calvinistic Methodists Association.

estimate in later years.[43] Apparently he subsequently embraced the ideas and practice of Mysticism. Hodges attended many of the Conferences, including the first in 1744.

Secondly there was, in many instances a language barrier. The Welsh tongue was strange to Wesley and he 'marvelled' when he heard his fellow-clergy preaching in it. Thirdly, there was undoubtedly an important influence gained from the visits to Wales and his meetings with the Evangelicals there. He would have noted that itinerancy was common to most of them and this would confirm him in his own practice of it, recalling that the Welsh revival began before his own movement. He cannot have failed to notice, too, that Davies employed lay-preachers and that Harris who remained in the Anglican Church to the end, was an itinerating lay-preacher, without any episcopal sanction. Whatever may be thought to be the origin of Wesley's system of lay-preaching, there is little doubt that one of the first and lasting impressions in this respect can be traced to his association with Harris.

Charles Wesley seems to have had even less contact with the Welsh Revivalists. His main contact with Wales appeared to have been with Mr Marmaduke Gwynne, a convert of Howell Harris. Charles married Gwynne's daughter on Saturday 8 April 1749. Why he does not seem to have had any friendship with the famous hymn writer of the Revival, William Williams of Pentecelyn,[44] it is hard to understand. Probably doctrine and languages were the barriers and Williams did for the Welsh what Charles did for the English Methodists.

The principal beneficed Evangelical of the North was, without doubt, William Grimshaw of Haworth. Of the Wesley brothers, Charles was the

---

43. J.W.J. (Vol.5, p.28.) Wesley said that on Sunday 28 August 1763 when he visited Hodges' church, the latter read the prayers like 'an old song, in a cold, dry, careless manner'.
44. Williams was a medical student at Hay. He was converted under Harris and then took Deacon's Order in the Church. He was not such a prolific hymn writer as Charles.

first to meet him. This meeting took place on 22 October 1746[45] and there was a further visit by Charles on 22 January 1747.[46] John met Grimshaw at Haworth on the first of May of the same year and a firm friendship was formed.[47] Next day, Wesley 'examined' W.D.'s (William Darney's) societies. Darney was a Scot who had begun itinerant preaching in the Haworth neighbourhood and forming societies. He received the support of Grimshaw who was quickly dubbed 'Mad Grimshaw, Scotch Will's Clerk'.

William Grimshaw (1708-63) was converted chiefly through reading two Puritan works: Brook's *Precious Remedies against Satan's Devices* and Owen *On Justification*. Appointed to the living of Haworth in 1742, he began a ministry which included many irregular features, such as preaching in houses, barns, quarries and by the roadside, and, furthermore, on many occasions, outside his own parish. His 'circuit' extended from Leeds to Chester, from Manchester to many of the Lancashire industrial towns, and societies were organized in most of the places he visited. Of all the Evangelical clergy, Grimshaw can safely be said to be the most irregular. On one occasion, when he was in trouble on account of his extra-parochial labours, he declared that if he were to be expelled from his living, he would take his saddle-bag and join Wesley, offering to work in one of the latter's 'poorest circuits'. This, however, was not to take place, and he remained in his own peculiar 'Methodist' circuit.

The first recorded instance of a joint itinerancy between Grimshaw and Wesley was on Thursday 25 August 1748[48] when they rode to Ronghlee, Colne, Heptonstall, Todmorden, among other places. At Colne, they were subjected to rough treatment at the instigation of George White, Curate of the parish. According to the Journal for Sunday 30

---

45. Jackson, Thomas *The Life of the Revd Charles Wesley* (London, 1841, Vol.1, p.452.) See also Hardy, R. Spence *William Grimshaw of Haworth* (London, 1860, p.65.)
46. *op. cit.* (Vol. 1, pp.460-1.)
47. J.W.J. (Vol.3, p.293.)
48. J.W.J. (Vol.3, p.295.)

July,[49] Wesley was assisted by Grimshaw at Kingswood, and a footnote suggests that the latter had taken his children there to be educated.

The Wesleys were always welcome preachers at Haworth Church and then to undertake a preaching tour of the surrounding district.[50] A tribute to Grimshaw was written in the *Journal* for Friday 2 April 1762,[51] though the former did not pass away until 7 April 1763,[52] and noteworthy was Wesley's emphasis on the fact of his preaching outside his own parish. On another occasion Wesley had described him as an Israelite indeed. A few such as him, he declared, would make any nation tremble.

'A Second Grimshaw' is the apt description of one other beneficed Evangelical in the North distinguished by his ecclesiastical irregularities, who deserves attention for his friendship with Wesley. The Revd John Baddiley,[53] Vicar of Hayfield in Derbyshire, was visited by Wesley for the first time on 8 April 1755 (Tuesday)[54] just before which Baddiley's favourite daughter had died. Two days later it was John's duty to officiate at her funeral.[55]

Baddiley warmly approved of Wesley's doctrines, having 'weighed' the orthodoxy of the published sermons with 'primitive Christianity'. Wesley in turn, declared that his friend was not effective until he became irregular.[56] Wesley was always welcome to preach in Hayfield Church whenever he visited the parish and it will be seen later that Baddiley was

---

49. J.W.J. (Vol.3, p.422.) Dated 30 July 1749.
50. *ibid.* (Vol.4, pp.68;212;310;332;447.) It appeared that Wesley preached at Haworth after Grimshaw's death, presumably at the invitation of his successor - John Richardson, another Evangelical.
51. *ibid.* (Vol.4, pp.413-8.)
52. See J.W.L. (Vol.4, p.160.)
53. Tyerman, Luke *The Life and Times of John Wesley, MA* (London, 1871-2, Vol.2, p.195.) gives his name as William, but surely he is confusing him with William Baddiley of Nailsea? The name was sometimes given as Baddeley or Badeley. A visit to Hayfield Church has revealed no further information from the incumbent there. There is a memorial to Baddiley's faithful ministry erected on the west end of the North wall of the nave.
54, 55. J.W.J. (Vol.4, pp.110-111.)
56. J.W.L. (Vol. 3, p.151n.)

one of the Evangelicals whose great concern was that the Methodist movement should be kept within the Church.[57] However, in a note in the *Journal* for Saturday 23 April 1765,[58] it appeared that Baddiley had now died and that '...he ran well till one offence after another had swallowed him up...' Not only had Baddiley indulged in extra-parochial work, but he had established societies outside his own parish and employed lay-preachers.

> 'Here lie the remains of JOHN BERRIDGE, late Vicar of EVERTON, and an itinerant servant of Jesus Christ; who loved his Master and His Work; and, after running His errands many years, was called up to wait on Him above. Reader, art thou born again? No salvation without the New Birth! I was born in sin, February, 1716; Remained ignorant of my fallen state till 1730. Lived proudly on faith and works for salvation till 1754. Admitted to Everton Vicarage, 1751. Fled to Jesus alone for refuge, 1756. Fell asleep in Christ, 22 January 1793.'[59]

Thus his epitaph sufficiently describes his career, spiritually and ecclesiastically of John Berridge. A product of Clare Hall, Cambridge, he was presented with the living of Everton by his college, following six years' curacy at Stapleford. Academically brilliant, he possessed an unparalleled wit and distinctive powers of oratory. In many respects, though certainly much more eccentric, he appeared to have resembled Grimshaw.[60]

Once spiritually awakened, he soon pursued an itinerant ministry

---

57. See next chapter for a further note on 'separation'.
58. J.W.J. (Vol.5, p.109.) The 'offences' make one suspicious that Wesley was referring to a lapse into Calvinism.
59. Ryle J.C. *The Christian Leaders of the Eighteenth Century* (London, 1868, p.235.) or (London, 1960) *Five Christian Leaders of the Eighteenth Century* (London, 1960, p.132.) Berridge was buried in the yard of Everton Church.
60. Walker of Truro objected to Berridge's ministry on 'Scriptural grounds'.

throughout the counties of Bedfordshire, Cambridgeshire, Essex, Hertfordshire and Huntingdonshire, riding about a hundred miles a week, and preaching about ten to twelve sermons in the open air, in barns, or wherever he could procure hearers. It is interesting to note that when Brian Bury Collins, a clerical friend of the Wesleys' was dismissed from his curacy, Berridge offered to appoint him as his own curate and wrote thus:

'I heartily accept your offer to supply my church and some extra-parochial cures to, if you please!'[61]

He was a regular winter visitor to London where he often preached at the Tabernacle in Tottenham Court Road, and, on at least one occasion, assisted Wesley at Spitalfields.[62]

It was not until 9 November 1758[63] that the first meeting with Wesley took place. It was at Berridge's suggestion and was made known to John by the Mayor of Bedford. Soon after the introduction, Berridge and Wesley proceeded to a neighbouring cleric, Revd William Hicks of Wrestlingworth, in whose church Wesley was to preach on many future occasions,[64] as he was also to do at Everton.[65] Of Hicks, whose conversion was attributable to Berridge's influence and with whom he pursued his itinerant labours, Wesley later noted:

'So far, Mr Hicks, who told me that he was first convinced of sin, 1 August 1758, and, finding peace in about six weeks, first preached the Gospel in 17 September. From that time he was accounted a fool and a madman.'[66]

61. J.W.L. (Vol.7, p.22.)
62. J.W.J. (Vol.4, p.482.) for Friday 1 January, 1762.
63. *ibid.* (Vol.4, p.291.)
64. *ibid.* (Vol.4, pp.300,433; Vol.6, p.464; Vol.7, p.216.)
65. *ibid.* (Vol.4, pp.291;300;317-322;359;431;433;482.)
66. *ibid.* (Vol.4, p.482.)

On another occasion he described him as '...a burning and shining light, full of love and zeal for God.'[67]

Revival is certainly the correct term to associate with Berridge and Hicks. From the first visit, Wesley witnessed this: 'Two thousand souls,' he declared, 'awakened in twelve months.'[68] It was during this first visit on 9 November, Wesley preached in Wrestlingworth, officiating again the next morning, only to witness scenes which he thought would never occur again.[69]In the middle of the sermon a woman '...dropped down as dead – deeply sensible of her want of Christ.'[70]This marked the beginning of a fresh series of strange phenomena after a lapse, apart from rare occurrences, of almost nineteen years.

Similar happenings took place in Everton Church the same evening. Wesley's comment on Berridge, who, with Hicks, had already witnessed similar phenomena, is significant:

> 'For many years, he was seeking to be justified by his works, but a few months ago, he was thoroughly convinced that "by grace we are saved through faith". Immediately he began to proclaim aloud the redemption that is in Jesus; and God confirmed His own word exactly as He did at Bristol, in the beginning, by working repentance and faith in the hearers, and with the same violent outward symptoms.'[71]

A full description of the Revival (apart from Wesley's visit), by an eye-witness is inserted in the *Journal* for Sunday 20 May, 1759,[72] including a letter to that person from Berridge. Another letter from

67. J.W.L. (Vol.7, p.23.) To Brian Bury Collins 14 June 1780.
68. J.W.J. (Vol.4, p.335.)
69. See Chapter Two, p.48.
70. J.W.J. (Vol.4, p.291.) It appeared that there had been a quarrel between Hicks and Berridge but it had soon been healed. See also J.W.J. (Vol.4, p.344) and J.W.L. (Vol.4, p.93.)
71. J.W.J. (Vol.4, p.291.)
72. *ibid.* (Vol.4, p.317.)

Berridge to Wesley, dated 16 July 1759 indicated that the joint ministry of Hicks and himself was attended by many instances of those outward signs. There is no doubt that they regarded this as being of God, '...who magnifies His Love as well as power amongst them by releasing souls out of bondage'.[73] Wesley was to witness similar happenings again when he visited Everton in August of the following year[74] and had, on that occasion, opportunity to examine some who had several times been in trances. They all agreed, said Wesley:

> '(i) that when they went away, as they termed it, it was always at the time when they were fullest of the love of God.
> (ii) that it came upon them in a moment, without any previous notice, and took away all their senses and strength.
> (iii) that there were some exceptions, but in general from that moment they were in another world, knowing nothing of what was done or said by all that were round them.'[75]

The same afternoon, further happenings of a similar kind, occurred, yet, in the evening, apart from one or two who '...cried out, there was a marked absence of such scenes.'[76]

In Bristol, Kingswood and Newcastle upon Tyne, these cases normally took place in barns, fields and private meetings. Now they occurred in churches. Wesley noted:

> 'I have generally observed more or less of these outward symptoms to attend the beginning of a general work of God. So it was in New England, Scotland, Holland, Ireland and many parts of England; but, after a time, they gradually decrease, and the work goes on more quietly and silently. Those whom it pleases God to employ in His work ought to be

73. *Methodist Magazine* (1780, p.611.)
74. J.W.J. (Vol.4, p.344.)
75. *ibid.* (Vol.4, p.344.)
76. *ibid.* (Vol.4, p.347.)

quite passive in this respect; they should choose nothing, but leave entirely to Him all the circumstances of His own work.'[77]

True it was at Everton, for on Sunday 25 November 1759, Wesley noted:

> 'A remarkable difference since I was here before as to the manner of the work. None now were in trances, none cried out, none fell down or were convulsed; only some trembled exceedingly – a low murmur was heard and many were refreshed with the multitude of peace.'[78]

Wesley proceeded to emphasize that there was a danger of regarding these trances, outcries and convulsions as essential to the work. Another danger was to regard them 'too little' or condemn them altogether. There was, he felt, sudden conviction of sin which caused the outcries, whereas visions and trances encouraged the believers. In some instances, after a time, '...nature mixed with grace, Satan could be mimicking this work of God in order to discredit the whole work. Even if the element of pretence entered, the real work of the Spirit should neither be denied or undervalued. We should, he concluded, 'diligently exhort all to be little in their own eyes, knowing that nothing avails with God but humble love. But still, to slight or censure visions in general would be both irrational and unchristian.'

Unfortunately Charles Wesley seems to have enjoyed little contact with either Berridge or Hicks, but it would be interesting to know what his view[79] of this aspect of the Everton Revival would have been, bearing in mind what he had to say of similar phenomena at Bristol and

---

77. *ibid.* (Vol.4, p.343.)
78. J.W.J. (Vol.4, p.359.)
79. J.W.L. (Vol.5, p.53.) According to the *Journal* (Vol.4, p.535) William Romaine and Martin Madan, two other Evangelicals of note, were 'in doubt about the work of God here', but were convinced on Friday 13 July 1759 by the relating of their experiences by two teenage girls.

Newcastle.[80]

Wesley's opinion of Berridge was not dissimilar to that he had of Hicks. In a letter to the Countess of Huntingdon, dated 10 March 1759,[81] he described him as '...one of the most simple as well as most sensible men of all whom it has pleased God to employ in reviving primitive Christianity... His word is with power; he speaks as plain and home as John Nelson, but with all the propriety of Mr Romaine and tenderness of Mr Hervey.'

The friendship between Berridge and Wesley was, inevitably, subject at times to disruption. The strong adherence of Berridge to certain Calvinistic tenets did not make for complete harmony and his views will be referred to later in quotations from one of his only two published works, namely *The Christian World Unmasked; Pray Come and Peep.* The other work was *Zion's Songs* and it was in this volume that some offence was caused to Wesley. In his preface to this work, Berridge claimed that 'All the hymns have been revised and many of them almost new made – The greatest and best part of them have been selected from the hymns of the Revd Mr John and Charles Wesley.' At least he had been honest about his sources! This was too much for John, however, who wrote on 18 April 1760[82] a letter in which he declared that he had hesitated to complain, for, in any case, Berridge was always hard to convince. The latter was too self-sufficient for had he not asserted that he cared for no man and could stand alone? He came to the heart of the matter:

> 'After we had been once singing a hymn at Everton, I was just going to say, "I wish Mr Whitefield would not try to mend my brother's hymns. He cannot do this. How vilely he has murdered that hymn, weakening the sense as well as marring the poetry!" But how was I afterwards surprised to hear it was not Mr

---

80. J.W.J. (Vol.4, p.335.)
81. J.W.L. (Vol.4, p.58.)
82. J.W.L. (Vol.4, p.91.)

Whitefield, but Mr B. In very deed it is not easy to mend his hymns any more than to imitate them... Has not this aptness to find fault frequently shown itself in abundance of other instances?'

Another cause of dissension was Berridge's notion that no other works than the Bible and Homilies should be read.[83] Wesley certainly had his answer to this idea:

'Nay, but get off the consequence who can: if they ought to read nothing but the Bible, they ought to hear nothing but the Bible, away with sermons, whether spoken or written! I can hardly imagine that you discourage reading even our little tracts, out of jealousy lest we should undermine you or steal away the affections of the people. I think you cannot easily suspect this. I myself did not desire to come among them; but you desired me to come. I should not have obtruded myself either upon them or you... I never repented of that (time) I spent at Everton, and I trust it was not spent in vain...'[84]

But this was not the only instance of differences between the two. In a letter to the Countess of Huntingdon on 20 March 1763,[85] Berridge was listed as being among those who were against Wesley though this was no doubt due to doctrinal issues. One thing is certain, that this opposition

---

83. Berridge had declared: 'I find they who read many books usually neglect the Bible and soon become eager disputants and in the end turn out Predestinarians.' See J.W.L. (Vol.4, p.91.) Berridge was the last person to criticize others for becoming Predestinarians! In any case, it appeared that he could find *only one* instance of this by way of proof!

84. J.W.L. (Vol.5, p.359.) Letter to Dr Rutherford 28 March 1768: 'In your first charge you undertake to prove that "Christianity does not reject the aid of human learning" (page 1). Mr Berridge thinks it does. But I am not accountable for him, from whom in this I totally differ.' Compare this with the letter just quoted

85. J.W.L. (Vol.4, p.206.)

would not be based, as in the case of many of the other Evangelicals, on the grounds of disagreement with itinerancy. Although Berridge and Hicks, both beneficed clergymen had their differences with Wesley, they proved to be at this time, two of his greatest friends, and, in a limited sphere, adopted Wesley's methods. Later, Berridge was to separate from Wesley but Hicks remained faithful to the end.[86]

On the other hand, there were far more evangelical clergy who, whilst one with the Wesleys and Whitefield in their zeal, and, to some extent, their doctrines, refused to pursue their labours beyond their lawful parish boundaries. In some cases, they definitely were hostile to the Wesleys and their irregular friends. Among these can be named Henry Venn of Huddersfield,[87] Samuel Walker of Truro, Thomas Adam of Winteringham in Lincolnshire and William Romaine. All these, and others, based their objections far more on the employment of lay-preachers who itinerated, rather than on the personal travels of the Wesley brothers and Whitefield. There is one notable exception, who, though he certainly had much to say against lay-preaching, protested for a considerable time against the itinerancy as such. He was James Hervey who had been a member of the Oxford 'Holy Club'.[88] His main indebtedness to Wesley, whose pupil at Lincoln College he had been, appeared to be Wesley's help in teaching Hervey the Hebrew language. Hervey had despaired of ever becoming proficient in this tongue but thanks to Wesley he had now been able to master it – an ability which is still no mean achievement! Before Hervey's

---

86. One of Berridge's converts was Elizabeth Hurrell who later preached with Wesley's approval. Her own converts included William Warriner who was the first Methodist Missionary to the West Indies and also Henry Foster who became one of Wesley's preachers.

87. It is on record that Venn on one occasion preached 'irregularly' when at Yelling in Huntingdonshire where he lived a life of semi-retirement after leaving Huddersfield. The brothers Richard and Rowland Hill also indulged in itinerancy but did not cooperate with the Wesleys (See Chapter Eleven).

88. Graduated BA. Ordained by Dr Potter in Christ Church Cathedral, Oxford, as Deacon in 1736. Priested Exeter, 1739. He entered Oxford at 17 years of age, holding a Crewe exhibition.

ordination, he began holding 'catechetical lectures' as he called them, in his father's house at Hardingstone, Northamptonshire. Wesley and Hervey continued their association after they had both left Oxford. In 1736, a letter from Hervey dated 2 September revealed that he had read Wesley's *Journal* and paid tribute to the fact that he was what he was because of John's 'never to be forgotten example'.[89]

Hervey became curate to another of the Oxford Methodists – Charles Kinchin, late of Corpus Christi, and now of Dummer near Basingstoke. It should be noted that his services were not confined to this village. These Oxford Methodists seemed to some extent to have been itinerants in these early days, but quite well within the law i.e. by a frequent exchange of pulpits, involving not only Hervey and Kinchin, but Gambold and Broughton. They were, of course, invading the parish of no minister without his consent. It is a pity that no further information about these exchanges is available.

In 1738, owing to failing health,[90] he accepted the invitation to reside at Stoke Abbey in North Devon, the home of Paul Orchard. It was whilst he was there, with plenty of time to think and little to do, that he heard of the Wesleys' evangelical awakening and their successful labours. Also he had been informed of Whitefield's progress which he mentioned in a 'congratulatory address' to 'the friend of my soul', i.e. Wesley, on the latter's return from America.[91] A further letter sent by Hervey to Wesley on 1 December of the same year stated that he had heard that the Wesleys were setters forth of strange doctrines that were contrary to Scripture and repugnant to the Articles of the Church. He believed that these rumours were untrue but he would remain uneasy until he had them refuted by one of the brothers.[92]

On 20 March[93] of the following year, John Wesley replied in a lengthy

---

89. Tyerman, Luke *The Oxford Methodists* (London, 1873, p.212.)
90. Further biographical details of Hervey can be found in Chapters One, Eight and Nine of this study.
91. Tyerman *op.cit.* (p.213.) Letter dated 21 March 1738.
92. Tyerman, Luke *The Oxford Methodists* (London, 1873, pp.217-8.)
93. J.W.L. (Vol.1, pp.284-7.)

epistle in which he defended himself against the criticisms reported by Hervey concerning his doctrinal views and the practice of itinerant preaching. In this letter he ignored the subject of lay-preaching and also rejected the idea that being in Holy Orders necessitated involvement in parochial work. The concept of the World Parish was uncompromisingly stated:

'If you ask on what principle, then, I acted, it was this: A desire to be a Christian; and a conviction that, whatever I judge conducive thereto, that I am bound to do; wherever I judge I can best answer this end, thither it is my duty to go. On this principle I set out for America, on this I visited the Moravian Church, and on the same I am ready now (God being my helper) to go to Abyssinia, or China, or whithersoever it shall please God by this conviction to call me.

'As to your advice, that I should settle in college, I have no business there, having now no office and no pupils. And whether the other branch of your proposal be expedient for me, namely: "To accept of a cure of souls", it will be time enough to consider when one is offered to me.

'But in the meantime you think I ought to be still; because otherwise I should invade another's office if I interfered with other peoples' business and intermeddled with souls that did not belong to me. You accordingly ask, "How is it that I assemble Christians, who are none of my charge, to sing psalms and pray and hear the scriptures expounded?" and think it hard to justify this in other men's parishes upon catholic principles.

'Permit me to speak plainly. If by catholic principles, you mean any other than scripture, they weigh nothing with me. I allow no other rule, whether of faith and practice, than the Holy Scriptures; but on scriptural principles, I do not think it hard to justify whatever I do. God in scripture commands me, according to my power, to instruct, reform the wicked, confirm the virtuous. Man forbids me to do this in another's parish: that is, in effect to do it at all; seeing I have now no parish of my own, nor probably ever shall. Whom then, shall I hear, God or man? "If it be just to obey man rather than God, judge you. A dispensation of the Gospel is committed to me; and woe is me if I preach not the Gospel."

'But where shall I preach it, upon the principles you mention? Why, not in Europe, Asia, Africa, or America; not in any of the Christian parts, at least, of the habitable earth; for all these are, after a sort, divided into parishes. If it be said, "Go back then, to the heathens from whence you came," nay, but neither could I now (on your principles) preach to them, for all heathens in Georgia belong to the parish either of Savannah or Frederica.

'Suffer me now to tell you my principles in this matter. I look upon all the world as my parish; thus far I mean, that in whatever part of it I am I judge it meet, right and my bounden duty to declare unto all that are willing to hear, the glad tidings of salvation. This is the work which I know God has called me to; and sure I am that His blessing attends to. Great encouragement have I, therefore, to be faithful in fulfilling the work He hath given me to do. His servant I am; and, as such, am employed according to the plain direction of His word – "as I have opportunity, doing good unto all men". And His providence clearly concurs with His word, which has disengaged me from all things else that I might attend on this very thing," and go about doing good.'

There is no doubt that Wesley would have replied in the same strain to any other critic of his parish-invading preaching.

It was not, however, about Wesley alone, that Hervey had heard rumours whilst residing at his country seat. On 18 April 1739 he wrote a very lengthy letter to his former rector, Charles Kinchin saying that he had heard he was soon to leave the Established Church and become an itinerant preacher. He mentioned his concern too about Wesley who, he reminded Kinchin, had once before found himself to have been led astray by the opinions of others and therefore was not readily to be followed. Twelve octavo pages followed these remarks and then he continued:

> 'There was a time when Mr Wesley was a warm and able advocate of primitive institutions. I marvel that he is so soon removed to another opinion. This is a fresh conviction – how variable his mind is, and, though burning with zeal for God, yet, given to change. And, having altered so often already, why may he not alter again, and new mould his present sentiments as well as his former?'[94]

Hervey counselled Kinchin to have patience and wait before deciding in favour of Wesley and his friends. Furthermore, he was concerned that his former rector had been persuaded by those people to leave 'our excellent church' and become an itinerant preacher. He refused to believe that this 'wandering into the wide world and preaching in a variety of places is preferable. Hervey, of course, must have been misinformed here – neither Wesley nor Whitefield ever desired to leave the Established Church nor would they have encouraged anyone else to do so. That they had suggested itinerancy to Kinchin, was, of course, a distinct possibility.

There was evidence that Hervey's suspicions were more deeply grounded in his letter to Whitefield dated 10 May 1739. In this he feared that the latter was being 'seduced'.[95] He had heard that among the new notions being expounded was that describing the Orders, Degrees and Robes of the University as being Anti-Christian. Also he had heard that human learning unfitted a man to preach the Gospel. Furthermore, he had been informed that the Established Church ministry was but an invention of men and the Church and its authority were founded upon a lie. What answer Whitefield gave, if any, is unfortunately not available.

---

94. Tyerman, Luke *The Oxford Methodists* (London, 1873, pp.220-222.)
95. Tyerman Luke *The Oxford Methodists* (London, 1873, pp.222-3.)

John Wesley never received a reply to his letter of 20 March and enquired the reason from Hervey. He wondered whether or not the idle stories which Hervey had heard had prevailed upon him. He advised Hervey to leave his secluded retreat and join the band of itinerants! Hervey was quick to reply and explain.[96] His health did not fit him for such an exacting task as that of a field-preacher. He had not even the right strength of voice to thunder to the heavens! If Wesley valued primitive institutions, he would, as did some of those early Apostles, settle somewhere and be content to labour there. 'Be a living Ouranius.'[97] What an example he could have been to neighbouring ministers: what a blessing to his people and theirs!

There were other Evangelicals to whom Wesley justified his conduct in strong terms, as he did to many more who were not of that persuasion. To Thomas Adam, Rector of Winteringham, in a letter dated 31 October 1765, he made a dogmatic stand:

> 'We know Mr Piers,[98] Perronet,[99] Manning,[100] and several
> regular clergy who do preach the genuine gospel, but to no
> effect at all. There is one exception in *England* – Mr Walker
> of Truro. We do not know one more who has converted one
> soul in his own parish. If it be said, "Has not Mr Grimshaw

---

96. See J.W.L. (Vol.1, pp. 332-4.)
97. 'Ouranius', according to the Editor of the Standard edition of Wesley's *Letters* is taken from Law's *Serious Call*. (See Chapter XXI). He is 'an holy priest', full of the Spirit of the Gospel, watching, labouring, and praying for a poor country village. Every soul in it is as dear to him as himself, and he loves them all as he loves himself, because he prays for them all as often as he prays for himself.
98. Vicar of Bexley, converted through Charles Wesley and attended the first Conference in 1744.
99. Sometimes referred to as the 'Archbishop of Methodism', Vicar of Shoreham. Introduced to Wesley by Piers.
100. Charles Manning was Vicar of Hayes; attended his first Conference in 1747. It is said he conducted John Wesley's marriage service. As time certainly told - this was not the most useful service he could have performed for John! All these clergymen were regular ministers. See J.W.L. (Vol. 3, pp. 147 ff.)

and Mr Baddiley?" No, not one, till they were *irregular* – till
both the one and the other formed irregular societies and took
in laymen to assist them. Can there be a stronger proof that
God is pleased with irregular even more than with regular
preaching?'

One could rightly and quickly have taken issue with Wesley about this
extravagant statement. Adam himself was truly no great success as an
incumbent, but the ministers of such Evangelicals as Hervey, Romaine
and Venn were outstanding and were beyond any criticism of Wesley or
any other as to their effectiveness.[101] Such an attitude as this could well
have done much harm to Wesley's methods and work, nor should it
occasion any surprise that many Evangelicals showed little desire to cooperate in the light of such a statement as this. Moreover, Henry Piers,
Charles Manning and Vincent Perronet were Arminian-Methodist clergy
who were lifelong and trusty friends of Wesley and whilst remaining
'regular' always welcomed him to preach in their churches. Wesley's
statement was especially unkind in respect of these men.

More justifiable, however, was his retort to Henry Venn on 22 June
1763 that those who caused irregularity were the very ones who complained
about it:

> 'Will they throw a man into the dirt and beat him because he is
> dirty? Of all men living those clergymen ought not to complain
> who believe I preach the Gospel (as to the substance of it). If
> they do not ask me to preach in their churches, *they* are
> accountable for my preaching in the fields.'[102]

A further comment in one of his letters summed up the position that the

---

101. Venn John (*The Life of Revd Henry Venn, MA &c* (London, 1837, p.387.) 'Dear
    Mr Adam finished his course at Winteringham three weeks ago, after being fifty-
    nine years rector of that parish. Exceedingly small was his success amongst his
    people after preaching the Gospel thirty years.' He died in 1784.
102. J.W.L. (Vol.4, p.217.)

grand breach between the irregular and regular clergy is that the latter said "...Stand by yourselves; we are better than you!" and a good man is continuing exhorting them so to do, whose steady advice is so very *civil* to the Methodists. But we have nothing to do with them. And this man of war is a dying man – it is poor honest Mr Walker...'[103]

John Newton was another Evangelical who had little faith in an itinerant ministry. Writing to an anonymous correspondent on 4 September 1777, he declared that a parish with a converted minister is blessed indeed.[104] Again on 7 March 1765, writing to an unnamed aspirant to the ministry, he said he had been tempted when he first felt called to the ministry, to preach in the streets, but he was thankful to God that he had altered his views. Had he adopted the practice of open-air preaching, he would have been rendered to 'a state of uselessness'. He went on to urge this potential ordinand to seek a regular ministry in the Established Church. Itinerancy could be useful, he said, but he '...more and more observed great inconveniences which follow in that way.'[105]

* * *

An impartial observer will quickly see that little purpose would be served by stressing the obvious illegality and irregularity of an itinerant ministry or 'field-preaching' where the permission of the incumbent concerned had not been obtained. On ecclesiastical grounds, the action of the Wesleys and Whitefield was indefensible. Of course, it must be said that whilst Whitefield introduced the practice to Wesley, he did not

---

103. J.W.L. (Vol.4, p.143.) Written to James Rouquet, 30 March 1761.
104. Newton, John *Cardiphonia, or The Utterance of the Heart in the Course of a Real Correspondence* (London, 1780, pp.237-8.)
105. *ibid.* (p.287 Cf. also pp.303,394-6 for similar views.) Newton owed his conversion to Methodist preaching in Liverpool, where he was employed as a tide-surveyor after pursuing his notoriously wicked career as the captain of a slave ship during which he was a declared unbeliever. Yet, although friendly with Wesley he never offered him his pulpit either at Olney, Bucks, or London.

originate it. He can, however, be given credit for the vision of the 'World Parish'. A precedent had already been set by the Erskines in Scotland and the Welsh Evangelicals who were at work before the enlightenment of either the Wesleys or Whitefield.

Spiritually there was much to be said for itinerancy. Apart from the undisputed good work which was being done by Evangelicals who never left their respective parishes, how would the great Evangelical movement have spread if it had been confined within church walls? It was a case of the mountain which would not go to Muhammed. Wesley and his itinerating colleagues had to go where the unchurched crowds were and speak to them there. Visualizing Kingswood as it was in the eighteenth century, one could think of more fruitful spheres. Yet it was here that revival broke out and the most unexpected happenings took place. The work was of the Spirit of God and this cannot always be forced through man-made channels. Wesley had made out an excellent case, spiritually, if not ecclesiastically.

However, a word must be said in defence of the majority of Evangelicals who rejected the idea of a travelling ministry. Only a handful of them joined Wesley in this method and there were one or two others who acted quite independently. Itinerancy amongst the Evangelicals was to die out before the century closed.

The aim of the Wesleys and Whitefield was also that of the parish-bound Evangelical and the latter was not to be despised.[106] A number of reasons, apart from the important matters of doctrinal differences which will be dealt with in due course, could be given for their not agreeing with, or participating in Wesley's itinerancy system. There was the obvious one of the illegality of this method. Moreover, some of these men were only curates to absentee incumbents and therefore opened themselves to the risk of ecclesiastical censure. Parish boundaries also served as a useful limit to their endeavours and afforded an area which they could reasonably manage themselves. Consequently they never entertained the

---

106. See p.341ff. for a further defence of the parish system of the majority of the Evangelicals.

idea of employing lay-helpers[107] and this subject was also to divide them even more from the Wesleys.

However, the vision of the World Parish had materialized in the Revival. In Methodism it had come to stay. It also brought with it further problems which invited lengthy debate. Having claimed the world for his parish, Wesley was forced to turn to others for help, whereas had he settled in a typical Anglican parish, this need would not have arisen. Hence his abortive appeal to the clergy for assistance including the majority of the Evangelicals.[108] If the clergy would not help, then he had to resort to lay-help. They were needed for two principal reasons – to become travelling preachers like himself and also to give pastoral oversight to the growing numbers of converts. This practice was to the clergy of his day, as big a novelty on field-preaching and it was to bring even more problems to Wesley, especially when, in due course, their relationship with the ordained clergy had to be faced up to and resolved.[109]

---

107. With the exception, of course, of Grimshaw, Baddiley and Howell Davies.
108. See Appendix Two (pp.375-378) and also pp.302-303 for the 'Scarborough Eirenicon'.
109. See Chapters Four and Five of this study, pp.81-103.

CHAPTER FOUR

SOCIETIES AND PREACHERS: THE CONCEPTION OF THE MINISTRY

There is little doubt that the Evangelicals of neither camp visualized the need of lay-preachers and helpers when first they were conscious of the impulse to preach what they felt was the true Gospel. They were Anglicans and the Anglican Church knew little or nothing of lay-preaching. It is true that machinery existing for the practice of lay-preaching in the reign of Elizabeth I had not been repealed. Nor is there any evidence that it was put into use.

The duties of such potential preachers,[1] however, bore little resemblance to the labours of those involved in the Evangelical Revival.[2] The proposed preachers were not to serve in 'any great cure', but could bury the dead and purify women after childbirth. Their 'preaching' would really have consisted of reading prescribed works.

It so happened that certain events which took place at the religious society meeting in Fetter Lane, did not endear either the Wesleys or Whitefield to the possibility of lay-preaching.[3] Two men, Shaw and Bowers (or Bowes), claimed to have special inspiration from the Holy Spirit. Because of this, laymen though they were, they claimed the right

---

1. See my book *John Wesley and The Christian Ministry* (London, 1963, p.27) for a full account of this.
2. See *Visitation Articles and Injunctions of the period of the Reformation III* 1559-75, edited by W.E. Frere (London, 1910.)
3. It has been said that John Wesley employed lay-preachers in America during his Georgian ministry, but there is little evidence to support this.

of priesthood and authority to administer the sacraments. Charles Wesley seemed to have become more involved with them than either John or Whitefield. According to his *Journal* for Wednesday 18 April 1739, Charles said he met Shaw at James's[4] where the malcontent insisted that there was no priesthood. He also claimed that he could baptize and administer the Holy Communion, the right being his as much as that of any priest.[5] On Wednesday 23 April he was told by Whitefield of the harmful effects of Shaw's doctrine at Oxford and this perturbed Charles. On 28 April (Saturday), Shaw interrupted George Whitefield's preaching at Islington churchyard. Charles tried to prevent Shaw, but without success.[6]

Charles recorded on Monday 4 June that he met Shaw 'the self-ordained priest' who was 'brimful of proud wrath and fierceness', his 'spirit suited to his principles'.[7] 'I could do him no good,' confessed Charles, 'but was kept calm and benevolent towards him; therefore he could do me no harm.' The next day, Shaw was described with Bowers as following Charles and George '...drunk with the spirit of delusion'[8] George declared them to be 'two grand enthusiasts'.[9]

Shaw pleaded his right to prophesy at Fetter Lane the next day and he and Bowers publicly declared that Charles Wesley made his followers '...more children of the devil than before'.[10] Charles complained on the Friday of the same week of the damage done by Bowers at Wycombe by preaching in the streets there and on Thursday, 16 August found that the churches were closed to himself for the same reason.[11] What is more, Bowers and Shaw, together with two other men named Wolf and Bray

---

4. Charles does not reveal the identity of 'James'.
5. C.W.J. (1736-9) p.228. Bowers lived in George Yard, Little Britain. He was a wholesale dealer in 'cloaks' or 'clocks'.
6. C.W.J. (1736-9) p.231. Charles mentioned this but Whitefield has made no reference to it in his *Journals*.
7. C.W.J. (1736-9) pp.234-5.
8. C.W.J. (1736-9) p.235.
9. C.W.J. (p.235.) Note it was Charles who recorded George's words.
10. C.W.J. (p.241.)
11. C.W.J. (p.248.)

had been supporters of the group called the 'French Prophets' who had come into the society and disrupted it. They also supported a self-styled 'prophetess' – a woman named Lavington whose grossly immoral conduct was soon to be exposed.

Charles Wesley said on 13 June 1739 that whilst Bray and Bowers 'were humbled', Shaw and Wolf were expelled from the society because they had declared themselves no longer members of the Church of England.[12] Bowers, too was not to be long before he parted company with the Wesleys. He became a subscriber to the Moravian idea of 'stillness', i.e. that until a man has experienced the New Birth, he should not attend church, hear preaching, read the Bible or partake of the Sacraments. According to John's *Journal*,[13] Bowers had affirmed that he had used the ordinances regularly but did not find Christ. Yet, when he left them off, for only a few weeks, he found Him. Said he: 'I am now as close united to Him as my arm is to my body.'

The Editor of the Standard edition of the *Journal* adds a note[14] to this incident – that Bowers set a precedent for lay-preaching. On the contrary, it could be expected that the trouble caused by Bowers and his friends would be more likely to convince the Wesleys, Whitefield and others of the potential dangers of unauthorised lay-preaching, especially of untrained men.

It was to be expected that, as a result of their evangelistic labours, converts would need spiritual oversight. This, of course, could not always be expected from the local clergyman especially when their parishes had been 'invaded'. It was inevitable that the Wesleys would have to enlist help from others and the only others available were laymen, apart from the few clergymen who were in sympathy with them. One of the duties of such lay-helpers was to 'expound'. By that term, Wesley meant elementary Bible teaching to small groups and nothing more.

The story of the first lay-preacher in Methodism is well known and

---

12. C.W.J. (pp.248ff.)
13. J.W.J. (Vol.2, p.366, Wednesday 16 July 1740.)
14. J.W.J. (Vol.3, p.258, Monday 8 September 1746.)

illustrated also the continual influence of Susannah, the mother of the Wesleys, in ecclesiastical matters. One such lay-helper, Thomas Maxfield was left by Wesley in charge of the London society whilst he journeyed to Bristol. During Wesley's absence, Maxfield took it upon himself to preach to the whole congregation and not only to teach the classes of members. Hearing of this, Wesley returned in order to rebuke him, but was quickly restrained by Susannah who bade John hear the man himself before he came to a decision. 'He is surely called of God to preach as you are,' she added. Wesley took his Mother's advice and was compelled to admit: 'It is the Lord; Let him do what seemeth good.'[15] Maybe Wesley also bore in mind the fact that Maxfield had been considerably influenced by the Countess of Huntingdon who had urged Maxfield to 'use his gifts'. Whether this was so or not, Lady Huntingdon later wrote to Wesley and described Maxfield as 'one of the great instances of God's peculiar favour that I know – highly favoured of the Lord.'[16]

Charles Wesley, it must be noted, was not convinced that this was an instance of Divine calling, but he was speedily answered by John on 2 April 1741:

> 'I am not clear that Brother Maxfield should not expound at
> Greyhound Lane, nor can I yet do without him. Our clergymen
> have miscarried full as much as the laymen...'[17]

Later, when quite an old man, Wesley stated that a man called Joseph Humphreys was his first lay-preacher, having begun in 1738. This cannot be true because, as Stevens points out,[18] Humphreys preceded Maxfield. If, therefore, Wesley was exercised in mind about Maxfield's preaching he certainly would not have permitted that of Humphrey.

15. Moore, Henry *The Life of the Revd John Wesley, MA* (London, 1824, Vol.1, pp.505-6.) Moore is the sole authority for this episode.
16. *ibid.* (Vol.1, p.509.)
17. J.W.L. (Vol.1, p.353.)
18. Stevens, Abel *The History of the Religious Movement of the Eighteenth Century called Methodism, to the Death of Wesley* (London, 1862, p.127.)

Perhaps Wesley was referring to Humphrey as being merely an exhorter or expounder to the classes and not as a lay-preacher. One lay-preacher whose work Wesley countenanced from the beginning, without referring to him as such, was John Cennick, a master at Wesley's Kingswood School, who later became a Calvinist and then a Moravian.

Needless to say, lay-preaching soon became firmly established as part of the growing Methodist organization. At the Conference of 1744, there were present at least four of the lay-preachers: Thomas Maxfield, Thomas Richards, John Bennet and John Downes. At this, the first Methodist Conference, it was stated on Thursday 28 August that the following officials belonged to each society: The Ministers, Assistants, Stewards, Leaders of Bands, Leaders of Classes, Visitors of the Sick, Schoolmasters, Housekeepers. The following day, the status and work of the Lay-Assistants were discussed. Most of the information available is given in the 'Bennet Minutes' but Henry Moore in his biography of Wesley, also has an account of the Conference.[19] Moore gives a question with answer, not found in Bennet's account for 1744, but, strangely enough, given for 1746. It seems likely that this would have referred to the 1744 gathering:

'Q. In what view may we and our "helpers' be considered?
A. Perhaps as extraordinary messengers (i.e. out of the ordinary way) designed – (1) To provoke the regular ministers to jealousy (2) To supply their lack of service, towards those who are perishing for lack of knowledge.'[20]

The Bennet Minutes recorded the following:[21]

'Q.Are Lay-Assistants allowable?
A.Only in case of necessity.
Q.What is the office of our Assistants?

19. *The Life of the Revd John Wesley* (London, 1824, Vol.2, pp.41ff.)
20. *ibid.* (Vol.2, p.55.)
21. The Bennet *Minutes* (London, 1896, pp.15ff.)

A.In the absence of the Minister to feed and guide, to teach and govern the flock.
1. To expound every morning and evening.
2. To meet the United Societies, the Bands, The Select Societies and the Penitents every week.
3. To visit the classes (London and Bristol excepted) once a month.
4. To hear and decide all differences.
5. To put the disorderly back on trial, and to receive on trial for the Bands or Society.
6. To see that the Steward and the Leaders, Schoolmasters and Housekeepers... faithfully discharge their several offices.
7. To meet the Stewards, the Leaders of the Bands and Classes weekly, and overlook their accounts.'

Moore, in his biography[22] supplies a further question with answer which he places before those quoted above:

'Q. Who is *the Assistant*?
A. That preacher in each circuit, who is appointed from time to time, to take charge of the Societies and the other preachers therein.'

It is to Bennet that one is indebted for the record of the actual duties of an Assistant. These are headed:

'What are the Rules of an Assistant?

1. Be diligent, never be unemployed a moment, never be triflingly employed (never while away time) spend no more

---

22. *op.cit.* (Vol.2, p.57.) Moore gives an important footnote to this '...in the absence of the Minister'. See also J.W.L. (Vol.2, pp.297ff.) which contains a similar list of duties. No actual date for this letter is given – only the year 1748.

time at any place than is strictly necessary.

2. Be serious. Let your motto be, "Holiness unto the Lord." Avoid all lightness as you would hell-fire and laughing as you would cursing and swearing.

3. Touch no woman; be as loving as you will, but hold your hand off 'em. Custom is nothing to us.

4. Believe evil of no one. If you see it done, well; else take heed of how you credit it. Put the best constructions on everything. You know the judge is always allowed (supposed)[23] to be on the prisoner's side.

5. Speak evil of no one; else your word especially would eat as doth a canker. Keep your thoughts within your (own) breast, till you come to the person concerned.

6. Tell everyone what you think wrong in him, that plainly, and as soon as may be, else it will fester in your heart. Make all haste, therefore to cast the fire out of your bosom.

7. Do nothing as a gentleman; you have no more to do with this character than with that of a dancing-master. You are the servant of all, therefore.

8. Be ashamed of nothing but sin; not of fetching wood or drawing water, if the time permit; not of cleaning your own shoes or your neighbour's.

9. Take no money of any one. If they give you food when you are hungry or clothes when you need them, it is good. But not

---

23. Corrected in Wesley's handwriting.

silver or gold. Let there be no pretence to say, we grow rich by the Gospel.

10. Contract no debt without my knowledge.

11. Be punctual; do everything exactly at the time; and in general do not mend our rules, but keep them, not for wrath but for conscience sake.

12. Act in all things not according to your own will, but as a son in the Gospel. As such it is your part to employ your time in the manner which we direct: partly in visiting the flock from house to house (the sick in particular); partly in such a course of Reading, Meditation and Prayer, as we advise from time to time. Above all, if you labour with us in Our Lord's vineyard, it is needful you should do that part of the work (which) we prescribe (direct)[24] at those times and places which we judge most for His glory.

Q. Should all our Assistants keep journals?
A. By all means, as well for our satisfaction as for the profit of their own souls.[25]

Q. Shall we now fix where each labourer shall be (if God permit) till we meet again?
A. Yes: (which was accordingly done).'[26]

---

24. Corrected in Wesley's handwriting.
25. A list of prescribed reading is appended. Wesley gave each preacher £5 as in order to purchase books. If they had no taste for reading, they had 'to contract one' or return to their trades. Although Wesley was a man of one book, he was against the idea that Bible study was sufficient in itself. See p.69 for his letter to Berridge about this.
26. Bennet *Minutes* (p.16.)

By the conference of 1744, there were thirty-five itinerant preachers and three local helpers or 'Assistants'.[27]

Fourteen named Assistants or lay-preachers were present at the Second Conference in 1745 when a further addition to the 'Rules' was given by way of question and answer:

'Q. What general method of spending their time may our Assistants have?

A. They may spend the mornings (from 6 to 12) in reading, writing and prayer; from 12 to 5, visit the sick and well; and from 5 to 6 use private prayer.'

At both Conferences it was asked whether a 'Seminary' could be provided for 'labourers' but the Question was laid aside by deciding to wait '...until God gives us a proper tutor.'[28]

It is natural that the first Evangelical, other than the Wesleys, to be associated with the principle of lay-preaching was Whitefield. However, he was by no means in agreement with it at first, due to his encounter with the extravagances of Shaw, Wolf and Bray.[29]

By 1741, a breach had occurred between Wesley and himself over the doctrines of Calvinism – a matter which will occupy the major portion of the second part of this study. Whitefield secured a piece of land not far from Wesley's preaching-place at the Foundry and built his celebrated Tabernacle. Immediately he secured the assistance of lay-preachers. What is most interesting is the fact that his two first assistants were none other than those who vied for the position of being Wesley's first helper, namely Cennick and Humphreys![30] Cennick left Wesley because of his adoption of Calvinism, though as has already been pointed out, he was

27. These were not to be thought of as being the same as the modern local-preacher, but were non-itinerant preachers who had full pastoral charge of the local society.
28. The Orphan House at Newcastle and Kingswood School were used as 'schools' for the preachers.
29. See pages pp.81-83 of this study.
30. See page 85 of this study.

not to remain with Whitefield for long. He found his final spiritual home with the Moravians. He died in 1755.

In 1739, Whitefield had shown hesitation about Cennick's being allowed to preach:

> 'I suspend my judgment of Brother Watkin's and Cennick's behaviour till I am better acquainted with the circumstances of their proceeding. I think there is a great difference between them and Howell Harris. He has offered thrice for holy orders; him therefore and our friends at Cambridge, I shall encourage; others I cannot countenance in acting in so public a manner. The consequences of beginning to teach so soon will be exceeding bad...'[31]

Nevertheless, by 1741, he seemed glad enough of Cennick's assistance.

Joseph Humphreys owed his conversion to Whitefield in London in June 1739. He had been studying at a Dissenting Academy for the ministry but was expelled because of his 'seriousness' about religion! He joined an Academy belonging to Mr J. Eames at Moorfields and ministered regularly to religious societies in Deptford, Greenwich and Ratcliffe. Not without significance is the fact that during his preaching, numbers of his hearers were thrown into convulsions similar to those which occurred under Wesley's ministry in Bristol. However, Humphreys was obliged to separate from Wesley and on 25 April 1741 joined Whitefield for the same reason as Cennick did. Soon he disagreed with Whitefield and obtained Presbyterian ordination. Not being content with that, he sought and procured ordination in the Church of England. In spite of his former evangelical successes, he finally abandoned belief in inward and personal religion.

Another of Whitefield's early helpers was Joseph Periam who after his conversion, which he owed to George's influence, was immediately

---

31. Tyerman Luke *The Life and Times of John Wesley* (London, 1871-2, Vol.1, p.277.)

regarded as insane and thrust into the Bethlehem Hospital (i.e. Bedlam). After languishing there for about two months, Whitefield used his influence to secure his release.[32]

Turning now to Whitefield's acceptance of the principle of lay-preaching, it could be accounted for in three ways.

Firstly, like the Wesleys (especially John) whatever his views may have been at first, the expedience of employing laymen as evangelists obviously proved itself as the Revival progressed. Also he would have realized how much slower the work would have advanced without their help.

Secondly, he must have been greatly influenced by the example of two of his closest friends – Benjamin Ingham, his former Oxford Methodist colleague and Howell Harris, the Welsh Evangelist whose successful labours were accomplished in spite of his being denied episcopal ordination. Ingham had been much more attracted to the Moravians than the Wesleys and Whitefield, and he soon joined them, retaining a good relationship with the latter. His main work was in Yorkshire, the county of his birth. He founded approximately eighty societies, although only thirteen remained after the disruption due to the spread amongst them of Sandemanian[33] doctrines. Ingham employed lay-preachers, though there is no information available about their training (if there was any) or about their organization. As for Harris, nowhere did Whitefield utter one word of criticism or surprise. His relationship with Harris was much closer than that between Wesley and Harris. Whitefield never failed to express his thankfulness for all Harris was able to do, particularly in the Principality. A mention will be made later about Harris's own lay-

---

32. For the whole sad story, see Tyerman, Luke *The Life of George Whitefield* (London, 1890, Vol.1, pp.227-230.)

33. Sandeman and his father-in-law, John Glass (founders of the Glas(s)ites or Sandemanians) taught that a National Church was unscriptural and that faith was solely sufficient for salvation to the extent that they laid themselves open to the charge of Antinomianism. Ingham married Lady Margaret Hastings, the sister-in-law of Lady Huntingdon. See Tyerman, Luke *The Life of George Whitefield*, (London, 1890, Vol.1, p.159) for Whitefield's introduction to Lady Huntingdon.

helpers.

A third reason is undoubtedly the most important. This is Whitefield's close association with, and almost servile admiration for, Selina, Countess of Huntingdon. A detailed account of her own system of organizing her lay-helpers and preparing men for ordination will be given in the next section of this chapter.

When Bishop Benson of Gloucester, who had ordained Whitefield, dared to criticize him to her, she quickly and pointedly replied: 'My Lord, mark my words; when you are on your dying bed, that will be one of the few ordinations which you will reflect upon with complacence,'[34] a prophecy which, tradition holds, came true!

Whitefield, unfortunately was no organizer and this would account for the fact that there never was any proper oversight of his lay-helpers. It could be said of him that he neither encouraged them to work for him, nor discouraged them, but accepted their services when offered. This may well have been the reason that he was so rarely attacked for employing lay-preachers whereas Wesley found it a common basis for criticism. A list of Whitefield's preachers is given in Tyerman's *Life of George Whitefield* with a description of their successes.[35] A few pages further on, their sufferings, too, are narrated.[36] Various 'Associations' of Calvinistic Methodists were held from time to time and it was at these that preaching arrangements were made for the various centres.[37] What organization existed for stationing preachers seems to have been left to the Associations, for Whitefield was so often absent from them. Sometimes, Howell Harris acted as George's locum tenens.

Whilst Whitefield was still not in agreement with the employment of ignorant, unlettered preachers, it is difficult to trace what training was

---

34. Tyerman, Luke *The Life of George Whitefield* (London, 1890, Vol.1, p.159.)
35. (London, 1890, Vol.2, p.113.) The names included these of George Cross, F. Pugh, Herbert Jenkins and John Cennick for 1744-5.
36. (Vol.2, p.160.) The names here included those of James Relly, John Edwards and Thomas Adams for 1747-8.
37. One of the centres was Exeter and at this time, only Whitefield's branch of Methodism existed here.

afforded his own lay-helpers. He declared the same year:

> 'It has long been my judgment that it would be best for many
> of the present preachers to have a tutor, and retire for awhile,
> and be content with preaching now and then, till they are a
> little more informed; otherwise I fear many who now make a
> temporary figure, for want of a proper foundation, will run
> themselves out of breath, will grow weary of the work, and
> leave it.'[38]

However, every endeavour was pursued for amicable relations between
lay-preachers of Wesley and those of Whitefield. At one 'Association'
held in Bristol on 22 January 1747,[39] Wesley and four of his assistants
were present and it was enquired:

> '1. How we may remove any hindrances of brotherly love
> which occurred?
> 2. How we may prevent any arising hereafter?'

It was agreed that Wesley's and Whitefield's preachers should
'...endeavour to strengthen each other's hands, and prevent separations
in the several societies.' Harris was also requested to go West to '...heal
the breach there made, and to insist on a spirit of love and its fruits among
the people.'

A similar spirit was evident in 1780 in the advice he gave to some of
Wesley's preachers who consulted him about their leader's discipline. He
replied he was utterly unconcerned in the discipline of Wesley's societies
and therefore could not be a competent judge of their affairs. If the
preachers were to meet more frequently and tell each other their grievances
and opinions, it might be of service. It could be done in a friendly way and

---

38. Andrews, J.R. *George Whitefield – A Light Rising in Obscurity* (London, 1930,
    p.247.)
39. Tyerman, Luke *The Life of George Whitefield* (London, 1890, Vol.2, p.160.)

thus dispense with any uneasiness. After all, those who live in peace must agree to disagree in many things with their fellow-labourers, and '...not let little things part or disunite them.'[40]

However, according to Tyerman,[41] who quotes Thomas Olivers, one of Wesley's best known preachers, Whitefield, later in life, did all he could to encourage Wesley's preachers. He entertained them, sometimes attended their Conferences and preached to them. 'Strange as it may seem,' said Olivers, 'he has been known to say, that he found more *Christian freedom* among Mr Wesley's people than he did among his own in London... He never seemed happier than when he had a number of them about him...'

Lady Huntingdon, formerly Lady Selina Shirley, had been introduced to Methodism by her sister, Lady Margaret (Betty) Hastings. Selina's conversion cannot be said to have been owed directly to the Wesleys or any of the Methodists, but occurred during a short, sharp illness during which she thought over seriously what her sister had told her they preached. She cast in her lot with the Methodists and received her share of the usual resentment and abuse which accompanied such association. She soon became on friendly terms with the Nonconformists, corresponding freely with such prominent personalities as Isaac Watts and Philip Doddridge. Such friendship obviously opened up to her the enormous potentialities of the service to evangelism by lay-workers. Was it not she who commended Thomas Maxfield's preaching to Wesley and mentioned without hesitation the benefit she had received from the preaching and the prayers of laymen?

Left a widow and the possessor of a large fortune, she was determined to use all in her power to further the spread of the Gospel. Her particular mission, she felt, was to her own society. She used her privileged position to greet 'proprietary chapels' to which she appointed chaplains. These were to be found in such towns as York and Huddersfield in the North,

---

40. Andrews, J.R. *George Whitefield – A Light Rising in Obscurity* (London, 1930, pp.246-7.)
41. *The Life of George Whitefield* (London, 1890, Vol.2, p.531.)

Gloucester, Worcester, Lewes and Brighton in the South. Resorts and spas including Bath, Cheltenham, Bristol and Tunbridge Wells were also catered for. Her chaplains were evangelical clergymen, carefully chosen and over whom she had supreme control. Together with these was a host of lay-workers. Some of the clergymen were settled in their own livings but many preached in the various chapels in rotation and soon a 'Connexion' on similar lines to that of the Wesleys was built up over which she exercised what can best be called 'episcopal authority'.

Her lay-preachers were trained and organized in a manner with which none other could compare, and, which must indeed, have been a source of some envy to Wesley. In 1767, she purchased Trevecca House[42] in Breconshire with the intention of turning it into a college for the lay-preachers. She invited John Fletcher,[43] Vicar of Madeley in Shropshire, to become Superintendent of the college. It was duly opened on 24 August 1768, Lady Huntingdon's fiftieth birthday. A clergyman named Joseph Easterbrook, later Vicar of the Temple Church, Bristol was assistant Superintendent or 'President'.

A plan for the examination of the young men who wished to enter the college, was drawn up and Wesley, Romaine and Venn were consulted before it was finally adopted. The first candidate accepted was James Glazebrook, a collier and 'getter of iron stone in Madeley Wood' as Fletcher described him.[44] He was a parishioner of Fletcher's and entered Trevecca on his recommendation. On the completion of his course, Lady Huntingdon procured for him Anglican ordination. After a number of curacies, he wished to be settled in a living. She offered him a post as one of her travelling ministers but he declined. It was only after her death that her daughter, Lady Moira secured for him the living of Belton in

---

42. After the death of Lady Huntingdon in 1791, the college was merged with Cheshunt College, Cambridge in accordance with her wishes.
43. Fletcher was one of Wesley's closest ministerial colleagues and was later to be his apologist against Lady Huntingdon and her associates in the great Calvinistic 'Minute' controversy of 1771-2.
44. A Member of the Houses of Shirley and Hastings *The Life and Time of Selina, Countess of Huntingdon* (London, 1839, Vol.1, p.81.)

Leicestershire.

The students were expected to remain at the college for three years, during which they were to receive free education and 'every necessary of life'. A suit of clothes would be provided once a year. After training, they were free to enter either the ministry of the Established Church or some Protestant Dissenting Church.[45] Their training appeared to have been thorough, at least, judging by the proposed scheme suggested by Fletcher in his letter to Lady Selina, dated 3 January 1768.[46] Apart from obtaining proficiency in the ancient languages, grammar, logic, rhetoric, Ecclesiastical history, 'a little natural philosophy', geography, with a 'great deal of practical divinity' were all included. To this list of subjects, a formidable list of prescribed books was appended. Obviously her college was to be a substitute for the usual courses at Oxford, Cambridge or the Dissenting Academics. One cannot say that this step could be criticized as 'irregular' but the fact that their training consisted of preaching throughout her Connexion, both in her chapels and the various 'rounds' (or 'circuits' as Wesley would have called them),[47] certainly left room for official objection. This practice was, of course, consistent with Dissenting procedure, but certainly irregular for those who aspired to Anglican orders.

After the first anniversary, Fletcher used his influence with Her Ladyship to secure the post of headmaster of the college for Joseph Benson. Benson had been at Oxford with the intention of entering orders, but once it was known that he was in sympathy with the Methodists, he was forced to leave. He became classics master at Kingswood. However, with Wesley's consent, he took up residence at Trevecca in the spring of 1770. He remained there for scarcely eighteen months, when, like Fletcher he was compelled to leave owing to his position in the 'Minute Controversy'

---

45. A Member of the Houses of Shirley and Hastings *The Life and Times of Selina, Countess of Huntingdon* (London, 1839, Vol.2, p.79.)
46. *ibid.* (Vol.2, p.85.)
47. Several horses were kept at Trevecca for the use of the student preachers for their itineraries.

of 1771,[48] which raged for some considerable time, causing an irreparable breach between the Countess and her followers on one hand, and Wesley's branch of Methodism on the other. This, however, will be dealt with more fully in a later Chapter.[49]

Grimshaw of Haworth, in common with the Wesleys and Whitefield, was not at first enamoured with the idea of availing himself of the assistance of lay-preachers. When John Nelson, one of Wesley's chief lay-helpers preached in the Old Hall at Haworth in 1744, Grimshaw warned his people not to go to hear him as he understood that wherever they went, the Methodists turned everything 'upside down'.[50] Yet, in a letter of 1784 to Dr Gillies of Glasgow,[51] Grimshaw wrote appreciatively of the work of Thomas Calbeck, the second Class-Leader and lay-preacher at Keighley and also of Jonathan Maskew, Paul Greenwood and others. He mentioned in the letter that their work was done in 1744. A letter of 21 July 1746, written about Grimshaw to a clergyman, the Revd Malachi Blake of Blandford, Dorset, by Mr Joseph Williams of Kidderminster,[52] said Grimshaw acknowledged that he had received a great deal of assistance from two laymen in the parish, who, with his approbation, expounded the Scriptures, and gave exhortation to great numbers, who, almost every day, attended on them in private houses, and had added, 'with an air of pleasure' that he believed God had converted as many by their services as by his own.

The chief assistant to Grimshaw was William Darney who had come

---

48. See Chapter Eleven of this study, p.306ff. Berridge was the only Evangelical critic of the Trevecca scheme from the beginning. 'The soil you have chosen is proper,' he said, 'Welsh mountains afford a brisk air for a student; and the rules are excellent; but I doubt the success of your project and fear it will occasion you more trouble than all your other undertakings beside.' (See A Member of the Houses of Shirley and Hastings *The Life and Times of Selina, Countess of Huntingdon* (London, 1839, Vol.2, p.92.)
49. See Chapter Eleven of this study (p.330ff.)
50. Laycock, J.W. *Methodist Heroes of the Great Haworth Round 1734-1784* (Keighley, 1909, p.21.)
51. *ibid.* (p.21.)
52. *ibid.* (p.132.)

to Haworth from Kilsyth. This man had been converted and became a preacher *before* Grimshaw knew him. Darney founded societies throughout the 'Haworth Round' as Grimshaw's greatly extended and irregular parish was known. Grimshaw ministered to these societies and himself acted as Wesley's assistant in what really was the 'Haworth Circuit'. In 1747, Wesley was asked to 'examine' Darney's societies. At the Conference of the following year, Darney became one of Wesley's helpers, though still serving in the 'Haworth Round'. Greenwood also became one of Wesley's preachers. By 1747, according to a letter written by Grimshaw to Wesley,[53] the people were crying out for more preachers, as so many new classes had been formed.

At the very edge of the 'Haworth Round' on the south-eastern side, the Vicar of Hayfield in Derbyshire, William Baddiley,[54] was also employing lay preachers, according to the *Methodist Magazine* of 1779[55] although nowhere did Wesley mention the fact. It is a pity that no information about these preachers, their organization, extent of work and district covered is available.[56]

What is definite, is that according to a letter written by Baddiley to Wesley in 1755, when the latter's preachers were clamouring for the right to administer the sacraments, the former warned against allowing this by pertinently pointing out that his own preachers had no sacramental powers.

One Evangelical who courageously defended the use of lay-preachers, especially in the case of Wesley, yet never employed them himself, was John Milner, Vicar of Chipping in North Lancashire. There had been opposition to Wesley's being invited to preach in Chipping Church,

53. Laycock, J.W. *Methodist Heroes in the Great Haworth Round, 1734-1784* (Keighley, 1909, p.57.)
54. In Hayfield Church, the name is spelt 'Badeley'.
55. See also Tyerman, Luke *The Life and Times of the Revd John Wesley, MA* (London, 1871-2, Vol.2, pp.205ff.) Also Denny-Urlin, R. *A Churchman's Life of Wesley* (London, 1880, p.130.)
56. A personal visit to Hayfield and enquiries there, were of no avail.

which resulted in Milner's being called before his Bishop. In a letter to Jonathan Maskew, a preacher of Grimshaw's, he related the incident:

> 'You have probably heard of my being called before the Bishop, for the high offence of letting Mr Wesley preach in my pulpit. I came off triumphantly, and my adversaries have just cause to be shamed. The Bishop heard me with so much mildness and candour, and I told him plainly and fully, the happy efficacy and success of the preaching, even of the lay-preachers, that I have great hopes he will not be an enemy, but a friend.'

He went on to say to Maskew:

> '...if you knew what Mr Wesley said of you, that "ten such would carry the world before them"...'[57]

As so much of the success of the Welsh Revival was due to the itinerant ministry of Howell Harris, himself a layman, it was to be expected that he would have no compunction in securing the assistance of other laymen. However, he was not the only Welsh Evangelist to do so. The other known employer of lay-assistants was Howell Davies, often referred to as the 'Apostle of Pembrokeshire',[58] and a clergyman. Little or nothing is known of his method of organizing these men or what training, if any, they received, but Wesley's views were certainly recorded.[59] In the *Journal* for Wednesday, 2 September 1769, he declared that the work of God had been hindered by Davies' lay-preachers who

---

57. Laycock, J.W. *Methodist Heroes in the Great Haworth Round 1734-1784* (Keighley, 1909, p.81.) *John* Milner must not be confused with Joseph Milner, Vicar of Holy Trinity Church Hull, and his younger brother, Isaac Milner who became Dean of Carlisle, both of whom were prominent Evangelicals. They were not related in any way.
58. See Chapter Three (Section Two) of this study.
59. J.W.J. (Vol.5, pp.229-230.)

opposed his own men. To avoid unnecessary and damaging contention, he advised his own preachers to let all the people sacredly abstain from backbiting, tale-bearing and evil-speaking; to let all his own preachers abstain from 'railing for railing', either in public or private, as well as from disputing; to let them never preach controversy, but plain practical and experiential religion.

Perhaps the earliest expression of evangelical disapproval of the practice of employing lay-preachers was from James Hervey. He was of a frail constitution and was recuperating from an illness at Stoke Abbey near Hartland in North Devon. Obviously he had been hearing rumours for he wrote on 1 December 1738 to Wesley:

> 'Dear Sir,
>   Will you permit me to inform you what is said, though I verily believe slanderously said, of you?...that you endeavour to dissuade honest tradesmen from following their occupations, and persuade them to turn preachers...'[60]

Wesley replied on 20 March 1739 in a long letter answering other criticisms but ignoring what Hervey had said about the employment of lay-preachers.[61]

It was inevitable that, sooner or later the question would arise of the need or rightness of Wesley's preachers working in the parish of an evangelical incumbent. Such was the case of Henry Venn, Vicar of Huddersfield, who, himself, employed no such laymen. The matter was discussed between the two men, apparently in an atmosphere of embarrassment on Wednesday 15 July 1761.[62] Wesley described the situation in a letter to Ebenezer Blackwell. Apparently some of his

---

60. Tyerman, Luke *The Oxford Methodists* (London, 1873, pp.217-8.) Also *The Evangelical Magazine* (1778, p.132.)

61. J.W.L. (Vol.1, pp.244-7.) See also pp.70-75 of this study for further details of this letter.

62. J.W.L. (Vol.4, p.160.) Letter to Ebenezer Blackwell, dated 16 July 1761. Blackwell was a friend of Wesley who lived at Lewisham.

preachers had gone to Huddersfield before Venn's incumbency and founded a small society. Now that Venn, an Evangelical, had arrived, the question arose – should the society cease? These preachers held Venn in esteem and in fact attended his church, but Wesley insisted that these helpers supplied what was 'missing' in Venn's ministry, though he did not make clear what it was that was missing! The new converts of Wesley's men requested that the preachers stayed. Wesley desired peace but to recall the preachers was too great a price to pay for it.

In a further letter to Ebenezer Blackwell[63] dated 15 August 1761, Wesley says he was pleased to announce a compromise, namely, that the preachers should limit their labours to 'once a month'.

John Pawson, later to be one of Wesley's own ordinands for his work in Scotland, gave his own account of the affair in *An Affectionate Address to the Members of the Methodist Societies, 1795*:

> 'For some years (and at the hazard of their lives) our preachers had preached in Huddersfield, where they formed a society and procured peace. Through the interest of our people, Revd Mr Venn got to be Vicar of that parish and for some time was made very useful. But in a while he petitioned Mr Wesley to withdraw the preachers from his parish, as he thought himself quite sufficient for the work without them. Mr Wesley did so for several years, to the unspeakable grief of our Society, till in the year 1765 we began to visit that place again without Wesley's knowledge, and by this means a door was opened into that dreadful wilderness beyond Huddersfield, where much good has been done. Mr Venn's curate took the pains to go from house to house to entreat the people not to come to hear us, but he lost his bad labour.'[64]

Wesley got to know about the renewed preaching at Huddersfield,

63. J.W.L. (Vol.4, p.161.)
64. John Riland was curate to Venn in 1763 when this reintroduction of preaching took place.

obviously from Venn himself, for in a lengthy letter addressed to the latter, Wesley, who had been attacked, not only for irregularities but particularly for doctrinal differences, agreed to suspend the preachers' activities there for another period:

> 'I come now directly to your letter, in hopes of establishing a good understanding between us. I agreed to suspend for a twelve month our stated preaching at Huddersfield, which had been there these many years. If this answered your end, I am glad; my end it did not answer at all. I heard of it from every quarter; though few knew that I did, for I saw no cause to speak against *you* because you did *against me*. I wanted you to do more, not less good, and therefore durst not do or say anything to hinder. And, lest I should hinder, I will make a further trial and suspend the preaching at Huddersfield for another year.'[65]

Another evangelical clergyman who took a similar attitude to that of Venn,[66] was Henry Crook who was curate of Hunslet near Leeds. He complained to Wesley when the latter was at Newark, that some of John's preachers had frequently expounded in Crook's parish.

Crook's judgement was that their preaching at Hunslet had done some good, but it had done more harm, because those who attended it had only turned from one wickedness to another. They had only exchanged Sabbath-breaking, swearing or drunkenness, for slandering, backbiting and evil-speaking; and those who did not attend it were provoked hereby to return evil for evil; so that the former were, in effect, no better, the latter, worse than before.[67]

Wesley admitted the same objections had been made in many other

---

65. J.W.L. (Vol. 4, pp.214-218.) Dated 22 June 1763.
66. J.W.J. (Vol.3, pp.279-280.)
67. Two sermons written by Crook were read by John Pawson and resulted in the latter's conversion. Pawson became one of Wesley's best known preachers and later Wesley 'ordained' him for work in Scotland.

places and his answer recorded on the very next page of the *Journal*, showed that he came to the conclusion that the sins of backbiting, slandering and evil-speaking were not altogether uncommon amongst either the clergy or the preachers. So could one expect their hearers to attain any higher standard of conduct?[68]

* * *

There is little point in emphasizing further the illegality of ordained unbeneficed clergy such as the Wesleys, Whitefield and also other clergy who did possess livings, employing lay-preachers. The precedent for lay-preaching which had existed in Elizabethan times, though never used, bore little relevance to the type of lay-preacher and his work in the eighteenth century.

In evangelical parishes, there was something to be said for the views of Venn and Crook. Lay-preachers maybe were not required. Societies would exist for the converts. Rather, lay-preaching originated from a need to assist the Wesleys and their coadjutors in the great 'World Parish' which they undertook to serve. Where the local clergy proved hostile, converts had to be provided for spiritually in local societies and, on the whole, apart from occasional visits from the Wesleys, they were to be served by the travelling laymen.[69] Local laymen became their immediate leaders or 'Class-Leaders' whilst the preaching was provided mainly by the itinerant preachers or 'Helpers'. If field-preaching and the itinerant ministry were 'of the Spirit' one could justifiably say that lay-preaching

---

68. Compare the attitudes of Crook and Venn with that of Joseph Easterbrook who was a member of the staff at Trevecca College. When he became incumbent of the Temple, Bristol, he handed over his converts to Wesley's societies.

69. A generation later, Rowland Hill who assented to the practice of lay-preaching never countenanced the slightest interference by itinerant preachers with '...the sphere of a clergyman whose doctrines and zeal were admitted by him.' See Sidney, Edwin *The Life of the Revd Rowland Hill AM* (London, 1834.) Hill himself had for some time been an itinerant.

was the same. It arose out of necessity and one cannot say that either the Wesleys or Whitefield were in agreement with the practice in the beginning. They simply accepted it as inevitable as the Evangelical movement grew.

Another factor which made lay-preaching a permanent feature of the revival was the contribution of Lady Huntingdon and her College at Trevecca. It was remarkably well organized and it could hardly be said of her preachers that they were ignorant and unlettered.

However, the practice was not to continue without providing difficulties which, in Wesley's case, especially, were to contribute to the final separation of Methodism from the Established Church. As the number of lay-preachers grew, their demand for greater authority grew also. The prevailing hostility among the greater part of the parish clergy to the Methodists and the refusal to dispense to them the sacraments added to the agitation on the part of the lay-preachers for greater power. In this they were encouraged by the local folk whom they served. Why could not the sacraments be administered to the people by their own preachers? The years 1754-1784 (when the first Methodist 'ordinations' took place) bear record to an increasing demand for authority in the form of ordination and the resistance to such demands by Wesley, who was strongly supported in this by his brother Charles.

In the next chapter it will be seen how this demand grew and how it was dealt with, first by attempting to procure regular Anglican ordination for the preachers, and then by the doubtful employment of a Greek bishop and, finally, by Wesley himself. Long before 1784 he had persuaded himself by his reading of two books[70] that he was a real spiritual episkopos with the power to ordain. Compared with Wesley's methods are those employed by Lady Huntingdon and the Evangelicals. Only the latter went about the task of procuring ordination in a legal and regular manner and many of their methods exist today.

---

70. The two books were Lord Peter King's *Primitive Church* and Bishop Stillingfleet's *Eirenicon*. See my book: *John Wesley and the Christian Ministry: The Sources and Development of his Opinions and Practice* (London, 1963, Chapter Three, pp.47-70) where a full summary of these works is given and the use which Wesley made of them.

CHAPTER FIVE

LAY-PREACHERS AND THE QUESTION OF ORDINATION

By the middle of the eighteenth century the relationship of the lay-preachers to the ordained ministry had to be faced. As the subject is studied in this chapter, it will be seen to be unavoidably linked with the possibility of separation of Methodism from the Established Church.

In so many parishes, the Methodists were refused the sacraments in their local church. Moreover, they could not understand why their own preachers could not administer the sacraments to them in their own preaching-houses.

On the other hand, the preachers themselves were becoming a problem to Wesley. They were putting pressure on him to allow them to administer. John's principle, however, was that there should be no administration without ordination;[1] hence his attempt to procure regular ordination from Anglican bishops. If only ordination could thus be obtained it would fulfil the requirements of the Methodist people and would make his preachers more useful. It would have solved the question of administering the sacraments where the local clergy refused to cooperate. However, there

---

1. See my book *John Wesley and the Christian Ministry* (London, 1963, pp108-118) for fuller details of Wesley's difficulties with his lay-preachers in respect of administering in the societies. Allegations had been made against the preachers that some of them had already administered the sacraments without Wesley's permission.

was one point which he disagreed with, namely, that such ordained preachers be 'fixed' in one place: his desire for ordination was for itinerant work. Nor was he agreeable to handing over his societies to a local incumbent, even though he might have been an Evangelical. To have done so would have caused the separation he intended to avoid.

Another reason for Wesley's seeking episcopal ordination was to end a practice which, by its very nature, pointed Methodism along the way of Dissent. That was the necessity of licensing Methodist preaching-places as 'Meeting-Houses' and preachers as 'Dissenting Ministers':

> 'Do not license yourself until you are constrained; and then not as a Dissenter, but as a Methodist preacher. It is time enough when you are prosecuted, to take the oaths. Thereby you are licensed.'[2]

It was not, however, as easily done as this. Arguing the case of the preachers to Thomas Adam, Rector of Winteringham, an Evangelical to whom reference has already been made, and whose sympathy with Wesley was waning, John cited an instance in London of the Justices being forced to grant a licence even though the preachers declared themselves to be 'of the church'. Yet others, Wesley admitted, were refused licences except as Dissenting ministers, so the fact that they had no choice was not their own fault. Wesley's argument to Adam was weak:

> 'They *did* call them so (i.e. Dissenters) in their certificate, but this did not *make* them so...'[3]

As was often the case, the driving force behind Wesley's endeavouring to keep on the straight and narrow Anglican path, was in the influence of his brother Charles. To Charles it was simply a straight choice. The

2. Minutes of the Conference, 1763.
3. J.W.L. (Vol.5, pp.97ff.) Dated 19 July 1768.

preachers must become either Church ministers or Dissenting ministers. His own choice needed no emphasis. In a letter to John Nelson, dated 27 March 1760, he wrote:

> 'I think you are no weathercock. What think you of licensing yourself as a Protestant Dissenter?...John, I love thee from my heart; yet rather than see thee a Dissenting minister, I wish to see thee smiling in thy coffin...'[4]

What was more, some of the preachers had begun to take upon themselves the right to administer both sacraments without Wesley's consent, or at least, so Charles alleged. He cited an incident of such misconduct in 1755, suspecting that the preachers concerned might even have received 'ordination' by the imposition of John's hands.[5] Hence it was time to give serious thought to the subject of ordination and to the whole question of the discipline of the preachers.

Naturally, Wesley turned to his evangelical colleagues for advice, though one receives the impression on reading through the correspondence that he had already decided what answer he wanted and what, in any case, he would do.

His greatest and most important correspondence was with Thomas Adam of Winteringham and Samuel Walker,[6] perpetual curate of Truro. Wesley had always admired Walker and on one occasion declared that he was the only *regular* minister who was successful[7] in converting souls in his parish. Yet Walker was very suspicious of Methodism and refused to have anything to do with the movement. He acknowledged their zeal and the good they had done but did not always approve of their methods. 'I trust,' he said, 'we shall keep our people in the generality clear from the

---

4. Jackson, Thomas *The Life of the Revd Charles Wesley MA* (London, 1841, Vol.2, p.185.)
5. Jackson, Thomas *The Life of the Revd Charles Wesley MA* (London, Vol.2, p.70.)
6. See also my book *John Wesley and the Christian Ministry* (London, 1963, pp.112-166.)
7. See also Chapter Three of this study.

peculiarities of Methodism'.[8] By 1759 he was able to say in a letter to Adam: 'There is an old society of John Wesley's in the parish. It will be a nice matter neither to quarrel nor join with them.' Walker had already established religious societies of his own by 1754, which, as they were within his own parish, broke no rule of the church. As a society, he felt, '...we shall be better able to glorify God; for hereby we shall bear a more public and convincing testimony to the case of Christ.' Another reason was to '...quicken, comfort and build themselves up in their holy faith.'[9] This letter was dated 22 October 1759.

Both Walker and Adam knew that the subject of lay-preachers and the possibility of separation from the Church had occupied a large part of the Conference of 1755 which had met in Leeds. After all the debate, the decision was that 'Whether separation was *lawful* or not, it was not *expedient.*' This did not appear strong enough for Charles Wesley who immediately composed a poetical *Epistle to the Revd Mr John Wesley* which he printed in a 12mo tract of 16 pages and put into circulation.

Wesley had already asked Walker for his opinion on a pamphlet which the former had published on the subject of separation from the church. On 3 September 1755,[10] Walker replied that if it was not lawful for them to depart, it could not in the nature of things be necessary or expedient. Wesley had to ask himself the following questions:

(i)   Whether it was lawful to separate?

(ii)   What is, and what is not separation?

(iii) Whether, if he determines it is not lawful, he has taken any steps towards it already?

(iv)   If so, and separation be unlawful, whether he ought not to put a stop to them?

(v)   In this view, what is he to do with lay-preachers? (A

---

8.   Sidney, Edwin *The Life and Ministry of the Revd Samuel Walker BA of Truro* (London, 1838, pp.50-1 & 156.)

9.   Sidney, Edwin *The Life and Ministry of the Revd Samuel Walker BA of Truro* (London, 1838, p.495.)

10. *ibid.* (pp.59 and 60.)

tender point.) There is no doubt 'a handle' had been given here for separation.

Wesley's middle way of 'permitting' rather than appointing preachers, put the matter quite out of his hands and deprived him of all influence; but as long as they were permitted or appointed, here was a *partial* separation from the Church. In any case, why did they want to leave the Church? They did not disagree with her doctrine, laws or administration nor had they been thrust out. Walker gave Wesley five more questions to ponder over, all dealing with the weakening of effectiveness if he quitted the Church. It would be a stumbling block to others and a cause for rejoicing by his enemies. What was more, he suggested, Wesley should state his case to some other person not immediately connected with him, for example, Mr Adam. Before Wesley's reply was received, Walker communicated to Adam his sentiments.

Wesley replied on 24 September 1755,[11] thanking Walker for his advice. He personally felt that separation would be unlawful but some of his people had said they could not agree with the Book of Common Prayer in some of the things which were stated therein. Also in the Decretals and Canons of the Church, there remained the 'very dregs of Popery'. Many of the Church's ministers had justifiably come in for criticism as had their doctrines. As for himself, he knew the origins of the doctrines of the church were sound and her worship pure and scriptural. The Methodists, as yet, had neither renounced the Church's teaching nor refused to join her worship. All they had done was to (i) Preach abroad; (ii) Pray extempore; (iii) Form societies; (iv) Permit preachers who were not episcopally ordained. Therefore, declared Wesley, if they could not stop a separation without stopping lay-preachers, the case was clear, they could not stop it at all. If they permitted the preachers they might as well appoint them. What Wesley now wanted to know was whether it was lawful for presbyters like themselves to appoint other ministers.

On 20 October 1755 Walker answered the comments about the

11. J.W.L. (Vol.3, pp.143-7.)

Methodist preachers as Wesley had given them. Wesley, however, had to do what was right and fear no consequences. It must be pointed out that Walker said nothing to Wesley about the latter's query, about presbyteral ordination. Copies of both Walker's and Wesley's letters were sent by Walker to Adam for the latter's comment, with the remark 'Do you think Mr Wesley will stand his ground? For my part, I fear not.' Walker inclined to the idea that Wesley had deviated too far already from the discipline of the church. Again he wrote to Mr Adam on 25 March 1756,[12] confirming his own view that there were many faithful and evangelical clergy in the church.[13] Of course, in all fairness, it must be granted that Wesley, travelling around the country as he did, would be in a better position than either Walker or Adam to know whether or not the clergy were helpful or otherwise.

The Bristol Conference of the following year spent a great deal of time, like the previous one, on the subject of separation from the church. A more positive resolution was passed – a solemn description of their purpose 'never to separate from the church'. The upshot of this declaration was that one or two preachers turned Independent ministers, taking their congregations (or societies) with them.

Just before this Conference, Charles Wesley wrote to Walker on 7 August 1756. He was able to inform Walker that he had been successful in getting John and certain of the preachers to sign a declaration reaffirming their allegiance to the Church of England.[14] If this had not been done, wrote Charles, he would have broken off from his brother and the Methodists. He felt that another letter from Walker to John might 'confirm him in his calling'. John, he suggested, should arrange for three lines of action to be carried out:

---

12. Sidney, Edwin *The Life and Ministry of the Revd Samuel Walker BA, of Truro* (London, 1838, p.182.)
13. Sidney *op.cit.* (p.182.)
14. It was signed by the following: John Jones; John Downes; John Nelson; Wm Kent – in addition to the Wesley brothers.

1. That the unsound, unrecoverable preachers should be let depart just now.
2. That the wavering should be confirmed, if possible, and established in their calling.
3. That the sound ones should be received into the strictest union and confidence, and, as soon as may be, *prepared for orders*.

This done, he should also then:

1. Take all proper pains to instruct and ground both his preachers and his flock in the same.
2. Wait with him (Charles) on the Archbishop who has desired to see him (John) to tell him 'our whole design'.
3. Advise, as far as they think proper, with such of our brethren the clergy as know the truth, and do nothing without their approbation.[15]

Walker did as Charles suggested and wrote to John.[16] He used the line that John ought to settle things as he would wish them to be after his death. He must keep in mind the interests of practical religion over and above the interests either of the Church of England or Methodism. It was unlawful to separate from the Church and he should not dispute with those who disagree. At the next Conference he must not only do this but determine which of the preachers who were fit for it might be considered for ordination. Those who were not ordained should be 'fixed' to certain societies as inspectors and readers rather than preachers. These arrangements should be carried out so as not to give offence to Dissenters of 'any denomination' – a rather unusual piece of advice to be given in this context.

---

15. Sidney *op.cit.* (p.202.) Charles also mentioned that the Countess of Huntingdon advised him long ago to write to Walker.
16. *ibid.* (p.202.) This letter is undated.

It is now time to consider Walker's reply to Charles.[17] He had been hesitant in writing to John but the thought of possible separation from the Church had driven him to it. Walker defined the Church to Charles as '...a congregation of Christian people, where the pure word of God is preached and the sacraments duly administered.' All that was left to a particular church was to settle government and modes of worship, because all other things were settled by Christ. Lay preaching was contrary to the rules of the Church of England, therefore, it constituted a separation from it. Walker was a little less logical when he admitted that the practice may well have been agreeable to the Spirit though such preachers would have felt easier in mind about their work, had they received 'an outward call'. But even if such preachers were needful, they were inconsistent with the Establishment, therefore if they continued, there would be a completion of the separation already begun. There would be no unity with the Church until lay-preaching was set aside. The practice had caused a bar to be made between regular clergymen and the Methodists. He pinpointed a real difficulty when he said that lay-preaching resulted in two disunited ministrations of the word in the same place, both by people claiming to be of the Church of England.

Quoting Mr Vivian[18] of Cornwood, he proposed the following scheme:

(i)   That as many of the lay-preachers as are fit for, and can be procured ordination, be ordained.

(ii) That those who remain be not allowed to preach, but be set over the societies as inspectors and assistants to those who are ordained.

(iii) That they be not moved from place to place, to the end they may be personally acquainted with all the members of such societies.

---

17. Sidney *op.cit.* (p.207.) The letter is undated.
18. Thomas Vivian of Cornwood informed Wesley in 1748 that he owed him a debt of gratitude for the blessing which came upon his soul after reading Wesley's writings. However, at a later date, Wesley declared that Vivian had '...fallen into the pit of the Decrees and knew him no more.'

(iv) That their business may be to purge and edify the societies under their care, to the end that no person be continued a member, whose conversation is not orderly and of good report.

The raw, unqualified and sadly misbehaved preachers were doing much harm to Methodism, maintained Walker, and was probably quite right in this judgment. In fact, he prophesied that lay-preaching would be the ruin of Methodism.

A private letter had gone to Charles at the same time[19] in which Walker declared he had little faith in the written agreement between the Wesleys and the preachers on the matter of separation.[20] He agreed that the brothers should see the Archbishop of Canterbury as soon as possible in the interests of peace. It was obvious that Walker's practical suggestions to John Wesley as outlined above found their origin in Charles' own ideas as seen in his previous letters.[21]

Lay-preaching, replied Charles, may be a partial separation but did not need to be a total one. He stayed with his brother, not so much to do good, but to prevent evil. He tried to prevent his brother's violent counsellors influencing him too much. He wanted John to put a stop to their hopes of leaving the Church of England and also prevent the employment of any new preachers until John entirely regulated, disciplined and secured the old ones.

Another letter, again unfortunately undated was written by Walker to Charles. It was similar in strain to his previous epistles, namely, that if it were not sinful to abide in a particular Church, it would be sinful to separate. It would be far better to remain in the Church if good were to result. Copies of this and his previous letters were sent to Adam at Winteringham. He pointed out to Adam the difficulties of the Wesley brothers. It was a pity that so many of these men who were preaching the Gospel were tinctured with unsound notions not in harmony with Scripture.

---

19. Sidney *op.cit.* (p.213.) This letter is undated.
20. See p.110 of this study.
21. Sidney *op.cit.* (p.215.)

If the Wesleys left the Church, then their usefulness would be at an end and such an occurrence would dampen the zeal of the regular clergy who were 'standing up in the gap'.

However, Adam could not countenance Walker's suggestions to Charles Wesley. He was sorry to differ with Walker, Conon[22] and Vivian, but Methodism was such a deviation from the Church of England that all attempts to render it consistent must be in vain. Lay-preaching was a manifest irregularity and would not be endured in any Christian society. As for ordaining any of them, they would probably not consent to it. If they did, for what purpose was it to be administered? To preach in fields or private houses and hold separate meetings. They must all return to the Establishment. John Wesley, he felt, would not give up lay-preaching for it would be giving up all. 'He must cry *peccavi*, and his heart will hold him a tug before he comes to that.' In any case, if Wesley did relinquish the practice, his followers would not.

Commenting on the second suggestion of Walker's that those preachers not to be ordained should be inspectors of societies, he asked, 'What societies?' These societies were disunited from their proper minister. How would Walker like this to happen in his own parish?[23]

To the third and fourth suggestions, namely that the ordained preachers settle in a place and that the unordained ones' work was to purge the societies, he could not see how the ordained ones would remain in one place – rather they would itinerate as was the Methodist custom. The unordained were bound to settle because of their secular employment. It was too late to do anything about reforming Methodism. Walker's best plan was to leave it alone!

The correspondence drew to a close with a final letter to Walker from Charles,[24] outlining the results of the Conference of 1756. It had been declared that the Methodists would remain in the Church of England and John was preparing a treatise on keeping them there. John's last letter to

---

22. Conon was the schoolmaster at Truro under whom Walker was converted.
23. J.W.J. (Vol.3, p.194.)
24. Sidney *op.cit.* (p.224). Letter dated 24 September 1756.

Walker, dated 3 September 1756[25] described the beginnings of lay-preaching. It came to be, because of the opposition of the clergy. They were called of God and permitted to travel abroad, preaching, confirming, comforting, exhorting and instructing, because more needed them. Great blessings had attended their work. Wesley had already kept the first of Walker's suggestions, namely, considering the interests of the Church of England and he also agreed with the inadvisability of separation. They had all declared themselves to remain within the Church. Wesley did not disagree with procuring ordination for them but he would not agree to their being fixed in one place. If this happened, their usefulness would cease. A frequent change of preachers was best, otherwise they would 'grow dead'. All have their respective talents and no one was sufficient in himself for '...beginning, continuing and perfecting the work of grace in a whole congregation.' He dismissed the idea of those not suitable for ordination being appointed inspectors and readers in a society. Who would minister the word to the people? The local clergy? He could not forbid his preachers to do what God had called them to do.

By 7 October 1756, according to another letter to Adam,[26] Walker was going to have no more to do with Wesley unless further advice was requested. Adam replied on 19 November[27] to the effect that the proceedings of the Methodists would have been condemned in any age of Church history. How could Charles Wesley reconcile his views on lay-preaching with his strict notions of conformity? Never mind what good the Methodists may, or may not have done. That was not the issue. The fact remained; the Methodists were already out of the Church.

Walker's final position was made amply clear in his advice to an active layman on one occasion:[28]

---

25. J.W.L. (Vol.3, pp.192.ff.)
26. Sidney *op.cit.* (p.309.)
27. Sidney *op.cit.* (p.309.)
28. Sidney *op.cit.* (p.322.) Sidney, commenting on this statement, carefully distinguishes between lay-preaching and lay-agency. The latter is '...an essential help to the minister; the former is an encroachment on his peculiar province.'

'There can be no objection made to your meeting by persons of common sense; but you see what the world is waiting for, that they may be able to blame you that you should undertake to preach. God hath so remarkably blessed our *regular*[29] scheme, that from thence, as well as from the unjustifiableness of any other, we can never keep too clear of the imputation lying upon the Methodists, that they set up lay-preachers...'

Walker, Adam and Vivian were not the only Evangelicals to see the possibility of separation from the Church beginning with lay-preaching.

Grimshaw, in a letter to Mrs Gallatin, dated 2 May 1755[30] said of the Methodist preachers' desire to administer the sacraments themselves:

'As to the lay-preachers' new scheme, I've no relish for it, nor is it expedient, but rather evidently clogging our Connection (*sic*) with several grievous difficulties. Their main design, as I understand, is to take upon them the office of administering the Lord's Supper. But this, as I conceive, is not expedient, because few of the clergy deny this sacrament to our people.[31] Nor is the reception of it from a carnal minister's[32] hand any objection thereto, or any obstruction to the communicant's blessing, provided he receives in faith...'

He went on to say that the permitting of the lay-preachers to administer would only cause a rupture with the Established Church and then the Methodists would become Dissenters. Moreover, he felt John Wesley's own writings were against such a separation. He (Grimshaw) would have to leave the Methodists if the preachers' scheme was carried through.

---

29. i.e. the regular parish members of ministry.
30. Laycock, J.W. *Methodist Heroes in the Great Haworth Round. 1734-1784* (pp.145ff.)
31. This was decidedly untrue in far too many cases.
32. This, of course, is provided for in Article No.26 in the Book of Common Prayer.

'I can,' he continued, 'harmoniously, as matters have hitherto been carried on, be a member of our Church and a Methodist preacher, and thus I could wish to live and die. But if my fellow labourers will needs be innovating, I must adhere to the former and decline the latter.'

Grimshaw, it must be noted, went deliberately to the Conference of 1756 to strengthen Wesley's hands on the question of leaving the Church. Baddiley of Hayfield also gave advice to Wesley on this same matter. He wrote from Hayfield on 7 June 1755, as follows:

'I would speak with regard to the case debated in your last Conference at Leeds. Some of your lay itinerant preachers had a desire, as such, to administer the sacraments of baptism and the Lord's Supper. How might it not be justly said unto them: *"Seemeth it but a small thing unto you, that God hath separated you from among the congregation to bring you near to Himself, that ye thus seek the priesthood also? Alas! Alas! Ye take too much upon you, ye sons of Levi!"*

'What could the event be, but settling in such places as seem most commodious to them, and then settling upon their lees? Has not this been the general bane of scriptural Christianity? Has it not eaten out the life of religion, and caused the power of godliness to dwindle in Dissenters of every denomination?

'For who – who can bear ease and fullness of bread? Be not, dear sir, estranged in your affection, nor straitened in your bowels of love to the mother that bare you, and still continues, notwithstanding small irregularities in you, to dangle you upon her knees. O! labour, watch and pray, with all your might, that no such breach be made. Wherefore should the pickthank heathen have cause to say "Where is now their

God?" I query much, if upon dissenting from the Established Church, the divisions and subdivisions of the Methodists among themselves would not exceed those of the anabaptists in Germany.'[33]

This is indeed a significant epistle from one whose own irregularities, including that of employing laymen to preach, were comparable with those of Wesley!

> 'Moved by our long continued cry
> Some apostolic father raise,
> Our want of labourers to supply
> To admit the vessels of Thy grace
> To lay on hands, o'erruled by Thine
> And recognize the call divine.'[34]

Such a hope expressed by Charles Wesley was a pious one indeed. More realistic was Joseph Cownley, a lay-preacher of John's, whom he later ordained. In a letter to Charles[35] he predicted the separation of Methodism from the Church of England after the death of the brothers:

> 'Unless,' said he, 'you get them fastened where they are by prevailing on one or more of the Bishops to ordain them. But then, what Bishop either in England or Ireland, will ever do this? – will ordain a Methodist preacher to be a Methodist preacher? For my part, as poor and worthless wretch as I am, I could not submit to it on the terms on which most of my brethren have hitherto got it.'

Yet it was for the very purpose of the itinerant ministry that John

---

33. Tyerman Luke *The Life and Times of Revd John Wesley* (London, 1871-2, Vol.2, p.205.)
34. Wesley, John and Charles *The Poetical Works of* (London, 1868-1872, Vol.6, p.119.)
35. Tyerman Luke *op.cit.* (Vol.2, p.387.)

desired episcopal ordination and it seemed incredible that he should be surprised when his requests received rebuffs almost without exception. The outstanding example of Wesley's very rare successes in this endeavour was when Thomas Maxfield, one of Wesley's first lay-preachers was ordained by the Bishop of Derry. According to Wesley,[36] the Bishop had said to Maxfield:

> 'Mr Maxfield, I ordain you to assist that good man, that he may not work himself to death.'

Wesley was little more successful in getting ordination for men who intended to settle in parishes, though he would realize that their itinerant usefulness would normally be at an end.

In 1764, Wesley chanced to meet with a supposed Greek Bishop, by name Erasmus, from Arcadia. Trying to procure ordination for another preacher, John Jones, a master at the Kingswood School, Wesley asked the Bishop if he would oblige in this case and his request was granted. Wesley was quite satisfied with the genuineness of the prelate's credentials.[37] Charles's rage knew no bounds when he heard of this step and he refused to recognize the ordination. Unfortunately for John, six other preachers,[38] without consulting him, paid the bishop to ordain them. This action received press publicity and this was due as much to the protests of certain other Anglican Evangelicals such as Romaine, Madan and Shirley,[39] as to any others. John had to disassociate himself from this action. Not only were the ordinations not recognized by him as valid, but he erased their names from the list of preachers and expelled them from membership of the Methodist societies. But this was not the

---

36. J.W.L. (Vol.4, pp.209ff.) Dated May 1763 (No day is given.)
37. Doubts have been cast on the genuineness of this 'bishop'. See Williams, Colin *John Wesley's Theology Today* (London, 1960, p.224.) and my book *John Wesley and The Christian Ministry* (London, 1963, pp.119-124.)
38. J.W.L. (Vol.3, p.291.)
39. De Coetlogon, Madan's colleague at the Lock chapel refused to join in the condemnation of Wesley.

end. It was here where Augustus Montague Toplady,[40] a young evangelical clergyman, then Vicar of Broad Hembury aired his views. Earlier, he had been on friendly terms with Wesley, even to the point of making John his confidante when a student at Trinity College, Dublin. Toplady claimed to have seen the certificate given by this 'vagrant' as he called the Greek Bishop, to these preachers. He entered into a most acrimonious correspondence with Wesley, finally accusing him of having asked Erasmus to consecrate him a bishop.[41] Fortunately, Wesley's defence was undertaken by one of his helpers, Thomas Olivers, and the matter died a natural death.

In 1775, Joseph Benson, another preacher of Wesley's attempted to bring before Conference a plan to secure greater efficiency among the preachers.[42] It advocated presbyterial ordination by the Wesley brothers and their training at Kingswood school. Benson consulted John Fletcher of Madeley about these proposals. Fletcher warned Benson that his scheme for training these men would not necessarily add to their usefulness, whilst the presbyterial ordination would cut them off from the Church of England, and this he could not countenance. His attitude to the suggestion for training makes strange reading when it is remembered that not only was he himself academically well endowed but that he had been President of Lady Huntingdon's College for preachers at Trevecca. Fletcher advised Wesley to try again to secure ordination for the preachers from the Archbishop before taking such an irregular step as ordaining them himself. The ordinands would be subjected to a strict doctrinal undertaking, including such emphases as the scripture doctrine of grace; justifying faith and Christian Perfection. They were also to consider themselves members of the Church of England, differing as little from her as possible.

By 1783, the final rift between the Countess of Huntingdon and the Established Church took place. Using her supposed right to possess and

40. Southey, R. *Life of Wesley and the Rise of Methodism* (London, 1881, p.487.)
41. Tyerman, Luke *The Life and Times of Revd John Wesley MA* (London, 1871-2, Vol.2, pp.487-8.)
42. J.W.J. (Vol.8, pp.328-34.)

build her own chapels, employing chaplains whenever and wherever she wished, she had already established her own 'Connexion' in the country. Her attention was drawn to the possibility of purchasing the Pantheon in Spafields, London. This was a building which had been used for amusement, mostly on Sundays. Toplady and Shirley[43] discouraged the idea by affording all the possible reasons why the plan would be a failure. However, she decided to buy the building and convert it into a chapel. Unfortunately, however, the local incumbent, the Revd William Sellon, minister of St James's Clerkenwell, objected to the new chapel and made legal claims on Her Ladyship including that of having a right to minister there when he so desired. A pluralist of the worst kind and avaricious for money, he further demanded payment of £40 per annum for permitting two of the Countess's chaplains to serve there. The sacramental collections and four other collections yearly were to be given to his charity school. Furthermore, the proprietors had to sign a bond for £1,000.[44]

Naturally, the Countess and her advisers protested. The matter was discussed with Lord Dartmouth, himself an evangelical laymen, and others, and it was decided to proceed with the project. The chapel, successively named Northampton Chapel and Spafields Chapel, was opened on 28 March 1779 when the preacher was a noted Evangelical – Thomas Haweis, Vicar of Aldwincle in Northamptonshire, one of Her Ladyship's chaplains. The controversy was taken to an Ecclesiastical Court by Sellon who obtained verdicts against the Countess and her officiating clergy. Not only was she wrong in respect of Spafields, but also in the matter of all her other places of worship. There was only one course she could take, other than cancel her whole Connexion, and that was to take shelter under the Act of Toleration. All her chapels were duly registered as Dissenting Meeting Houses.

Two of her chaplains, the Revd Thomas Wills and the Revd William Taylor, decided to secede from the Church of England and took oaths as Dissenting ministers. It was agreed that they should then ordain others to

---

43. Berridge, on the other hand, did all he could to encourage her in this project.
44. Shirley and Hastings, A Member of the Houses of *The Life and Times of Selina, Countess of Huntingdon* (London, 1839, Vol.2, pp.311ff.)

the ministry. Accordingly, on 9 March 1783, six young men were duly ordained to the ministry of what could rightly be called 'The Countess of Huntingdon's Connexion'.

Inevitably, many of Her Ladyship's chaplains withdrew from her service, including such notable names as Shirley, Romaine, Venn, Jesse[45] and Townsend.[46] Among those who continued with her, without renouncing Anglican orders, were Haweis and Thomas Pentycross.[47]

Thus ended the career of Selina, Lady Huntingdon – Anglican. Whilst still in the Establishment, she had found far less difficulty in obtaining Anglican ordination for her Trevecca students than did Wesley for his lay-preachers. Much of her success was due to her position as a peeress of the realm. This she used to influence other members of the nobility who, if not themselves patrons of livings, were certainly on intimate terms with many who were. Lord Dartmouth, especially could be cited here. However, now that she was a Dissenter, all was not lost. At least, it could be said that she was mistress in her own spiritual house, head of a 'Connexion' completely her own and with no further need to exercise care and caution not to offend against Ecclesiastical Law.

Wesley's quest for ordination for his own lay-preachers could well have been influenced by Lady Huntingdon's final move to settle her own problem. Whilst Wesley nowhere referred to the incident mentioned above, it was not without significance that the following year, 1784, saw the first of his own presbyteral ordinations. It was quite possible that the precedent set by Lady Huntingdon was one of the determining factors for his own act. The need for ordained men in America was given as the reason for his first ordinations. The year 1785 was marked by ordination for work in Scotland. Ordinations for overseas work other than America, took place the following year. In 1788, ordinations for work in England were performed. No doubt, John had waited to take the final step until

---

45. Vicar of West Bromwich.
46. Rector of Pewsey, Wilts.
47. Pentycross was Vicar of St Mary's, Wallingford – one of Selina's most popular preachers.

after his brother's death earlier in the year. Thus, the main source of opposition was then removed.

As far back as 1745, Wesley's reading of Lord Peter King's *Primitive Church* had convinced him that presbyter and bishop, whilst different in function, were one in essence. By 1755, his reading of Bishop Edward Stillingfleet's *Eirenicon (*or *Irenicum)* persuaded him that Christ left no instructions authorizing any particular form of Church government or ministry.[48]

One thing is certain. Between 1745 and 1784, Wesley had heeded all opposition to his using this supposed power. Such opposition came not only from Charles but from many of the Evangelicals because in such a step they saw the danger of the separation of Methodism from the Church of England. It was only when it seemed that his life's work was to come to a standstill, that he showed he preferred to risk the possibility of separation. There was to be no curtailment of Methodist evangelistic endeavour.

William Law, who had exercised such a profound initial influence on both the Wesleys and many of the evangelical clergy, had ventured to remark to Charles Wesley in August 1739, that he hoped the Methodists would have been '...dispersed by little and little into livings, and have leavened the whole lump.'[49] It will have been seen already that the great majority of the Evangelicals strove to do just this. It is no cause for surprise that the better known Evangelicals were those who indulged in some measure of irregularity. Irregularity in any sphere never fails to reward with some degree of notoriety. But most of the Evangelicals confined themselves for most of the time, to their own parishes. Thus they were often lost in obscurity and little note has been made of them. As G.R. Balleine has said,[50] whilst the Wesleys and their coadjutors made the world their parish, the Evangelicals made their parish their world.

---

48. For a full treatment of this, see my book *John Wesley and The Christian Ministry* (London, 1963, pp.47-70.)
49. C.W.J. (1736-9, p.246.)
50. *A History of The Evangelical Party in the Church of England* (London, 1951, p.40.)

Therefore they were dedicated to strengthening the existing parish ministry. The aim was for more evangelical clergy – a twofold aim: To further Evangelicalism among the present incumbents and to encourage young Evangelicals to enter the ministry of the Church. This was done firstly by the establishing of Clerical Clubs or Societies. The best known of these was the one founded by Samuel Walker of Truro who has featured so much in previous pages. He had already achieved success in organizing religious societies for the lay-folk. Now he had formed his 'Clerical Club' or 'Parsons' Club' as it was sometimes called. It was, according to Sidney,[51] for the '...mutual edification, encouragement, and advice as to pastoral duties.' The Members assembled once a month in each other's houses to '...consult upon the business of their calling.' According to Sidney, it began in 1755, though G.C.B. Davies[52] would trace its origin to 1753 and thinks it continued until at least 1759. One of its candidates for ordination was a young medical student – Thomas Haweis whose preparatory studies prior to going to Oxford in 1755 were carefully guided by Walker. Haweis, like Walker, was spiritually indebted to the schoolmaster, Conon. He was later Rector of Aldwincle in Northamptonshire and remained faithful to Lady Huntingdon after she forsook Anglicanism.[53]

Another of the several clerical associations began in 1767 under the leadership of Henry Venn of Huddersfield. The society met at his home until he removed to the country living of Yelling in 1771. It was a harmonious society and its numbers were restricted to those of a similar mind and outlook. It had a wide representation including York, Lancaster, Chester and Derby. When Venn left the district, the society removed to Ellend, a smaller nearby town. Here it came under the leadership of

---

51. Sidney, E. *The Life and Ministry of Samuel Walker of Truro* (2nd ed, London, 1838, pp.75-76.)
52. Davies, G.C.B. *The Early Cornish Evangelicals 1735-1780* (London, 1951, p.75.)
53. See Wood, A. Skevington *Thomas Haweis 1734-1820 (London, 1957)* for a full account of his life and ministry.

George Burnett,[54] the perpetual curate of Elland. This club met at Elland for seventy years and was known as the 'Elland Clerical Society'. It continued during the ministry of Burnett's two immediate successors and then its venue was Halifax, the next town. From there it returned to Huddersfield where it still meets! Its attention became drawn to the need of encouraging young men to enter the ministry in the year 1777. Such candidates were helped both during their ordinary education and their university courses. The society enjoyed a great measure of success and amongst the names of those who were thus helped were Thomas Thomason, Chaplain to the Honourable East India Company in Calcutta, and Samuel Marsden, first chaplain at Botany Bay, who was sometimes referred to as 'Apostle of New Zealand'. Another beneficiary, Charles Jarram of Cobham in Surrey, when in old age, intimated that when he was in college, no fewer than eight or ten 'were on the Society's books' at Cambridge.[55]

There was an even more effective method of securing an increase of Evangelical fervour and witness in the Church. John Wesley recorded that on Monday 20 December 1784 he had '...the satisfaction of meeting Mr Simeon, Fellow of King's College in Cambridge.'[56] He noted that Simeon had spent some time with Fletcher of Madeley and that they were kindred souls, resembling each other in fervour of spirit and in the 'earnestness of their address'. Wesley also recorded that he was pleased to hear that there were three parish churches in the town wherein the true scriptural religion was preached. Simeon was also a close friend of Venn, Berridge, Pentycross of Wallingford and other Evangelicals.[57] He had

---

54. Burnett owed his conversion to Walker of Truro. A Scotsman from Aberdeen, he had been brought to assist at Truro Grammar School by Conon. Burnett and Haweis were close friends. Thus Burnett would already have had some experience of Clerical Clubs whilst at Truro.

55. See Greenwood D. and A. *A History of Elland Church* (Huddersfield, 1954, pp.52-53.)

56. J.W.J. (Vol.7, p.39.) See also Vol.7, p.339 for Wesley's second meeting with Simeon.

57. His most famous protégé was Henry Martyn, celebrated missionary-martyr of

been appointed Vicar of Holy Trinity Church in Cambridge in 1783 where he remained until his death in 1836. At first he was met by hostility from both the University and his congregation because of his Evangelical views. His influence over the undergraduate body at Cambridge University was immense and the number of these who subsequently entered the Christian ministry cannot be numbered. However, his main contribution to securing livings for Evangelicals, once ordained, was his 'Trust' later called the 'Simeon Trust' which still exists. A man of considerable fortune, he spent much of it in the purchase of advowsons so that Evangelicals could always be afforded a living. Not only was he successful in procuring support from other wealthy sources, he finally left the remainder of his own personal fortune, £5,000, to the trust which he had created.

Charles Simeon was perhaps the greatest example of faith in the parish system of the Church of England. He was possessed of a determined churchmanship. He exalted the Christian ministry and was a loyal subscriber to the Prayer Book and Articles of the Church. It was said of him, in annoyance, that he was '...more of a Churchman than a Gospel-Man.'[58]

The Evangelicals, as distinct from the Methodists, became more determined to remain loyal to the Church and therefore to the existing parish system, intent on making it work. The irregularities of the Wesleys and the Countess of Huntingdon only served to increase their determination to this end. What is more, they succeeded and in the Church, their successors remain. It has been shown, however, that much was owed in the early days to Lady Huntingdon's provision at Trevecca of suitable training for ordinands for the Church as well as for Dissent. It would have benefited the Wesleys and their contemporary Evangelical clergy friends who employed lay-preachers, to have devised some similar system of training; but the more lasting method was obviously that of the Clerical societies and Simeon's in particular. These could be said to have

---

58. Overton, J.H. and Relton, F. *The English Church from the Accession of George I to the End of the Eighteenth (1714-1800)* (London, 1906, p.240.)

taken the place of Lady Huntingdon's system as far as the Evangelical branch of the Church was concerned. A precedent had now been set for the regular provision of Evangelical incumbents and livings.

Wesley had desired ordination purely for irregular itinerant work. Lady Huntingdon desired it for both regular and irregular use. Few could fail to have some sympathy with the members of the episcopal bench who refused to oblige! The Evangelicals sought ordination purely for the intention of reviving a languishing and spiritually impoverished church to which they belonged.

The accusation of irregularity cannot be levelled solely at Wesley and his followers. Apart from the more notorious examples of Berridge, Grimshaw and Baddiley, it must be remembered that even Romaine confessed to having *once* preached irregularly, whilst Henry Venn often officiated at Surry Chapel in London, a building erected for Rowland Hill, an Anglican evangelical clergyman who had received only deacon's orders.[59] The reason for the provision of the chapel was that Hill could find no useful avenue of service within the Church. In fact, the many clergy who had become Lady Huntingdon's chaplains and preached in her various chapels, had all been acting irregularly, notwithstanding that they did this in all innocence. The subsequent Ecclesiastical Court case proved this. Some, like Thomas Halweis continued deliberately after Lady Huntingdon's separation from the Church and also cooperated with all denominations.[60]

One thing was certain. A man was either a believer in the regular or the irregular ministry.[61] It is difficult when one looks at the eighteenth-century situation to see how a compromise between the two could have been effected. Opinions were too strong for that.

Did social snobbery play any part in the attitudes displayed? It must

---

59. Venn, John *The Life and a Selection from the Letters of the Revd Henry Venn, MA* (London, 1837, p.117.) He also preached in houses and barns in Yelling.
60. Wood, A. Skevington *Thomas Haweis 1734-1820* (London, 1957, pp.210-211.) See Index of this book for further references.
61. See Conclusion at the end of Chapter 11 of this study where the matter is again referred to.

have been a strange sight to see Wesley, a former Oxford Don addressing the ignorant, unlettered Kingswood colliers in a way they could understand and to which they could respond. Equally strange was the success Whitefield enjoyed amongst the aristocracy of the land. He was the son of the widow of an inn-keeper, yet, to use a favourite expression of his, he was 'winning coronets for Christ'. One would normally have expected the respective roles to have been reversed.

In any case, the whole conception of lay-preaching such as that used by Wesley, and, to a smaller extent, by Whitefield, would be frowned upon, not only because of its illegality but because of the *type* of person employed. It is true that the average lay-preacher was from an artisan background, uneducated and often indiscreet in his conduct. Wesley had tried to train them and not always with success. He provided them with books and insisted that they did plenty of reading or else they had to leave him. To each he gave the sum of £5 for the purchase of books. This fact made no difference to many in the Church, but the Wesleys stood their ground. A conversation between Robinson, Archbishop of Armagh and Charles Wesley amply illustrated this:

> Robinson: '...One thing in your conduct I could never account for, your employing laymen.' 'My Lord,' said Charles, 'the fault is yours and your brethren's.' 'How so?' asked the Primate. 'Because you hold your peace, and the stones cry out.' 'But I am told,' his Grace continued, 'that they are unlearned men.' 'Some are,' replied Charles, 'and so the dumb ass rebukes the prophet.'[62]

One facet of this subject not yet referred to, which must be dealt with before this part of the study closes, is the cordial relationship of many of the evangelical clergy to the Dissenters. The Wesleys had little connection with Dissent at any time. Admitted, John Wesley in his famous sermon on *The Catholic Spirit* did recognize Dissenters whatever their sect, as

---

62. *Methodist Magazine* (London, 1822, p.783.)

brothers in Christ, and maintained that they had a right to their own modes of government and worship; but he was cautious to add that he believed the government of his own church was scriptural and apostolic.[63] Yet, for all this, he is rarely recorded as having preached in a Dissenting Meeting-House, and there is little doubt that he preferred field-preaching to this. It will be recalled how both Charles and John strove to avoid the inevitable practice of licensing their preachers as Dissenting ministers, and their preaching places as Dissenting Meeting Houses. Whitefield, on the other hand, enjoyed free and full cooperation with Nonconformists. In 1737 he recorded that some of his enemies were irritated because of his 'free conversation with many of the serious Dissenters' who invited him to their houses and told him that 'If the doctrine of the New Birth and Justification by Faith was preached powerfully in the Church, there would be but few Dissenters in England.'[64] He preached often in their meeting-houses on both sides of the Atlantic and it is not without significance that his last resting-place was in a Presbyterian Church.[65]

Another incident which shocked Wesley was the action of Henry Venn as he prepared to leave Huddersfield for his semi-retirement at Yelling. In case Venn's successor was not an Evangelical, a number of his people determined to build a chapel in Huddersfield where they could have their own pastor. Venn, surprisingly enough not only gave his sanction, but made a contribution towards the erection of the building. It was his wish that the Liturgy be used there and he bade the people attend the chapel, which they did. As his son pointed out[66] (but regretfully), this was a mistake, as the successor soon left and the following incumbent was one of Venn's own outlook. Few of the parishioners, however, returned to the parish church.

---

63. J.W.S. (Vol.2, p.139.)
64. G.W.J. (p.90.)
65. At Newburyport, Mass. U.S.A.
66. Venn, John *The Life and a Selection from the Letters of the Revd Henry Venn, MA* (London, 1837, pp.174-5.)

'I dare not, like Mr Venn,' commented Wesley,[67] 'leave the parish church where I am, to go to an Independent meeting. I dare not advise others to go thither rather than the church. I advise all over whom I have any influence steadily to keep to the Church...'

Grimshaw acted similarly in 1762. Titue Knight was a Methodist preacher who changed his doctrinal views and set up as an Independent minister in Halifax. A chapel had to be built for him and Grimshaw not only made a contribution but undertook to beg for it! Through Grimshaw's influence, Lady Huntingdon made a substantial gift towards the cost.

'He was no bigot; he made no distinction of sect or party the measure of his love to Christians,' wrote J.W. Laycock. 'He used to say, "I love Christians, true Christians, of all parties; I do love them, I will love them, and none shall make me otherwise."'[68]

However, in spite of these acts of ecclesiastical indiscretion, the Evangelicals, as a whole, remained within the Church. Any separation they caused was, like the cases of Huddersfield and Halifax, purely local. Wesley, on the other hand, indulged permanently in two irregularities of practice which laid the foundations for a complete separation from the Church, even though, to the end, he protested his loyalty to her and his

---

67. J.W.L. (Vol.5, p.98.) Dated 19 July 1768. The chapel concerned was erected in Highfield and later became Highfield United Reformed (formerly Congregational) Church. Its pastor for over fifty years from the beginning was William Woodhouse. Venn's son (*op.cit.* pp.174-5) said his father was no advocate of irregularity in others and only indulged in it because he thought he might do good, but finally repented of his actions.
68. Laycock, J.W. *Methodist Heroes in the Great Haworth Round 1734-1784* (Keighley, 1909, pp.234-5.) The church became The Square (formerly Congregational), Halifax. It was the church in which the celebrated preacher John Henry Jowett was brought up. The building is now used as a theatre.

determination never to leave. Thomas Adam's declaration[69] that the Methodists were to all extent and purposes outside the Church, harsh though it may have seemed, was quite near the truth, whilst Joseph Cownley's prediction that when the Wesleys died, the Methodists would, in any case, leave the Church, was certainly fulfilled.[70] The Evangelicals, whatever their temporary aberrations may have been, staked all on the existing parish system of their church. Their choice was not without its success, for their influence abides in the Church to this day in the Conservative evangelical wing of Anglicanism.

---

69. See page 115 of this study.
70. See page 118 of this study.

PART TWO

THEOLOGICAL

CHAPTER SIX

DOCTRINAL FOUNDATIONS

It can, with certainty, be stated that the theological ideas of the Wesleys were shaped by two important factors – the views of their parents and the influence of books. Both these were far more decisive in the realms of theology than in that of ecclesiastical order which has just been dealt with.

The Wesley home at Epworth was a curious mixture of High Church Anglicanism and Puritanism. The Wesleys' ancestors had been strong Puritans. Their paternal great-grandfather, Bartholomew Wesley, and grandfather, John Wesley, had both been ejected from their livings in Dorset by the 1662 Act of Uniformity. Their grandmother on the same side of the family, was a daughter of John White of Dorchester, a member of the Westminster Assembly of Divines who had been persecuted for preaching against Arminianism! On their mother's side, their great-grandfather, another John White, was a leader of the Puritans in the City of London, whilst their grandfather, Dr Samuel Annesley, was a celebrated Puritan preacher in the same city. Both Samuel Wesley and Susannah Annesley had been brought up as Dissenters, the former having been educated first of all at a Dissenting Academy. Yet both left Nonconformity to join the Anglican Church from which their respective ancestors had been expelled.

Puritan theology was Calvinistic and the seventeenth century had borne witness to the hostility between the Puritans and the Arminian clergy, who had found favour with both Archbishop Laud and the King.[1] It could be said that whilst Samuel and Susannah had revolted against the harsher tenets of Calvinism, such as Predestination and Reprobation, much of the Puritan 'ethos' remained in them. This is amply evidenced in the strict and methodical ordering of the Epworth homestead, especially in respect of the bringing up of the family. It was Puritan in spirit but not in theology. That the Wesley brothers should have adopted the Arminian standpoint should occasion no surprise. Their decision was arrived at rationally and honestly.

Susannah Wesley exercised the greater influence on the brothers, especially in the case of John. It was to her that he addressed his theological queries. She had written to him on 21 July 1725 about repentance by which she seems to have meant 'regeneration':

> 'What then,' her son replied, 'shall I say of Predestination?
> An everlasting purpose of God to deliver some from damnation
> does, I suppose, exclude all from that deliverance who are not
> chosen, and if it was decreed from eternity that such a
> determinate part of mankind should be saved, and none beside
> them, a vast majority of the world were only born to eternal
> death, without so much as the possibility of avoiding it. How
> is this consistent with either the Divine justice or mercy? Is it
> merciful to ordain a creature to everlasting misery? Is it just to
> punish man for crimes which he could not but commit? How
> is man, if necessarily determined to one way of acting, a free
> agent? To lie under either a physical or a moral necessity is
> entirely repugnant to human liberty. But that God should be
> the author of sin and injustice (which must, I think, be the
> consequence of maintaining this opinion) is a contradiction to
> the clearest ideas we have of the divine nature and perfections.'[2]

---

1.   Charles I.
2.   J.W.L. (Vol.1, pp.22-23.) Dated 29 July 1725.

He called faith 'an assent upon rational grounds' because he held divine testimony to be the most reasonable of all evidence whatever. Faith must necessarily at length be resolved into reason. *God* is true; therefore what *He* says is true. He has said this; therefore it is true. When anyone can bring Wesley more reasonable propositions than these he would be ready to assent to them. Until then, it would be highly unreasonable to change his opinion.

> 'I used to think that the difficulty of Predestination might be solved by supposing that it was indeed decreed from eternity, that a remnant should be elected, but that it was in every man's power to be of that remnant.'

He continued:

> 'But the word of Our Articles will not bear that sense. I see no other way but to allow that some may be saved who were not always of the number of the elected.'

He asked his mother for her sentiments on this point and to show if and when he might have been in error.
Susannah replied on 18 August 1725:

> 'Divine faith is an assent to whatever God has revealed to us, because he has revealed it. And this is that virtue of faith which is one of two conditions to our salvation by Jesus Christ. I have often wondered that men should be vain as to amuse themselves with searching into the decrees of God, which no human wit can fathom, and do not rather employ their time and powers in working out their salvation. Such studies tend more to confound than to inform the understanding, and young people had better let them alone. But since I find you have some scruples concerning our article,[3] *Of*

---

3.   Article XVII *Of Predestination and Election*

Predestination. I will tell you my thoughts of the matter. If they satisfy not, you may desire your father's direction, who is surely better qualified for a casuist than I.

'The doctrine of Predestination, as maintained by the rigid Calvinists, is very shocking, and ought to be abhorred, because it directly charges the most High God with being the author of sin. I think you reason well and justly against it; for it is certainly inconsistent with the justice and goodness of God to lay any man under either a physical or moral necessity of committing sin, and then to punish him for doing it.

'I firmly believe that God, from eternity, has elected some to eternal life; but then I humbly conceive that this election is founded in His foreknowledge, according to Romans viii 29,30. Whom, in his eternal prescience, God saw would make a right use of their powers, and accept of offered mercy, he did predestinate and adopt for His children. And that they may be conformed to the image of His only Son, he calls them to Himself, through the preaching of the gospel, and, internally, by His Holy Spirit; which call, they obeying, repenting of their sins and believing in the Lord Jesus, He justified them, absolved them from the guilt of all their sins, and acknowledges them as just and righteous persons, through the merits and mediation of Jesus Christ. And having thus justified, He received them to glory to heaven.

'This is the Sum of what I believe concerning Predestination, which I think is agreeable to the analogy of faith; since it does in no wise derogate from the glory of God's free grace, nor impair the liberty of man. Nor can it with more reason be supposed that the prescience of God is the cause that so many finally perish, than that one knowing the sun will rise tomorrow is the cause of its rising.'[4]

---

4.   Tyerman, Luke *The Life and Times of John Wesley* (London, Vol.1, pp.39-40.)

This is a long letter and the necessity to quote it in full will be obvious when it is realized that John adopted his mother's views on this subject which was to be such a bone of contention for the greater part of his ministry.

On 19 December 1729, he took up with his father the subject of the origin of evil. *Unde Malum*, he said, had been a 'mighty question'. The conclusion of the letter shows that he rejected the notion of dualism, and the origin of evil was accounted for from the possibility of a '...various use of our liberty, even as that capacity or possibility is ultimately rounded on the defectability and finiteness of a created nature.'

The first books (other than the Bible) which moved Wesley to his new life was Thomas à Kempis's *Imitation of Christ*. He wrote:

'When I was about twenty-two, my father pressed me to enter into holy orders. At the same time the providence of God directing me to Kempis's *Christian Pattern*, I began to see that true religion was seated in the heart, and that God's laws extended to all our thoughts as well as words and actions. I was, however, angry at à Kempis for being too strict; though I read him only in Dean Stanhope's translation. Yet I had frequently much sensible comfort in reading him, such as I was an utter stranger to before.'[5]

However, he experienced difficulties in his reading of à Kempis and wrote to his mother requesting her advice. On 8 June 1725 she replied[6] indicating his difficulties which were about the Intention of God:

'I have Kempis by me; but have not read him lately. I cannot recollect the passages you mention; but, believing you do him justice, I do positively aver that he is extremely in the wrong in that impious – I am about to say blasphemous, suggestion,

---

5. J.W.J. (Vol.1, p.466.)
6. Tyerman *op.cit.* (Vol.1, p.34.)

that God, by an irreversible decree, has determined any man
to be miserable even in this world. His intentions, as Himself,
are holy, just and good; and all the miseries incident to me
here or hereafter proceed from themselves. I take Kempis to
have been an honest weak man, that had more zeal than
knowledge...'

Nevertheless he was later to write an important pronouncement on his
reading of à Kempis, the last sentences of which speak for themselves:

'In the year 1726[7] I met with Kempis's *Christian Pattern*.
The nature and extent of inward religion, the religion of the
heart, now appeared to me in a stronger light than ever it had
been done before. I saw that giving even all my life to God
(supposing it possible to do this, and go on farther) would
profit me nothing, unless I gave my heart, yea, all my heart, to
Him. I sought after this [Christian Perfection] from that
hour.'[8]

Jeremy Taylor had a limited influence over him. In the *Journal*
(Preface to the First Edition)[9] he recorded that:

'It was in pursuance of an Advice given by Bishop Taylor, in
His Rules for Holy Living and Dying, that about fifteen years
ago, I began to take a more exact Account than I had done
before, of the manner wherein I spent my Time, writing down
how I had employed every Hour.'

Taylor disappointed him in his account of hope, of which he said:
'Faith believes the revelation; Hope expects his promises; Faith gives our

---

7.   Surely, the year is 1725!
8.   J.W.W. (Vol.11, p.185.)
9.   J.W.J. (Vol.1, p.83.)

understandings to God; Hope, our passions and affections. Faith is opposed to infidelity; Hope to despair.' Yet, in another place, complained Wesley, he said that Faith differed from Hope in the extension of its object and the intension (*sic*) of its degree; Faith belonged to all things revealed, Hope only to things that were good, future and concerning ourselves. The objection to this, Wesley maintained, was that Taylor made Hope a part or species of Faith, and consequently contained in it, as was every part of its whole. Whatever Hope was, he affirmed, it was certainly distinct from Faith as well as Charity.

However, he liked very much Taylor's account of the pardon of sins, which, he declared, was the clearest he had ever met. Pardon of sins, in the Gospel, Taylor had written in his *Holy Dying*, was sanctification. Forgiveness of sins was not a secret sentence, a word, or a record, but it was a state of change affected upon them.

Wesley, nevertheless, felt that there were contradictions in Taylor's works, which were certainly militating against the already forming doctrine of 'Assurance' or conscious salvation. He complained of them to his mother on 18 June 1725:[10]

'Dr Taylor in his *Holy Living and Dying* says, "Whether God has forgiven us or not, we know not, therefore, be sorrowful for ever having sinned." This seems to contradict his own words in the next section, where he says that "by the Lord's Supper, all the members are united to one another, and to Christ the Head. The Holy Ghost confers on us the graces necessary for, and our souls receive the seed of, an immortal life."

'Now surely these graces are of not so little force as that we cannot perceive whether we have them or not. If we dwell in Christ, and Christ in us (which He will not do unless we are regenerate), certainly we must be sensible of it. If we can never have any certainty of our being in a state of salvation,

---

10. J.W.L. (Vol 1, pp. 19-20.)

good reason it is that every moment should be spent, not in joy, but in fear and trembling; and then, undoubtedly, in this life we are of all men the most miserable. God deliver us from such a fearful expectation as this!'

Far greater than all other literary influences was that of William Law the Non-Juror. John's expenses for 1732, when a Fellow of Lincoln, shows that he bought Law's *Serious Call to a Devout and Holy Life* for five shillings. It was a work on which he attempted to model his own life, for Law had persuaded him that it was an impossibility merely to be 'half a Christian'. Previously he had read *Christian Perfection* by Law soon after its publication in 1726.

It is incumbent upon the reader at this point to look at Law's teaching on this subject because it became one of the Wesleys' most important teachings, and, in a later chapter, to compare it with their own views.[11]

Law maintained that Christian Perfection did not consist in any singular state or conditions of life, or in a particular set of duties, but in the holy and religious conduct of ourselves in every state of life. It called no one to the cloister, but to a right and full performance of those duties which were necessary for all Christians, and common to all states of life. He called this perfection for two reasons, first because he hoped that it contained a full representation of that height of holiness and purity to which Christianity called all its members; secondly, that the title might invite the reader to peruse it with diligence and find a 'regular draught' for 'those holy tempers' which were the perfect measure and standard of Christian piety.[12]

All Christians were called to the one end and the same perfection and were equally obliged to labour after it.[13] Last he should be accused, after a cursory reading of the first chapter, of promoting a false idea of

---

11. See Chapter Ten of this Study.
12. Law, William *A Practical Treatise upon Christian Perfection* (London, 1728, pp.2 and 3.)
13. *ibid.* (p.13.)

salvation by good works, the second chapter insisted on the need for Christian conversion. The sole end of Christianity, he said, was to deliver us from the misery and disorder of this present state and raise us to a blissful enjoyment of the Divine nature. Christianity was not a school for the teaching of moral virtues, the polishing of manners, or forming us to live a life of this world with decency and gentility. It was deeper and more divine in its designs and had much nobler ends than these; it implied on *entire change of life*.[14] Nothing less than this great change of heart and mind could give any one assurance that he was truly turned to God. There was but this one term of salvation, 'He that is in Christ, is a new creature.'[15]

The third, fourth and fifth chapters all dealt with the necessity of renouncing the world and worldly tempers, whilst the sixth chapter stated that Christianity called all men to a state of self-denial and mortification, the subject being continued in the next chapter and chapter eight.

According to the ninth chapter,[16] Divine Grace was necessary for attainment of Christian Perfection, for it implied several duties which the Christian was to perform. Humility took high rank among these. As an inspired person in whom the Spirit of God dwelt, the Christian's heart must be renewed by that Spirit, which prompted him to self-denial, Temperance, Abstinence, Care and Watchfulness. Any single thing which came into his life must set forth the glory of God, inspired by the Spirit so that it was a good proof that the Spirit of God dwelt within him.

The succeeding chapter again emphasized the necessity of Divine Grace and laid obligation on all Christian people to constant purity and holiness of conversation. Law further stated that the great danger here was the reading of 'vain, impertinent books'. Whilst the actual books were not cited, Law obviously had in mind some of the 'lewd and unedifying' publications of his day. He also referred to a type of play which could be seen regularly at the theatre which he felt would not be

---

14. Law *ibid.* (p.41.)
15. *ibid.* (p.67.)
16. *ibid.* (pp.250ff.)

helpful to spiritual development, for in the following chapter, he asserted that a sincere Christian would avoid the 'entertainment of the stage' which was corrupt and sinful. Rather Christians were called[17] to a constant state of prayer and devotion and to imitate the life and example of Jesus Christ.[18] The work closed with an exhortation to Christian Perfection. What good would it do to a man? The good it would do, declared Law, was to change him from the enjoyments of an animal life to an infinite happiness in eternity.[19] Three other reasons emerged, namely:

(i) The world had nothing else to offer instead of it.[20]

(ii) The necessity of it. Law asserted that there were different degrees of holiness, but we could not state these different degrees ourselves, but must all labour to be as eminent as we could and then our different improvements must be left to God.[21]

(iii) To induce one to aspire after Christian Perfection was the double advantage[22] of it in this life and that which was to come.

A similar idea was expressed in the conclusion of his *Serious Call*.[23] There, he said it was as reasonable to suppose that it was the desire of all Christians to arrive at Christian Perfection as to suppose that all sick men desired to be restored to perfect health. As he had already showed in the Treatise, Christian Perfection called no one necessarily to the cloister but rather to those duties which are necessary for all Christians and common

---

17. Law *op.cit.* (Ch.12, pp.414-457.)
18. *ibid.* (Ch.13, pp.458-495.)
19. *ibid.* (pp.513-4.)
20. *ibid.* (p.523.)
21. *ibid.* (pp.513-4.)
22. *ibid.* (p.523.)
23. Law, William *Serious Call to a Devout and Holy Life* (London, 1750, Ch.24, p.341.)

to all states of life.[24]

Nevertheless, whilst virginity, voluntary poverty and such other restraints of lawful things, were not necessary to Christian Perfection, they were much to be commended in those who chose them as helps and means of grace for a more safe and speedy arrival at it.

It was only in this manner and in this sense that he would recommend any particular way of life; not as if Perfection consisted *in it*, but because of its great tendency to produce and support the true spirit of Christian Perfection.

Being the prolific reader he was, Wesley read and found help in innumerable volumes, including works of Beveridge, Nelson, Hickes, George Herbert, and, by no means least, Henry Scougal in his *Life of God in the Soul of Man*, a work to which George Whitefield owed much.

However it is to the great Reformer, Luther, to whom one must now look for an abiding influence. It was by no means a direct one, for the great impact of the doctrine of Salvation and Justification by Faith was conveyed to the Wesleys through their association with the Moravians and, in particular, Peter Boehler, their leader in England.

Whilst the Moravians convinced him of the truth of this teaching, he was by no means ignorant of it before this time. The Wesleys were very familiar with the doctrines of their church and in particular the teachings of the *Book of Homilies*. In his *Journal*, John recorded a conversation with Boehler on the subject. He quoted the Sermon in the *Homilies* on '*The Salvation of Mankind*':[25]

'I had now no objection to what he (Boehler) said of the nature of faith; namely, that is (to use the words of our Church) "A sure trust and confidence which a man hath in God, that through the merits of Christ his sins are forgiven and is reconciled to the favour of God".[26] Neither could I deny either

24. *ibid.* (Chapter 2.)
25. *Sermons or Homilies Appointed to be read in Churches in the Time of Queen Elizabeth of Famous Memory* (London, 1824, pp.19-30.)
26. *ibid.* (p.29.)

the happiness or holiness which he described as fruits of this
living faith...'[27]

It will be seen in due course that this great doctrine – the teaching of
the Church of England, even though it took the Moravians to convince
him of the truth of it, was the doctrine which formed the basis of
Methodist teaching to the present time.

The sermon in the *Homilies* was in three parts. The first declared that
three things must go together in our justification: Upon God's part, His
great mercy and grace; upon Christ's part, justice, that was, the satisfaction
of God's justice, or the price of our redemption, by the offering of his
body, and shedding of his blood, with fulfilling of the Law perfectly and
thoroughly: and upon our part, true and lively faith in the merits of Jesus
Christ; which yet was not ours, but by God's working in us.[28] Faith
justifies without works,[29] a doctrine supported by the 'Old Doctors' such
as Hilary, Basil and Ambrose.[30] But there was also the warning, so often
to be found in Wesley's later writings, namely that Justification by Faith
did not 'teach carnal liberty' or that we should do no good works.[31]
Rather, a justified man would demonstrate good works by the new life
which had been effected.

Describing what took place on 24 May 1738, Wesley stated in the
Journal that 'Faith... [i.e. the faith which justifies] was the gift, the free
gift of God.' Therefore, he said:

'I was not thoroughly convinced; and by the grace of God, I
resolved to seek it unto the end, (i) By absolutely renouncing
all dependence, in whole or in part, upon *my own* works or

27. J.W.J. (Vol.1, p.455.)
28. *Sermons or Homilies Appointed to be read in Churches in the Time of Queen
     Elizabeth of Famous Memory* (London, 1824, p.21.)
29. *ibid.* (p.22.)
30. *ibid.* (p.23.)
31. *ibid.* (p.28.)

righteousness; on which I had really grounded my hope of salvation, though I knew it not, from my youth up; (ii) by adding to the constant use of all the other means of grace, a continual prayer for this very thing, justifying, saving faith, a full reliance on the blood of Christ shed for *me*, a trust in Him as *my* Christ, as *my* sole justification, sanctification, and redemption.'[32]

Another subject on which Boehler had convinced Wesley, was that of instantaneous conversion i.e. that faith was given in a moment and man was changed in that instant. 'I could not comprehend what he spoke of – *an instantaneous work* – I could not understand how this faith should be given in a moment; how a man could at once be thus turned from darkness to light, from sin and misery to righteousness and joy in the Holy Ghost.'[33] Searching the Scriptures, however, he was 'astonished' to find *no other* than instantaneous conversions, but wondered if times had changed since then. Boehler obliged by providing group after group of 'living witnesses' to bear out this fact to him.

Before leaving the subject of Wesley's theological foundations, there was one further tenet of his for which he was indebted to the Moravians, namely that of Assurance.

Wesley had sought elsewhere, e.g. Taylor, for an assurance of forgiveness of sins, but in vain. His mother was of no help here, for it was not until 1739 that she experienced this herself, when her son-in-law, Westley-Hall was delivering the cup to her during the Communion service.

Wesley was unable, during his voyage to America, to give answers in the affirmative when questioned about his spiritual state, by August Gotlieb Spangenburg:

'He told me he could say nothing till he had asked me two or

---

32. J.W.J. (Vol.1, p.472.)
33. J.W.J. (Vol.1, pp.454-5.)

three questions. "Do you know yourself? Have you the witness within yourself? Does the Spirit of God bear witness with your Spirit that you are a child of God?" I was surprised, and knew not what to answer. He observed it, and asked, "Do you know Jesus Christ?" I paused, and said, "I know He is the Saviour of the world," "True," he replied, "but do you know He has saved you?" I answered: "I hope He has died to save me." He only added, "Do you know yourself?" I said, "I do." But I fear they were vain words.'[34]

His experience of 24 May 1738 was, as A.S. Yates asserts,[35] his own personal assurance. Believing was one thing; Knowing was another:

'I felt I did trust in Christ, Christ alone for salvation; and as assurance was given me that He had taken away *my* sins, even *mine* and saved me from the law of sin and death.'[36]

He was to find himself in agreement with the authentic voice of the Church of England in the person of Edmund Gibson, Bishop of London when interviewed by the prelate when the latter was investigating complaints that their[37] doctrine was unsound and that they were contravening the discipline of the Church. Gibson found nothing wrong with the Wesleys' teaching about Justification by Faith alone because they had offset any tendencies to Antinomianism by stressing the necessity of good works following justification. Wesley did not claim 'absolute assurance' which would have implied, like the notion of 'perseverance', that there could be no backsliding. The Wesleys agreed with Gibson's own definition of assurance, namely '...an inward persuasion whereby a

34. J.W.J. (Vol.1, p.151.)
35. Yates, A.S. *The Doctrine of Assurance: With special Reference to John Wesley* (London, 1952, p.11.)
36. J.W.J. (Vol.1, p.476.)
37. Both brothers had been reported to His Lordship.

man is conscious in himself after examining his life by the law of God, and weighing his own sincerity, that he is in a state of salvation and acceptable to God.'[38]

The question must now surely arise; did Wesley ever read any of the works of Arminius or Calvin? As H.A.S. Pask points out, Wesley was too exact a scholar to be content with second-hand knowledge.[39] The first indication that Wesley was familiar with Remonstrant literature was given in a letter to him from his father dated 26 January 1725[40] when Samuel declared that John should read Grotius as he was the best, for the 'most part, on the Old Testament' and it could be assumed that John took this advice. The second reference is in the *Journal* for 6 July 1741[41] when, by mistake he took down from the shelves of the Library of Lincoln College, the works of Episcopius which gave him an account of the proceedings of the Synod of Dort. He exclaimed:

> 'I believed it might be useful to read it through. But what a
> scene is here disclosed! I wonder not at the heavy curse of
> God, which so soon after fell on our Church and nation. What
> a pity it is, that the *Holy Synod* of Trent, and that of Dort, did
> not sit at the same time; nearly allied as they were, not only as
> to the *purity of doctrine*, which each of them established, but
> also as to the *spirit* wherewith they acted; if the latter did not
> exceed!'

Pask is correct when he asserts that nowhere in the writings of John Wesley does he give the title of any single Remonstrant work. Yet, in

---

38. J.W.J. (Vol.2, p.93.)

39. I am indebted for much of the information contained in this paragraph, and the next, to Dr H.A.S. Pask of North Shields who kindly loaned me his unpublished Ph.D. Thesis of Edinburgh University entitled *The Influence of Arminius Upon the Theology of John Wesley*. See Chap. VI. The thesis is dated 1937.

40. Moore, Henry *The Life of the Revd John Wesley, MA* (London, 1824, Vol.1, p.123.)

41. J.W.J. (Vol.2, p.473.)

1770 during the last great Calvinistic Controversy,[42] Wesley published a pamphlet *What is an Arminian?*[43] In this he gave a very brief account of Jacobus Arminius (James Harmens). Wesley related that Arminius was first one of the Ministers of Amsterdam, and afterwards Professor of Divinity at Leyden. He was educated at Geneva; but in the year 1591, began to doubt of the principles which he had till then received. And being more and more convinced that they were wrong, when he was vested with the Professorship, he publicly taught what he believed of the truth, till in the year 1609 he died in peace. A short account of Arminian beliefs was given and then a list of Calvinistic tenets followed. In 1778, Wesley's own magazine *The Arminian Magazine* was published. In the preface to the first part, dated 1 November, he stated that the aim of the Magazine was to maintain that 'God willeth all men to be saved, by arguments drawn partly from Scripture, partly from reason; proposed in as indifferent manner as the nature of the thing will permit.' In the first edition of the Magazine he included *A Sketch of the Life of Arminius* taken from Peter Bertius's Funeral Oration on the interment of Arminius which took place at Leyde on 22 October 1609. Where had Wesley read this? At Lincoln College? Nowhere did he give any indication of his sources.[44]

Did Wesley read any of Calvin's works? Again one is left in some doubt what was read. Dr Frank H. Baker, the noted Methodist historian, insists that nothing of Calvin's works were read during the Oxford years. The *Journal* certainly bears this out. An examination of Wesley's

---

42. See Chapter Eleven of this study, pp. 301-354.
43. J.W.W. (Vol.15, pp.26-7.)
44. I am indebted to the Revd S.C. Thexton who was in charge of the college property at Richmond where a large part of Wesley's library was stored, and to Revd Dr John C. Bowmer who later had charge of it at the Methodist Archives Centre for the information that no works of Arminius or Calvin are to be found in it. Dr Baker in a personal letter dated 24 April 1973 states that the only copy to be found is in the Kingswood Library and that is in Latin and was purely for use by the students. Both Dr Baker and Dr Pask believe that it would be impossible to establish which editions of Arminius or Calvin Wesley used.

Predestination Calmly Considered[45] implies, according to Dr Baker, the use of an English edition of Calvin's *Institutes*. In the *Journal* for 9 July 1741, Wesley mentioned that he came across Calvin's account of Michael Servetus, whose execution Calvin had consented to, but this gave no information about doctrinal sources.

It will be noticed that Wesley in his early probings into theology was more concerned with the claims of Calvinism and, having rejected these, he owed his introduction, as Dr Pask asserts, to 'English Arminianism' more to native sources than any direct from Holland.[46] Also two of those 'native sources' must never be overlooked. They were, so Geoffrey Nuttall points out, his own parents, Samuel and Susannah:

'From his parents, indeed Wesley not only learned Arminian doctrine directly. He learned something far rarer and more remarkable, and, which, it may be argued, profoundly affected his Arminianism and his reasons for holding it so firmly – This was his missionary outlook...'[47]

The sources matter less than the doctrines themselves and their practical application. To Wesley, a man was saved and justified by his own faith – alone. He accepted it purely as a gift (it cannot be earned). The same man had a right and a freedom to spurn it altogether! But he could, by the Spirit, grow in perfect love of God and man and this was and had to be, demonstrated by the fruits of the good life, i.e. good works. The onus was on man. The offer was God's.

It is now time to look at the logical basis of the opposite camp of the eighteenth-century Evangelicals. One must obviously begin with

---

45. For a summary of this work, see pp.188-191 of this study.
46. This is contained in a personal letter from Dr Pask dated 21 May 1973. In a further letter dated 6 June 1973 he says, 'Wesley didn't (I think) feel it very necessary to check up too closely on Arminius himself. What he read – *whatever* he read about the Dutch origins simply confirmed what he already held – hence, to his day, he said, "I am an Arminian."'
47. Nuttall, Geoffrey *The Puritan Spirit* (London, 1967, p.76.)

Whitefield, for his influence among these Evangelicals was inestimable and he was the first to expound his views polemically, especially against the Wesleys. The way in which certain other Evangelicals came to their theological position will be dealt with as they enter this study from time to time.

Whitefield, like Wesley, was to compile his own system of theology but the basic disagreement between the two was also the foundation of the truly sorry story to be recounted in the next chapters. George, however, had no theological preferences before his conversion. His family could make no pretensions to either saintliness or erudition. Of his father, little is known and his mother was not the lady of the parsonage but the keeper of the Bell Inn at Gloucester. In this, he had an unfavourable start when compared with the Wesley brothers.

However, before his conversion, he had, as a youth in Bristol, pondered over à Kempis's *Imitation of Christ*, and, preparatory to entering Oxford when only 17 years of age, he perused *The Christian's Defence against the Fears of Death*. Once in Oxford, Law's *Serious Call* and *Treatise on Christian Perfection* were read and they had a profound effect upon him, especially the latter, but his interest in Perfection was not to last. It was here that Charles Wesley met Whitefield and, besides introducing him to the new 'Holy Club', lent him a few volumes. Amongst these were Professor Francke's *Treatise Against the Fear of Man* and *The Country Parson's Advice to His Parishioners*. Charles, at this time, whilst helping George in respect of books, hindered him by guiding him on Quietist lines, with the accompanying deprecation of human activity and responsibility.

His new teacher (whom, afterwards, he always referred to as 'his never-to-be-forgotten friend') loaned him another volume. This was one which was to have a greater effect upon him than all the previous ones. It was Henry Scougall's *The Life of God in the Soul of Man*.[48] This taught him that 'Some falsely-placed religion in going to church and doing hurt to no one, but being constant in the duties of the closet, and now and then

---

48. Formerly Professor of Divinity at Aberdeen University.

reaching out their hands to give alms to their poor neighbours.' He continued to read 'That true religion was a union of the souls with God or Christ formed within us.' He rejoiced at this and recalled that 'A ray of Divine Light instantaneously darted in upon his soul, and from that moment, but not till then, did he know that he must be a new creature.'[49]

So it was, that in 1733, when he was 19 years of age, the light dawned on Whitefield.

It has been asserted by Tyerman[50] that by 1737 there were no traces in his sermons or other writings of Whitefield's Calvinistic leanings and that these dogmas were to be learned later among the Presbyterians and Independents of America. The truth of this statement is open to question. Arnold A. Dallimore in his essay on George Whitefield,[51] quotes Whitefield's utterance a few months before his death when he spoke of the believer's eternal security:

> 'O, my dear hearers, this is no new doctrine. I set out with this doctrine. The second sermon I ever preached was on these words: "He that is in Christ is a new creature." I was then about twenty-and-a-half years old. The next sermon I preached was upon "Ye are justified", and the next "Ye are glorified", which shows that although I am nearly fifty-five years old, I am so far from changing my principles, which I am sure I was taught by God's word and God's Spirit.'

These were the doctrines of Grace. Although, as Dallimore goes on to say, Whitefield was not clear about these matters during the first year or two of his ministry, he was so afterwards. In his biography, Tyerman rightly points out that in his first seven sermons published in 1737, Whitefield scarcely mentioned the doctrine of Justification by Faith,

---

49. O.W.J. (p.47.)

50. Tyerman, Luke *The Life of George Whitefield* (London, 1890, Vol.1, p.102.)

51. Dallimore, Arnold A. *George Whitefield Evangelical Library Bulletin* (Autumn, 1964, page 7.)

although it had been a personal experience for him. That he soon did preach it was obvious. However, his Calvinistic leanings were evident in at least two sermons published in 1737. Dallimore reminds his readers, that whilst crossing to America in 1739, George wrote distinctly about Election, Predestination and Final Perseverance:

> 'This is my comfort. "Jesus Christ, the same yesterday, today and forever!" He saw me from eternity; He gave me my being; He called me in time; He has freely justified me through faith in His blood; He has in part sanctified me by His Spirit; He will preserve me under the everlasting arms till time shall be no more. O, the blessedness of these evangelical truths! They are indeed Gospel; they are tidings of great joy to all who have ears to hear. These bring the creature out of himself. They make him hang upon the promises, and cause his obedience to flow from a principle of love.'[52]

The initial Calvinistic influence was twofold:

Firstly, there was the literary influence of Scougall; the *Works of Matthew Henry*;[53] Richard Alleine's *Alarm to the Unconverted*[54] and Richard Baxter's *Call to the Unconverted*. These were Puritan works; the Puritans were Calvinists to a man and their books did their work well. As J.C. Ryle, in his brief biography[55] says, these books coupled with the 'reading of the Word of God on his knees', brought Whitefield 'the glorious liberty of Christ's Gospel' and he 'never again turned to asceticism, legalism, mysticism or strange views of Christian Perfection.'

Secondly, surely the 'heart correspondence' as Tyerman calls it[56] which Whitefield had with the brothers Ralph and Ebenezer Erskine, and

---

52. *Evangelical Library Bulletin* (London, Autumn 1964, p.7.)
53. A presbyterian minister at Chester noted for his Biblical Commentary.
54. Educated at Oxford. Rector of Batcombe, Somerset. Ejected under the Act of Uniformity. Wesley adopted and revised his 'Covenant Service' (still used).
55. *George Whitefield and His Ministry* (London, 1958, p.13.)
56. Tyerman, Luke *The Life of George Whitefield* (London, 1890, Vol.1, p.274.)

later his visits to them, had no small influence on his theological thinking. Both these men were field-preachers and later secessionists from the Church of Scotland, becoming notable exponents of a rigid Calvinism. The correspondence began in May 1739. Tyerman says Whitefield's Calvinism was 'suddenly born in June 1739'.[57] A letter to Ralph Erskine dated 23 July, 1739[58] expressed thankfulness that Erskine approved of George's sermon. On the other hand, Erskine's own sermons were a much consulted help to George. Coupled with the Scottish influence, there was the growing friendship with Howell Harris, the Welsh preacher whose theology had swung from Arminianism to Calvinism. Writing to Harris in 1739 (the year in which he had first met Howell), Whitefield admitted his Calvinism:

> 'Since I saw you, God has been pleased to enlighten me in that comfortable doctrine of *Election*, etc. At my return, I hope to be more explicit than I have been...'[59]

He certainly was! It will be noted, that whilst he was already in America for the second time, he had not yet met with the American Calvinists who were supposed to have introduced him to these ideas.

There were further works read in 1739 which added to his already formed views. The *Journals* for Friday 22 June 1739[60] state that he had read Jenks' *Submission to the Righteousness of Christ*, a volume which dealt with the doctrine of the Imputation of Christ's Righteousness – a cardinal notion of the Calvinists and one which was to cause so much subsequent disagreement between the Evangelicals and the Wesleys. During the voyage to America on the second visit, he took the opportunity to read Jonathan Warne's *The Church of England man turned Dissenter* and *Arminianism the Backdoor to Popery*, both taken from *The Preacher* by Dr Edwards of Cambridge. 'These are noble testimonies given before

57. Tyerman, Luke *The Life of George Whitefield* (London, 1890, Vol.1, p.274.)
58. *ibid.* (Vol.1, pp.268-9.)
59. *ibid.* (Vol.1, p.314.)
60. G.W.J. (p.292.)

than University,' wrote Whitefield, 'of Justification by Faith only, the Imputed Righteousness of Christ, our having no freewill etc...'[61] Whitefield declared, '...that they deserve to be written in letters of gold.'

The next day he wrote that 'The outward righteousness of Christ Jesus imputed to us, I believe, is the sole foundation and cause of all the inward communication which we receive from the Spirit of God.[62]

Naturally his subsequent visits to America and his friendship with the dour Calvinist, Jonathan Edwards, Gilbert and William Tennent (the latter was a friend of the Erskines) certainly strengthened the views Whitefield already held. Edwards was a Congregational minister; The Tennents were Presbyterians. Whilst a minister of the Church, in Northampton, Mass., Edwards had tried hard to stem the popular drift towards Arminianism, but his extremities led to his expulsion from his church in 1749. The next year he began a missionary crusade at Stockbridge. Here he wrote three important works: His essay on *Original Sin; The Nature of True Virtue* and *Inquiry into the Modern Prevailing Notions respecting that Freedom of the Will, which is supposed to be essential to Moral Agency* (1754). He denied freedom of the will as unphilosophical and absurd and it was his intention to defend the extreme position of Election.

When it was realized that Edwards and Whitefield worked together in missionary enterprise leading to 'The Great Awakening' in New England in 1740-3, it was not surprising that Whitefield emerged as a fully-fledged Calvinist and eager to defend his position – hence the disagreement with the Wesleys shortly to be considered.

However, it is doubtful whether Edwards or Whitefield ever fully understood the tenets they so stoutly defended. Whitefield, it must be remembered, was primarily an evangelist offering Christ and calling men to repentance. He was no erudite scholar and it is often true that a successful evangelist is not always an academic! Nevertheless, had he not leaned to Calvinism, many opportunities and contacts would have been denied him. His popularity and success both in Wales and Scotland

---

61. G.W.J. (p.335.) Dated Saturday 29 September 1739.
62. G.W.J. (p.335.)

would have been as small as those of Wesley. Moreover, he would have lacked the important patronage of the Countess of Huntingdon and thereby would have been denied the exercise of a great influence over such evangelical clergy as Hervey, Venn, Romaine and Berridge. Equally important was his ability to move among the Dissenting congregations of the land, because here, his Calvinistic tenets were welcome.

The results of the English Reformation were embodied in the Thirty-Nine Articles of Religion. Whilst they required no limit to the most liberal thinking consistent with belief in Revelation, they repudiated anything which savoured of the exclusiveness of Rome. Their teaching was based on Scripture and they safeguarded certain points of doctrine from medieval and sixteenth-century exaggerations. They were explanations and safeguards, pacificatory rather than to be accepted literally. They were also intended to include the maximum number of subscribers. It was soon seen how elastic they were, allowing a greater latitude of interpretation than would have been expected or intended. It was a discovery made long before the days of John Henry Newman and the Tractarian Movement!

It is necessary, briefly to look at these Articles, having in mind the statements of both Wesley and Whitefield that they preached no doctrine but that of the Church of England.

Articles VI and XVIII stated that the Scriptures were sufficient for salvation and that was in the name of Christ only. Original Sin was not, as the Pelagians averred, in the following of Adam[63] but was the fault and corruption of the nature of every man, their being inclined by it to evil.

Man, had, however, free will but that will was not exercised by ourselves completely. 'A man cannot turn and prepare himself' by his own natural strength and good works, to faith and calling in God.[64] The grace of Christ assisted man in this. This grace was both an inward assistance and a 'preventing' grace by which the will was first moved and disposed to turn to God,[65] for example the conversion of Paul. Two

---

63. Article IX.
64. Article X.
65. Burnet, Gilbert *An Exposition of the XXXIX Articles of the Church of England* (Oxon, 1796, p. 155.) Burnet was Bishop of Salisbury and this work was first published in 1699.

different ways of regarding its efficacy were possible, namely that it never failed to convert those to whom it was given and secondly, though it enabled men to turn to God, they could also resist it. Gilbert Burnet said that those holding it to be efficacious in itself, restrained it to the number of those who were elected and converted by it.[66]

The Justification of Man[67] by faith only meant that he was accounted righteous before God through the merits of Christ and not because of his works. Good works, however, were the fruits of faith and followed after Justification, though they did 'not put away our sins'. Good works done before Justification were 'not pleasing to God' because they did not arise from a man's faith. They were not done as God had willed nor did they make men ready to receive the Grace of Christ.

Most important is Article XVII 'Of Predestination and Election'. 'Predestination to life, is the everlasting purpose of God, before the foundations of the world were laid, he hath constantly decreed by his counsel, secret to us, to deliver from curse and damnation, those whom he hath chosen in Christ out of Mankind, and to bring them by Christ to everlasting salvation...'

Burnet asked the question: 'Upon what views did God form his purposes and decrees concerning mankind? Did he do it merely to advance His own glory or did he leave the decision to man's free rational thought?[68] In the latter case, he would *foresee* their decisions.

Those who held the former view that God did this to advance His own glory were Supralapsarians who believed God decreed the fall of Adam and that those he decreed to save would confer glory on Himself. Those, on the other hand who felt Adam sinned freely were Sublapsarians and for them, God sent His grace to *some* who were converted and kept in a state of *perseverance* to the end, whilst the rest were left in the lapsed state.

A third opinion was possible, namely that of the Remonstrants, who held that God created all men free but foresaw how men would use that

---

66. Burnet *ibid.* (p.155.)
67. Article XI.
68. Burnet *op.cit.* (p.189ff.)

freedom. Christ died for all men, but they had to decide whether they would use the assistances which were offered to them. This was the Arminian position.

Burnet dealt with both kinds of Calvinistic view and also with that of the Arminians. Both had advantages and disadvantages. A Calvinist, he said,[69] was taught by his opinions, to think meanly of himself, and to ascribe the honour of all to God. A Remonstrant or Arminian, on the other hand, was engaged to awaken and improve his faculties, to fill his mind with good notions, to raise them in himself by frequent reflection, and by a constant attention to his own actions – he would see cause to reproach himself for his sins, and to set about his duty and purpose.

As to disadvantages, the Calvinist was tempted to a false security and 'sloth'; The Arminian may be tempted to trust too much in himself and too little in God. If the Arminian was zealous to affect liberty, it was because he could not see how there could be good or evil in the world without it. A Calvinist seemed to break in on liberty because he could not reconcile it with the Sovereignty of God and the freedom of His grace. Burnet continued to say that the common fault on both sides was, to charge one another with the consequences of their opinions, as if they were truly their tenets. They both spoke too boldly of God. It was a very daring presumption to pretend to assign the order of all the acts of God, the ends proposed in them, and the methods by which they were executed. The hard thing to be digested in this whole matter, he said, was reprobation. Many Calvinists tried to avoid the logical reason for this if they held election but rather than give up the latter, they would bear the responsibility of asserting the former. On the other side, those who persuaded themselves that the doctrine of reprobation was false, did not see how they could deny it, and yet ascribe a free election to God. Some had tried a middle way, of ascribing all that was good to God and all that was evil to man. 'Let us arrogate no good to ourselves, they say, and impute no evil to God,' is the way Burnet described this suggestion. So they allowed the

---

69. Burnet, Gilbert *An Exposition of the XXXIX Articles of The Church of England* (Oxon, 1796, p.417.)

matter to rest in a way which Burnet agreed, was lazy, yet safe.

Summing up, Burnet felt that the Article was *against* the Supralapsarians. It mentioned, nowhere, any reference to Reprobation. It did assert the efficiency of grace but did not define it. It was very probable, he said, that those who wrote this Article meant that the decree of Predestination was absolute, but since they had not said it, no one was bound to believe that it was thus intended. Whilst the Arminians who did not deny that God had foreseen what all mankind would do or not do, could also subscribe to the Article, without renouncing their opinions on freewill. However, the Calvinists had less ground for scruple, as the Article seemed to favour them.

Burnet, having dealt with the controversy admirably, finished by declaring that the Church had not been peremptory but had left latitude for different opinions. 'And I,' he concluded, 'leave the choice as free to my readers as the Church has done.'[70]

So here, in a work, originally published in 1699, which would be known both to Whitefield and his Calvinist friends and also to the Wesleys and their supporters, was a scholarly compromise on which both sides could rest their case as well as upon their interpretation of Scripture.

Whilst considering the theological basis for the teaching of both sides, one is in a better position to judge the statement of both Whitefield and Wesley that they taught nothing but what was the teaching of the Church of England. It was one of the easiest truths to arrive at because both parties found the support there for their viewpoint.[71] Yet it will be quickly seen that this brief study of the Articles surely shows the controversies between the two schools of thoughts to be less purposeful and necessary than their respective propagators believed.

---

70. Bishop Burnet's Exposition of the Articles has been used here because in the eighteenth century this was the classic and standard commentary on the Articles and known to Wesley and the Evangelicals – in fact to all the clergy.
71. The succeeding chapters of this study will illustrate how this freedom of interpretation was used to the full and the unfortunate results which came from it.

CHAPTER SEVEN

THE FIRST CALVINISTIC CONTROVERSY
THE NEW BIRTH AND REGENERATION:
UNIVERSAL OR PARTICULAR REDEMPTION?

In this chapter the first of the doctrinal disputes in which Wesley was involved, will be dealt with, namely that which took place between himself and George Whitefield.

Wesley, as will have been seen in the previous chapter, was confirmed in his belief in Arminian tenets and was content with nothing less than having these precisely defined. In Arminianism, he had found a workable and understandable system of theology. It could be briefly stated thus:

God did decree to confer salvation on those whom he foresaw would maintain their faith in Christ Jesus inviolate until death, and, on the other hand, to consign over to eternal punishment, the unbelieving who resisted his invitations to the end of their lives. Jesus Christ, by His death, made expiation for the sins of all and every one of mankind; yet none but believers could become partakers of its divine benefit. No one of himself could, by the powers of his own freewill, produce or generate faith in his own mind, because being by nature evil, and incompetent (ineptus) both to think and do good, it was necessary he should be born again and renewed by God, for Christ's sake, through the Holy Spirit. The Divine grace or energy which healed the soul of man, perfected all that could be truly called good in him, yet this grace compelled no man against his will, though he could be repelled by his will. Those who were thus united to

161

Christ by faith were furnished with sufficient strength to overcome sin; but it was possible for a man to lose his faith and fall from a state of grace.

This, then, represented Wesley's Arminianism which was the basis of his teaching and preaching to the end of his days.

It was Wesley's conception of God and His purpose which caused him to reject Calvinism[1] – even that of a moderate type – which was all that many of his antagonists claimed. It was not enough to say to him that in predestinating the elect to be saved, God simply passed by the reprobates and left them to their own inclinations and deserts. Predestinating the elect to be saved meant to him reprobating the non-elect to be positively damned. Furthermore, the final perseverance of the elect whatever they did, to final salvation, was, to Wesley, a dangerous affront to morals. This is why he was, for many years, to point out that Antinomianism (i.e. the setting aside, without compunction, the moral law, knowing that one was quite safe in the end) could arise from this idea. There was the growing in grace to perfect love of God and man, as found in his teaching on Christian Perfection. Wesley felt that a convinced Calvinist had seen no need for this.

Sooner or later, it was inevitable that the opposing teachings of Wesley and Whitefield would be brought into the open. Strange to relate, the beginnings of this first dispute had roots in Wesley's *lack* of strictness. Although a firm Arminian himself, he had never required subscription to Arminianism from those desirous of membership of his societies. This was to prove very troublesome for him. A man named Acourt joined one of the London societies. Charles Wesley excluded the man from the meetings because he debated the subject of election in meetings designed for devotional purposes. The man appealed to John, saying that he had

1. See Wesley's essay *What is an Arminian?* (J.W.W. Vol.15, p.27.) In it he drew all the obvious and well-known differences between Arminianism and Calvinism but warned every Arminian preacher *never* in public or private to use the word *Calvinist* as a term of reproach and to try to prevent others from doing this. The Calvinists should also treat the term *Arminian* in the same way!

been expelled because of his opinions. John naturally enquired what these opinions were. Acourt replied, 'Election – I hold that a certain number are elected from eternity, and they must be saved, and the rest of mankind must and shall be damned.' He mentioned that there were others in the society who believed the same. Wesley insisted that whilst the man could believe this, he must keep his opinions to himself. 'Nay, but I will dispute about them,' he answered. 'You are all wrong and I am determined to set you right.'[2] Wesley felt that no useful purpose would be served by Acourt's remaining in the society and it was made clear that he had better leave. Acourt prophesied that within a fortnight they would all be in confusion and that the Wesleys were false prophets.

Matters came to a head when Wesley found that John Cennick to whom he had entrusted the work of 'helper' and teacher at his Kingswood School, had turned Calvinist. At this time, 1740, Cennick had ceased to preach Universal Redemption and led a party against the doctrine and against his patron. After useless attempts at reconciliation, Cennick had to be excluded. He had written a number of letters to Whitefield asking him to return and refute the idea of Universal Redemption. Cennick left Wesley and took with him about ninety of John's followers and they joined Whitefield's movement. Cennick, however, found his true spiritual home soon afterwards, with the Moravians.[3]

Wesley had now little choice but to make a firm stand on doctrine and to do so publicly. The outcome was a sermon – on *Free Grace* – a term beloved of Whitefield! This publication needs to be looked at closely for it was to become the bone of contention which led to the temporary estrangement between Wesley and George.

It will be noted that this sermon does not appear in the *Standard Sermons*[4] but in Benson's edition of Wesley's *Works* it appears as Sermon No. LV.[5] The text was from Romans Chapter viii verse 32: 'He

2.   J.W.J. (Vol.2, p.353.) Dated: Thursday 11 June 1740.
3.   *ibid.* (Vol.2, p.433.) Dated: 6 March 1741.
4.   Edited by E.H. Sugden (London, 1933.)
5.   i.e. *The Works of the Reverend John Wesley* (Edited by Joseph Benson) (London, 1809, Vol.8, pp.408-423.)

that spared not his own Son but delivered him up for us all, how shall he not with him also freely give us all things?'

Free Grace was all in all! The Grace or Love of God, whence came our salvation, was free in all, and free for all. First, said Wesley, it was free in all to whom it was given. It did not depend on the power or merit of man. But, Wesley asked, is it free *for* all as well as *in* all? There were some who would answer 'NO' – it was only free for those whom God had ordained to life and those are few. The rest were decreed to die eternally. God, according to the Calvinists, willed this. This, Wesley declared, was the decree of Predestination. Some, of course, would say, 'This is not the predestination I hold – I hold only the election to Grace. Those not elected to salvation are merely left to themselves and thus finally punished.' But, queried John, 'Was this all the Predestination which they held?' Surely if some were predestined to life, the rest *must* be predestined to eternal punishment? If God left them unelected and finally punished them, was this not also a decree of reprobation? Call it what you like, he continued, 'Election, Preterition, Predestination or Reprobation,' it all came to the same thing in the end.

Now if this were so, Wesley argued, all preaching was in vain. The elected would not need it; the reprobated were infallibly damned in any case and no preaching would ever alter the fact. This then, he maintained, was plain proof, that the doctrine of Predestination was not a doctrine of God. Secondly, it directly tended to destroy that holiness, which was the end of all the ordinances of God. The motive for holiness was taken away. Several particular branches of holiness were likewise destroyed, namely, meekness and love, for example love of one's enemies. Furthermore, the elect could well adopt the attitude of coldness and contempt to those who were the supposed outcasts of God. Even if the decree of reprobation was not held, it would inevitably follow that certain people would be regarded as reprobates. Thirdly, the doctrine tended to destroy the comfort and happiness of Christianity, especially for those who were not elected to new life. What was the happiness of the elect? Not just a notion or an idea, but a full assurance of faith, NOT an assurance of final perseverance.

Another objection to election was its obstruction to the Witness of the Spirit, not only to the reprobates but also to those who had fallen from the state of grace, which was a real possibility. Even the elect must have been entertaining doubts and fears concerning election and perseverance. The Christian who did not hold the view of election did not concern himself as to whether he would persevere in the future. He had the witness *now* and abided in Him by faith from hour to hour. Fourthly, this uncomfortable doctrine directly tended to destroy zeal for good works. For whatever lessened love, must also lessen the desire to do good to mankind. Fifthly, this notion had a tendency to overthrow the whole Christian Revelation. This was just what the enemies of the faith desired! To believe that thousands were damned from eternity was to deny revelation – as if it had not existed.

If then, not all men were to be saved, why was this? By the decree of God? No! the fact springs from personal and voluntary rejection on the part of man. 'They will not come unto me that they may have life [John V v.40].' Jesus thus became a hypocrite, for he regretted that there were some who would not come to him when they *could not* because they were decreed to act thus. That was blasphemy. The doctrine of Predestination was blasphemy. 'You cannot charge your death on Him,' declared Wesley, '"Have I any pleasure at all, that the wicked should die" said the Lord God – "I have no pleasure in the death of him that dieth" said the Lord God [Ezekiel xxviii. v.11].'

Although this was an impassioned writing composed out of a deep conviction, one cannot help but appreciate its simple unanswerable logic and its reasoning from Scripture.

The latest editor of Whitefield's *Journals* is surely wrong when he says[6] that the first hint of doctrinal difference leading to serious results was in a letter by George to John dated 25 June 1739. The first such letter was rather the one dated 24 May 1740 written at Cape Lopen:

---

6.   i.e. *George Whitefield's Journals* (Edited by Ian Murray) (London, 1960, p.565.)

'Honoured Sir,

I cannot entertain prejudice against your conduct and principles any longer, without informing you. The more I examine the writings of the most experienced men, and the experiences of most established Christians, the more I differ from your notion about not committing sin, and your denying the doctrine of election and final perseverance of the saints. I dread coming to England, unless you are resolved to oppose these truths with less warmth, then when I was there last...'[7]

Whitefield pointed out, quite correctly that he might stay in America for he was enjoying success there and because the folk there were of one mind!

Certainly on 25 June 1740 there was the request of Whitefield that Wesley should never speak against Election in his sermons. 'No one can say,' he claimed, 'that I ever mention it in public discourses, whatever my private sentiments may be.'[8]

There was also a letter on 2 July of the same year, which the Editor of Whitefield's *Journals* gives, but which Tyerman omits. It was obvious by now, that Wesley's *Free Grace* sermon had reached George – no doubt having been sent by Wesley's enemies:

'Dear Honoured Sir,

If you have any regard for the peace of the church, keep in your sermon on predestination. But you have cast a lot...'[9]

Again on 25 August 1740:

'Only give me leave, with all humility, to exhort you not to be strenuous in opposing the doctrines of election and final

---

7.   Tyerman, Luke *The Life of George Whitefield* (London, 1890, Vol.1, pp.389-390.)
8.   Tyerman, Luke *The Life of George Whitefield* (London, 1890, Vol.1, pp.394-5.)
9.   G.W.J. (p.565.) It was Wesley's practice at this time to cast lots when in doubt as to what his action should be.

perseverance, when, by your own confession, "you have not the witness of the Spirit within yourself" and consequently are not a proper judge. I remember, dear brother E— told me one day, he was "convinced of the perseverance of the saints", I told him you were not. He replied, "But he will be convinced when he has got the Spirit himself." For some years, God has given me this living witness in my soul...Dear and honoured Sir, I write this not to enter into disputation. I hope I feel something of the meekness and gentleness of Christ. I cannot bear the thought of opposing you; but how can I avoid it, if you go about, as your brother Charles once said, to drive John Calvin out of Bristol? Alas! I never read anything that Calvin wrote. My doctrines I had from Christ and His Apostles. I was taught them of God; and as God was pleased to send me out first, and to enlighten me first, so I think he still continues to do it...'[10]

What an admission from so great an exponent of 'Calvinism'![11]

On 1 September 1740, Charles wrote[12] to Whitefield abhorring the possibility of a separation between George and themselves. George replied, maintaining still, that sinless perfection was unattainable in this life and that indwelling sin remained in a man until death. To affirm perfection and deny final perseverance was absurd. But surely Whitefield was wrong here. Wesley did not hold to *sinless* or moral perfection, but rather *perfect love* of God and man.[13]

On 25 September, George wrote to John in the same vein, pointing out that sinless perfection was unscriptural and referred to John's sermon on *Free Grace*, now obviously in print:[14]

---

10. Tyerman *op.cit.* (Vol.1, pp.403-4.)
11. See page 178 of this study where this statement is discussed.
12. Tyerman, Luke *The Life of George Whitefield* (London, 1890, Vol.1, pp.411-2.)
13. See Chapter Ten of this study.
14. Tyerman, Luke *op.cit.* (Vol.1, p.414.)

'I find your sermon has had its expected success; it has set the nation disputing. You will have enough to do now to answer pamphlets. Two I have already seen...'[15]

Only three days afterwards, he wrote again, what was perhaps the curtest letter from him to John:

'What mean you by disputing in all your letters? May God give you to know yourself; and then you will not plead for *absolute perfection,* or call the doctrine of *election* a "doctrine of devils"...Let God teach you!...'[16]

Two letters only are recorded as having been written by John to George. The first was on 9 August 1740[17] in which John simply stated that there were bigots both for Predestination and against it and that he was sending a message to both but neither would receive it. 'Therefore for a time you are suffered to be of one opinion and I of another. But when His time is come, God will do what man cannot – namely, make us both of one mind...'

Apparently the second letter which was dated 27 April 1741 and sent from London, dealt first of all with some petty criticism of the furnishings of the Society Room at Bristol, but the latter part of the epistle exposed Whitefield's theological ignorance once again:

'Indeed, among the latter [i.e. heretics] you publicly place me; for you rank all the maintainers of universal redemption with Socinians themselves. Alas! my brother, do you not know even this – that the Socinians allow *no redemption* at all; that Socinius himself speaks thus – *Tota redemptionis nostrae per Christum metaphora?*[18] and says expressly, Christ did

---

15. It is to be regretted that Whitefield did not give the titles of these pamphlets.
16. Tyerman, Luke *op.cit.* (Vol.1, p.414.)
17. J.W.L. (Vol.1, p.351.)
18. i.e. 'The whole of our redemption by Christ is a metaphor'.

not die *as a ransom* for any, but only as an *example* for all mankind? How easy were it for me to hit many other palpable blots in that which you call an answer to my sermon! And how above measure contemptible would you then appear to all impartial men, either of sense or learning! But I spare you...'[19]

An unfortunate incident was to happen to Whitefield. In 1739, there was published *An Abstract of the Life and Death of Mr Thomas Halyburton* with a *Recommendatory Epistle* by Whitefield and a '*Preface*' of six pages by Wesley. In this Preface, Wesley introduced his ideas of Christian Perfection and because Whitefield's *Epistle* stood in such close connection with this, he was accused by a group who called themselves 'The Querists', of subscribing to Wesley's doctrine of perfection!

'As for your insinuating that I countenance Mr Wesley in his errors, I do no such thing,' replied George indignantly!

He quickly pointed out that he prefaced Halyburton's Memoirs before he had seen what Wesley had written. Had he known what John was going to say he wouldn't have prefaced the work at all. In fact he had torn off part of Wesley's *Preface* from several of the books which he had given away recently and had told Wesley in no uncertain manner the error of his ways.

A further letter of complaint was received from George dated 24 November 1740 in which he wished for harmony but he said it could not be so since Wesley held 'Universal Redemption'.[20]

A more important letter was written on 24 December 1740 – one important enough to constitute an Appendix in the latest edition of Whitefield's *Journals* where it is printed in full, complete with Preface.[21]

---

19. J.W.L. (Vol.1, p.357.)
20. Tyerman, Luke *The Life of George Whitefield* (London, 1890, Vol.1, pp.439-440.)
21. G.W.J. (pp.571-588.) See also Tyerman *op.cit* (Vol.1, pp.469-471) but in his account he omits the *im*personal parts of the letter.

It is far too long to include here and a summary must suffice.

Whitefield began by expressing his regret that differences had arisen between himself and the Wesleys and that so many had been led into error. He objected to the Wesleys having propagated the doctrine of Universal Redemption. He had been silent too long and whatever the cost, he had now to speak. He did not agree with John's practice of deciding his course by casting lots and what was more, it had not always worked. As for the text [Romans viii], it was an unfortunate choice as it was here where the doctrine of election was so clearly seen. The word 'All' meant only those in Christ and the grace that was given was the Grace to persevere to the end. Wesley's very sermon has had the effect of confirming him in his belief in election. Wesley had deliberately stirred up dislike of the doctrine of reprobation in the hope that equal dislike would be engendered against election. For, he admitted, 'The doctrine of election and reprobation must stand or fall together.' Whitefield agreed with the idea of reprobation:

> 'I believe the doctrine of reprobation, in this view that God intends to give saving grace, through Jesus Christ, only to a certain number, and that the rest of mankind, after the Fall of Adam, being justly left of God to continue in sin, will at last suffer that eternal death, which is its proper wages... This is the established doctrine of Scripture, and acknowledged as such in the Seventeenth Article of the Church of England, as Bishop Burnet himself confesses...yet dear Mr Wesley absolutely denies it.'

How wrong Whitefield was here.[22] Burnet did not take sides but merely stated the case of each side impartially. Wesley would be equally familiar with Burnet.

Whitefield then proceeded to answer Wesley's points in the order in which he had made them:

---

22. See previous Chapter of this study, Section 3.

1) 'If this be so [i.e. if there be an election] then is all preaching vain etc...'

George replied that God who had elected, had also ordained preaching. No one knows who the elect were and therefore 'promiscuous' preaching was necessary. For the elect, it was the power of God to their salvation; to the non-elect it was the restraining influence against much wickedness and sin.

2) 'The doctrines of election and reprobation tend to destroy that holiness, which is the end of all the ordinances of God.'

A man who carried perfection 'to such an exalted pitch as dear Mr Wesley does' would know that a true lover of the Lord Jesus Christ would strive to be holy for the sake of being holy and work for Christ out of love and gratitude without any regard to the rewards of heaven, or fear of hell. The elect knew that the more good works they did, the greater would be their reward, and holiness was a mark of election. As for election 'destroying several particular branches of holiness, such as meekness, love, etc.', Wesley must have been in contact with some very narrow-spirited Predestinarians whereas there were many more also, who, knowing that they were elect, were meek, lowly and pitiful. In any case, the same argument could be used against Universal Redemption.

3) 'The doctrine tends to destroy the comforts of religion and the happiness of Christianity etc..'

Whitefield seemed to score a point here. He immediately quoted Article XVII: 'That the godly consideration of predestination, and election in Christ, is full of sweet, pleasant, unspeakable comfort to godly persons, and such as feel in themselves the working of the Spirit of Christ...' Moreover it was his own spiritual support. Whitefield could not continue if he had not known that he was chosen from *before* the foundation of the world. What, conversely, did one say of the reprobates to whom these comforts were lost? Whitefield said that none living, especially none who were desirous of salvation, could know they were not of the number of God's elect. None but the unconverted could have any just reason, so much as to fear it. Election had a natural tendency to rouze (*sic*) the soul out of its carnal security. Therefore many 'carnal men' cried out against it.

Wesley had objected that the Witness of the Spirit could be obscured by this doctrine and that this was borne out by experience. Whitefield asked – whose experience? Obviously not Wesley's! Wesley had not got this, so he was no judge and this by his own confession. Wesley had said that many, and, in fact, every man who did not hold the view of election enjoyed the uninterrupted witness of the Spirit. But how did Mr Wesley know this? Had he consulted the experience of the very many in all parts of the earth? No – and the Church asserted that this doctrine 'greatly confirms and establishes a true Christian's faith of eternal salvation through Christ.'

Full assurance of faith could only arise from a belief of God's electing everlasting love. Furthermore the Christian could not be kept in a state of salvation by his own freewill, otherwise he would soon entertain grave doubts and fears, once he fell into sin. Man did sin after conversion. A man who claimed 'sinless perfection' was speaking against the Holy Spirit who condemned those who say that they had no sin, making God a liar. [1.John 8.10.] But here again, Whitefield was not trying to understand Wesley's doctrine – *not* of *sinless* perfection but of *perfect love.*

4) Wesley had said 'How uncomfortable a thought is this, that thousands and millions of men, without any preceding offence or fault of theirs, were unchangeably doomed to everlasting burnings?' Whitefield replied: 'But who said that this was so?' Surely Wesley would admit God's justice, in imputing Adam's sin to his posterity. God might have passed *all* by, therefore it was just that he might pass by *some.* If Wesley did own this, he had to acknowledge the doctrine of election and

reprobation. If not, he had not understood the notion of Original Sin aright.

5) 'This doctrine has a direct manifest tendency to overthrow the whole Christian religion. For, supposing that eternal unchangeable decree – one part of mankind must be saved, though the Christian Revelation were not in being: and the other part of mankind must be damned, notwithstanding that Revelation; and what would an infidel desire more?'

Whitefield asked – how was this? God's absolute purpose of saving his chosen did not preclude the necessity of the gospel revelation. Having received it, we were under a joyful obligation to spread it so that it can be God's way of bringing home his elect.

Wesley had further said that the assertors of election made revelation contradict itself. Cannot God hate the fallen in Adam, asked Whitefield, yet do the reprobate no wrong whilst loving the elect? God could be love without showing mercy at all. Wesley had argued that God was no respecter of persons. Certainly, agreed Whitefield, he was not a respecter of persons, upon the account of any outward condition or circumstances in life whatever. But as a Sovereign Lord of all, who was debtor to none, he had a right to do what He will with His own and to dispense His favours to what objects He saw fit, merely at His pleasure.

Wesley had said that Predestination to life was in no way dependent on the foreknowledge of God, according to Calvinists. If foreknowledge signified approbation, as it did in several parts of scripture then we had to confess that Predestination and Election did depend on God's foreknowledge. But if by God's foreknowledge, one understood God's foreseeing some good works done by his creatures as the foundation or reason of chusing (*sic*) them, and therefore electing them, then we had to say, that in this sense, Predestination did not in any way depend on God's foreknowledge.

As for the text Wesley had used to prove God did not delight in the sinner's death, Whitefield agreed he did not take delight simply in their death but did delight in the justice which condemned them so to die. Wesley has averred that Election was blasphemy. Rather, retorted George, it was Universal Redemption which was the highest reproach upon the dignity of the Son of God, by saying 'Christ not only died for those that are saved, but also for those that perish.' If this were the case, all the damned souls would be brought out of hell, for how could all be universally redeemed, if all were not finally saved?

Whitefield closed this long letter by accusing Wesley of dishonouring God by denying Election. He made salvation depend, not on God's *free grace*, but on man's *free will*. A certain number were given to Christ as the purchase and reward of his obedience and death. For these, and these only, he was now interceding, and with their salvation, he would be fully satisfied.

He continued:

> 'Be a little child; and then; instead of pawning your salvation, as you have done in a later hymn book, if the doctrine of *Universal Redemption* be not true, instead of talking of *sinless perfection*, as you have done in the preface to that hymn book, and making man's salvation to depend on his own *free will*, as you have done in this sermon; you will compose an hymn in praise of sovereign distinguishing love. You will caution believers against striving to work a perfection out of their own hearts, and print another sermon the reverse of this, and entitle it *Free Grace Indeed!*[23] Free, not because free to all, because

---

23. In his *Preface*, Wesley noted but declined to answer a pamphlet entitled *Free Grace Indeed.* 'I dare not,' he said, 'speak of the deep things of God in the spirit of a prize-fighter or a stage-player.' No author was mentioned. Could Whitefield have been the author in view of the fact that later here, he bade Wesley compose another sermon with this very title?

God may withhold or give it to whom and when he pleases.'

Moreover, continued Whitefield, it was all very well for Wesley to censure the clergy for not keeping to the Articles of the Church when he himself denied Articles IX, X and XVII! At the Judgement, he would see Wesley convinced of Election and everlasting love!

On 1 February 1741, Whitefield wrote a letter to both the brothers:

> 'Why did you throw out the bone of contention? Why did you print that sermon against predestination? Why did you, in particular, my dear Brother Charles, affix your hymn, and join in putting out your late hymn-book? How can you say, you will not dispute with me about Election, and yet print such hymns, and your brother send his sermon against election to Mr Garden and others in America... But I must preach the gospel of Christ, and that I cannot *now* do, without speaking of election...'[24]

The hymn to which George referred was affixed to the *original* edition of the sermon on *Free Grace*, but not when the sermon was included in Wesley's *Works*, and contained thirty-six stanzas. It was part of the collection published in 1740 entitled *Hymns and Sacred Poems*. Published by John Wesley MA, Fellow of Lincoln College, Oxford and Charles Wesley, MA Student of Christ Church, Oxford, London: Printed by W. Strahan and sold by James Hutton, 1740 (12mo-207pp.) The preface contained a statement on Christian Perfection, which, as will have been noted, caused offence in itself to George Whitefield. However, this particular hymn, of which the following verses must suffice as an introduction, caused equal hurt to Whitefield as did the sermon to which it was attached:

---

24. Tyerman, Luke *The Life of George Whitefield* (London, 1890, Vol.1, p.465.)

'*For every man He tasted death,*[25]
  He suffered once for all;
He calls as many souls as breathe,
  And all *may* hear the call.

A power to choose, a will to obey,
  Freely His grace restores;
We all *may* find the living way,
  And call the Saviour ours.

When God invites, shall men *repel*?
  Shall man the exception make?
"Come freely come, *whoever will*,
  And living water take."

Thou canst not mock the sons of man;
  Invite us to draw nigh,
Offer Thy grace to all, and then
  Thy grace to most deny!

Horror to think that God is hate!
  Fury in God can dwell!
God could in a helpless world create,
  To thrust them into hell!

Down there an endless death to die,
  From which they could not flee:-
No, Lord Thine inmost bowels cry
  Against the dire decree!'

---

25. From Charles Wesley's *Hymns on God's Everlasting Love.* The hymn is entitled *The Cry of a Reprobate.* A thorough study of his hymns on this subject would have been helpful to a greater understanding of the Wesleys' position on Universal Redemption, but space does not permit this.

However, on 11 March 1741, Whitefield landed in England, at Falmouth. One of his first acts was to publish an official answer to Wesley's sermon on *Free Grace*. The title was *A Letter to The Revd Mr John Wesley, in Answer to his Sermon entitled 'Free Grace' by George Whitefield. A.B. late of Pembroke College,* Oxford. London. Printed by W. Strahan, for T. Cooper (8vo.31.pp.) Included in the publication were the Articles of the Church of England on: 'Original or Birth Sin', 'Free Will' and 'Predestination and Election' together with a hymn by Dr Isaac Watts, the start of which was:

'Behold the potter and the clay,
   He forms his vessels as he pleases;
Such is our God, and such are we,
   The subjects of His high decrees.'

Abel Stevens says this publication was printed at Boston and also at Charleston, South Carolina.[26] If this was so, was it a copy of the London edition or a surreptitious edition which was distributed amongst Wesley's followers in London and caused so much odium for Whitefield when he arrived there? In any case, the copies received by Wesley's people as they arrived at the Foundry were torn up during the service following the example of Wesley himself, who did so at the preaching desk. Whitefield found he had many enemies but he still insisted that he must preach against the Wesleys. Charles reminded him of his recent promise that he would do no such thing.[27] George admitted that his intention was an error and withdrew it. After a period of inevitable dissension, the Wesley brothers and Whitefield were reconciled and turned their energies against the common enemy instead of each other. However, in spite of their renewed friendship, there were now two distinct brands of Methodism – that of Wesley and that of Whitefield. Evangelical Calvinists flocked to

---

26. Stevens, Abel, Ll.D *The History of the Religious Movement of the Eighteenth Century called Methodism* (London, 1862, p.112.)
27. Charles composed special verses to mark the reconciliation.

support Whitefield and soon his popularity was regained. Furthermore, after the separation of Whitefield from the Wesleys, the Countess of Huntingdon, whose home at Donnington Hall had often been visited by Wesley who preached there, was now also attracted by George's Calvinistic tenets and she appointed him her chaplain. Further successes for Whitefield were to be made in Calvinistic Wales and Scotland.

However, Whitefield's subsequent career does not concern one here, though it is necessary to look again at his theological position by comparison with that of the Wesleys.

It must be said that, on the whole, his position was untenable. He preached Calvinism, yet admitted that he had never read a single work of Calvin's. His views were borrowed, firstly from the Erskines of Scotland and then confirmed and amplified by his contacts in America, especially by the Tennents and Jonathan Edwards. His unsatisfactory answers to Wesley's questioning about the fate of the non-elect showed how muddled his thinking was. He enthused about election but was hesitant to be dogmatic about reprobation. Personal experience was claimed as a seal on his theological position, though he said little which would indicate the influence of others upon him. His deep sense of his own sinfulness and the fact that he was the first of the Oxford Methodists to experience evangelical conversion, not forgetting the influence of all those Puritan works which he had read, confirmed him in the belief that he was 'elected from eternity' for his mission. It is true that, on the whole, he did not preach Calvinistic doctrines in his sermons, but his preaching he felt, was necessary to make the elect conscious of their election and respond.

To the Wesleys, the Justice and Mercy of God were at stake as both sermons and hymns show. The Calvinists held that preaching was illogical because surely, the elect would be saved in any case. Logic was surely on their side for had their own theology not been worked out rationally long since? Whitefield was certainly *the* 'preacher' of the three, but the other two were the scholars and also the competent organizers.

The second part of the chapter must now be used to show the results of this controversy which might well be called 'The First Calvinistic Controversy', on the Wesleys, especially John. During the year 1740-1 various Anti-Calvinistic works were published by him. The years 1745 and 1751 also brought forth isolated works and then there was little until 1770 when the 'Minute Controversy' began.[28] All these works show the measure of importance Wesley attached to this subject. The fact that his Conference discussed the matter confirms this.

The first work was: *Serious Considerations concerning the Doctrine of Election and Reprobation. Extract from a Late Author [Dr Watts] with an Address To the reader by John Wesley.*12.pp. 12mo. London. 1740. It was an extract taken from Watts's Essay: *The Ruin and Recovery of Mankind*, Question XIII: 'How far has the glorious undertaking of Our Lord Jesus Christ provided any hope of salvation for those who were not eternally chosen, and given into the hands of Christ, to be redeemed and saved?[29] Watts had dealt with the subject quite reasonably and impartially, and, whilst it is difficult to see which school of thought it was to which he belonged, his criticism was mainly of the Calvinistic idea. In the *Memoirs of Dr Watts* which the Revd George Burder affixed to Watts's *Works*, he said it was Watts's intention in these essays, to 'soften and relieve the hard and obnoxious' scripture doctrines on original sin.[30] If this contention of Burder's was true, then it is a matter of opinion whether or not Watts's intention was a laudable one!

Very early in 1741 there appeared the following pamphlet: *The Scripture Doctrine concerning Predestination, Election and Reprobation. Extracted from a late Author by John Wesley.* 16.pp. 12mo. London. Printed by W. Strahan, 1741. Who is the author mentioned? Abel Stevens,[31] who gives a chronological list of all Wesley's Works, gives no indication who it is. However, the copy of this treatise in Wesley's *Works*

---

28. See Chapter Eleven of this study.
29. Burder, Revd George (Editor) *The Works of the Reverend and Learned Isaac Watts* (London, 1811, Vol.1, pp.48-162.)
30. *ibid.* (Vol.1, p.xxxix.)
31. Stevens, Abel *The History of the Religious Movement of The Eighteenth Century called Methodism* (London, 1862, p.787.)

[Ed. Benson, J. 1809] bears no mention that it had been extracted from the work of anyone else and appears as simply one of Wesley's own compositions.[32]

From texts which he quoted, the author [Wesley?] said it was plain that 'God chose some to life and glory before or from, the foundation of the world.' Just as Christ was actually not slain for thousands of years afterwards, so men could be said to have been 'elected from the foundation of the world' and not elected *until* their conversion. They were, as St Peter said, 'Elect, according to the foreknowledge of God, through sanctification of the Spirit, unto obedience', i.e. not chosen until they were sanctified. [Cf. 'God calleth things that are not, as though they were'.] They were chosen to salvation through believing the truth which had to be proclaimed through the gospel. According to Scripture, then, Predestination was: God's fore-appointing obedient believers to salvation, not without, but 'According to his foreknowledge' of all their works, 'from the foundation of the world'. Just so, he predestined or fore-appointed all disobedient unbelievers to damnation, not without, but according to his foreknowledge of all *their* works.

God, from the foundation of the world, foreknew all men's believing or not believing. And, according to this, his foreknowledge, he chose or *elected* all obedient believers to salvation and refused or *reprobated* all disobedient unbelievers to damnation. There could, of course have been the objection that the author held our faith and obedience to be the cause of God's electing us to glory. This, he answered, by declaring that faith in Christ producing obedience to him was the cause without which God elected none to glory. It could be shown like this:

'What is the cause of my obedience? My Love to Christ.
What is the cause of my love to Christ? My faith in Christ.

32. J.W.W. (Vol.14, pp.382-396.) However, I am indebted to the Revd Dr H. McGonigle, Principal of the Nazarene College, Manchester, (letter dated 22 January 1992) who states that Wesley extracted it from a work entitled *The Order of Causes* by a Baptist, Henry Haggar, 1654.

What is the cause of my faith in Christ? The preaching of the gospel of Christ.
What is the cause of the preaching of the gospel to us? Christ's dying for us.
What is the cause of Christ's dying for us? God's great love and pity wherewith he loved us, even when we were dead in trespasses and sins.'

The author thus felt he had proved that he did not hold that God chose any man to life and salvation, for any good which he had done, or for any which was in him, before He put it there.

Using Scripture, Wesley confirmed this, summarizing his findings thus:

1. God's love was the cause of his sending His Son to die for sinners.
2. Christ's dying for sinners is the cause of the Gospel's being preached.
3. The preaching of the Gospel is the cause (or means) of our believing.
4. Our believing is the cause (or condition) of our justification.
5. The knowing ourselves justified through his blood, is the cause of our love to Christ.
6. Our love to Christ is the cause of our obedience to him.
7. Our obedience to Christ is the cause of his becoming the Author of eternal salvation to us.

He said that the following should also be considered:

1. There was a necessity of God's love in sending His Son to die for us, without which he had not come to die.
2. There was a necessity of Christ's love in dying for us, without which the Gospel could not have been preached.
3. There was a necessity of the Gospel's being preached,

without which there could have been no believing.

4. There is a necessity of our believing the Gospel, without which we cannot be justified.

5. There is a necessity of our being justified by faith in the blood of Christ, without which we cannot come to know that he 'loved us and washed us from our sins in his own blood'.

6. There is a necessity of our knowing his love, who first loved us, without which we cannot love him again.

7. There is a necessity of our loving him, without which we cannot keep his commandments.

But for whose sin did Christ die? Did he die for *all men*, or but for some? The author set out to answer this by reference to Scripture – from Isaiah [Liii.vs.4-6]: 'The Lord hath laid on him the iniquity of us *all*'; from John the Baptist 'Behold the Lamb of God which taketh away *the sins of the world*'; from the Angel at the Nativity: 'Glad tidings...which shall be to *all* people'; from the words of Christ himself: 'Whosoever believeth in him should not perish...' Some would say that '*all men*' meant only the *elect*. To this shameless evasion, the author answered that the Scripture spoke of *the world* not a *world of believers*. Christ died for all mankind because the Scripture affirmed it and nowhere did it speak of his dying only for *some*. Furthermore, Christ commended the gospel to be preached to every creature and all men were called to repent. Those who perished were damned for *not believing in the name of the only begotten Son of God*, therefore he must have died for them, or else they would have been damned *for not believing a lie*.

He then proceeded to show the absurdities of saying that *Christ died only for the elect:*

If Christ died not for all, then:

1. Unbelief is not sin on those who perish.

2. Then it would be a sin in the greatest part of mankind to believe he died for them. It would be believing a lie.

3. Then they who are damned are not damned for *unbelief.*

4. Then those who obey Christ by going and preaching the Gospel to every creature go with a lie in their mouth.
5. Then God is not in earnest in calling all men everywhere to repent.
6. Then why does Christ say 'He is not willing that any should perish'?
7. How shall God judge the world by the man Christ Jesus if he did not die for the world?

But some were bound to say, 'If Christ died for all, why are not all saved? The answer was that they did not believe. God called them and they refused to answer. It would then be accused. 'Oh then you are an Arminian! You are a Free-Willer! You hold free will in man!' The author held nothing that was not in Scripture. Man had no will or power of himself, but by the Grace of God he might do all things. Might all men be saved if they would? The answer is:

1. What should hinder them if they be willing?
2. God is not willing that any should perish.
3. He is willing that all men should be saved.

If they are not saved it was because they would not come to Him as lamented over Jerusalem.[33]

Then came a little later in 1741, Wesley's *Serious Considerations on Absolute Predestination. Extracted from a late Author* [Barclay's *Apology for the Quakers*] *by John Wesley*. 24.pp.12mo. Bristol. 1741. This is not in the collected *Works* of Wesley, but if it was taken from Barclay's *Apology for the True Christian Religion, as the same is set forth and preached by the People called in Scorn, 'Quakers', 1678,* then Wesley had used a work containing a strong attack on Calvinism.[34]

---

33. This formed part of Wesley's *Preservative against Unsettled Notions in Religion* which will be referred to again in the next two chapters of this study.
34. See Cross, F.L. (Ed) *The Oxford Dictionary of the Christian Church* (Oxon, 1958, p.130.)

In the same year (1741) there was published the *Dialogue between a Predestinarian and His Friend.* Published by John Wesley. The second edition was enlarged and contained a *Preface to all Predestinarians.* (12.pp.12mo. 1741).[35]

In the *Preface* Wesley answered in advance the accusations that the quotations he would use were false and that Predestinarians would not speak in this way. 'Your fundamental principle is this,' he said, 'God, from eternity ordained whatsoever should come to pass.' Either, then, they had to equivocate, evade the question and prevaricate 'without end'. Otherwise they must swallow the above assertions together and honestly avow them, or perhaps renounce them altogether and believe in Christ, the *Saviour of all.*

Wesley made the Predestinarians affirm that God from all eternity unchangeably ordained whatsoever came to pass with no exception and this extended to the actions of men whose wills were governed by the Will of God which was efficacious and irresistible. Furthermore, he asserted that sin was the will of God and so was the Fall of Adam. In fact, according to the Calvinists, he was even made by God for the purpose of the Fall. But, objected the Friend, was this not rather the foreknowledge of God than His Will? No, replied the Predestinarian, God foresaw nothing but what he decreed. 'A horrible decree,' replied the Friend and the Predestinarian agreed and went on to remark that God *elected some* to life and *reprobated others* to everlasting punishment. All men were not created for the same end.

The Friend asked if God's Predestinating men to life or death was grounded on his foreknowledge? The reply was that God as he foresaw every man, knew what every man would deserve and therefore elected him to life or death and damnation. But, queried the Friend, if God had positively decreed to damn the greater part of mankind, why did he call

---

35. Abel Stevens in his *The History of the Religious Movement of The Eighteenth Century called Methodism* (London 1862, p.788) says that Wesley was accused of plagiarizing this title from *Dialogue between a Presbyterian and a Baptist* but adds that there were no grounds for supposing this to be true.

upon them to repent and be saved? The answer was that God had his effectual call whereby he gave the elect the salvation to which he had ordained them; so he had his judgments towards the reprobates, whereby he executed his decree concerning them. Why then, asked the Friend, did He call to them to turn and live? The Predestinarian replied that He called them that they may be more deaf; he kindled a light that they may be more blind. But yet, God was not the author of sin even though he had reprobated many to sin. Even the sins of the elect were foreordained. 'God is the author of that action, which is sinful, by his irresistible will, but you cannot charge God with sin. God only necessitated them to the act of sin, not to the deformity of sin. They could not sin further than he had permitted and commanded.' The Predestinarian quoted Judas and Esau as those who were predestined to damnation but the Friend would not own this. The Predestination said Esau and his posterity were damned for their unbelief. The Friend asked 'By what faith are you saved?' 'By faith in Christ,' was the answer, 'who gave himself for me.' The Predestinarian now asked a question: 'What then, do you mean by the words *Election* and *Reprobation*?' The Friend replied: 'I mean this: First, God did decree from the beginning to elect or choose (in Christ) all that should believe, to salvation. Secondly God did from the beginning decree, to reprobate all, who should obstinately and finally continue in unbelief.'

> Pred: What then do you think of *absolute, unconditional election and reprobation*?
> Friend: I think it cannot be found in Holy Writ, and that it is a plant which bears dismal fruit. An instance of which we have in Calvin himself; who confesses that he procured the burning death of Michael Servetus, a wise and holy man, purely for differing from him in opinion, in matters of religion.

In this treatise, Wesley could easily have been accused of overstating his case. The type of Predestinarian illustrated here was of the extreme Supralapsarian type. Whitefield, at his furthest extreme was certainly not one of these nor were those Evangelicals who have already featured in this present study. Even Toplady, who was one of Wesley's most bitter and extreme antagonists, and whose works will be studied in a later chapter,[36] could not be numbered among Predestinarians of this kind.

It should occasion no surprise that in the very same year (1741), Charles Wesley published his *Hymns on God's Everlasting Love: To Which is added The Cry of the Reprobate*. 48.pp.12mo.[37] A second part was published in the same year in one tract of 84.pp.12mo. A second edition of the two parts was brought out in 1756. Part I consisted of 18 hymns; Part II of 20 hymns, the last five of which were headed *Gloria Patri*. A third edition was published in 1770 and a fourth in 1790.

However, on a different note, one can read in Wesley's *Journal*[38] for Wednesday 24 August 1743 a 'desire to unite with Mr Whitefield as far as possible' to avoid needless dispute. Dealing firstly with Unconditional Election, he stated his belief that God before the foundation of the world, did unconditionally elect certain persons to do certain works, for example Paul to preach the Gospel; Elected some nations to receive peculiar privileges like the Jewish nation or some nations to hear the Gospel like England and Scotland. What was more, he may well have unconditionally elected some persons to eternal glory. However, he could not believe that those not thus elected must perish everlastingly.

As far as Irresistible Grace was concerned, the grace which brought faith and thereby salvation into the soul was irresistible at *that* moment but not *generally* irresistible so that one has no choice whether or not to comply with it. As for the third tenet, namely Final Perseverance, he was inclined to believe that there was a state attainable in this life, from which one could not finally fall. He that has attained this is one who could say: 'Old things are passed away; all things in me "are become new".' But to believe that the *Elect* would infallibly persevere to the end, he could not accept.

---

36. See Chapter Eleven of this study.
37. Wesley, John and Charles *Poetical Works of* (Ed. George Osborn) (London, 1868-72, Vol.6, p.311-312.)
38. J.W.J. (Vol.3, pp.84-6.)

If Wesley believed that writing the above statement was to constitute an eirenicon, he must surely have shortly realized that for once he had failed! The Minutes of the first Conference held in 1744 quickly proved this. On the very first day, 25 June 1744, a discussion on Justification by Faith was held.[39] The question (No.17) was asked:

'Have we not then, unawares, leaned too much towards Calvinism?'

The answer was quickly given: 'We are afraid we have.'

It is as well to give here the remainder of the debate:

'Q.18 Have we not also leaned towards Antinomianism?
A.   We are afraid we have.
Q.19. What is Antinomianism?
A.   The doctrine that makes void the law through faith.
Q.20. What are the main pillars hereof?
A.   1. That Christ abolished the moral law.
       2. That therefore Christians are not obliged to observe it.
       3. That one branch of Christian liberty, is liberty from obeying the commandments of God.
       4. That it is bondage to do a thing, because it is commanded, or forbear it because it is forbidden.
       5. That a believer is not obliged to use the ordinances of God, or do good works.
       6. That a preacher ought not to exhort to good works; not unbelievers, because it is hurtful; not believers, because it is needless.
Q.21. What was the occasion of St Paul's writing his Epistle

---

39. Minutes of the Late Conversations between Revd Messrs Wesley and others. *The Bennet Minutes* (pp.10 and 11.)

to the Galatians?

A.   The coming of certain men amongst the Galatians, who taught, "Except ye be circumcised, and keep the law of Moses, ye cannot be saved."

Q.22.   What is his main design therein?

A.   To prove 1. That no man can be justified, or saved, by the works of the law, either moral or ritual. 2. That every believer is justified, by faith in Christ, without the works of the law.

Q.23.   What does he mean by "the works of the law"? (Gal.ii.v.16 &c.)

A.   All works which do not spring from faith in Christ.

Q.24.   What [is meant] by being under the law? (Gal. iii.23.)

A.   Under the Mosaic dispensation.

Q.25.   What law has Christ abolished?

A.   The ritual law of Moses.

Q.26.   What is meant by liberty? Gal.v.verse.1.

A.   Liberty, 1. From that law, 2. From sin.

Thus was expressed Wesley's main objection to Calvinism, namely Antinomianism or the setting aside of the moral law as unnecessary. Wesley did not say that the Calvinists taught Antinomianism, but simply stated that to the Calvinist it was a possible temptation and attitude.

The following year saw a treatise published by Wesley similar to *A Dialogue between a Predestinarian and his Friend*, namely: *A Dialogue between an Antinomian and his Friend.* 12.pp.12mo. [Dated 24 August 1745]. An extract only from this together with the other *Dialogue* was given in Wesley's *Preservative*.

The next work on Calvinism did not appear until 1751: *Serious Thoughts on the Perseverance of the Saints* 24.pp.12mo. London. December 1751. This was a most important document but a consideration of this will be given in Chapter Ten of this study where the subject of Perseverance is dealt with at length.

The year 1752 brought forth his *Predestination Calmly Considered*

by John Wesley. 83.pp.12mo. London, 1752.[40] A later edition was
published with the hymn entitled *The Horrible Decree* – 15 stanzas of
eight lines each, attached. Dr Gill[41] replied to this tract. It was also
republished in the *Arminian Magazine* Vol.ii. Wesley replied to Gill in
1754 in a published tract: *An Answer to all which the Revd Dr Gill has
printed on the Final Perseverance of Saints. By the Revd Mr Wesley.*
12.pp.12mo. London. Trye (December). 1754.

In his *Predestination Calmly Considered*, Wesley began by affirming
that many, because of their own personal experience felt that the Grace of
God always worked irresistibly in every believer and that He gave this to
some only and not to others because it was his own will.[42] Quoting from
the Protestant Confession of Faith drawn up in Paris in 1559, and the
Synod of Dort (1618), he stated the doctrine of Election by God to eternal
life or 'Predestination' – implied some were elected to eternal damnation,
this latter doctrine being called 'Reprobation'. He finally cited Calvin's
own words.[43]

Some, declared Wesley, held to the idea of Election but not Reprobation
and he attempted to show that this was illogical as one implied the
other.[44] The next sections[45] contained Wesley's own interpretations of St
Paul's 'Election' doctrine. It was (i) a divine appointment of some
particular men to do some particular work in the world. (ii) a divine
appointment of some men to eternal happiness. But the election was
conditional, dependent upon a man's faith. Without Reprobation the idea

---

40. J.W.W. (Vol.14, pp.316-381.)
41. Dr John Gill was pastor of a Baptist Church in Southwark. Gill wrote two pamphlets
    against Wesley. He described Wesley's *Predestination Calmly Considered* and
    Wesley's reply to him as 'miserable'. Gill was a man of great learning and on whom
    the University of Aberdeen had conferred the degree of Doctor of Divinity.
42. Wesley *op.cit.* (Sections I-IV.) It might be noted that Wesley wrote this work in
    ninety numbered sections which makes it rather tedious reading.
43. Sections V-VII.
44. *op.cit.* (Sections VIII-XV.)
45. *op.cit.* (Sections XVI-XVII.)

of Election could not stand.[46] He could not believe that these doctrines could be found in Scripture. Conversely, he found in Scripture support for the opposite views. Reprobation, he declared, was a travesty of the justice of God.[47] He dealt briefly with Our Lord's parable of the labourers in the vineyard [Matthew Ch.20] and at great length with Romans chapter 9.[48] One should never have assigned God's sovereignty as the cause why any man was punished with everlasting destruction. The Calvinist, maintained Wesley, was putting eternal happiness and misery on an unscriptural footing.[49] The Sovereignty of God was never to be brought to supersede his justice.[50] The Election which implied Reprobation did not agree with the Scripture account of God's justice.[51] Christ died for all and this could not be denied.[52] He enlisted the support of Dr Isaac Watts to show that there is no such thing as the sincerity of God in sending his ministers into the world to call men to repent if there were some who were predestined never to do so.[53] In fact *there could be no God* if some were to remain un-elected.[54] Wesley felt that the Calvinists were afraid that should they discard the doctrine of Election they would thereby be suspected of being Arminians or Pelagians, holding the idea of man's free will, and that would rob God of the glory in man's salvation.[55]

Man must, he affirmed, cooperate with God in the working out of his own salvation. There would be far less glory attributable to God if He saved man irresistibly than there would be in saving him as a free agent.

---

46. Augustine, from whom Calvin developed so much of his ideas, held only to the doctrine of Election. The actual stating of reprobation in such strong terms was more the work of Calvin's successors who interpreted his doctrine. It was more Calvinism than Calvin.
47. Wesley *op.cit.* (Section XXII.)
48. *op.cit.* (Sections XXIII-XXX.)
49. Section XXX.
50. Sections XXXI-XXXVII.
51. Section XXXVIII.
52. Section XXXIX.
53. Sections XL-XLI.
54. Sections XLIII-XLV.
55. Sections XLVII-LIV.

Free will accorded more with the Wisdom, Justice, Love and Mercy of God. Neither was there disharmony with the other attributes of God, namely, unchangeableness, sovereignty and faithfulness.[56]

Wesley then showed[57] that the Covenants made between God and man both in the Old and New Testaments were conditional. It was not against the faithfulness of God that some who have believed finally fell away. The faithfulness of God was the same – it was man who became unfaithful. He worked through the same list as he began with in his treatise – of those who could and often did, fall away from a state of grace, citing further texts[58] to prove his point. Salvation was neither conditional nor unconditional.[59] God could sometimes work irresistibly in some soul and did, but many were saved without this.[60] Only the love of God humbled man,[61] and it was a fallacy to suppose that it was the doctrine of Election which made a man love God.[62] The idea of Reprobation was not only unscriptural but it had a pernicious effect on men because they accepted what was, as inevitable and took no care over their souls.[63]

It was no use lying to further the cause of God. 'Strive,' said Wesley, 'after that holiness, without which, no man shall see the Lord.'[64]

The argument, as will be seen, rested on the interpretation of Scripture. Wesley obviously regarded, for example, St Paul's use of the word 'election'[65] purely to imply vocation. It was not to be taken to its extreme meaning as did the Calvinists. By all his works on the subject, Wesley made his position quite clear and it will be seen subsequently, that he never altered his position. How far he was right in furthering a damaging

---

56. Wesley *op.cit.* (Sections LV-LX.)
57. Sections LXI-LXVII.
58. Section LXXXIX.
59. Section LXXX.
60. Sections LXXXI-LXXXIII.
61. Section LXXXIV.
62. Section LXXXV.
63. Sections LXXXVI-LXXXVIII.
64. Wesley *op.cit.* (Sections LXXXIX-XC.)
65. See again e.g. Romans Chapters 9 and 11 and also I. Thessalonians, Chapter 1 etc.

controversy and how far he was justified in so doing because of a real fear of Antinomianism, will be discussed in later chapters.

By the time the last of the above mentioned works was published, Wesley had involved himself in the beginning of what rightly must be called the Second Calvinistic Controversy – purely a literary one – with James Hervey, principally concerning the Calvinistic doctrine of Imputed Righteousness of Christ. This sorry episode which continued long after Hervey's death, will be told in the next two chapters.

CHAPTER EIGHT

THE SECOND CALVINISTIC CONTROVERSY
'THE IMPUTED RIGHTEOUSNESS OF CHRIST'

(Wesley and James Hervey)

(I)

Imputation, theologically speaking, is to attribute anything to a person or persons and lay it to their account either as a reward or punishment. There is, of course, the doctrine of the Imputation of Adam's sin to his posterity. This forms one aspect of Augustine's doctrine of Original Sin – one which determined the general view of Western Catholicism. Thomas Aquinas repeats it but goes further and points out that since original sin involves guilt before God, and guilt implies a voluntary act, it is therefore not enough to say that Adam handed on a corrupt nature. But he does concede that Adam's descendents are involved in his *voluntary* act of transgression. However, the issue here is not the imputation of sin but of Christ's Righteousness to the sinner. It implies the infusion of Christ's righteousness into the believer, since God's imputation is necessarily according to truth. The imputation of Adam's sin and the imputation of Christ's righteousness are closely connected. The one is set over against the other.

The Scriptural basis for both these dogmas is supposedly found principally in the Epistles of Saint Paul, the main passage being Romans Chapter Five, verses 12-21 where the effects of Adam's sin and of Christ's righteousness are contrasted. As sin flows from man, righteousness flows from Christ. However, on a thorough examination of this passage, it is difficult to see that these two doctrines are taught at all. Whilst Paul obviously believed in the Divine imputation of sin from Adam's transgression, it is by no means clear that he held the immediate imputation of Christ's righteousness.[1] Again, Chapter Five verses 18ff. are by no means theologically precise. Certainly Paul traces back the condemnation of men to the trespass of Adam but the connection with Christ's righteousness is left very vague. The exact meaning of righteousness (δικαιόσυνη) is uncertain. It could mean the righteous act *or* the merit of Christ, *or* the justifying sentence. How the sin of Adam and the obedience of Christ bring about the imputation of sin or of righteousness respectively, is left unexplained.

However, according to the Calvinistic system, all human works are evil, though covered and not counted as sins in the case of the Christian elect through the imputed merits of Christ.[2]

Naturally, there were objections to both doctrines. The Pelagians and Socinians entirely repudiated the doctrines of the imputed guilt of Adam's sin. The Socinians and Arminians objected to the doctrine of the imputation of Christ's Righteousness. Rather, the latter spoke of Paul's teaching of the imputation of *faith for righteousness.* Christ's merits are not imputed but *imparted* to man and produce a real change from the state of sin to the state of grace.

Although the Articles and Homilies[3] of the Church nowhere supported

---

1.   See Romans Chapter Five, verse 13 which is inconsistent with this.
2.   It must be remembered that the idea of the ascription to a person, by deliberate substitution of the righteousness or guilt of another plays an important part in the Lutheran doctrine of Justification by Faith which asserts that a man is formally justified by the imputation of Christ, without becoming possessed of any personal righteousness of his own.
3.   See *Sermons or Homilies Appointed to be read in Churches in the Time of Queen Elizabeth of Famous Memory* (London, 1824, pp.26ff.)

the doctrine of the imputation of Christ's righteousness, the Calvinistic Evangelicals expounded it, especially Whitefield. The latter's views were contained primarily in his sermons and, to a considerable extent, in his letters to the Wesley brothers, as will have already been noticed. True, pride of place in his controversial letters was given to the ideas of Election, Predestination and Perseverance of the Saints. Whitefield believed the offence of Adam was imputed to man but the righteousness of Christ was imputed to believers for their justification.[4] Before one could have peace with God, one must be justified by faith through the Lord Jesus Christ. Christ must be applied to the heart and brought home to the soul. Thus *His* righteousness became *our* righteousness, and His merits may be imputed to our souls.[5] Furthermore, Christ's righteousness delivered believers from the guilt of sin. By having Christ's righteousness imputed to them, they were dead to the law, as a covenant of works. Christ had fulfilled it for them, and in their stead. God had given them the victory by imputing to them the righteousness of the Lord Jesus.[6] In another sermon of Whitefield's, it will be seen that one of the most important aspects of this doctrine which was to play such a great part in the Hervey–Wesley dispute, was that of distinguishing between the active and passive obedience of Christ. The active obedience was so often overlooked in His life and work. His passive obedience, of course, referred to His sacrificial death. These together[7] made up that righteousness in its completeness which was imputed to a man. In another exposition, the term 'righteousness' was defined. It was said to be, according to Whitefield, the inward holiness wrought in us by the blessed Spirit of God.[8] But an Arminian or 'an enemy' to free grace would call it moral honesty or doing justice

---

4. Whitefield, George *Select Sermons* (London, 1958, pp.36-7.)
5. Cf. Newton, John *Cardiphonia or The Utterance of The Heart* (London, 1780, pp.143-161.)
6. Whitefield, George *Select Sermons* (London, 1958, p.65.)
7. Whitefield *op.cit.* (p.74.)
8. Whitefield, George *Sermons on Important Subjects* (London, 1833, Sermon No.197): 'The Righteousness of Christ, an everlasting Righteousness.' (Daniel, Chapter 9, verse 24.)

between man and man! In no wise, did the doctrine of imputation destroy the desire to do good works or lead to licentiousness. Good works were excluded from being the cause of our Justification, but they were required as *proof* of our having His righteousness imputed to us.[9]

Grimshaw, another noted exponent of this doctrine added in his *Creed* that this very righteousness which was sufficient to redeem all mankind would be imputed to every penitent soul, and that to all intents and purposes, as if *he*, as indeed he should have done, had himself performed it.[10]

Thomas Adam of Winteringham declared that 'The maintainers of Imputed Righteousness must be content to undergo the mortification of being thought opposers or discouragers of good works, though they constantly plead for them, and for their own doctrine, as the best, if not the only sure way of attaining to them; do not come a whit behind their adversaries in the performance of them; and perform them more freely and sincerely, and upon more generous principles of love, gratitude, and obedience, than those who venture all upon their own actions, and make them the ground of their acceptance.'[11]

Apart from Hervey, the other clearest indication of the Calvinistic interpretation of Romans Chapter Five was given by Samuel Walker of Truro. He accused Wesley and his followers of not even believing in the apostasy of man and therefore rejecting the imputation of Christ's righteousness, thus ascribing the merit of Justification 'to faith and not to Him (Christ)'.[12]

One now turns to the one Evangelical whose literary work on this subject soon became a classic and also the basis for what may be called

9. Whitefield, George *Select Sermons* (London, 1958, p.75.)
10. Cragg, G.C. *Grimshaw of Haworth* (London, 1947, p.111.) Cf. Romaine, William *Treatise on the Life, Walk and Triumph of Faith* (Glasgow, 1838) where the whole subject is treated exactly in the same manner. See pp.545-552: 'The Believer's Triumph in the Lord his Righteousness'.
11. *Private Thoughts on Religion* (Glasgow, 1824, p.199.)
12. Sidney E. *The Life and Ministry of the Revd Samuel Walker, BA* (London, 1838, p.158.)

'The Second Calvinistic Controversy'.

Biographical details of the early life of Hervey have already been supplied in earlier chapters.[13] As was stated, he did not embrace the full evangelical faith until 1739. Asked in a letter from Whitefield dated 4 April 1739 if the Spirit of God bore witness with his spirit that he was a child of God, Hervey gave an evasive answer. He said this was a most searching question and that in truth he could not tell.[14] Did he find peace and joy in the Holy Ghost? Sometimes he did rejoice but the bright prospect was soon overcome by clouds of fear. He agreed that one was justified by faith alone. Works could have no share in our justification because 'there is iniquity in holy things.' Yet a few lines further on he amended his thought and wanted to alter his reply and say that not by faith *only* but by works (in conjunction with it) a man was justified.

However, not long after, in the same year, in a further epistle to Whitefield, Hervey indicated that he had embraced the doctrine of salvation by faith *only* and that George's *Sermons* and *Journals* seemed to have played no small part in the change:

> 'You are pleased to ask, How the Holy Ghost convinced me of self-righteousness, and drove me out of my false rests? Indeed, Sir, I cannot precisely tell. The light was not instantaneous, but gradual. It did not flash upon my soul, but arose like the dawning day. A little book, wrote [*sic*] by *Jenks*, upon *Submission to the Righteousness of God* was made serviceable to me. Your *Journals*, dear Sir, and especially that sweet sermon on "What think ye of Christ?" were a means of bringing me to a knowledge of the truth. And another excellent piece has been, and I hope will be, as so much precious eye-salve, to my dim clouded understanding – I mean *Marshall's Gospel Mystery of Sanctification.*'[15]

---

13. See Chapters 1 and 3.
14. Tyerman, Luke *The Oxford Methodist* (London, 1873, pp.219-220.)
15. Tyerman, Luke *The Oxford Methodists* (London, 1873, pp.223-4.) No date. Also *Evangelical Magazine* (1794, page 503.)

He then admitted that no longer did he trust in his own good works –
they were no hiding place in the storm! They were a refuge of lies. His
intentions now are to work for his Master's service, not *for* but *from*
salvation. He sought this blessing, not as a *condition*, but, as a *part* – a
choice and inestimable part of that complete salvation, which Jesus
purchased for him.

Hervey wrote[16] *A Recommendatory Letter from Mr Hervey to the
Publisher of a New Edition of Marshall on Sanctification.* Hervey paid
tribute to the instruction, consolation and spiritual improvement '...which
I myself have received from that solid and judicious treatise.' He hoped it
would prove the same to others. He mentioned that he was recommending
the treatise in his own work: *Theron and Aspasio* and looked upon
Marshall as being 'no improper *supplement*' to his dialogues and letters.
It appears by the letters prefixed to his defence of *Theron and Aspasio*
that he intended to make an improvement on Marshall's work. A fourth
edition of *Theron and Aspasio* was thus intended but was never produced.

Note the following first reference to his interest in the 'Righteousness
of Christ' as a cherished doctrine:

> 'I endeavour to put no confidence in these bruised reeds, but
> to rest upon the Rock of Ages. Not in these, most blessed
> Jesus, but in Thy robes of righteousness, let me be found,
> when "God shall call the heavens from above, and the earth,
> that He may judge His people..." The righteousness of Thy
> obedience, O Lord Redeemer, is everlasting.'[17]

In 1741 a correspondence with Whitefield written when Hervey was
curate of Bideford in North Devon is illuminating. Hervey hoped that the
triumphs of free grace would prevail mightily over their unbelief. Too
long had he been a blind leader of the blind. He had perverted the good
ways of God and darkened the glory of redeeming merit and sovereign

---

16. Hervey, James *Aspasio Vindicated &c* (1771, pp.454-5.)
17. Tyerman, Luke *The Oxford Methodist* (London, 1873, pp.223-4.)

grace. He had presumed to give works a share in the redemption and recovery of a lost sinner '...and has placed those filthy rags upon the throne of the Lamb.'[18]

Hervey remained curate of Bideford from 1740 until July 1743, enjoying no small measure of popularity, only to be dismissed by the new vicar. Two literary works were embarked upon here. Kilkhampton churchyard afforded inspiration for his *Meditations among the Tombs*. The summer house of a pleasant garden belonging to his host at Stoke Abbey near Hartland, suggested his *Reflections on a Flower Garden*.[19] He had founded a religious society in Bideford which continued to meet for over forty years.

Wesley had written to Hervey on 8 August 1739 bidding him to come out of his country retreat and begin field-preaching[20] but Hervey had protested that this was impossible because of his feeble state of health. He had withdrawn into a corner because of '...a languid flow of spirits, and an enervated state of body...' He still cherished his friendship with Wesley. Tyerman records that Hervey probably heard Wesley preach in London during his stay there because he referred to the preaching on 'The Gift of the Holy Ghost' by 'our old acquaintance' – 'May I never forget what was uttered this night. Might I but experience it and I should bless the day in which I was born.'[21]

Then, in the same letter came the first real hint that there were some theological differences between them:

> 'As for points of doubtful disputation – those especially which relate to *particular* or *universal* redemption – I profess myself attached neither to the one nor the other, I neither think of them myself, nor preach of them to others. If they happen to

18. Tyerman, Luke *The Oxford Methodists* (London, 1873, pp.223-4.)
19. These two were later bound up with *Descant upon Creation* and *Contemplations on the Night* and *Contemplations on the Starry Heavens*. These 'Meditations' drew forth from Samuel Johnson his parody *Meditation on a Pudding*.
20. J.W.L. (Vol.1, pp.331-333.) See also p.75 of this study.
21. Tyerman, Luke *The Oxford Methodists* (London, 1873, p.238.)

be started in conversation, I always endeavour to divert the discourse to some more edifying topic. I have often observed them to breed animosity and division, but never knew them to be productive of love and unanimity. I have further remarked, that in forming their sentiments on these doctrines, persons may be diametrically opposed, and yet in high favour of God, and eminently owned by Him in their ministry. Therefore, I rest satisfied in this general and indisputable truth, that, the Judge of all the earth will assuredly do right; and whosoever cometh to Him, under the gracious character of a Saviour, will in no wise be cast out.'

This was quite a reasonable, gracious and fair letter but as subsequent pages will show, this generous and charitable spirit was soon to wane. It is of inestimable importance to this study that both Marshall[22] and Whitefield had done their work well – Hervey was now a Calvinist, howbeit, a moderate one by comparison with some – to the end of his days.

In October 1743, he became curate to his father at Weston Favell, a small village, then of some 300-400 inhabitants, near Northampton, where later, he succeeded his father as vicar and remained there until his death in 1758. Here he pursued his work faithfully, as a parish priest, doing all he could to care for his parishioners. In November 1749 Whitefield, concerned for James's health, suggested that he took advantage of the offer of the Countess of Huntingdon to have him at her home for a week.[23] Previously there had been little correspondence between Lady Huntingdon and Hervey although she had a great regard for him. However, a regular exchange of letters took place between them from February 1750 until his death. Of course, this pleased Whitefield, who wrote to say, 'I am glad you have opened a correspondence with our elect lady.

---

22. Walter Marshall, whose work Hervey had commended was a Presbyterian divine and Calvinist; Scholar of Winchester; Fellow of New College, Oxford 1650. Incumbent of Hursley but ejected 1662. Later minister at Gosport (b.1628; d.1680).
23. Tyerman, Luke *The Oxford Methodists* (London, 1873, p.257.)

Keep it open, I entreat you, my dear friend.' His visit to her home inevitably brought him in contact with other evangelical clergy,[24] meeting Romaine for the first time, and also numerous distinguished persons. Arriving in June 1750, he later remained in London[25] at the home of his brother until the death of his father in May 1752, spending much of his time in literary pursuits. He enlarged and corrected his *Meditations and Contemplations* and began his work on *Theron and Aspasio*. 'I was,' he said in one of his long series of letters to Lady Frances Shirley, 'writing a little treatise upon some of the most important doctrines of Christianity; to be disposed partly into dialogue, partly into letters; and rendered entertaining by several descriptive pictures in nature and its everpleasing scenes.'[26]

There is no evidence that Hervey had any interview with the Wesleys until 1751 and even Whitefield seemed to be absent from the scene during that interval. Writing again to Lady Shirley early in 1752 he confessed that he was one with the Methodists but withheld from acting '...by a languishing constitution.'[27]

This being 'one with the Methodists' poses the problem whether it referred to Whitefield's or Wesley's branch of Methodism. Hervey was already differing theologically with the Wesleys and there is no evidence that he now approved either of itinerant preaching or the employing of lay-preachers.

The first theological controversy between Hervey and John Wesley began in 1751-2 by the latter's publishing his two pamphlets: *Serious Thoughts Upon the Perseverance of the Saints* and *Predestination Calmly Considered.*[28] That Hervey took exception to them is evident in a letter he wrote to someone unnamed, dated 24 March 1752:

24. Tyerman, Luke *The Oxford Methodists* (London, 1873, p.257.)
25. Charles Wesley said in his Diary for 14 September 1750; 'I met James Hervey at the Tabernacle and in the fellowship of the spirit of love.'
26. Hervey, James *Works* (London, 1797, Vol.6, p.226.)
27. Hervey *op.cit.* (Vol.6, p.250.)
28. See page 181 and pages 179-192 of this study for summaries of these two works of Wesley's.

'Mr Wesley's last piece I have not read though I can't say I am fond of that controversy. The doctrine of the perseverance of Christ's servants, Christ's children, Christ's spouse, Christ's members, I am thoroughly persuaded of. Predestination and reprobation I think of with fear and trembling. And if I should attempt to study them, I should attempt to study them on my knees.'[29]

No criticism could be levelled at Hervey on that declaration. His controversy with Wesley was never about these two subjects but solely about 'Imputation of Christ's Righteousness'.

However, mutual literary criticism seems to have been the basis of the relationship between the two men at this time, in spite of their differences. In 1754, Wesley sent to Hervey his *Notes on the New Testament* for the latter's comment, prior to publication. These *Notes* were founded on Bengel's *Gnomon* and therefore were very concise,[30] hence Hervey's criticism. They were intended for use amongst the preachers and are still part of the accepted body of doctrine of Methodism and compulsory reading for lay-preachers and ministers. Wesley also acknowledged his indebtedness to the Lectures of Dr Heylyn and the *Expositor* of Dr Doddridge. Hervey obliged with his remarks on 29 June of the same year:

'Dear Sir,
I have read your *Notes* and have returned them with such observations as occur to my mind. I think, in general, you are too sparing of your remarks and improvements. Many

---

29. Tyerman, Luke *The Oxford Methodists* (London, 1873, p.270.) He says that Hervey was 'thoroughly opposed to Wesley on Perseverance of the Saints but on Predestination he was dubious.'
30. Five editions were issued during Wesley's lifetime. Dr Adam Clarke in the General Preface to his own Commentary says of Wesley's *Notes* (1825): 'Though short, the notes are always judicious, accurate, spiritual, terse, and impressive and possess the happy and rare property of leading the reader immediately to God and his own heart.'

expositions are too corpulent; yours are rather too lean. May the good hand of the Lord be with them and their author.'[31]

In 1755, there was published by Hervey his work *Theron and Aspasio*[32] which became the basis of contention between himself and Wesley.

From time to time, Hervey had sent out portions of this work to friends in whom he had confidence, in order that he might benefit by their criticism. Had Philip Doddridge, a former near neighbour at Northampton still been alive, he would undoubtedly have been numbered among these friends. However, Hervey had now made another friend from Dissenting circles – Mr John Ryland, a Baptist minister. A long correspondence with Ryland took place in which *Theron and Aspasio* was frequently discussed.[33] Some of the dialogues were sent to Whitefield for his views. Hervey, one might suppose, felt obliged to do so, having done Whitefield the favour of examining some of George's sermons. Accompanying his scripts to George, was a letter promising him £30 for the purchase of a negro slave! What a revelation on the views of both of them on the subject of slavery![34] Whitefield replied on 9 June 1752:

'My very dear friend,

I have received and read your manuscripts; but for me to play the critic upon them, would be like holding up a candle to the sun. However, before I leave town, I will just mark a few places as you desire, and then send the manuscripts to your brother. I foretell their fate; nothing but your scenery can screen you. Self will never bear to die, though slain in so genteel a manner, without showing some resentment against

31. Tyerman, Luke *The Life and Times of John Wesley* (Vol.2, p.227.) See Tyerman's *Oxford Methodists* (pp.290-1.)
32. See Bibliography at the end of this study for full title.
33. Hervey, James *Works* (London, 1787, Vol.7, pp.3-108.)
34. See Chapter Eleven (Section viii) for the subject of the Evangelicals and Slavery.

its artful murderer.'[35]

One cannot help feeling that John Wesley was somehow being thought of when the prophecy about the fate of the manuscripts was made! Whitefield's prowess as a literary critic could scarcely be compared with that of Hervey, was one of his final comments as he returned the papers. Of course, Whitefield would be well aware of the possible controversy which could arise by the intrinsic Calvinism contained in Hervey's writings. It would not require much brilliance to 'foretell their fate'. He, of all people, would know the reaction against them of the Arminians. Hervey surely could not have been blind to their debatable content, or else he would not have been so eager to send the scripts out to various friends for criticism.

A further letter was received by Hervey from Whitefield on 14 November 1752:

> 'Surely, God hath raised my dear friend up, to let the polite world see how amiable are the doctrines of the Gospel. Why will you weary the world, and your friends, by delaying to publish your other long-wished-for performance [*Theron and Aspasio*]. I shall be glad to peruse any of the Dialogues. The savour of the last is not of my mind. Pray let them see the light this winter. They will delight and warm many a heart...'[36]

It was obvious that more manuscripts were sent to Whitefield for review, according to the following letter addressed to Hervey on 27 January 1753. It was important, if only to show the characteristic distinction between the classes which existed in Whitefield's mind:

> 'How many pardons shall I ask for mangling, and, I fear,

---

35. Gillies, John D.D. *Memoirs of the Life of the Reverend George Whitefield, MA*, (London, 1772, p.200.)
36. Tyerman, Luke *The Oxford Methodists* (London, 1873, p.278.)

murdering your dear *Theron and Aspasio*? You will see by Monday's coach, which will bring a parcel directed to you. It contains one of your *Dialogues* and two more of my sermons...I write for the poor; you for the polite and noble. God will assuredly bless you for what you write...As yet I have only time to peruse one of your sweet *Dialogues*. As fast as possible, I shall read the rest. I am more than paid for my trouble by reading them...'[37]

What form the 'mangling' took would be interesting to read, but unfortunately there was no record of it.

Then came the worst mistake poor Hervey ever made! He sent the MSS of three of the *Dialogues* from *Theron and Aspasio*, consisting of 129 pages out of a total of 1300 contained in the whole work, to John Wesley for criticism. John spent what leisure time he had at his disposal between 28 October 1754 and 16 February 1755 studying these and analysing them.[38] After his revision, he returned them with '...a few inconsiderable corrections'. This did not satisfy James. 'You are not my friend,' he complained, 'if you do not take more liberty with me.'[39] Wesley then promised to repeat the task, but this time, he performed it more thoroughly. He made far more important corrections, though there is no trace of the letter containing these in the Standard Edition of Wesley's *Letters*. Hervey was offended. He had indeed asked for criticism and, whilst he had been dissatisfied with insufficient revision, he disliked the other extreme. Wesley was not consulted again and a friendship, once an exemplary instance of ministerial brotherliness, was now on the wane.

The criticisms of Wesley and others notwithstanding, 18 February 1755 saw the first edition published. Its 6000 copies were soon sold and a second edition was called for. Within nine months, a third edition was

---

37. Gillies, John D.D. *Memoirs of the Life of the Reverend George Whitefield, MA* (London, 1772, p.201.)
38. J.W.J. (Vol.4, p.103n.)
39. Tyerman, Luke *The Oxford Methodists* (London, 1873, p.290.)

required.[40]

The main purpose behind these three volumes of *Theron and Aspasio* was the recommending to 'people of manners and polite accomplishments',[41] the theology of Calvin and, in particular, the doctrine of the Imputed Righteousness of Christ. In his *Preface*, he declared with pleasure that every doctrine 'of note' maintained in the *Dialogues* and *Letters* was implied in the Anglican liturgy, asserted in the Articles, or taught in the *Homilies*. Moreover, he claimed that the same sentiments were to be found in Milton's *Paradise Lost*. It was Hervey's intention to make religious conversation fashionable and judging by the success of its distribution, he seemed to have achieved this. He had hoped to receive permission from the Countess of Huntingdon to dedicate the work to her, but it was refused. She had obliged, unsuited as she was to such work, by reading the MSS of Hervey's writings and in turn passing them over to more competent critics for their comments. This pleased James though he was naturally disappointed because she would not accept the dedication. However, in the end, a relative of hers, Lady Frances Shirley, already a friend of Hervey's, agreed to have it dedicated to her.[42] She also had acted as invited critic.

Theron and Aspasio constituted a work of three fairly large volumes and space permits only a brief summary. The main points of the work must suffice.

The first dialogue outlined the characters of the two speakers whose names afforded the title and who were portrayed as country gentry. Theron was the more provocative. An after dinner conversation turned to the elegance and dignity of the Scriptures. Then came[43] a walk through

---

40. See Hervey, James *Works* (London, 1787, Vol.7, p.427) where, in a letter dated 10 September 1755, he planned a supplement to *Theron and Aspasio*.

41. Hervey *Works op.cit.* (Vol.7, p.10.) Letter to Mr Ryland: 'I do not pretend, nor indeed do I wish to write one new truth. The utmost of my aim, is, to represent old Doctrines in a pleasing light, and dress them in a fashionable or genteel manner.'

42. Hervey entered into a long correspondence with Lady Shirley. See his *Works* (London, 1787, Vol.6, pp.189-451.)

43. Hervey, James *Theron and Aspasio &c* (London, 1755, Vol.1, Dialogue II, pp.41ff.)

the gardens and remarks were made on the beautiful frame and beneficent ordering of things. The talk then turned to the main topic of the work, Justification with the imputation of our sins upon Christ and the imputation of His Righteousness. On these doctrines, asserted Hervey (through Aspasio, whose ideas were his indeed) hung all the privileges and whole glory of the Gospel.[44] Justice was an act of God Almighty's grace, whereby he acquitted his people from guilt and accounted them righteous for the sake of Christ's Righteousness which was wrought for them, and was imputed to them.

What did he understand by Christ's Righteousness? asked Theron, and what was the meaning of 'imputed'?

> Aspasio replied:
> 'By Christ's righteousness, I understand, all the various instances of His active and passive Obedience; springing from the perfect holiness of His heart; continued through the whole progress of His life; and extending to the very last pang of death. By the word imputed I would signify, that this righteousness, though performed by Our Lord, is placed to our account; is reckoned, or adjudged by God as our own. Insomuch that we may plead it, and rely on it, for the pardon of our sins; for the adoption into His family; for the enjoyments of life eternal.'[45]

This was further illustrated in the story of Onesimus, the runaway slave who stole his master's goods, yet because of his encounter with Saint Paul, became a convert to Christianity. He was thus sent back, with a commendatory letter to his master, Philemon, pleading the slave's case: 'If he hath wronged thee, oweth thee ought, put that on mine account. I Paul have written it with mine own hand. I will repay it.'

As a meadow was the setting now[46] – Christ's satisfaction was thus

---

44. Hervey, James *Theron and Aspasio &c* (Vol.1, pp56ff.)
45. Hervey *op.cit.* (Vol.1, pp.58-9.)
46. *op.cit.* (Vol.1, p.75ff.)

stated:

> 'The second Person of the ever-blessed Trinity unites the
> human Nature to the Divine; submits Himself to the obligations
> of His people; and becomes *responsible* for all their Guilt. In
> this capacity, He performs a perfect obedience, and undergoes
> sentence of death: makes a full expiation of their sins, and re-
> establishes their title to life. By which means, the Law is
> satisfied; Justice is magnified; and the richest grace exercised.
> Man enjoys a *great Salvation*, not to the discredit of any, but
> to the unspeakable glory of all, the divine attributes.'[47]

This satisfaction Aspasio considered as a 'Redemption-price', and he
traced this idea through the Old Testament. Christ's death was further
considered in Dialogue Four[48] which had a park containing a 'romantic
mount' as a background. Christ suffered the death which our sins
deserved, 'by taking our place and enduring what we deserved.' Through
Theron, ancient and modern objections to this theory of the Atonement
were asked and Aspasio answered each one of them.

Now, an elegant arbour in a flower garden was the scene for a further
discussion on Imputed Obedience and Righteousness.[49] The foundation
of the doctrine of Imputation was found in St Paul's teaching that Christ
was the second man and last Adam. Adam was a public person and acted
in [sic] behalf of all his People.'

> 'That, as Adam was the first general representative of this
> kind, Christ was the second and the last; there never was, and
> there never will be, any other – That, what they severally did,
> in this capacity, was not intended to terminate in themselves,
> but to effect as many as they respectively represented.'[50]

47. *op.cit.* (Vol.1, Section4, pp.80-1.)
48. *op.cit.* (Vol.1, pp.130ff.)
49. Hervey *op.cit.* (Vol.1, pp.192ff.)
50. *op.cit.* (Vol.1, p.207.)

Again, objections from reason were brought forth and answered. One of Theron's mistakes, according to Aspasio, was the neglecting to distinguish inherent and imputed righteousness:

> 'We never suppose,' he said, 'that a profane person is devout or an intemperate person sober. This is *inherent* righteousness – But we maintain, that the profane and intemperate, being convinced of their iniquity, and betaking themselves to the all-sufficient SAVIOUR for redemption, are interested in the merit both of His life and of His death. This is *imputed* righteousness.'[51]

It was this imputed righteousness which made a man whole before God. Theron now questioned the necessity of personal obedience. Aspasio replied that we were no longer under a necessity of obeying the law, in *order to* establish our Justification, 'or lay the foundation of our final acceptance' but we were under obligation to obey the commandments of Our Lord. Did we then make void the law, through faith in the imputed righteousness of Our Lord? 'God forbid,' said Aspasio:

> 'Not content to deny this false insinuation, the Christian maintains the very reverse, Yes, *we establish* the law. Considered as the original covenant of life; we provide for its honour, by the perfect obedience of Christ. Considered as an invariable *standard* of duty; we enforce its observance, by the most rational, manly and endearing motives.'[52]

After a lengthy conversation[53] about Theron's study and picture gallery in which it took place, the matter of imputation was resumed. Theron confessed that he had searched the Scriptures, but found no

---

51. *op.cit.* (Vol.1, p.227.)
52. Hervey *op.cit.* (Vol.1, p.227.)
53. *op.cit.* (Vol.1, pp.246ff.)

reference to the term imputed righteousness. Aspasio agreed that the expression was not there but the doctrine 'abundantly taught' just as in the Pentateuch, the word *resurrection* did not occur, nor did *satisfaction* in the New Testament, yet Our Lord proved the truth of the former from Moses, and the latter was acknowledged to be the 'unanimous sense of the Apostles and Evangelists'.[54] Other objections from Scripture were 'urged and refuted'.

Beginning with a survey of haymaking and a contemplating on the pleasures of nature freely enjoyed, Theron proceeded to outline his plan of 'acceptance with God' which consisted of sincerity, repentance and good works, recommended by the merits of Christ. However, Aspasio showed this idea to be a false foundation – there were no such things as good works, until we were accepted through the *Redeemer*.

After a digression on duelling, the spirituality and extent of the Divine law and the infinite purity of God were dealt with.

Dialogue IX was the first in Volume Two of *Theron and Aspasio* and here, Justification was taught as not being available by our own works. There was no relaxation of the Divine law, as to the precepts or the penalty. It had an inflexible strictness and principal ends:

> 'The law hath concluded all mankind under sin. Yet not with an intention, that any should be encouraged now, or perish for ever: but that every one may see his inexpressible need of a Saviour's death and a Saviour's obedience. That, being thus prepared, both to value and receive so precious a blessing, the promise of justification by faith in Jesus Christ may be given to them that believe.'[55]

Theron made his last effort to demolish the evangelical scheme of Justification.[56] Among other objections, more plausible and refined than

---

54. *op.cit.* (Vol.1, p.290.)
55. Hervey, *op.cit.* (Vol.2, pp.39-40.)
56. *op.cit.* (Vol.2, pp.42ff.)

the preceding, he strenuously insisted that Faith is our righteousness. Aspasio maintained that justification was not upon faith but upon its author; not upon Our Lord's righteousness considered only as passive, but upon his active and passive obedience united.[57]

The ruins of Babylon were considered[58] and a passage of John Howe's treatise, *The Living Temple* was quoted at length. This led on to the stating of the doctrine of Original Sin – the depravity and ruin of human nature.

An extremely hot day caused the speakers to take shelter in a 'shady bower'[59] in which a true method of deriving benefit from the Classics was outlined, but the main topic was the wonderful structure of the human body.

The depravity of human nature was again referred to and[60] laid open and proved from experience. Thereon was now found alone in the fields,[61] enjoying the charms of nature and reflecting on these past conversations. He was driven to think again of Aspasio's commendation of the doctrine of imputed righteousness. Aspasio came on the scene and confirmed to his friend that by this doctrine, the perfections of God were glorified, the claims of the law were answered, the interests of morality were secured. He further recommended self-examination, the keeping of a diary, disappointed that Theron had still not become a convert to his favourite doctrine and extracted from his friend a promise to correspond.

Now began a series of twelve letters[62] after which there were three final dialogues. The first letter which opened the correspondence showed Aspasio pointing out some important articles of duty designed to facilitate self-examination and promote conviction of sin. In this endeavour, Aspasio seems to have succeeded by what can be read in the second epistle.[63]

---

57. *op.cit.* (Vol.2, p.92.)
58. Hervey *op.cit.* (Vol.2, pp.94ff.) Howe (1630-1705) was a Puritan divine. Vicar of Torrington, North Devon, but ejected in 1662.
59. *op.cit.* (Vol.2, pp.160ff.)
60. *op.cit.* (Vol.2, pp.222ff.)
61. *op.cit.* (Vol.2, p.308ff.)
62. *op.cit.* (Vol.2, pp.335ff.)
63. Hervey *op.cit.* (Vol.2, pp.361ff.)

Theron was convicted of the error of his ways and 'evil of his heart'. He saw the necessity of a better righteousness than his own. He now desired a further explanation and a fuller proof of the doctrine under debate. Aspasio, naturally, obliged in the next letter,[64] and felt he had proved his point from the Liturgy, Articles, Homilies and from Patristic writings. From the Liturgy, he chose the Prayer of Humble access in the service of Holy Communion: 'We do not presume to come to this Thy table, O merciful Lord, *trusting in our own righteousness.*' The collect for the Circumcision had this expression: 'Almighty God, whose blessed Son was *obedient to the Law for Man.*' The Eleventh Article affirmed: 'We are accounted righteous before God only for the merits of Our Lord and Saviour Jesus Christ.' Thus can man appear righteous before God, not on account of any *native* righteousness, or *acquired righteousness* but that which is imputed. Of course, as in Scripture, Hervey, under the guise of Aspasio was putting his own interpretation on the Articles as the Calvinistic Evangelicals generally were doing on the Scriptures, especially Romans, Chapter Five. The Homily concerning *Salvation of Mankind*[65] was cited for further support, whilst Clement, Justin Martyr and Chrysostom were the Fathers quoted.

Scripture proof came next[66] and the Old Testament was dealt with, followed in the next letter[67] by reference to a remarkable panic instanced by rumours of press-gang activity which had been spread among the congregation in a church. Aspasio used this scene as illustrative of the great Day of Judgment but Hervey apologized for using such a 'plebeian illustration'. Imputed Righteousness was then demonstrated from the New Testament quotations.

The third volume began with Letter VI[68] which was from Theron to Aspasio. He took a cursory view of the habitable creation, tracing the perfections of nature, through the earth, air and fire, noting the

---

64. *op.cit.* (Vol.2, pp.369ff.)
65. *op.cit.* (Vol.2, pp.386ff.)
66. Hervey *op.cit.* (pp.386ff.)
67. *op.cit.* (Vol.2, pp.413ff.)
68. *op.cit.* (Vol.3, pp.1ff.)

advantageous effects of these elements.

Aspasio took the opportunity of replying,[69] displaying the no less admirable perfection of Christ's righteousness, its principle and extent in 'perseverance'.

Aspasio then[70] described a drought and the majesty of the sun after a night of rain. From this he proceeded to describe the meritorious excellency of Christ's righteousness, illustrated from the magnificence of His works and the divinity of His person. Theron took over in the next letter[71] to describe the western cliffs; the wonders of the ocean and the benefits of navigation. Aspasio now took the chance to follow this by enumerating the much richer benefits resulting from the imputation of Christ's righteousness. He showed their happy influence on holiness of heart and obedience of life.[72] He continued to exemplify the last fact,[73] especially in the conduct of Abraham when called upon to offer up his son Isaac. Finally he spoke of union with Christ – how it was described in Scripture – its blessed and glorious effects.[74]

The dialogues now began again[75] and Aspasio visited Theron and found him under anxiety of spirit. Partly to entertain, partly to comfort his friend, Aspasio enlarged upon the bounty of the Creator, visible both to the animal and vegetable world. The new convert was slow of heart to believe. Aspasio then enlarged on the evangelical motives to faith.

A Harvest scene began Dialogue XVI,[76] followed by a description of Philenor's garden with its statues which they were now visiting. The nature of true faith was described; its true foundation and sovereignty supported. The last dialogue[77] took place on a river voyage. The happiness,

---

69. *op.cit.* (Vol.3, pp.39ff.)
70. *op.cit.* (Vol.3, pp.65ff.)
71. Hervey *op.cit.* (Vol.3, p.105ff.)
72. *op.cit.* (Vol.3, pp.170ff.)
73. *op.cit.* (Vol.3, pp.203ff.)
74. *op.cit.* (Vol.3. pp.228ff.)
75. *op.cit.* (Vol.3, pp.245ff.)
76. *op.cit.* (Vol.3, pp.307ff.)
77. *op.cit.* (Vol.3, pp.375ff.)

peace and blessings which came from the application of Christ's righteousness to every case of distress and in any time of need were then described.

He closed:

> 'What a gift, then, is Righteousness of Christ? Blessed be God, for all the indulgent dispensations of Providence! Blessed be God for all the beneficial productions of nature! But above all, blessed be God, for the transcendent and unspeakable gift – of Christ and His Righteousness.'[78]

During 1755, Wesley had found opportunity to read the whole of *Theron and Aspasio* and wrote to Hervey submitting further comments on the latter's work, but received no reply.[79] 15 October 1756 saw a similar, but a very long letter from Wesley to his friend giving a whole resumé of the work. As this letter elicited no reply, Wesley published it as the twelfth pamphlet in a series of thirteen, for the use of Wesley's preachers, entitled: *A Preservative against Unsettled Notions in Religion*.[80] Wesley said:[81]

> 'A considerable time since, I sent you a few hasty thoughts which occurred to me on reading the *Dialogues between Theron and Aspasio*. I have not been favoured with any answer. Yet upon another and a more careful perusal of them, I could not but set down some obvious reflections, which I would rather have communicated before these Dialogues were

78. Hervey, J. *Theron and Aspasio etc.* (Vol.3, pp.446.)
79. This letter is not traceable in the Standard edition of Wesley's *Letters*, but it is known to have been written because Hervey sent it to Ryland and in August 1755 asked for its return.
80. Published at Bristol, 1758, 246pp.12mo, price 2/- per copy.
81. The full text of this letter of 15 October 1756 is given in Appendix One of this study.

published.'

He proceeded to deal with Hervey's work, dialogue by dialogue and letter by letter. In this enormous letter, Wesley dealt with *Theron and Aspasio* as one would have expected him to do, objecting to the unnecessary length of the work just in order to labour a doctrine[82] which he felt had no Scriptural basis. He attacked the affected language. But to be fair to Wesley, there were many parts of the work which he could commend and did so, but only those substantiated in Scripture. Some of the *Dialogues* and *Letters* were most useful; some were totally unnecessary. The latter only tended to encourage Antinomianism. Wesley disagreed with Hervey's definition of Justification by Faith. What is more, there was no encouragement for the pursuit of personal holiness. Hervey, according to John had confused the Righteousness of God with the merits of Christ and had said that even notorious transgressors in themselves had a sinless obedience in Christ. Wesley could see this being a welcome doctrine to some of his own former preachers who have left him, e.g. James Wheatley, Thomas Williams and James Relly. A careful perusal of this letter in its fullness is absolutely essential to the understanding of the further troubles which lay ahead for Wesley due to his attitude to *Theron and Aspasio*.

Note Wesley's conclusion of his letter:

'Upon the whole, I cannot but wish that the plan of those Dialogues had been executed in a different manner. Most of the grand truths of Christianity are herein both explained and proved with great strength and clearness. Why was anything intermixed which could prevent any serious Christian's recommending them to all mankind? anything which must necessarily render them exceptionable to so many thousands of the children of God? In practical writings I studiously

---

82. Perhaps Wesley was also aware that Hervey had also printed a sermon on this subject, based on the text: 'Many made righteous by the obedience of one' (Romans, Chapter Five. verse 19).

abstain from the very shadow of controversy' nay, even in controversial, I do not knowingly write one line to which any but my opponent would object. For opinions, shall I destroy the work of God? Then am I a bigot indeed. Much more, if I would not drop any mode of expression rather than offend either Jew or Gentile or the Church of God. I am, with great sincerity, dear Sir,

Your affectionate brother and servant.[83]

That Hervey had received Wesley's epistle, there is no doubt because Tyerman refers to a letter written by Hervey to an unknown recipient asking for this to be returned:

'Pray return Mr W–'s letter. I find, by private intelligence, that he has shewn it in London; and has thought proper to animadvert upon me, by Name, from his pulpit. I am inclined to take no notice either of his preaching or his writing.'[84]

Later in this letter he mentioned that Whitefield was at his house, and, Tyerman thinks, that as George and the Wesleys had recently experienced a misunderstanding about Methodist affairs at Norwich, Whitefield would no doubt be the bearer of the 'private intelligence'.

It is now necessary to examine the reasons for Wesley's attitude to Hervey's *Theron and Aspasio.*[85]

Firstly, Hervey was a self-confessed Calvinist. 'I am,' he said, 'what people would call, a moderate Calvinist; but I can assure you, I can bear, I shall delight, to have my notions sifted; nor am I so attached to any favourite scheme, but I can readily relinquish it, when Scripture and

83. The letter which forms Appendix One of this present study is taken from J.W.L. (Vol.3, pp.371-388.)
84. Tyerman, Luke *The Oxford Methodists* (London, 1873, pp.302-3.)
85. It is assumed, of course, that the reader has read fully the whole of Wesley's letter given in Appendix One of this study.

reason convince me it is wrong.'[86] The latter part of this statement was fair enough, but herein in was the main reason for Wesley's opposition, namely was this doctrine in Scripture and *was* it reasonable? Hervey was hardly sincere in declaring that he could 'bear to have his notions sifted'. It was all too obvious that this was something he just could not bear to do, at least by Wesley and sulked when the attempt was made. Furthermore to have said that he was attached to no favourite scheme was certainly not true or else why did he go to the trouble of publishing these three fair-sized volumes to extol but one particular aspect of Calvinism, namely the Imputed Righteousness of Christ? This fact did not endear him to Wesley for he had dwelt on a subject which to John was a dangerous one, which, like Election, Predestination and the Perseverance of the Saints, tended to encourage Antinomianism – the idea that Christians were by grace, set free from the need to observe any moral law.[87] Antinomianism, to Wesley, was the 'arch-enemy'. In a letter to Samuel Furly written from Kingswood, dated 14 October 1757,[88] Wesley described Hervey as a 'deep rooted Antinomian...that is, a Calvinist consistent with himself (which Mr Whitefield is not, nor Robert Bolton nor any Calvinist who is not a latitudinarian.)' Now with regard to this latter criticism, Wesley was unjust in calling Hervey an Antinomian, whatever the dangers of commending 'imputation' might be. If one looks back[89] one will readily notice that Hervey in no way underestimated the moral law and the necessity to keep it. He went out of his way to stress obedience to the Divine Law.

Secondly, Wesley attacked Hervey on the matter of style and presentation. Hervey, in a letter to a friend, dated 18 August 1753 said:

'That is most likely to win our approbation, which extenuates

---

86. Tyerman, Luke *The Oxford Methodists* (London, 1873, p.290.) Also Hervey, James *Works* (1787, Vol.5, pp.353ff.) This is quoted from a letter dated 18 May 1753.
87. See this study pages 185-188 and Bennet's *Minutes* for 1744.
88. J.W.L.(Vol.3, p.230.)
89. See this study pp.207-9.

the fancy, without fatiguing the attention. Since this is the disposition of the age, let us endeavour to catch men by guile; turn even a foible to their advantage; and bait the gospel hook agreeably to the prevailing taste; In this sense, "become all things to all men".'[90]

It is interesting to note that in a letter to Revd Mr Pearsall of Taunton dated 29 May 1751, Hervey criticized the latter's style, advising him to use the 'pruning knife' and 'cut off several of the shoots' – the style was 'too luxuriant and pretty'! It is a pity, of course, that Hervey could not provide examples of such advice in his own works which were notorious for these very faults.[91]

Wesley had his own style which he commended without reserve. '*Easiness*...is the first, second and third point; and *stiffness*, *apparent* exactness, *artificialness* of style the main defect to be avoided, next to solecism and impropriety.' Again – 'What,' he asked, 'is it that constitutes a good style? Perspicuity and purity, propriety, strength and easiness, joined together.'[92]

> 'That "poor people understand long sentences better than short" is an entire mistake. I have carefully tried the experiment for thirty years, and I find the very reverse to be true.'[93]

That *Theron and Aspasio* was Calvinism dressed up in literary niceties was no recommendation to Wesley. If anything, it would make him more strongly opposed to it than ever. Whilst there was every indication that Hervey's preaching style, when in his own pulpit was plain and simple,[94] he had set out deliberately in this work to attract the 'polite' and those of

---

90. Hervey, J. *Works* (London, 1787, Vol.6, p.436.)
91. Tyerman, Luke *The Oxford Methodists* (London, 1873, p.265.)
92. J.W.L. (Vol.4, p.232 and Vol. 4, p.256.)
93. J.W.L. (Vol.4, p.267.)
94. See Tyerman, Luke *The Oxford Methodists* (London, 1873, pp.309/310) where Ryland confirmed this.

'accomplished manners'. 'My writings,' he said to Lady Shirley, 'are not fit for ordinary people; I never give them to such persons, and dissuade this class of men from procuring them. O that they may be of some service to the more refined part of the world.'[95] There may well have been some justification for writing to 'the refined' classes, but somehow the hint of snobbery which kept creeping in from time to time among the Calvinistic Evangelicals is apt to give the reader a shudder of dismay.

Wesley, like Whitefield (obviously simple in his writings even if he did pay undue deference to the 'refined'), wrote for the 'humble poor'. Late in life, Wesley declared that:

> 'I could, even now write as floridly and rhetorically as even the admired Dr B–; but I dare not, because I seek the honour that cometh of God only. What is the praise of men to me, that have one foot in the grave, and am stepping into the land whence I shall not return. Therefore, I dare no more write in a *fine style*[96] than wear a fine coat. But were it otherwise, had I time to spare, I should still write as I do. I should purposely decline, what many admire, a highly ornamental style...'[97]

Finally, how strange it is that Augustus M. Toplady, soon after this time, a student at Trinity College, Dublin, according to a letter published by Tyerman dated 13 September 1758, agreed with Wesley's censures:

> 'Your remarks on Mr Hervey's style are too just; and I think a writer would be much to blame for imitating it; or indeed the style of any other; for if he has any abilities of his own, he

---

95. Hervey, James *Works* (London, 1787, Vol.6, p.436.)
96. See *The Oxford Companion to English Literature* (ed. Sir Paul Harvey) (London, 1950, p.371) where it is said that whilst Hervey's works were popular, they were marked by a 'pompous and affected style'.
97. Tyerman, Luke *The Life and Times of John Wesley* (London, 1871-2, Vol.3, p.521.)

ought to use them. I believe Mr Hervey's mentioning the active, exclusive from the passive, obedience of Christ, is rather a casual than intentional omission; but an author cannot be too careful how he expresses himself on a point of so much importance. I have been long convinced, that self-righteousness and antinomianism are equally pernicious; and that to insist on the imputation of Christ's righteousness, as alone requisite to salvation, is only strewing the way to hell with flowers. I have myself known some make shipwreck of faith and love and a good conscience, on this specious quicksand.'[98]

It will be seen later in this study how Toplady was to change his doctrine so that he agreed with Hervey.[99] Moreover, one may also note with some amazement how Toplady later turned on Wesley for criticizing Hervey's style.[100] It must, of course, be remembered that when Augustus wrote the above letter, he was but a youth of eighteen years of age.

A third point needs to be considered when examining Wesley's attitude to Hervey's work. John had been James's tutor at Oxford and on this account he may have taken full advantage of this relationship to be blunt and pointed with his former pupil when asked for literary criticism. Hervey had indeed received that for which he had asked and then resented it. Wesley, it must be remembered, had been roughened by his continual experience of riding around the country on horseback, facing endless opposition and attacked by countless mobs. Here, he was dealing with a sick,[101] in fact a dying, man, sensitive to a degree, hidden away and

---

98. Tyerman, Luke *The Oxford Methodists* (London, 1873, p.315.)
99. See Chapter Eleven of this study.
100. Abbey C.J. and Overton J.H. *The English Church in the Eighteenth Century* (London, 1878, Vol.2, p.175.)
101. Dr A.G. Brown, my local physician, who has made a special study of the psychological effects upon patients suffering from terminal illnesses has read William Romaine's brief biography of Hervey prefixed to Hervey's *Meditations and Contemplations* (London, 1812). Dr Brown remarks that whilst little is said of the symptoms of Hervey's last illness, it is probable that he was suffering either

protected from the rigours of itinerant life, in his country vicarage, committed to a minimum of ministerial labours. It may well be that Wesley acted as though he were still Hervey's tutor and thereby have felt somewhat responsible for his former pupil's theological views. Hence his criticism and correction in short plain words of the work of one who chose a more delicate and refined expression of his views.

The damage, however, was done, and it was never repaired. The biographer of Hervey[102] says of John:

'He gave his opinion without tenderness or reserve. He condemned the language, reprobated the doctrines, and endeavoured to invalidate the proofs by which they were supported. Whatever good sense there might be in some of his remarks, the dogmatical language, the dictorial [sic] style in which they were delivered, entirely prevented the effect...'

As has already been mentioned, Hervey was no ultra-Calvinist but a self-confessed 'moderate'. Nor was he fond of controversy, or so he said in a letter to Lady Shirley dated 25 November 1755 where he stated he could freely converse or correspond with persons who either adopted or discarded Predestination; provided they would not '...drag in the litigated proposition and force me to engage in disputation.' But on the other hand, if those people were determined to obtrude the bone of contention, he had much rather remain alone and in silence. He readily confessed that he was not master of the subject. Therefore it would be very inadvisable for him to undertake either its establishment or refutation.[103]

---

from Tuberculosis or Carcinoma of the lung. Seeing that Hervey had always been of a sensitive nature and then in his latter days became hyper-sensitive, the Doctor inclines to the view that this points to TB of the lung. A characteristic of the terminal stage of this disease is often hyper-sensitivity and a tendency to take offence where none is meant. This is precisely what happened as a result of Wesley's letter of 15 October 1756. (See Appendix One of this study.)

102. See longer biography in *Meditations and Contemplations* (London, 1803.)
103. Hervey, James *Works* (London, 1787, Vol.6, pp.393-4.)

If Hervey was truthful here, he was, as he claimed, no strong Calvinist and maybe Wesley treated him a little too roughly. No wonder then, that Hervey remained silent in his country retreat and did not reply to Wesley's two epistles, unless, of course, the 'Eleven Letters', presumed to have been his, and published posthumously, really were his final reply. These letters and the controversy which raged about them were to do irreparable damage to the evangelical cause and this subject will be dealt with in the next chapter.

Did Hervey, however, complain to others about Wesley's treatment which he so much resented? There were a number of letters written by Hervey which suggest this. Of particular interest is a letter dated 9 January 1755[104] to Lady Frances Shirley which could only have been written soon after Wesley's first letter containing the 'inconsiderable corrections' which failed to satisfy James, had been received. (The longer letter containing the fuller criticisms was dated 15 October 1756.) But here is a difficulty. It will be remembered,[105] however, that Wesley had spent what leisure time he had at his disposal between 28 October 1754 and 16 February 1755 reading through the MSS of *Theron and Aspasio* which Hervey had sent for criticism. It was after this that the letter containing the 'inconsiderable corrections' was sent. Was there another letter sent by John to Hervey about the latter's doctrinal outlook prior to January 1755? There is no trace of one in the Standard *Letters*. Now the letter sent to Lady Shirley plainly gave a hint that Hervey had *already* taken offence because of something Wesley had said:

> 'Mr John Wesley...takes me very roundly to task on the score
> of Predestination. At which I am surprised. Because a reader,
> ten times less penetrating than he is, may easily see, that this
> doctrine (be it true or false) makes no part of my scheme;
> never comes under consideration; it is purposely and carefully
> avoided. I cannot but fear, he has some sinister design. Put the

---

104. Hervey, James *Works* (London, 1787, Vol.6, pp.373ff.)
105. See Page 205 of this study.

wolf's skin on the sheep and the flock will shun him. I do not charge such an artifice, but sometimes I cannot help forming a suspicion. If I live to do myself the honour of writing again to your Ladyship, I hope you will give me leave to relate the whole affair as it stands between Mr Wesley and myself...'

One can only ask why, if this is how Hervey felt about Wesley before the latter's 'inconsiderable corrections', why did he trouble to write to John and ask for a fuller and deeper criticism, knowing full well that a more detailed and severe analysis would be received? This difficulty poses a question for which there is no answer.

The relationship between Hervey and Wesley was not improved by a further friendship cultivated by Hervey with William Cudworth, the minister of an Independent congregation in Margaret Street, London. This was unfortunate for the simple reason that Wesley and Cudworth had become enemies some ten years previously.[106] Cudworth himself had written a *Dialogue* to which Wesley had replied by his two *Dialogues between an Antinomian and his Friend*. Wesley, rightly or wrongly, regarded Cudworth as an Antinomian and dealt with him severely. It does not overtax the imagination to realize the effect of this newly formed friendship of Cudworth and Hervey on the latter's attitude to Wesley. As late as 27 April 1759, Wesley had lost none of his dislike for Cudworth. He recorded: 'I had an interview with Mr Cudworth. I observed upon the whole (i) that his opinions are all his own, quite new, and his phrases as new as his opinions; (ii) that all these opinions, yes, and phrases too, he affirms to be necessary to salvation; maintaining that all who do not receive them worship another God, and (iii) that he is as incapable as a brute beast of being convinced even in the smallest point'.[107] Wesley regarded him as an avowed enemy of the law of God, for Cudworth termed all those who preached the 'law' as 'legalists'. To preach the 'law', to him was an abomination. What was more, the feeling between

---

106. J.W.J. (Vol.4, p.303.)
107. J.W.J. (Vol.4, p.303.)

Wesley and Cudworth was mutual. The latter disliked the former as he did '...the Pope and ten times more than he did the devil.' Further details of such a relationship are hardly called for!

When the second edition of *Theron and Aspasio* was being prepared,[108] Hervey realized, not upon many helpers as he had done for the first edition, but mainly on Ryland and Cudworth. Hervey could not have wished for a better supporter of his notion of imputed righteousness than Cudworth. This was shown in his letter to Cudworth of 22 April 1755.[109] In this, Hervey, whilst showing his pleasure at Cudworth's approval of his doctrine, admitted that his [Hervey's] own writings were not 'relished by everybody', not even by 'many pious people'. He had enclosed a couple of letters containing objections.[110] He wanted them considered and in Cudworth's 'concise' way, which he admires. The 'attacks' had not shaken Hervey's opinion but he wanted to deliver it even more clearly and firmly in another edition. After wishing Cudworth success in the publication of a collection of evangelical literature, he remarked unkindly on a similar venture by Wesley:

> 'Mr Wesley has huddled over his performance[111] in a most precipitate, and therefore, most imperfect manner. One would think, his aim was, not to select the best and noblest passages,

108. 3,000 copies had been agreed upon but the publishers took the liberty of extending the edition by a further 1,000 because of the demand.
109. *Aspasio Vindicated etc.* (London, 1771, p.377.)
110. No doubt Hervey was referring to Wesley's objection as contained in an untraceable letter written to him by John sometime early in 1755 after his first reading of the unpublished MSS of *Theron and Aspasio.* Hervey did speak of 'a couple of letters' here and the other could well have been from one of the many critics of the work.
111. This referred to Wesley's *Christian Library consisting of Extracts and Abridgements of the Choicest Pieces of Practical Divinity which have been published in the English tongue* (51 vols, 12mo. Begun 1749 and completed 1756.) Cf. letter from Hervey to Cudworth (Hervey Works Vol.4, p.334) where he spoke of Cudworth's proposed publications: 'I could wish to have it judiciously executed and not performed in that confused, inaccurate, slovenly manner, which must be a continual discredit to Mr W——'s *Christian Library.*'

but to reprint those which came first to hand.'

A further proof that the friendship between Hervey and Wesley had terminated even before the arrival of the letter of 15 October 1756, or even the one of August, 1755 could be seen in James's letter to Lady Shirley of 5 July 1755. This year had seen a crisis in the Methodist societies and the two Wesley brothers had differed over the role of the lay-preachers. Charles had just published his famous poetical *Epistle from Charles Wesley to the Revd Mr John Wesley.* Hervey told Her Ladyship that he had recently read an advertisement of this 'Epistle' and had she seen it? If so, could she inform him of the actual design and contents of it?

> 'I hope,' he continued, 'there is no hostility commenced between the brothers. I have no connection, nor correspondence with them, but should be sorry for such an event.'[112]

Hervey must have anticipated a further letter of criticism from Wesley because in a letter written to Ryland on 7 August 1756, he mentioned having received intimation (no indication was given as to the writer) that Wesley was bringing a charge against him. Wesley was '...going to unmask his battery and play his artillery upon me in public. Two persons, formerly his preachers, inform me, that he is now in Ireland, and preparing an answer to *Theron and Aspasio.*'[113]

The October letter of Wesley's had obviously arrived according to the following letter which Hervey sent to Ryland on 29 November 1756:

> 'Herewith you have the grand attack from Mr W. of which I apprized you some time ago. Examine it closely; return it speedily; and if you please, confute it effectually; demolish

112. Hervey, James *Works* (London, 1787, Vol.6, *Letters, to Lady Shirley* No.LXXXIII, p.389.)
113. *ibid.* (Vol.7, p.41, Letter XXI.)

the battery, and spike up the cannon. I have not answered in any shape; and when I do answer with my pen, I propose nothing more than a general acknowledgement, and an inquiry, whether he proposes to print his animadversions.'[114]

It is interesting to read that in 1756,[115] Hervey's friends desired some formal recognition of his ability as a writer as displayed in *Theron and Aspasio*. The recognition proposed seems to have been the conferring of a Doctor's degree, but Hervey demurred and his thoughts still appeared to be on the impending attack which was going to be made on his work '...by a hand not well affected to the imputed righteousness of Our Lord, but remarkably zealous for the inherent righteousness and *perfection* of man.' There is little doubt that he was referring to the possibility of Wesley's publishing the letter of 15 October. His suspicions were confirmed for Wesley did just this, including this letter in his *Preservative*. Wesley began this in December 1756 and it was published in 1758. No doubt the preachers who had informed James of the forthcoming October letter also warned him of its possible publication.

---

114. Hervey, James *Works* (London, 1787, Vol.7, pp.45-6, Letter XXIII.)
115. Tyerman, Luke *The Oxford Methodists* (London, 1873, pp.310-311.)

CHAPTER NINE

THE SECOND CALVINISTIC CONTROVERSY

'THE IMPUTED RIGHTEOUSNESS OF CHRIST'

(Wesley and James Hervey)

(II)

The year 1757 marked a new stage in the Hervey–Wesley relationship. In this year, a 500-page book appeared entitled: *Letters to the Author of Theron and Aspasio.*

This was written either by Robert Sandeman or John Glass, his father-in-law. Tyerman, in his *Oxford Methodists*[1] says it is the work of Sandeman, but in the same author's *The Life and Times of John Wesley*[2] he says it could have been written by either Sandeman or Glass. Robert Sandeman (1718-71) was minister at Perth in Scotland but later took over the leadership of the Glassites (or Glasites), a sect which his father-in-law had founded. His followers then assumed the title of Sandemanians. Glass was minister of the parish church at Tealing near Dundee until expelled from the Established Church of Scotland in 1728. He founded the Glassite sect, endeavouring to model his churches on those of early

---

1. Page 313.
2. (London, 1871-2, Vol.2, p.293.)

Christianity.[3] Their practices had notable differences from other churches, including, for example, the washing of each other's feet, the celebrating of the Eucharist by dining in each other's homes between morning and afternoon services; the celebration of the Agapé by drinking broth, and using the kiss of charity. Benjamin Ingham, one of members of the Oxford 'Holy Club' had been much impressed by his reading of *Theron and Aspasio*. However, by his examination of Glass's (or Sandeman's) work on Hervey's, he embraced Sandemanian views which resulted in his separation from his evangelical friends, Hervey and Wesley included. His action also resulted in the near ruin of his own Connexion, many of his Yorkshire societies leaving him to join with the Wesleyan body.

Wesley could not be sure whether Sandeman or Glass was the author of this treatise against Hervey. In any case, the writer had used the pseudonym 'Palaemon'.[4] Whoever wrote it revealed considerable ability. It contained severe attacks on the popular evangelical preachers of the day, all of whom, according to the author, maintained that 'Christian faith is not only an assent to the whole gospel of Christ but also a full reliance on the blood of Christ; a trust in the merits of His life, death and resurrection; a recumbency on Him as our stonement and our life, *as given for us and living in us.*[5] The writer of *Letters to the Author of Theron and Aspasio*[6] asserted that mere assent to the Gospel truth was sufficient. What Christ had done was that which pleased God; what He had done, was that which quietens the guilty conscience of man as soon as he knew it; so that when he heard of it, he had no occasion for any other question but this: "Is it true or not?" If he finds it is true he is happy;

---

3.   Michael Faraday the natural philosopher and physicist was a member of one of these communities. There were not many followers but a few churches were founded outside Scotland. There is a disused Sandemanian chapel, now a barn, on a farm near Kirkby Stephen in Cumbria.

4.   Remmius Palaemon was a celebrated and prosperous Roman schoolmaster and grammarian.

5.   Quoted from J.W.S. (Vol.1, pp.40-1.)   Sermon No.1: 'Salvation by Faith' (Ephesians. Ch.2. verse.8.)

6.   The work consisted of two volumes published in Edinburgh 1757.

if not, he can reap no comfort by it.'
He continued:

> 'Whatever doctrine teaches us to think, that by our acceptance
> with God is began [*sic*] by our own good endeavours, seconded
> by Divine aid, or even first prompted by the Divine influence,
> leads us to look for acceptance with God by our own
> righteousness; for whatsoever I do, however, assisted or
> prompted, is still my own work. Aspasio tells us, "Faith is a
> real persuasion that Christ died *for me*". This account of faith
> somewhat resembles the arch of a bridge thrown over a river,
> having the one end settled on a rock, and the other on sand or
> mud. That Christ died *for me*, is a point not so easily settled.
> This is a point which the Scripture nowhere ascertains...'[7]

Men were justified, the writer claimed, by the knowledge of 'a
righteousness finished in the days of Tiberius'; and this knowledge
operated upon them and led them to work righteousness.[8]

As for assurance, the doctrine especially emphasized by the Wesleys –
no man, said the writer, could be assured that his sins were forgiven him,
but in so far as he was 'freed from the service of sin, and led to work
righteousness'.[9]

A personal attack was then made upon Wesley in the following
paragraph:

> 'Perhaps it may be thought needful, that I should define what
> I mean by *popular doctrine*; especially as I have considered
> many as preachers thereof, who differ remarkably from each

---

7. *Letters on Theron and Aspasio to the Author of that Work* (This was an alternative title). (Vol.1, p.20.)
8. *ibid.* (Vol.2, p.190.)
9. *Letters on Theron and Aspasio to the Author of that Work* (Edinburgh, 1757, Vol.2, p.194.)

other; and particularly as I have ranked among them Mr
Wesley, who may justly be reckoned one of the most virulent
reproachers of God that this island has produced.'[10]

Wesley, having read this book, was quick to reply.[11] Tyerman[12]
regards his answer to Glass(?) as a defence of his friend Hervey. A glance
at the paragraph just quoted above will be sufficient to show that Wesley
was in need of defending *himself*!

His reply was dated Bristol 1 November 1757:

> 'Sir,' he began. 'It is not very material who you are. If Mr
> Glass is still alive, I suppose you are he.[13] If not, you are at
> least one of his humble admirers, and probably not very old;
> so your youth may in some measure plead your excuse for
> such a peculiar pertness, insolence, and self-sufficiency, with
> such an utter contempt of all mankind, as no other writer of
> the present age has shown. As you use no ceremony toward
> any man, so neither shall I use any toward you, but bluntly
> propose a few objections to your late performance, which
> stares man in the face as soon as he looks at it.'

This introductory paragraph set the tone for Wesley's detailed reply.
He used repeatedly the term 'slanderer' to describe his adversary. He
outlined three 'slanders', namely:

> (i) His speaking of Hervey that 'He shuts up our access to the
> divine righteousness by holding forth a preliminary human

---

10. *ibid.* (Vol.2, p.300.)
11. J.W.L. (Vol.3, pp.231-239.) Glass's(?) work called forth at least ten other replies
    apart from Cudworth's *A Defence of Theron and Aspasio against the Objections
    contained in a late Treatise entitled 'Letters on Theron and Aspasio'* which
    Hervey had commissioned him to write.
12. *The Life and Times of John Wesley* (London, 1871-2, Vol.2, p.293.)
13. This indicates Wesley's uncertainty whether Glass or Sandeman was the author.

one as necessary to our enjoying the benefit of it' (p.4) and that he thereby set men to work to do something in order to make their peace with God (p.9).

(ii) Glass's own words: 'As to that strange something which you call faith, after all you have told us about it, we are at as great a loss to tell distinctly what it is as when you began.'

(iii) The author has said that 'The popular preachers [he included Archbishop Tillotson] together with Drs Lucas, Crisp, Doddridge, Watts, Gill, Guthrie, Boston, Erskine, Willison, Flavel, Marshall, Griffith Jones, Hervey, Romaine, Whitefield and, of course, Wesley, never tell us what they mean by faith but by some laboured circumlocutions.'

Wesley added to these, three more 'slanders' which arose out of them, especially deprecating the 'great body of the people' who attended these popular preachers because they were of the world. Wesley declared Glass did not know himself what faith was and his attempt to define it was stark-staring nonsense. 'You can,' said Wesley, 'talk sense if you please. Why should you palm upon your readers such stuff as this?'

As for his theory of justification, Wesley declared that Glass '...justified his opponents and condemned himself as "damnably criminal" and it looked as if every devil in hell would be saved.'

Furthermore, there could not be any love for God or neighbour with Glass, because of the hatred, malevolence, rancour, bitterness which was shown in his opinion of all those who did not fall in with his ideas. Glass has said he abhorred all persecution but Wesley said he would be very loath to trust him! 'I doubt it,' he said, 'were it in your power, you would make more bonfires in Smithfield than Bonner and Gardiner put together.'

Towards the end of his letter, Wesley defended the 'popular' preachers whom Glass said worship another God and compared with whom '...no sinners are more hardened, none greater destroyers of mankind than they.' [p.98]

The last example of his 'unparalleled charity' was Glass's assertion that 'If anyone chooses to go to hell by a devout path, let him study any one of those four famous treatises. Mr Guthrie's *Trial of a Saving Interest in Christ*; Mr Marshall's *Gospel Mystery of Sanctification*;[14] Mr Boston's *Human Nature in its Fourfold State*; or Dr Doddridge's *Rise and Progress of Religion in the Soul*. If any profane person who desires to be converted enter into the spirit of those books, he thereby becomes twofold more a child of hell than he was before.' Wesley replied thus:

> 'Such is the doctrine, such is the spirit, of Palaemon! condemning the whole generation of God's children; sending all his opponents to hell at once, casting arrows, firebrands, death on every side! But I stop. God be merciful to thee a sinner; and show thee compassion, though thou hast none for thy fellow-servants! Otherwise it will be more tolerable, I will not say for Seneca or Epictetus, but for Nero or Domitian, in the Day of Judgement than for thee!'[15]

In a letter to Samuel Furly, dated 14 October 1757,[16] Wesley described 'Palaemon' as '...a man of admirable sense and learning, but a Calvinist and Antinomian to the bone; as you may judge from his vehement anger at Mr Erskine, Cudworth and Hervey for their legality.'

The last word, however, was not with Wesley. A threepenny pamphlet entitled *Remarks on the Revd John Wesley's Sufficient Answer to the author of the Letters on Theron and Aspasio by J.D.* appeared the same year in which Wesley was accused of having 'crowded more scandal, insolence, self-sufficiency, hatred, malevolence, rancour, bitterness and uncharitableness' into his penny tract than Hervey had put into his five-shilling book.[17] Hervey's was '...sarcastical, lively, volatile and pungent

---

14. It will be recalled that this was a favourite book of Hervey's. See Chapter Eight of this study, pp.193-226.
15. J.W.L. (Vol.3, pp.231-239.) This was published at 1d. per copy.
16. J.W.L. (Vol.3, p.230.)
17. Tyerman, Luke *The Oxford Methodists* (London, 1873, pp.293-4.)

as the ether; Wesley's was as dull as lead.'

A careful search through Hervey's *Works* reveals no mention whatsoever of Wesley's defence of *Theron and Aspasio*. Hervey must have known about it as it was published as a tract and, naturally would be interested in all the reviews, criticisms and comments on his work. If he did know of it, one might reasonably expect some word of appreciation, especially as Wesley had been personally attacked in both works, i.e. by Glass and J.D. Wesley did not set out purely to defend Hervey's work – he was defending himself as well. Also he could not conscientiously defend the whole of *Theron and Aspasio* because he disagreed with the purpose of it. However, he did defend the parts of it with which he agreed and this was commendable on the part of Wesley, considering Hervey's impoliteness to him. Also Wesley, to give him his due, would not sit back and allow Glass(?) or anyone else to misrepresent Hervey's work publicly.

Returning to Hervey's plans for replying to Wesley's strictures on his work, it was to Ryland and Cudworth he turned for help. Two letters of Hervey's were dated for 3 January 1758. To Ryland he said:

'You enquire after my intended answer to Mr Wesley. I am transcribing it for the press, but find it difficult to preserve the decency of a gentleman, and the meekness of the Christian: there is so much unfair dealing running through my opponent's objections, and the most magisterial air all along supplying the place of argument. Pray for me, dear friend, that I may not betray the blessed cause, by the weakness of my reasoning nor dishonour it by the badness of my temper. Whether I shall be able to finish this work is apparently uncertain...'[18]

It was uncertain, of course, by reason of his declining health.

---

18. Hervey, J *Works* (London, 1787, Vol.7, p.58.) Letter XXXIV.

The other letter of this date did not give the recipient's name[19] but it obviously referred to Wesley in its contents. He felt that his opponent, Wesley, was angry with him for speaking *too much* and *too openly*, (at least, in his critic's opinion) on the side of election, and particular redemption. He asked his friend to whom he wrote, for his opinion whether or not Wesley's criticisms were just. Hervey complained that Wesley had just published a large book at the price of six shillings on the doctrine of *Original Sin*; the greater part of which, was an abridgement of Dr Watts's *Ruin and Recovery*; and of another treatise written by Mr Hebden. In this new work, Wesley had taken the opportunity to quote two or three passages from his *Theron and Aspasio* – one from Vol.1, p.184 which he thus introduced:

> 'To explain this a little further in Mr Hervey's words, "By federal head I mean, that, as Adam was the first general representative (of *this kind*)," says Aspasio, but Mr Wesley makes him say "*of mankind*. Christ was," etc. He goes on to the bottom of the page, then turns back to the upper part, and represents me as forming a conclusion in these words, "All these expressions demonstrate, that, Adam, as well as Christ, was a representative of *all mankind*, and, that, what he did, in this capacity, did not terminate in himself, but affected all whom he represented."'

Hervey felt that this was a very injurious representation. One sentence was a palpable misquotation. He asked – would it be proper for him to take any notice of it? He was sometimes apprehensive that Wesley would draw him into a dispute about particular redemption. Hervey knew Wesley could say startling and horrid things on that subject and this, perhaps might be the most effectual method to prejudice people against

---

19. This cannot have been Cudworth because in *Aspasio Vindicated etc. 1771* there is a special collection of letters to Cudworth and there is no mention of this one.

his principal point.[20] However, Hervey's objections need deeper examination.

Upon examination of Wesley's treatise on *Original Sin*,[21] it would not be true to say with Hervey that the greater part of it was an abridgement of Watts's *Ruin and Recovery*[22] and Hebden's treatises which were four in number.[23] Watts's and Hebden's works and also those of Dr Jennings[24] were used but most of the work was Wesley's own. Wesley wrote it primarily as a reply to Dr Taylor's treatise: *The Scripture Doctrine of Original Sin proposed to Free and Candid Examination*, published in 1740. Taylor was a scholarly Presbyterian minister in Norwich and was also the first President of the Presbyterian Theological college at Warrington, holding this position until his death in 1761. He held Socinian views (i.e. Anti-Trinitarianism, denying the Divinity of Our Lord and any other doctrine which cannot be based on human reason). He also subscribed to the teaching of Pelagius [c.AD360-420] (i.e. that sin was not transmitted from Adam down through the human race, but that each child born into the world was morally clean; that if he sinned he did it by the force of example; that it was possible for him not to sin, and that for all his good deeds he accumulated merit with God.) Wesley, whilst disagreeing with Taylor, respected his learning and character. John did, however, come into conflict with some of Taylor's disciples in Bolton in

---

20. Hervey, J *Works* (London, 1787, Vol.6, Letter CXCVIII, pp.149-150.)
21. This was written in four parts and by 1771 there was an edition in seven parts. It was first published in 1757. The parts were dated from November 1756 to 17 August 1757 (Bristol). A sermon was later written and published by him as a twopenny pamphlet on the same subject. See J.W.W. (Vol.14, pp.1-315) for this treatise.
22. Wesley derived some strange views from Watts, e.g. that before the Flood, the earth was much more fruitful and that there was nothing but Spring and Summer weather. (*Original Sin.* Part IV.) It was the misunderstanding of Watts, who in any case was referring not to the Flood but to the Fall!
23. The Revd Samuel Hebden was minister at Wrentham in Suffolk and later at Boston. He was the author of the *Four-Fold State of Man.*
24. Dr David Jennings, a DD of St Andrews was a dissenting tutor and pastor of an Independent congregation at Wapping.

1748.[25] It is of interest to note that Wesley wrote on 9 December 1758[26] to A.M. Toplady who was later to be one of his fiercest opponents, that he believed that no single person since Mahomet had given such a wound to Christianity as Dr Taylor. Especially did he cite Taylor's work on *Original Sin*, which, with others, he had poisoned so many of the clergy, and, indeed '...the fountains themselves – the Universities in England, Scotland, Holland and Germany'.

Wherein did Wesley make use of Hervey's work? The first instance occurred in Part II, section 1 in which Wesley said Hervey discerned something more than Taylor did in the Mosaic account of the first parents' sin before God judged them. 'I make no apology,' he declared, 'for transcribing some of his words.'[27]

The second use of *Theron and Aspasio* was but a repetition of Hervey's quotation of Howe's *Living Temple* with which Wesley closed section 2 of Part II of his work.[28]

Thirdly, Dialogue II of Hervey's treatise was referred to in order to support Wesley in a technical quibble about the Hebrew of Job xi. verse 12 (i.e. 'a wild ass's colt').[29]

However, Wesley's use of *Theron and Aspasio* to which Hervey principally objected was in respect of Dialogue V (Part III, section 6 of Wesley's *Original Sin*). Hervey's actual words were:

> 'Aspasio: I mean what the Apostle teaches, when he calls CHRIST the second man (footnote=1.Cor.xv. verse 47), and the last Adam (footnote=1.Cor.xv. verse 45) – the second! The last! How? Not in a numerical sense. Not in the order of time. But in this respect – That, as Adam was a public person, and acted in the stead of all mankind, so CHRIST was a public person, and acted in behalf of all His People – That as

25. J.W.J. (Vol.3, p.374.)
26. J.W.L. (Vol.4, pp.47-49.)
27. J.W.W. (Vol.14, pp.57-8.)
28. *ibid.* (Vol.14, pp.109-111.)
29. *ibid.* (Vol.14, p.125.)

Adam was the first general representative of this kind, CHRIST was the second and last: there never was, and there never will be, any other – That, what they severally did, in this capacity, was not intended to terminate in themselves, but to affect as many as they respectively represented.'[30]

Wesley's words can be seen by a careful comparison with the above[31] to have been different in the following instances:

(i) Wesley missed out 'the second' after the reference to Corinthians above.
(ii) As Hervey noted, Wesley unfortunately had used 'mankind' instead of 'this kind'.

The latter did indeed alter the meaning of the sentences concerned and Hervey was right to protest. Literary misquotation is always serious, for it is misrepresentation. Wesley later attempted to clear himself of this charge in the preface to his *A Treatise on Justification, extracted from Mr John Goodwin, by John Wesley, with a Preface, wherein all that is material in Letters just published under the name of the Revd Mr Hervey is answered.* This work of Wesley's is not to be found in Benson's edition of the Works, but in the third edition which was edited by Thomas Jackson.[32]

This treatise was published in 1765 at Bristol with a Preface dated Hoxton Square 16 November 1764 (207pp.12mo). The Letters referred to are the famous *Eleven Letters* which will be dealt with fully a little later in this chapter.

Wesley said: that both the misplacing of the commas, and the putting of 'mankind' for 'this kind' were the printer's errors, not his. Moreover, he was absent during the printing of the work. This excuse, of course,

---

30. Hervey, J. *Theron and Aspasio* (London, 1755, Vol.1, pp.206-7.)
31. J.W.W. (Vol.14, pp.162-3.)
32. i.e. 1828 (Vol.X, pp.304ff.)

could be quite valid and is still a common one! But who was at fault for not carefully checking the printer's proofs?

On the other hand, one could have expected some acknowledgement of Wesley's appreciation of part of *Theron and Aspasio* in the *Treatise on Original Sin*, for in the Treatise, no criticism of the former was embarked upon, because Wesley, of course, only used the passages with which he agreed, even if they were incorrectly printed. In his *Treatise*, Wesley said:

> 'Since the writing of this, I have seen several tracts, which I shall have occasion to take notice of hereafter. There are likewise many excellent remarks on this subject in Mr Hervey's Dialogues.'

Whilst these remarks should have pleased Hervey, it was possible that the latter would still take exception to Wesley's rejection of his favourite notion of Imputed Righteousness of Christ which he had done again in the *Treatise on Original Sin*.[33] It should be noted at this juncture that there was also another occasion when Wesley quoted favourably from *Theron and Aspasio*.[34] When writing his *Thoughts on the Imputed Righteousness of Christ*, his argument followed identical lines to those expressed in the letter of 15 October 1756. He said:

> 'Upon the whole, I cannot express my thoughts better, than in the words of that good man, Mr Hervey: "If people may be safe, and their inheritance secure, without any knowledge of these particularities, why should you offer to puzzle their heads with a few unnecessary terms?" "We are not very solicitous as to the credit, or the use, of any particular set of

---

33. J.W.W. (Vol.14, pp.232-237.) Tyerman, Luke *The Oxford Methodists* (London, 1873, p.315) is inclined to criticize Hervey for taking this attitude. He calls him ungenerous and suspicious.
34. J.W.W. (Vol.14, pp.432-3.)

phrases. Only let men be humbled as repenting criminals, at the Redeemer's feet; let them rely as devoted pensioners, on his precious merits, and they are undoubtedly in the way to a blissful immortality."[35]

Hervey's next letter to Ryland was on March (no day given) 1758, and showed that James was still hard at work on his lengthy answer to Wesley's objections:[36]

'My affectionate respects to Mr Carter; tell him I cannot spare Mr Wesley's book, because I am transcribing though very slowly, and with a most feeble hand, my remarks for the press; in executing which work, I have continual need of having his letter before me. He urges no argument, either to establish his own opinion, or to overthrow mine; only denies the validity of my reasons in such manner as the following: "How does it appear that Christ undertook this before the foundation of the world, and that by a positive covenant between Him and the Father?" "Neither of these texts, nor all of them prove, what they were brought to prove, that there ever was any such Covenant between the Father and the Son..."'

It is strange that Hervey yet again referred to the 'Covenant' objection in a letter to Ryland[37] just as if he had not previously mentioned it. It was written, as was the other, in March 1758 but, again, no day was given:

---

35. Hervey, J. *Theron and Aspasio* (London, 1755, Dialogue 1, Vol.1, pp.65-66.) (though Wesley has quoted from the Dublin edition).
36. Hervey, J. *Works* (London 1787, Vol.7, pp.60-1, Letter XXXXVI.) See Appendix One of this study for Wesley's reply to the 'Covenant'. It was here, he asserted, that Calvinism and Antinomianism met.
37. Hervey, J. *Works* (London, 1787, Vol.7, p.66.)

'Mr Wesley, among other objections to *Theron and Aspasio*, finds fault with the doctrine of a Covenant established between the father and the Son – calls upon me to prove it by Scripture, and defies me to prove that it was made from Eternity. I find, from reading Witsius,[38] that Dr Owen[39] has treated this subject very copiously, in his second volume, *Exercise* IV, page 49. I wish you would be so kind as to peruse this Dissertation and give me an extract of the thoughts that are most material, and the arguments that are most forcible.'

On 4 March he wrote to a friend:

'I have a long letter, containing two or three sheets, from Mr Wesley – it consists of Animadversions on my Dialogues and Letters, which I should be glad if you would peruse, and favour me with your opinion. He wrote me one before, more stinging and sarcastic than this. I have taken no notice of *either*, being very unwilling to embark in controversy; but for your judgment *on the last*[40] which is written with candour and temper, I should be much obliged, and have additional reason to be,

Dear Sir,

Your affectionate friend,

James Hervey[41]

---

38. See Appendix One where a note is given on Witsius (p.369).
39. Owen was a Puritan divine. Educated at Oxford. Chaplain to Oliver Cromwell; Dean of Christ Church, but expelled at the Restoration. Charles II allowed him to minister to an Independent congregation in Leadenhall Street, London.
40. Obviously Wesley's letter of 15 October 1756 was referred to. Apparently the previous letter from Wesley must have been written just after 16 February 1758 and, according to Hervey, must have been much more searching.
41. Hervey, J. *Works* (London, 1787, Vol.6, Letter CXCVI.) The letter was not to Cudworth for there is no trace of it in *Aspasio Vindicated etc. 1771* where the Hervey–Cudworth correspondence is given in full.

Now does this letter mean that Hervey was hesitant in publishing a reply to Wesley as it compares oddly with the letter to Ryland study.[42] Of course, as the latter epistle bore no day and the one immediately above gives the date of 4 March it may well indicate that in the meantime, Hervey had decided to reply and that the Ryland letters were written later in March. Yet on 23 June 1758 Hervey again showed hesitation in writing a public answer to Wesley. By this date, Wesley's letter of 15 October 1756 must have been published in the *Preservative* for Hervey complained about it to a friend:[43]

'I little thought when I put Mr Wesley's manuscript into your hand, that I should see it in print so soon. I took very little notice of it, and let it lie by me several months, without giving it an attentive consideration. It seemed to me so palpably weak, dealing only in positive assertions and positive denials, that I could not imagine he would adventure into the world without very great alterations. But it is now come abroad, just as you received it, in a two-shilling pamphlet, intitled [*sic*] *A Preservative against Unsettled Notions in Religion*. In this pamphlet, what he has wrote against me makes only a *small* part. Now then the *question* is, whether I shall attempt to answer it? Give me your opinion, as you have given me your assistance...'

What was causing Hervey to prevaricate about answering Wesley publicly? It would most likely be due to increasing physical weakness. Even if he had the desire, had he the strength to perform the task? Tyerman,[44] believes the 'friend' mentioned in the above letter to be Cudworth. However, in *Aspasio Vindicated etc. 1771* which contained

---

42. See pp.233 and 239.
43. Hervey, J. *Works op.cit.* (Vol.6, pp.97ff.)
44. Tyerman, Luke *The Oxford Methodists* (London, 1873, p.316.) Tyerman seems to be unaware of the indecision on the part of Hervey about replying to Wesley.

the full Hervey–Cudworth correspondence, there was no mention of it. There must have been another friend who at this time was affording Hervey literary help. It could not have been Ryland as two letters on the same matter had already been addressed to him. Wesley's letter had been written privately to Hervey who had declined to answer it within a reasonable space of time. Did Wesley know that Hervey had been contemplating replying to it in the press? If so, Wesley was fully justified in publishing his *Preservative*; if not, he was wrong to do so. If Wesley did know of Hervey's intention – where did he get his information from? He certainly would not receive it from Cudworth or Ryland who were at this time, Hervey's greatest literary helpers and no friends of John. In any case, to publish his letter to Hervey, Wesley ought to have known that he was asking for trouble – which he certainly received.

Wesley, in his Preface to his *Treatise on Justification*, said:[45]

'It is no wonder that, several of my objections, as Mr Hervey observes, "appear more like notes and memorandums than a just plea to the public". It is true. They appear like what they are – like what they were originally intended for. I had no thought of "a plea to the public" when I wrote, but "of notes and memorandums" to a private man.'

Hervey was correct when he pointed out that the *Preservative* only dealt with him in a very small part. This work was a collection of a few short letters and tracts by Wesley including, for example: *A Treatise on Baptism* [11 November 1756]: *A Letter to Mr Law, occasioned by some of his late writings (The Spirit of Prayer and the Spirit of Love)* [December 1755] and *Reasons against a separation from the Church of England*.

There was a letter in Hervey's *Aspasio Vindicated etc. 1771*[46] which was not contained in his *Works* of 1787, written by him to Cudworth

---

45.   J.W.W. Ed. T. Jackson (London, 1823, Vol.10, p.305.) As previously mentioned, Benson's edition which is used throughout this study does not contain this work.
46.   *op.cit.* (p.342.)

revealing that James had already completed part of his answer to Wesley's objections, and sought Cudworth's advice on it. A significant footnote was added by Cudworth who, himself edited the Hervey–Cudworth correspondence:

> 'This was an answer to Mr John Wesley's objections against *Theron and Aspasio* and is so valuable a defence of imputed righteousness, that its publication is much to be desired. It has been since published by Mr Hervey's brother, and may be seen in the preceding part of this volume.'

Further letters of 27 July and 2 August[47] dealt with the same manuscript, the former including the information that the work would be of about ten sheets in length and would make up a two-shilling pamphlet. By 9 August, two more sheets had been added and Hervey said:[48]

> 'Here I inclose [*sic*] two sheets more. They are very long. But I hope you will get time to revise them. Your last packet I received, and am much obliged for your remarks – I apprehend, the piece will make a two-shilling pamphlet. If you could suggest or insert anything to make it *edifying* and useful, I should be glad. Would it not be proper to print Mr W–'s letter, and prefix it to my answer?'[49]

Hervey could not have given Cudworth a more welcome opportunity to settle an old score with his antagonist Wesley, though how far this privilege was abused will be dealt with a little later.

Yet a further letter was addressed on 24 October 1758 to the anonymous

---

47. *ibid.* (p.343.)
48. *ibid.* (p.344.) A P.S. was added 'I suppose three sheets more will finish the work.' The next letter is dated 16 August 1758 and apparently only two sheets more would be required to finish the 'essay'. Hervey's reply (*The Eleven Letters*), in fact, was a very lengthy work.
49. *Aspasio Vindicated etc* (1771, p.344.)

friend who was also helping Hervey with his reply to Wesley:

> 'Let me repeat my thanks for the trouble you have taken, and
> for the *assistance* you have given me, in relation to my
> controversy with Mr Wesley. He is so unfair in his quotations,
> and so magisterial in his manner, that I find it no small
> difficulty to preserve the decency of the gentlemen, and the
> meekness of the Christian, in my intended answer... May our
> Divine Master aid me in *both* instances, or else not suffer me
> to write at all.'[50]

Anxious by the continued silence of his friend Hervey and obviously
having heard rumours of the impending literary battle being prepared
against him, Wesley wrote to him from London on 29 November 1758.
He related to Hervey that a week or so previously he had met with a
certain Mr Pierce of Bury who had informed him of a conversation he
had had a few days before with Mr Cudworth. Cudworth apparently had
mentioned that he had prevailed upon Hervey to write against Wesley. As
far as he (Wesley) was concerned, anyone was welcome to write what he
pleased about him. Hervey, however, should remember that before he
published anything against Wesley, Wesley had written a private letter to
him and no answer had been forthcoming. He felt he had written in a most
inoffensive manner and the whole purpose of his publication[51] was to
safeguard his own preachers from being tossed to and fro by various
doctrines. Wesley expected the same courtesy from Hervey, i.e. a private
letter first of all in which he could have stated his complaints. If they were
then not answered to his satisfaction, Hervey could publish them to the
whole world. But he did give Hervey a stern warning to give no countenance
to '...that insolent, scurrilous, virulent libel which bears the name of
William Cudworth.' How Hervey could possibly converse with such a

---

50. Hervey, James *Works* (London, 1787, Vol.6, p.104, Letter CLXXVII) 'To a
    friend.'
51. i.e. *Preservative against Unsettled Notions in Religion* (London, 1758.)

man, Wesley just could not understand. Hervey should not have left his old well-tried friends – the new ones were not comparable with them. Wesley was not concerned for himself but for Hervey. An evil man had influenced him just as he stepping 'into eternity'. Time was short for both of them and it should be employed in fostering peace and good will.

Unfortunately Wesley was too late. Hervey had neither strength nor inclination to reply. Between four and five o'clock in the afternoon on Christmas Day, 1758, Hervey passed to where the wicked cease from troubling; the weary are at rest, and, where, it is hoped, controversy is unknown.[52]

It is at this juncture that Charles Wesley is heard. He had either been ignorant of the difference between Hervey and his brother, or had deemed it prudent to keep clear of the quarrels which were taking place. Since Oxford days, he had met Hervey only occasionally and then on the happiest terms. Now, quite characteristically, he mourned his friend and expressed his sorrow poetically:

PART I

He's gone! The spotless soul is gone
    Triumphant to his place above;
The prison walls are broken down,
    The angels speed his swift remove,
And shouting on their wings he flies,
    And HERVEY rests in paradise.

---

52. J.W.L. (Vol.4, pp.46-7.) This letter was also printed in the *Arminian Magazine* 1778, p.136.) This was Wesley's last letter to Hervey. Whitefield wrote his last epistle from London to Hervey on 19 December. Hervey's last letters were to Lady Frances Shirley and Cudworth. To the latter he wrote on 15 December 1758: 'I am so weak I am scarce able to write my name'. (*Aspasio Vindicated etc.* 1771, p.346.)

Through the last dreadful conflict brought,
    Which shook so sore his dying breast,
Far happier for that bitter draught,
    With more transcendent raptures blest,
He finds for every patient groan,
    A jewel added to his crown.

Saved by the merit of his Lord,
    Salvation, praise to Christ he gives,
Yet still his merciful reward
    According to his work receives;
And with the seed he sow'd below,
    His bliss eternally shall grow.

Redeemed by righteousness divine,
    In God's own portraiture complete,
With brighter rays ordained to shine,
    He casts his crown at Jesu's feet,
And hails him sitting on the throne,
    For ever saved by grace alone.

PART II

FATHER, to us vouchsafe the grace,
    Which brought our friend victorious through;
Let us his shining footsteps trace,
    Let us his steadfast faith pursue,
Follow this follower of the Lamb,
    And conquer all through Jesu's name.

Through Jesu's name, and strength, and word,
    The well-fought fight our brother won;
Arm'd with the Saviour's blood and sword,

He cast the dire accuser down;
Compell'd the aliens to submit,
And trampled flesh beneath his feet.

In vain the Gnostic tempter tried
With guile his upright heart to ensnare;
His upright heart the fiend defied;
No room for sin when Christ was there;
No need of fancied liberty,
When Christ had made him truly free.

Free from the law of sin and death,
Free from the Antinomian leaven,[53]
He led his Master's life beneath;
And, labouring for the rest of heaven,
By active love, and watchful prayer,
He showed his heart already there.

How full of heaven his latest word,
'Thou bidd'st me now in peace depart,
For I have known my precious Lord,
Have clasped thee, Saviour, in my heart,
My eyes thy glorious joy have seen!'
He spake; he died, and enter'd in.

O might we all, like him, believe,
And keep the faith, and win the prize!
Father, prepare, and then, receive,

---

53. The trouble was, that with Cudworth as a close friend and influential adviser, Hervey was by no means free from the 'Antinomian leaven'. This proves that Charles did not (or gives the impression that he did not) know of the objections his brother had against Hervey on the grounds that the latter was taking too much heed of the Antinomian Cudworth.

> Our hallowed spirits to the skies,
> To chant, with all our friends above,
> Thy glorious, everlasting love.[54]

One could wish that the Hervey–Wesley saga had ended with the former's passing, but it was not to be. Six years Hervey had been at rest, when it appeared as though he had struck a blow at Wesley from the grave. It was obviously unexpected because Wesley seemed to have been willing to let the controversy fade out now that Hervey was dead. He had written to Samuel Furly from London on 9 December 1760 saying that he was determined not to publish anything against Hervey unless the latter's answer to Wesley was made public. 'Indeed,' he continued, 'it is Mr Cudworth's both as to matter and manner. So let it pass for the present.'[55]

A surreptitious edition of Hervey's reply to Wesley's criticism of *Theron and Aspasio* was published in the form of *Eleven Letters*.[56] The following year an authentic edition was issued by Hervey's brother William and this bore the following title:

Eleven Letters from the late Revd Mr Hervey, to Revd Mr John Wesley; containing an Answer to That Gentleman's Remarks on Theron and Aspasio. Published from the Author's Manuscript, left in possession of his brother, Mr Hervey, With a Preface showing the Reason for their being now printed. 2mo.297pp.

The unauthorized edition possessed a different title:

---

54. The full poem is in Jackson, Thomas *Centenary of Wesleyan Methodism* (London, 1839, pp.367-8.) A condensed version is given in Tyerman, Luke *The Oxford Methodists* (London, 1873, pp.323-4.)
55. J.W.L. (Vol.4, p.118.)
56. No printer's name is given and the brief Preface is signed by 'Philolethes'. The editor acknowledges that these letters have found their way into the world 'by stealth'.

Aspasio Vindicated, and the Scripture Doctrine of Imputed Righteousness Defended against the Objections and Animadversions of the Revd Mr John Wesley. In Eleven Letters and prepared for the Press by the late Mr J—s H—y, A.B.[57] 12mo.288pp.

William Hervey's preface to his brother's letters was important.[58] He represented his brother as having decided to ignore Wesley's letter of 15 October 1756[59] until he saw it printed in the *Preservative*. One is bound to agree with Tyerman here, that Wesley did not publish this until 23 June 1758 and as it will have been noted, Hervey was already intending answering Wesley's letter[60] much as he had wavered in his decision to do so.

Speaking of the *Preservative*, William Hervey said:

'This my brother looked upon as a summons to the bar of the public...'

William admitted that when he was sent for to attend his dying brother, he asked what he should do with James's letters which he was preparing in reply to Wesley – Should he publish them?

'By no means,' was the answer, 'because he had only transcribed about half of them fair for the press; but as the corrections and alterations of the latter part were mostly in

---

57. N.B. Hervey was an MA of Cambridge, a degree which he had applied for in addition to his BA of Oxford, in order to be able to hold the neighbouring livings of Weston Favell and Collingtree in plurality. Hervey entered into the transaction with reluctance.

58. Hervey, J. *Works* (London, 1787, Vol.7, pp.cxi-cxii) and *Aspasio Vindicated etc. 1771* pp.i-iv.)

59. See Appendix One of this study.

60. See pp.233 of this study for Hervey's letter to Ryland dated 3 January 1758, where Hervey intended to publish. See also p.239.

shorthand, it would be difficult to understand them, especially as some of the shorthand was entirely his own; and others could not make it out, therefore, he said, "as it is not a finished piece, I desire you will do no more about it."'[61]

William said that at first, he intended to keep his brother's wish in spite of the 'repeated solicitations of many of his friends' who desired them to be printed. The 'friends' concerned gave as their reason for urging publication, the allaying of the 'groundless prejudices' which the Preservative 'might occasion' in the 'minds of many'. It was only the surreptitious edition which occasioned his own publication. 'More,' he thought, 'will follow.'

'As this is the case,' he continued, 'I think it my duty to the memory of my late brother, to send forth as correct an edition as I possibly can; for as to *that* which has appeared (from what editor, I know not), it is so faulty and incorrect, that but little judgement can be formed from it, of the propriety and force of my brother's answers to Mr *Wesley*.

'As to the unfairness of publishing my brother's letters without my consent, and the injustice to his memory, in sending so mangled a performance out under his name, they are too apparent to need any proof: and though the editor, as I have been informed, gave away the whole impression, so that it is plain, lucre was not the motive of his proceeding, and I would charitably hope he did it with a view of benefitting his readers; yet it is so like *doing evil that good may come*, as, in my opinion, to be quite unjustifiable.'

However, as the only way now left to remedy in some way what had

---

61. Hervey, J. *Works* (Vol.4, p.iii) and Preface to *Aspasio Vindicated etc.* (pp.ii and iii.)

been done and to prevent a further imposition on the public, from worse motives than those which actuated that particular publisher, William had called 'a friend' to his assistance; and by this means he was able to present to the reader as perfect a copy of these letters as could be made from the manuscript in his hands:

> 'That the reader may judge more clearly of the state of the controversy between my late brother and Mr *Wesley*. I have thought it right to obtain Mr *Wesley*'s letter, word for word, as it stands in the *Preservative*.'

The Wesley letter was then reproduced and a significant footnote was given early in the letter to the effect that 'The reader will easily see that Mr *Wesley* has, in most cases, quoted very unfairly.'

After the letter, William Hervey continued his remarks, answering the possible objections, especially that of keeping alive a controversy which happened 'Long ago' and 'now probably forgotten'. His justification for publishing the eleven letters was that the *Preservative* was still on sale at the Foundry and was still recommended by Wesley to his preachers '...to be carefully read, then to be recommended and explained to the several societies where they labour.' To Hervey, then, the controversy was kept alive by Wesley himself 'in the most effectual manner, daily and hourly'.

He concluded:

> 'This proves very sufficiently, the *seasonableness*, and, as things have happened, the *expediency* of the present appearance of the following letters in public. How pertinent an answer they contain to Mr *Wesley*'s objections, is now to be left to the consideration of the candid reader.'
>
> W. Hervey

Miles Lane,
5 December 1764.

It is now necessary to examine the contents of these eleven letters which Hervey had prepared and Cudworth revised.

The first letter was interesting for its introduction which sets out Hervey's purpose in replying:

> 'I received the letter you mention, containing remarks on the dialogue between *Theron and Aspasio*. As, after a careful perusal, I saw very little to alter my sentiments, I laid aside your epistle without returning an answer, in hopes that my silence (which, it seems you mistook for obstinacy) would most emphatically speak my advice; which, had it been expressed more plainly, would have been delivered in the apostle's words, *That ye study*, or make it your ambition, *to be quiet.*
> Since you have, by printing these remarks, summoned me, though reluctant, to the bar of the Public, it should seem, that I ought not to discredit *the truth once delivered to the saints*, by a timid silence; and I am the more willing to answer for myself, as I have now the privilege of an unprejudiced judge, and an impartial jury. If my defence should be lost of my opponent, it may possibly make some useful impressions on the court, and candid audience. However, I will not absolutely despair of convincing Mr *Wesley* himself, because it is written, *Give admonition to a wise man, and he will yet be wiser.* On some very momentous and interesting points, I may probably be a little more copious than the strict laws of argument demand, in order to exhibit some of the great truths of the gospel, in so *clear* a light, that *he may run who readeth them*; in so *amiable* and *inviting* a light, that the believer may rejoice in them, and the sinner may long for them. For such disgressions, I promise myself an easy pardon, both from yourself and the reader.'

He then dealt with Wesley's criticism of Hervey's 'stiff and affected language' of the second Dialogue. Wesley should not have quoted from the Dublin edition but from the English, and the last printing of that one. Style, he felt, was but a small matter when the subject was the all-important one of justification.[62]

His main defence, naturally, was of his notion of Imputed Righteousness – a favourite one of his, he readily admitted, but he protested that Wesley's objections were 'an insinuation so depretiatory [*sic*] to the Righteousness of the Blessed Jesus,' that he uttered:

'I had much rather heard [them] in a Jewish synagogue than have seen [them] in Mr Wesley's writings.'[63]

Hervey's manner of defence warrants attention. He was uncharacteristically sarcastic. More than once he accused his opponent of misquoting Aspasio. Wesley put himself before and above Scripture.[64] He has only one irrefragable argument to use in order to triumph over Aspasio, namely: 'I cannot allow it at all' and that was delivered '...with the air of oracular response'. It mattered not whether Aspasio was supported by Scripture or reason or any other respectable authority.[65]

He had a tart reply to Wesley's suggestion that he had made 'a slip of the pen' on one occasion in Aspasio's utterances:

'Have you not then as much reason, to charge our Divine Master with a slip of the tongue as to charge Aspasio with a slip of the pen?'[66]

Noteworthy were Hervey's repeated attempts to expose Wesley as a

---

62. Hervey, J. *Aspasio Vindicated etc.* (1771, p.32.)
63. *ibid.* (p.75.)
64. *ibid.* (p.141.)
65. Hervey, J. *Aspasio Vindicated etc* (1771, p.145.) 'What fine work,' he said, 'could our adversaries make with the Scriptures, if we should allow them Mr Wesley's interpretations!' Cf. p.112 where 'St James affirms one thing, Mr Wesley affirms the contrary, and who am I, that I should decide between the two disputants?'
66. J.W.L. (Vol.3, p.374.)

supporter of Papist views and indicate the similarity of his ideas with the pronouncements of the Council of Trent. Constantly he threw doubts on Wesley's orthodoxy, maintaining in one instance that '...he scarcely distinguishes himself from the heretic.'[67]

In fact, it was Wesley who was the Antinomian for not holding the view that Christ had to fulfil the moral law.

As for Wesley's objections[68] they were more like notes and memoranda than a just plea to the public – a caveat than a confutation. They were brief negatives, laconic assertions and quick interrogatives. He demanded proof but rarely gave it.[69] His brevity was the cause of Hervey's prolixity. Furthermore, Wesley seemed incapable of distinguishing between the common and the uncommon and could not discern between 'any' and 'every'; and 'some' and 'all'. He rambled from the point and was too fond of hair-splitting.[70] A man like John should have known how to make a better use of pen, ink and paper than to litigate about letters and syllables.

Wesley's sermons[71] and his brother's hymns were regularly thrown back by way of confrontation. Bengelius[72] on whom Wesley had relied to a great degree for his *Notes on the New Testament* was also brought in evidence against him. He seemed also '...to have forgotten the *Principles of a Methodist* and if so, permit me to remind you of them.'

---

67. Hervey, J. *Aspasio Vindicated etc.* (1771, p.156 also p.137.) He had heard it was said that Wesley was a Jesuit in disguise. He rejected the statement but cannot acquit his principles from halting between Protestantism and Popery. They have stolen the hallowed fire and were infected with the leaven of AntiChrist.

68. Hervey *op.cit.* (pp.102ff.)

69. Hervey, J. *Aspasio Vindicated etc.* (1771, p.159.)

70. *ibid.* (p.216.) See also p.103 for an example of this. Aspasio had said: 'St Paul often mentions "a righteousness imputed".' Wesley had objected to this. See J.W.L. (Vol.3, p.374) where John replied: 'Not *a* righteousness, never once, but simply righteousness.' Hervey asked whether δικαιόσυνη was mentioned by St Paul without the article. If the article were omitted, then it could mean *a* righteousness. Greek grammar was certainly on the side of Hervey there.

71. Hervey, *op.cit.* (p.215.)

72. *ibid.* (p.283.)

Perhaps the classic example of sarcasm in the Eleven Letters was to be found on pages 239 and 240 of *Aspasio Vindicated etc. 1771*:

> 'Aspasio's interpretation of the phrase, authenticated by the language of Scripture, Mr Wesley set aside; and introduces another, whose only recommendation to the public, is, "I come from Mr Wesley's pen." "Do you so? then we will allow you all proper regard. But because you come from Mr Wesley's pen, must you therefore displace propriety and supplant truth? make an inspired writer argue incorrectly, nay, jar with himself? This is rather too much for you to assume, even though you came recommended by a greater name."'[73]

What did Hervey think of Wesley's attitude? First of all, he was dishonest. John stated in his letter that rather than believe The Almighty God was the tyrant of the doctrine of Reprobation, he would 'sooner be a Turk, A Deist, yes, an Atheist'[74] Hervey warned him:

> 'Let me give you a word of friendly advice. Before you turn Turk or Deist, or Atheist, see that first you become an honest man. They will all disown you, if you go over to their party destitute of common honesty.'[75]

Wesley was no gentleman else he would not have mentioned the names of some of his former preachers as those who would be glad to hear Aspasio's assertion that '...even notorious transgressors in themselves have a sinless obedience in Christ.'[76]

---

73. Hervey, J. *Aspasio Vindicated etc.* (1771, p.253.) 'But Mr Wesley cased in his own self-sufficiency...esteemeth all the aforementioned as mere nothing...' and again on the same page: 'Mr Wesley, supported by his greater self...is too censorious of others and too indulgent to himself.'
74. J.W.L. (Vol.3, p.387.)
75. Hervey *op.cit.* (p.279.)
76. *ibid.* (p.198.)

Wesley, in Hervey's opinion was replying with '...the solemnity of a censor and the authority of a dictator.'[77] He was difficult to please[78] and his hand was against himself as well as against everybody else.[79] Out of his own mouth he condemned himself.[80]

As for the Wesley letter itself, it could not, in Hervey's view have been intended for the general public, since:

> '...every reader is treated, not as his judge, no, nor as his equal, but as his pupil, not as one that is addressed with argument and convinced by reasoning, but as a tame disciple, that is to acquiesce in the great preceptor's solemn *SAY SO*.'[81]

Hervey finished, having quoted from 'Wesley's own pen':

> 'For neither our own inward nor outward righteousness is the ground of our justification. Holiness of heart, as well as holiness of life, is not the cause, but the effect of it. The *sole* cause of our acceptance with GOD, is the righteousness and death of CHRIST who fulfilled GOD's law and died in our stead. Excellent sentiments! In these may I ever abide! to these may you also return!'[82]

It was hardly to be expected that Wesley would leave this lengthy work unchallenged. He replied in two ways. The first was the publication of a *Treatise on Justification extracted from Mr John Goodwin, with a preface wherein all that is material in Letters just published under the name of the Revd Mr Hervey is answered* in 1765[83] (12mo.

---

77. Hervey, J. *Aspasio Vindicated etc. 1771* (p.112.)
78. *ibid.* (p.289.)
79. *ibid.* (p.202.)
80. *ibid.* (p.205.)
81. *ibid.* (p.153.)
82. *ibid.* (p.290.)
83. Goodwin was Vicar of St Stephen's, Coleman Street, London (1633-1645).

215.pp.London). Writing to Thomas Rankin on 2 November 1764, [84] Wesley stated that, at the request of several of the preachers, he had, at length, abridged *Goodwin's Treatise on Justification*. He expressed the hope that it would stop the mouths of gainsayers concerning imputed righteousness and teach them (at least, the most candid) to speak as '...the oracles of God.'

In the Preface to the work,[85] Wesley gave the reason why he had printed the letter of 15 October 1756 in his *Preservative*. He had 'frequently and strongly' recommended *Theron and Aspasio* and therefore felt it a duty to indicate those points with which he was in disagreement. Having learned that Hervey intended to reply, Wesley had requested to see the manuscript before it was published. If Hervey did not receive from him, a satisfactory answer within a year, then he could be free (with Wesley's full consent) to '...publish it to all the world.'

> 'I do not intend to answer Mr Hervey's book,' he said, 'shall my hand be upon that saint of God? No; let him rest in Abraham's bosom. When my warfare is accomplished may I rest with him till the resurrection of the just! I purpose only to speak a little on the personal accusations which are brought against me. The chief of these are twelve: 1. That I assert things without proof. 2. That I am self-sufficient, positive, magisterial. 3. That I reason loosely and wildly. 4. That I contradict myself. 5. That I do not understand criticism and divinity. 6. That I have acted in a manner unworthy of a gentleman, a Christian, or a man of sense. 7. That I am

---

84. J.W.L. (Vol.4, pp.274-5.)
85. See J.W.J. (Vol.5, p.102; note) Monday 12 December 1764: 'I retired to Hoxton, to answer what was personal in the letters ascribed to Mr Hervey. How amazing is the power of prejudice! Were it not for this, every one who knew him and me would have cried out with indignation. "Whatever Mr W. was, none can commend or excuse Mr H. Such bitterness he ought not to have shown to his most cruel enemy; how much less to the guide of his youth – to one he owns to have been his 'father and friend'."'

impudent. 8. That I deny justification by faith, and am an enemy to the righteousness of Christ. 9. That I am an heretic, and my doctrine is poisonous. 10. That I am an antinomian. 11. That I teach Popish doctrine. 12. That I am a knave, a dishonest man, of no truth, justice, or integrity.'

It is true that Hervey had accused Wesley of not being honest but there is no trace of the accusation of 'impudence' in the Eleven Letters. He continued:

'"And is this thy voice, my son David?" Is this thy tender, loving grateful spirit? No "the hand of Joab is in all this!" I acknowledge the hand, the heart, of William Cudworth. I perceive it was not an empty boast, which he uttered to Mr Pearse[86] at Bury, before my friend went to Paradise – "Mr Hervey has given me full power to *put in* what I please." But he too is gone hence; and he knows now whether I am an honest man or no. It cannot be long, even in the course of nature, before I shall follow them. I could wish till then to be at peace with all men; but the will of the Lord be done! Peace or war, ease or pain, life or death, is good, so I may but "finish my course with joy" and the ministry which I have received of the Lord Jesus to testify the gospel of the grace of God.'

Wesley's second reply was contained in a sermon to which he always attached great importance and which he directed his Assistants to possess and disperse. It was based on Jeremiah xxiii. verse 6: '*This is His name whereby He shall be called. The Lord Our Righteousness*' and its popular title was taken from the last four words of the text.[87] It was first preached at the chapel in West Street, Seven Dials on Sunday 24

---

86. Note the different spelling of the name of Mr *Pierce* of Bury. See page 244 of this study.
87. J.W.S. (Vol.2, pp.420-441.)

November 1765. He rightly began by deploring the 'innumerable contests which have arisen about religion not only among unbelievers, but by those who are the children of God.[88]

The righteousness of Christ was both Divine and Human; but it was the latter that could be said to be imputed to man. His active righteousness was seen in his sinless and obedient life. The passive righteousness was evident in his sacrificial death on the cross. How was it imputed and when?

> 'All believers are forgiven and accepted, not for the sake of anything in them or of anything that ever was, that is, or ever can be done by them, but wholly and solely for the sake of what Christ hath done and suffered for them... We are justified freely by His grace, through the redemption that is in Jesus Christ.'[89]

And again:

> 'If we take the phrase of imputing Christ's righteousness, for the teaching (as it were) the righteousness of Christ, including His obedience, as well passive and active, in the return of it, that is, in the privileges, blessings, and benefits purchased by it; so a believer may be said to be justified by the righteousness of Christ imputed. The meaning is, God justifies the believer for the sake of Christ's righteousness, and not for any righteousness of his own...'[90]

It was, as St Paul affirmed, a man's faith in Christ that was imputed to him for righteousness, having taken off his own first. He believed in inherent righteousness which he understood to be not that which was the

---

88. *ibid.* (Vol.2, pp.423-4.)
89. *ibid.* (Vol.2, p.430.)
90. J.W.S. (Vol.2, p.432.)

ground of our acceptance with God, but that which was consequent upon it. There was no question of putting faith in the place of Christ or His righteousness. Each took its proper place.[91] The sole danger of speaking of the imputed righteousness of Christ, as Wesley saw it, was that a man could feel it was a cover for his unrighteousness. Here was the tendency towards Antinomianism and the more vulgar presentation of Calvinism, namely: the elect of God were saved no matter what they might do subsequently, and this idea could encourage it. He concluded with an appeal for the right to use the expression 'imputation of Christ's righteousness', or if he saw the attendant dangers, to employ an alternative. But he begged his readers not to do this to represent him as a Papist, or 'an enemy to the righteousness of Christ'.

It might well be thought that the matter would by now have been definitely closed, as well it should have been, but it was to be raised again – for one of the most serious results of the Hervey–Wesley controversy was now to be revealed.

Dr John Erskine[92] of Edinburgh decided to republish the *Eleven Letters* with a preface of his own in which he made a venomous attack on Wesley. One of John's elderly itinerant preachers, John Kershaw rushed to the rescue by publishing in Edinburgh *An Earnest Appeal to the Public, in an honest, amicable and affectionate Reply* to Erskine's Preface. Erskine, not to be outdone, issued a 'defence' of his Preface attacking Wesley more violently than ever. Wesley himself wrote to Erskine on 24 April 1765, asking what was his motive for making all this trouble so long after Hervey's death? It was a reasonable letter and quite moderate in tone:

'You ushered into this part of the world, one of the most bitter

---

91. *ibid.* (Vol.2, pp.433-4.)
92. Erskine (b.1721. d.1803.) was a Glasgow DD. He was also a friend of Jonathan Edwards and George Whitefield. His relationship with the latter speaks for itself in respect of his theological views. He was joint minister of Old Greyfriars Church in Edinburgh.

libels that was ever written against me; written by a dying man (so far as it was written by poor well-meaning Mr Hervey) with a trembling hand, just as he was tottering on the margin of the grave...Mr Hervey, who had been a man of peace all his life, began a war not six months before he died. He drew his sword when he was just putting off his body. He then fell on one to whom he had the deepest obligations, (as his own letters, which I have now in my hands, testify) on one who had never intentionally wronged him, who had never spoken an unkind word of him, or to him, and who loved him as his own child. O tell it not in Gath! The good Mr Hervey (if these letters were his) died cursing his spiritual father.'[93]

A more spirited defence was supplied by one of Wesley's Assistants, Walter Sellon in 1767, and whilst well-meaning in his intentions, did Wesley more harm than good.[94] It was entitled: *An Answer to Aspasio Vindicated in Eleven Letters, said to be wrote by the late Revd Mr James Hervey.* In it Sellon threw discretion and courtesy to the winds. Hervey, he declared, was sunk in Antinomianism and weak, being managed by Cudworth. Hervey's brother must have planned his edition 'in the bottomless pit', inspired '...by the prince thereof and published by a knave.' It seemed that he had thought it his duty to patronise all '...the railing, scurrility, antinomianism, blasphemy, lies and lewdness contained in that book and make his brother's name stink to the latest posterity.'

Wesley's last written word on the whole controversy was again addressed to Erskine[95] and dated, Edinburgh May 1766. He had not time to write him a formal reply and he had lost all hope of convincing him. Yet he answered succinctly all Erskine's attacks on eight different points

---

93. J.W.L.(Vol.4, pp.294-6) in which Wesley says he writes 'out of love for him'.
94. Nowhere does Wesley comment upon Sellon's performance.
95. This letter does not appear in the Standard Edition of Wesley's *Letters*. See J.W.W. (Vol.13, pp.112-125.) He adds a postscript to this pamphlet which includes his letter of 24 April 1765.

and refused as he had done all along to believe that Hervey could possibly have been the author of the hurtful accusations in the *Eleven Letters*. He concluded with a reference to his regard for Hervey:

> 'If those related to me by so near, so tender ties, thus furiously rise up against me, how much more may a stranger, one of another nation? "O Absalom, my son, my son!"'[96]

It seems almost an impudence, that, at the time when this fracas was at its height, the friends of Hervey, appreciating Charles Wesley's poetical skill, approached him with a view to his writing and epitaph, presumably to be inscribed on his tomb. It will be remembered that when Hervey died, Charles had written numerous and appropriate, appreciative verses in commemoration of his old Oxford friend. Now it was different. He refused. Obviously he had now learnt of the prolonged and unnecessary controversy which had raged throughout the religious circles of the land. However, with commendable charity he penned the following verses as a compromise and out of a sense of decency. But it will be quickly observed that they were serving a far more useful purpose as a poetical defence of his brother's honour.[97]

> 'O'erreach'd, impell'd by a sly Gnostic's art,
>   To stab his father, guide and faithful friend,
> Would pious Hervey act the "accuser's" part?
>   And *could* a life like his in malice end?
>
> No: by redeeming love the snare is broke;
>   In death his rash ingratitude he blames;
> Desires and *wills* the evil to revoke,
>   And dooms the "unfinished libel" to the flames.

---

96. J.W.W. (Vol.13, p.121.)
97. Jackson, Thomas *The Life of the Revd Charles Wesley, MA* (London, 1841, Vol.2, pp.157-8.)

Who then, for filthy gain betray'd his trust,
        And show'd a kinsman's fault in open light?
Let *Him* adorn the monumental bust,
        The econium fair in brass or marble write.

Or if they need a nobler trophy raise,
        As long as Theron and Aspasio live,
Let Madan or Romaine record his praise;
        Enough that Wesley's brother can *forgive*!'

Charles had not featured much in the controversy but this short and perhaps negative step was not without significance. He had no doubt been grieved at this hindrance to his brother's usefulness, knowing how good he had been to Hervey in his younger days. It was not a step which Charles would take rashly or without thought and pain.

It is amazing how the busy Wesley found the time (and the dying Hervey, the strength), to engage in a literary battle of this magnitude in which it appears so little was at stake. Neither emerged victoriously. As one reads Hervey's *Vindication* of his *Theron and Aspasio* there was present throughout the atmosphere of nervous excitability[98] – an indication of having written the decisive and final word on every topic, yet, realizing, that having done so, it would profit him nothing. A last word, indeed it was, but a lasting one too! Its damage could not be easily assessed but an attempt must now be made to do so. Hervey had struck his old friend from the grave, and the blow was a grievous one.

How far, then, could Hervey be held responsible for the contents of the *Eleven Letters*? It seemed to be uncharacteristic of a sensitive nature like his to dip his pen so frequently for the purpose of virulent sarcasm. But a dying man, leading such a sheltered life, could easily have become increasingly sensitive and embittered by advancing weakness. He must be given this point in his favour, for had he not claimed on more than one occasion that he 'naturally disliked controversy' and had seldom found it

---

98. See pp.220-1 for the medical opinion on Hervey.

advantageous.[99] What is more important, had he not also instructed his brother, when on his death bed, not to publish the letters?

There arises another question here. Even if Hervey's temperament had worsened in his latter days and therefore he could have written all that was published in his name, there was the very real possibility that his letters were revised and the shorthand ones transcribed, by others after his death. Cudworth's name could not be kept out of this enquiry. Wesley held Cudworth responsible for much that was unpleasant in this work to which the latter had unrestricted access. Cudworth certainly had the motive, for charity between himself and John was almost at zero point. Writing to John Newton on 9 April 1765, Wesley complained:[100]

> 'A dying man has drawn a sword and wounded, if not me, yet many others, and *you* among the rest. Poor Mr Hervey (or Mr Cudworth rather) painting me like an hideous monster, with exquisite art both disfiguring my character and distorting my sentiments, had made even Mr Newton afraid of me, who once thought me at least an harmless animal. A quarrel he could not make between us; neither can anyone else. For *two* must go to a quarrel; and I declare to you I will not be one... "Oh but Mr Hervey says you are *half* a Papist." What if he *proved* it too? What if he had proved I was a whole Papist? (though he might as easily have proved me a Mahometan). Is not a Papist a child of God? Is Thomas à Kempis, Mr De Renty, Gregory Lopez gone to hell? Believe it who can. Yet still of such (though Papists), the same is my brother, sister and mother...'

Or again to the same recipient, 14 May 1765:

---

99. Hervey J. *Works* (London, 1787, Vol.5, p.192.)
100. J.W.L. (Vol.4, p.292.) Newton assured Wesley on 18 April that 'Mr Hervey's letters have not wounded me at all. In my personal regard for you they have made no abatement, in my sentiments in other respects, no alteration.'

'But do not wrest and wiredraw and colour my words as Mr Hervey (or Cudworth) has done in such a manner that when I look in that glass I do not know my own face! "Shall I call you?" says Mr Hervey, "my father or my friend? For you have been both to me!" So it was and you have as well requited me! It is as well my reward is with the Most High.'[101]

In all fairness to Cudworth, it could not, on the other hand, be proved that he did, in fact publish the first and spurious edition of the *Eleven Letters* or that he provided the most offensive parts of the authentic one.

Some important points arise which must not be overlooked. Firstly Hervey had other friends who had seen Wesley's letter of 15 October 1756 and to whom he had written requesting advice whether or not he should answer it and it will be remembered that not all were named. Ryland and Cudworth were certainly among them, but there was no evidence that Ryland had any axe to grind where Wesley was concerned. Cudworth had a score to settle. The fact that the latter died before the spurious version had been published by no means absolved him from suspicion.

Secondly, an interesting note is given in Wesley's *Journal* (Standard Edition) Vol.4, p.103 which says that the Revd J.C. Nattrass who had studied both MSS found that the passages which had deeply wounded Wesley were not the interpolations by Cudworth or some other person, but the work of Hervey himself. But how could Nattrass know which was Cudworth's work and which was that of Hervey? In any case there is no trace of the spurious copy today. Nattrass's judgment surely was pure assumption.

Thirdly, it will be recalled that Hervey when asked by his brother William whether or not he should publish the letters, answered in the negative as not all of them 'were fair for the press'. Some were in a shorthand of his own invention. Who then, translated this shorthand unless it were someone who was intimately acquainted with Hervey's

---

101. J.W.L. (Vol.4, p.300.)

Letters and method of shorthand?

Fourthly, William Hervey had said that he did not know who was the anonymous author of the first and false edition of his brother's work. Had it been Cudworth or Ryland, he surely would have known, though whether he would have made this public is entirely another matter. In the case of Ryland, Tyerman[102] has an interesting note on a remark of his. Ryland admitted that just upon the point of their (the *Letters*) being suppressed, and lost to the Christian world for ever, they were, soon after Hervey's death, put into his hands for twelve or fourteen weeks. He said that from a principle 'of foolish and false delicacy' he did not take a copy of them which he ought to have done. 'Happy for the Church, the manuscript fell into the hands of three of my friends who had more sincerity, zeal and courage than I had, and thus the manuscript was rescued from destruction and the original copy at last brought to light.' The reader may be left to judge how 'happy' the whole affair was to the Church and the extent to which such 'zeal, sincerity and courage' were required.

Fifthly, Tyerman notes also that a comparison of the two MSS reveals that, except in typographical corrections, the insertion of Hebrew words instead of English characters, the punctuation of sentences and the addition of a quotation from St Chrysostom in Greek, the authentic edition hardly differed from the surreptitious one. If this were so, there was little justification for a fresh edition by William Hervey to correct the unauthorized one.

Whoever wrote the surreptitious edition will remain for ever a mystery. Three or four names will always lie under suspicion. Without further definite proof, Hervey himself must take the major part of the blame for the authentic edition whatever instructions he may have given William when nearing his end. After all, Hervey *had written* them and he should have known that deathbed requests were not always honoured and it would have been as well if he had insisted on the destruction of the letters before his own eyes. One fact is clear, that Hervey was weak-willed, and,

102. Tyerman, Luke *The Oxford Methodists* (London, 1873, p.331.)

no doubt, as already indicated in the medical opinion, due to his illness and his sensitive nature, he was far too easily influenced by others. For the writing of these letters and the manner in which they were written, Cudworth and Ryland could certainly take a share of the blame, to say nothing of the possibility of others who acted as 'literary critics'.

Henry Moore in his biography of Wesley[103] says in a footnote that William Hervey did not profit by his disloyalty to his brother. William, unfortunately, was tempted to lend money to someone – an amount of about 1000 pounds (one wonders whether or not this sum was part of the royalties on the *Eleven Letters!*) The man to whom he had made the loan prosecuted William for taking more than the legal interest. The penalty for this offence was thrice the sum which was recovered. Mr Blackwell, a banker and a warm friend of Wesley's and known for his honesty, a fact which earned him the title of 'the rough diamond', was Hervey's banker. When William consulted him, Blackwell told him bluntly that he should have done what his brother James had bidden him to do namely: destroy the letters written against Wesley. Now he could count his gains! Moore remarks: 'That there were other persons besides Mr Wesley who believed in a particular and remunerative providence.'

Finally, was this literary battle a mere storm in a teacup? Were the results merely ephemeral? The answer, regrettably, is 'No'. Two serious results – lasting pieces of damage were unused. The first was upon Wesley's work in Scotland. Erskine was probably more successful than he had anticipated. Scotland, an essentially Calvinistic country would naturally heed one of its own ministers who defended Calvinistic doctrines rather than an English Wesley opposing them. Wesley and his teaching were suspect there for a long time.[104] The progress of Methodism was retarded for about twenty years.

---

103. Moore, Henry *Life of the Revd John Wesley MA* (London, 1825, Vol.2, p.248.)
104. See J.W.J. (Vol.5, p.111): 'I preached at Dunbar about noon, and in the evening at Edinburgh. My coming was quite seasonable (though unexpected), as those bad letters, published in the name of Mr Hervey, and reprinted here by Mr John Erskine, had made a great deal of noise.'

The second result was permanent. The controversy which appeared for a while to die down, broke out again with even greater bitterness culminating in the great Calvinistic dispute of 1770 onwards which did not abate until the death of Toplady in 1778. This was, as will be seen in the last chapter of this study, the final breach between the Calvinistic Evangelicals who remained in the Church, the 'Calvinistic Methodists' and others who turned Dissenters under the leadership and actions of the Countess of Huntingdon; and those who followed Wesley, who, later, when the latter passed on, were also to leave the church.

Looking back, the Hervey–Wesley story makes sorry reading. On one hand, Hervey, a sensitive, yet a brilliant scholar and literary genius, grateful beyond words to his former teacher, displayed one of the worst faults in human nature – an unjustifiable self-confidence. The *Eleven Letters* indicated the latter trait. Yet Hervey was really an enigma. The 'self-confidence' shown in the *Letters* has to be weighed against the plentiful evidence that he was far too easily influenced by 'many friends', some of whom had no scruples about seeing his friendship with Wesley dissolved. Too often he sought and heeded their 'advice'.

On the other hand, Wesley, once a tutor and always a tutor, roughened and hardened by his experiences and far busier than ever Hervey could have been, was asked by Hervey for his opinions. When Wesley gave them 'without polish or reserve', he thereby offended Hervey permanently. Instead of answering Wesley, Hervey was content to complain to others (a common enough fault amongst sensitive folk) and retreated into a sulky silence. This, however, did not absolve Wesley from publishing his originally private letter of 15 October 1756,[105] in the *Preservative* even though he gave a year's ultimatum to Hervey. Wesley unwittingly gave his enemies (Cudworth and Erskine included to say nothing of William Hervey, who appeared to be no friend) their golden opportunity of making trouble. Hervey's faults[106] notwithstanding, Wesley brought upon

---

105. See Appendix One of this study.
106. See *Concise Oxford Dictionary of National Biography* (Oxon, 1903, Note on Hervey.) 'His popularity as a writer never led him to take a false view of his own

himself a storm which proved to be one of a number of factors which later helped his movement to leave the Mother Church, in which, to his dying day, he had urged it to remain.

One final point to be noticed is that during the Hervey–Wesley controversy, most of the Anglican Calvinistic Evangelicals remained silent; but they missed nothing of what was going on. So much publicity had been given to the dispute that they could not fail to do so. Moreover the Third Calvinistic (or 'Minute') controversy followed so soon after this dispute was beginning to subside, that one cannot but feel that it was remembered all too well. Nor must it be overlooked that there would have been one person who followed the controversy closely and with great interest and that was Selina, Countess of Huntingdon, a great friend of Hervey. Was it not she who instigated the 'Minute Controversy' to be discussed in Chapter Eleven of this study? This may well have been in the minds of Her Ladyship and her evangelical coadjutors that they had kept a cowardly silence when the good name of a late Calvinistic colleague needed to be defended. The next time Wesley was to obtrude himself into debate about Calvinism, it was incumbent upon them to see that he was put into his rightful place. How far they were successful in doing this, will be for the reader to judge after a perusal of the last chapter of this study.

---

powers; when it was at its height, he frankly confessed that he was not a man of strong mind and that he had not power for arduous researches.'

CHAPTER TEN

PERFECTION OR PERSEVERANCE?

'I think it was the latter end of the year 1740 that I had a conversation with Dr Gibson, then Bishop of London, at Whitehall. He asked me what I meant by Perfection. I told him without any disguise or reserve. When I ceased speaking he said, "Mr Wesley, if this be all you mean, publish it to all the world. If any one then can confute what you say, he may have free leave." I answered, "My Lord, I will," and accordingly wrote and published the sermon on Christian Perfection.'[1]

What, then, was this doctrine of Perfection which the Wesleys so stoutly declared in sermon, writings and song and which was to cause them so much criticism from the Calvinistic wing of the Evangelicals? Was it a consistent teaching or was it modified with the passing of time?

In his *Plain Account of Christian Perfection*, Wesley gave a brief outline of the influences which brought him to adopt the doctrine.[2] In 1725, when twenty-three, he read Bishop Taylor's *Rules and Exercises on Holy Living and Dying*. These works related to purity of intention and

---

1.   J.W.W. (Vol.16, p.82.) See also modern edition of *Plain Account of Christian Perfection*, which is used in this chapter (London, 1960, p.16.) There is no reference to this interview in the Journal but see J.W.L. (Vol.5, p.172.)
2.   J.W.S. (Vol.2, pp.147-8; Introduction to sermon.)

on reading them, Wesley resolved to give all his life to God. Having read Thomas à Kempis's *Christian Pattern* (or *Imitation of Christ*) the following year, he realized that giving his life to God was useless unless he gave his whole heart. A few years after, William Law's *Treatise on Christian Perfection* and *Serious Call* were put into his hands. These convinced him of the absolute impossibility of being half a Christian. In 1729 his reading of the Bible showed him that it contained the only standard of truth and the only 'model' of religion. He saw that he must walk as Christ walked and have in him the mind that was in Christ.

From Wesley's writings, it is noted that the complete salvation of man takes place in three stages. Whilst Wesley did not seem to care for the term 'total depravity' and did not use it, nevertheless he agreed with the main idea that because Adam fell, his descendants inherited his corruption. This was 'sinfulness' as distinct from 'a sin' which was the 'voluntary transgression of a known law'. However, mankind had the offer of Divine Grace – prevenient grace, i.e. going before and predisposing the soul to salvation. The three stages, then, were:

'1. Justification by Faith alone. This is not done *in* a man, but *for* him. This removed the guilt of Adam's sin and brings reconciliation between him and God.

2. Regeneration. This is the change wrought in the believing soul by the Holy Spirit so that it is "adopted" by God and man becomes a redeemed child of God.

3. Sanctification. This is a purifying process which takes place in the believer after regeneration. When a man believes then sanctification begins. As faith increases, this holiness increases also.

Entire sanctification is the term given to the completion of the process.' (Wesley, perhaps unfortunately gave this experience the name 'Perfection'.)

It was inevitable that, as the Methodist movement progressed, not only would the Wesleys preach and write upon the theme but it would command the attention of the Methodist people.

Thus, on Tuesday morning, 26 June 1744, the first Conference discussed Sanctification:[3]

> Q.1. What is it to be sanctified?
> A. To be renewed in the image of God, in righteousness and true holiness.
> Q.2. Is faith the condition or the instrument of sanctification, or present salvation?
> A. It is both the condition and the instrument of it. When we begin to believe, then salvation begins. And as faith increases, holiness increases, till we are created anew.

And again:[4]

> Q.6. What is implied in being made perfect in love?
> A. The Loving the Lord our God will all our mind and soul and strength: Deut.vi.5., xxx.6., Ezek.xxxvi.

The following year, the subject was taken up again:

> Q.1. When does inward sanctification begin?
> A. In the moment we are justified, the seed of every virtue is then instantaneously sown in the soul. From that time the believer gradually dies to sin and grows in grace, Yet sin remains in him, yes, the seed of all sin, till he is sanctified throughout in spirit, soul and body.
> Q.2. What will become of a Heathen, a Papist, or a Church-of-England man, if he dies without being thus sanctified?
> A. He cannot see the Lord, but none who seeks it sincerely shall or can die without it; though possibly he may not attain it till the very article of death.

---

3. Bennet *Minutes* (London, 1896, pp.11 and 12.)
4. *ibid.* (pp.23-4.)

Q.3.   Is it ordinarily given till a little before death?

A.   It is not, to those who expect it no sooner nor probably ask for it.

Q.4.   But ought we to expect it sooner?

A.   Why not? Although we grant 1. That the generality of believers (whom we have hitherto known) are not so sanctified till near death. 2. That few of those to whom St Paul wrote his Epistles were so at that time he wrote. 3. Nor he himself at the time of writing his former Epistles; yet this does not prove that we may not today.

It was also asked whether or not a sanctified man could carry on in business and it was decided that he could because there need be no distraction. Marriage, too, was declared to be no obstacle. It was also decided that St John was amongst those who had experienced sanctification fully.[5] A justified man, however, could not recognize a sanctified person unless he possessed a 'peculiar gift of God' – for the spiritual man was judged of no man. What was more, they should beware of bearing hard on those who thought they had attained Entire Sanctification.

Q.10.   In what manner should we preach entire sanctification?

A.   Scarce at all to those who are not pressing forward; to those who are, always by way of promise, always drawing rather than driving.

Q.11.   How should we wait for the fulfilling of this promise?

A.   In universal obedience; in keeping all the commandments; In denying ourselves and taking up our cross daily. These are the general means which God hath ordained for our receiving His sanctifying grace. The particular are prayer, searching the Scriptures, communicating, and fasting.

---

5.   i.e. John Ch.iv.verse17: 'Herein (or through Him) is our love made perfect, that we may have boldness in the day of judgment, because as He is so are we in this world.'

In 1733, Wesley preached the first sermon which touched on the subject of Perfection. It was based on Romans Ch.2. verse 29 entitled: *Circumcision of the Heart.*[6] Circumcision of the heart was '...that habitual disposition of soul, which, in the sacred writings, is termed holiness; and which directly implies, the being cleansed from sin...being endued with those virtues which were also in Christ Jesus'; the being so 'renewed in the spirit of our mind,' as to be 'perfect as our Father in heaven is perfect.' Love was the fulfilling of the law, the end of the commandment. It was not only the first and great commandment, but all the commandments in one: 'Thou shalt love the Lord Thy God with all thy heart, and with all thy soul, and with all thy mind, and with all thy strength.'

A similar theme was worked out in the sermon *The Almost Christian.* Being 'altogether a Christian' implied love of God and love of neighbour.[7]

After the interview in 1740 with Bishop Gibson, Wesley proceeded to preach a sermon on *Christian Perfection.* He set out to show in what sense Christians were not perfect and in what sense they were.[8] Christians were not perfect in knowledge as to be free from ignorance, or from mistake or error. Neither could they be free from temptation or 'infirmities'. Christian Perfection was but another word for holiness. Christians were, however, perfect insofar as they did not 'continue in sin', i.e. were made free from outward sin. For this assertion, Wesley claimed the literal interpretation of the Scriptures, answering in his sermon, every possible objection. He said: 'In conformity, therefore, both to the doctrine of St John, and to the whole tenor of the New Testament, we fix this conclusion – *A Christian is so far perfect, as not to commit sin.*[9] Furthermore, the Christian was free from evil thoughts and evil tempers. These arose from

---

6. J.W.S. (Vol.1, pp.264-279.) Sermon preached before the University of Oxford at St Mary's Church.
7. J.W.S. (Vol.1, pp.61-63.) Sermon preached before the University of Oxford at St Mary's Church.
8. J.W.S. (Vol.2, p.150ff.) Based on Phil. Ch.3.verse.12: 'Not as though I had already attained, either were already perfect.'
9. *ibid.* (Vol.2, pp.168-9.)

the heart of man and if the heart of man be no longer evil, these could not proceed from it. The blood of Christ did not cleanse at the hour of death, or in the day of Judgment but cleansed at the present time and that from 'all sin'.[10] However, this freedom from sin was to be modified in its expression or at least explained in a different way as various criticisms were received by Wesley and this will shortly be dealt with at length.

Another modification Wesley made was about the time factor. It will be noticed that in the early days, he insisted upon the gradual work of grace in the Christian. He doubted that perfection could be given instantaneously, maybe, as Colin Williams suggests, because of his own failure to receive the gift.[11] However, after many had claimed to receive it in the year 1760, he began to emphasize instantaneous reception. He wrote:

> 'Neither dare we affirm, as some have done, that all this salvation is given at once. There is indeed an instantaneous, as well as a gradual, work of God in His children; and there wants not, we know, a cloud of witnesses who have received, in one moment, either a clear sense of the forgiveness of their sins, or the abiding witness of the Holy Spirit. But we do not know a single instance, in any place, of a person's receiving, in one and the same moment, remission of sins, the abiding witness of the Spirit, and a new clean heart.'[12]

Preceding the instantaneous gift was the gradual work but the emphasis was on the former. So Wesley, in his *Plain Account*, summed up his

10. Affixed to this sermon was Charles Wesley's hymn on Perfect Love: 'God of all Power, and Truth, and Grace,' the last verse of which ran:
   'Now let me gain perfection's height!
   Now let me into nothing fall!
   Be less than nothing in my sight,
   And feel that Christ is all in all!'
11. Williams, Colin W. *John Wesley's Theology Today* (London, 1960, p.184.)
12. Wesley, John *A Plain Account of Christian Perfection* (London, 1960, p.24.)

doctrine succinctly:

> '(i) That Christian perfection is that love of God and our
> neighbour which implies deliverance from *all sin*;
> (ii) That this is received merely by faith.
> (iii) That it is given *instantaneously* in one moment.'

The doctrine of Perfection was to cause Wesley more criticism than he received in respect of any other idea which he held. It is not surprising that his first critic was Whitefield. Both in letters and sermons, he opposed Wesley with fierceness, but also with genuine affection. In a letter, he remonstrated with John:

> 'I am sorry, honoured Sir, to hear by many letters that you
> seem to own a sinless perfection in this life attainable. I think
> I cannot answer you better than a venerable old minister in
> these parts answered a Quaker: "Bring me a man that hath
> really arrived to this, and I will pay his expenses, let him come
> from where he will." I know not what you may think; I do not
> expect to say indwelling sin is finished and destroyed in me till
> I bow down my head and give up the ghost. Besides, dear Sir,
> what a fond conceit it is to cry up perfection, and cry down the
> doctrine of final perseverance.'[13]

In another epistle he wrote:

> '*Sinless Perfection*, I think, is unattainable in this life,' he
> declared. 'Show me a man that could ever justly say, "I am
> perfect."'[14]

---

13. This letter is given only in Paterson Gladstone, James *George Whitefield. MA: Field-Preacher* (London, 1901, pp.150-1.) No date.
14. Written to Charles Wesley. Tyerman, Luke *The Life of the Revd George Whitefield* (London, 1890, Vol.1, p.413.) This, of course, was a travesty of Wesley's teaching.

Again, he declared, it was enough if it could be said when they bowed down their heads and gave up the ghost. Indwelling sin remained until death, even in the regenerate – a view which he claimed was consistent with the Articles of the Church. There was no man living who did not sin in thought, word and deed. It was absurd to affirm such a thing as perfection and yet deny final perseverances. To be incapable of sinning and capable of being finally damned was a contradiction in terms.

Another hortatory letter was written in similar terms on 28 September 1740.[15] The same tone prevailed in a further epistle of 9 November 1740 addressed to John:

'O that we were of one mind! for I am yet persuaded you greatly err. You have set a mark you will never arrive at, till you come to glory. I think few enjoy such continued manifestations of God's presence as I do, and have done for some years; but dare not pretend to say I shall be absolutely perfect.'[16]

Almost in desperation, Whitefield wrote yet another lengthy letter to Wesley suggesting, not very discreetly, an alternative to preaching perfection. The following quotation revealed his intention:

'I believe your fighting so strenuously against the doctrine of election, and pleading so vehemently for a sinless perfection, are among the reasons or culpable causes why you are kept out of the liberties of the gospel, and from that full assurance of faith, which they enjoy, who have experimentally tasted, and daily fed upon God's electing, everlasting love. Dear, dear Sir, O be not offended! For Christ's sake, be not rash! Give yourself to reading. Study the covenant of grace. Down

15. Tyerman, Luke *The Life of the Revd George Whitefield* (London, 1890, Vol.1, p.414.)
16. *ibid.* (Vol.1, pp.435-6.)

with your carnal reasoning! Be a little child, and then, instead of pawning your salvation, as you have done in a late hymnbook, if the doctrine of *universal redemption* be not true; instead of talking of sinless perfection, as you have done in the preface of that hymnbook; and instead of making man's salvation to depend on his own *free will*, as you have done in this sermon, you will compose a hymn in praise of sovereign distinguishing love. You will caution believers against striving to work a perfection out of their own hearts, and print another sermon the reverse of this, and entitle it, "Free Grace *Indeed*". Free, not because free to all; but free, because God may withhold or give it to whom and when He pleases.'[17]

However, according to a letter of 28 April 1741, addressed to Howel Harris, Whitefield, quite mistakenly seemed to think that he was one with the Wesleys in holding a sinless perfection:

'I speak thus, because you seem offended that some affirm there is no such thing as dominion over indwelling sin, nor rest from working for life wholly! We shall never have such a dominion over indwelling sin as to be entirely delivered from the stirring of it; and the greatest saint cannot be assured, but, some time or other, for his humiliation or punishment for unfaithfulness, God may permit it to break out into actual breach of His law, and in a gross way too. Let us not be high-minded, but fear. It is equally true, that we shall not rest wholly from working for life; for whilst there is any part of us unregenerate, that part will be always leading us to the old covenant. But I suppose you have been tinctured with the

---

17. Tyerman, Luke *The Life of the Revd George Whitefield* (London, 1890, Vol.1, pp.469-70.) N.B. Forty years afterwards, Wesley referred to this difference of opinion and said it was not only the doctrine which caused the separation, but Whitefield's manner in which he maintained his own ideas. The hymnbook referred to was the 1741 edition.

doctrine of sinless perfection. No wonder, therefore, you write thus...'[18]

Wesley was the object of further attacks, mainly during the period 1760-3, no doubt due to the extravagance of certain of his followers to which reference will be made later.

Henry Venn's objection to the doctrine called forth Wesley's reply on 22 June 1763. Wesley maintained that Venn's unwillingness to co-operate with him and allow Methodist societies to be established in his parish had, as a pretended reason, none other than his preaching 'Perfection':

'To this poor end, the doctrine of Perfection has been brought in head and shoulders. And when such concessions were made as would abundantly satisfy any fair and candid man, they were no nearer – rather farther off, for they had no desire to be satisfied. To make this *dear* breach wider and wider, stories were carefully gleaned up, improved, yes, invented and detailed, both concerning me and the "perfect ones". And when anything very bad has come to hand, some have rejoiced as though they had found great spoils... "But you hold Perfection" – True – that is, loving God with *all* our heart, and serving Him with *all* our strength. I teach nothing more, nothing less than this. And whatever infirmity, defect, ανομια, is consistent with this any man may teach, and I shall not contradict him...If I was as strenuous with regard to perfection on one side as you have been on the other, I should deny you to be a *sufficient* preacher; but this I never did...'[19]

---

18. *ibid.* (Vol.1, pp.478-490.)
19. J.W.L. (Vol.4, pp.214-8.) Venn's Calvinism and hostility to 'Perfection' seem to have been due to the influence of his second wife Mira. See Hennell, M. *John Venn and the Clapham Sect* (London, 1958) where Venn's change of views is discussed. Also see Venn, John *The Life and a Selection of Letters of the Late Henry Venn, MA* (London, 1837, pp.31-34.)

Grimshaw of Haworth was the one Evangelical who after having disagreed with Wesley and his teaching on Perfection, went out of his way to understand it fully and thus satisfy himself that it was Scripturally based. In a letter to Charles Wesley on 31 March 1760 he stated:

'The doctrine of perfection runs very high, just now, in these parts. About Otley and Leeds, I am told, not fewer than thirty profess sinless perfection; and thirty more, I expect, will pretend thereto shortly. If it be of God, it is well. Time will prove it. I wish they knew their own hearts. My perfection is, to see my own imperfection; my comfort, to feel that I have the world, flesh and devil to overthrow through the Spirit and merits of my dear Saviour; and my desire and hope is, to love God with all my heart, mind, soul, and strength, to the last gasp of my life. This is my perfection. I know no other, excepting to lay down my life and my sword together.'[20]

It is interesting to note that at this time, two of Grimshaw's lay-preachers, William Darney and James Wild in addition to a number of Wesley's own preachers, did not fully accept the doctrine of Christian Perfection *for fear it might be held to mean sinless*[21] *perfection.* Nevertheless Grimshaw continued to be somewhat disturbed by this teaching. On the 6 July 1761, Wesley entered the 'Haworth Round' and preached at Otley, carefully examining the society and especially those who professed Christian Perfection. The next day he wrote a letter to Alexander Coates, defining his doctrine:

'The perfection I teach is perfect love; loving God with all the heart: receiving Christ as prophet, priest, and king, to reign alone over all our thoughts, words, and actions...To say

---

20. Laycock, J.W. *Methodist Heroes in the Great Haworth Round AD 1734 to 1784* (Keighley, 1909, p.224.)
21. *ibid.* (p.214.)

Christ will not reign alone in our hearts, *in this life*, will not
enable us to give him *all* our hearts.'[22]

However, on Monday 13 July 1761, Wesley obligingly preached a
sermon at 5 o'clock in the morning at Haworth, on the manner of waiting
for 'perfect love'. This, he stated in his *Journal*,[23] was especially for the
satisfaction of Grimshaw; but Grimshaw was still not convinced. It
appeared, as on other occasions, that the doctrine was abused by certain
over-zealous Methodists who made exorbitant claims as to their attainment
of perfection.

He wrote:

'And as to the other [sinless perfection], your resolutions in
Conference are such, if John Emmet informs me right, as
seem to afford me sufficient satisfaction...I cannot be
reconciled...that he who disbelieves the doctrine of sinless
perfection is a child of the devil. That he is no true Christian,
who has not attained it, etc., etc...'[24]

He wished Wesley would admonish the preachers who were making
such statements:

'*Sinless* perfection is a grating term to many of our dear
brethren,' he continued, 'even to those who are as desirous
and solicitous to be truly holy in heart and life, as any,
perhaps of them who affect to speak in this unscriptural way.'

Grimshaw came to the heart of the matter when he suggested that the
term *sinless* be not used and a term 'less offensive' substituted, and

---

22. J.W.L. (Vol.4, pp.157-8.) Coates was a Scotsman and became Wesley's oldest
    itinerant.
23. J.W.J. (Vol.4, p.469.)
24. Laycock, J.W. *Methodist Heroes in the Great Haworth Round. AD 1734-1784*
    (Keighley, 1909, pp.220-221.)

which sufficiently expressed true Christian holiness:

> 'By this I mean,' he said, '(and why may I not tell you what I mean?) all that holiness of heart and life, which is *literally, plainly, abundantly,* taught us all over the Bible, and without which, no man, however justified through faith in the *righteousness of Christ,* can ever expect to see the Lord. That is that holiness, that Christian perfection, that sanctification, which, without affecting *strange, fulsome, offensive, unscriptural* expressions and representations, I, and I dare say, every true and sincere hearted member in our societies, and I hope, in all others, ardently desire and strenuously labour to attain. This is attainable; for this, therefore, let us contend; to this the more, as we see the day, the happy, the glorious day approaching...'

In a letter to Charles Wesley dated 6 March 1763, he reaffirmed his rejection of sinless perfection:

> 'Scriptural or Christian Perfection I allow and avow. Sinless Perfection I disclaim...'[25]

He wrote in a pastoral letter to the Societies in Newcastle on 27 January 1761:

> 'If the term sinless perfection be disgustful to some, true Christian perfection will be grateful to all who know Christ. 'Tis to love God with all our heart, mind, soul and strength. This is Scriptural perfection. This is the work of God.'[26]

---

25. Laycock, J.W. *Methodist Heroes in the Great Haworth Round. AD 1734-1784* (Keighley, 1909, p.238.)
26. Cragg, G.C. *Grimshaw of Haworth* (London, 1947, pp.51-2.)

Wesley had made his one and only convert to his concept of Christian Perfection among the Calvinistic Evangelicals!

It should be noted that Grimshaw wrote his own creed! and Article 22 averred:

> 'I believe it is by the spirit we are enabled not to eradicate, as some affirm (for that is absurd) but to subjugate the *old man*, to suppress, not extirpate, the exorbitances of our fleshly appetites; to resist and overcome the world and the devil, and to grow in grace gradually, not *repentively*, i.e. suddenly, *or all at once*, upon the perfect and eternal day. This is all I know or acknowledge, to be Christian perfection, or sanctification.'[27]

Not all Wesley's opponents wrote directly against him. Some implied in their writings their disagreement with him on this matter. John Newton had but one solitary passage in which he made his views known:

> 'Far, very far, am I from that unscriptural sentiment of sinless perfection in fallen man. To those who have a due sense of the spirituality and ground of the divine precepts, and of what passes in their own hearts, there will never be wanting causes of humiliation and self-abasement on the account of sin; yet still there is a liberty and privilege attainable by the gospel beyond what is ordinarily thought of.'[28]

Samuel Walker of Truro was another opponent of 'Perfection'. Whilst Wesley was not mentioned in his writings on perfection, the existence of the controversy was implied. Wesley had been perturbed by the condition

---

27. Cragg, G.C. *Grimshaw of Haworth* (London, 1947, p.112.) It will be noticed that whilst agreeing with Wesley's doctrine of perfection, he differs on the subsidiary point of instantaneous perfection to which Wesley held.
28. Newton, John *Cardiphonia, or The Utterance of the Heart in the Course of a Real Correspondence (Letters to a Nobleman)* (London, 1780, p.24.)

of his Cornish converts and felt that their need was the preaching of perfection. He wrote in the *Journal*:

> 'The more I converse with the believers in Cornwall, the more
> I am convinced that they have sustained great loss for want of
> hearing the doctrine of Christian Perfection clearly and strongly
> enforced. I see, wherever this is not done, the believers grow
> dead and cold. Nor can this be prevented but by keeping up in
> them an hourly expectation of being perfected in love. I say an
> hourly expectation; for to expect it at death, or some time
> hence, is much the same as not expecting it at all.'[29]

Walker disagreed with Wesley's teaching. He believed that perfect holiness was necessary to a Christian's happiness in God. It was a divine work of grace which developed gradually and was not complete until the future life.[30] Other sermons, under the title: *The Purifier* were no doubt published with Wesley's views in mind. Again, sanctification was gradual. It was a work of purification – the putting off the old man, and crucifying the flesh with the affections and lusts. The question was not whether a man was perfect, but whether he was regenerate – and not whether he had no corruption within him, but whether he had grace in him.[31] It was only the rising and advance of grace in the soul, which put out corruption until the whole soul was perfected after God's image. It was not achieved by man's own effort but the method used was suffering in order to call forth meekness, humility and patience.[32] He came, however, quite near to one of Wesley's precepts when he said that a regenerate man could not wilfully choose to sin on any motive. When he did sin, it was by surprise and infirmity. God lifted him up again, though it was by severe discipline.[33]

The question now arises, were the criticisms of the Evangelicals

29. J.W.J. (Vol.4, p.529.)
30. Walker, Samuel *Fifty-Two Sermons* (London, 1763, Vol.1, p.177.)
31. Walker, Samuel *Christ the Purifier* (London, 1824, p.18.)
32. *ibid.* (p.48.)
33. Walker, Samuel *Christ The Purifier* (London, 1824, p.169.)

justified? It must be stated quite fairly that to a considerable extent they were and that there were certainly a few faults on Wesley's side.

Nowhere did Wesley use the term 'sinless perfection' in his teaching, but his words and his terms certainly lay open to being misinterpreted as this.

One of his earliest sermons, viz: *The Almost Christian*,[34] declared that being 'altogether a Christian' implied love of God and love of neighbour. This love of God he stated:

> 'Is such...as engrosses the whole heart, as takes up all the affections, as fills the entire capacity of the soul, and employs the utmost extent of all its faculties...He is crucified to "the desire of the flesh, the desire of the eye, and the pride of life..."'

and again:

> 'It is a sure trust and confidence which a man hath in God, that, by the merits of Christ, his sins are forgiven, and he is reconciled to the favour of God; whereof doth follow a loving heart, to obey His commandments.'

Another sermon, *The Circumcision of the Heart*, preached earlier still,[35] said this circumcision consisted of:

> '...that habitual disposition of soul which, in the sacred writings, is termed holiness; and which directly implies, the being "cleansed from sin, from all filthiness both of flesh and spirit"; and by consequences, the being endued with those virtues which were also in Christ Jesus; the being so "renewed in the spirit of our mind", as to be perfect as our Father in

---

34. J.W.S. (Vol.1, p.62, Preached in 1741.)
35. *ibid.* (Vol.1, pp.268-9, Preached in 1733.)

heaven is perfect.'

Sinless Perfection in all but a word!

Another instance may be gathered from the sermon *The Witness of Our Own Spirit*, and, although no date was given, it was obviously an early one, purely because of its teaching on perfection:[36]

> 'And now we can perform, through God, what to man was impossible...We can do all things in light and power of that love, through Christ which strengtheneth us.'

and again:

> '...my conscience beareth me witness in the Holy Ghost by the light He continually pours in upon it, that I "walk worthy of the vocation wherewith I am called; that I abstain from all appearance of evil, fleeing from sin as from the face of a serpent".'

Now Wesley said in the *Plain Account*[37] that he scrupled not to call his view of religion as expressed in the *Circumcision of the Heart* – Christian Perfection. 'This was the view of religion I then had...This is the view I have of it now, without any material addition or diminution...'[38] If this were so, the Evangelicals who read those sermons and saw the Minutes of the 1744 Conference could be excused for believing Wesley taught Sinless Perfection – that once justified, the believer was entirely freed from sin, that it was a moral perfection.

However, only one Evangelical could really be thus excused – and that

---

36. J.W.S. (Vol.1, p.232.) Cf. Letter to Thomas Olivers, dated 24 March 1757. (J.W.L. Vol.3, p.212): 'One fruit given at the same instant (at least usually) is a direct, positive testimony of the Spirit that the work is done, that they cannot fall away – that they cannot sin.'
37. London, 1960, p.8.
38. J.W.S. (Vol.2, p.378.) Compare this reference with the above quotation.

was Whitefield who protested to Wesley during the period 1740-1742. It
will be seen that the other Evangelicals did their protesting after 1760 and
it was also after this date that Wesley gave a clearer indication of what he
meant by 'perfection'. In 1763, he wrote his sermon on *Sin in Believers*
in which he answered the question: 'Is there sin in him that is in Christ?':

> '...that, although we are renewed, cleansed, purified, sanctified,
> the moment we truly believe in Christ, yet we are not then
> renewed, cleansed, purified, altogether; but the flesh, the evil
> nature, still *remain* (though subdued), and wars against the
> Spirit...'[39]

Surely this was contradictory to Wesley's statement quoted above that
his views had not altered. The foregoing quotation was a serious
modification of his former teaching.

Instance too, his 1767 sermon on *The Repentance of Believers*:

> 'From what has been said we may easily learn the
> mischievousness of that opinion – that we are wholly sanctified
> when we are justified; that our hearts are then cleansed from
> all sin...it is by no means true that inward sin is then totally
> destroyed...we still retain a depth of sin...'[40]

In a letter to Mrs Maitland written on 12 May 1763 he explained:

> 'Absolute and infallible *perfection*? I never contended for it.
> *Sinless Perfection*? Neither do I contend *for this*, seeing the
> term is not scriptural. A perfection that perfectly fulfils the
> whole law, and so needs not the merits of Christ? I acknowledge
> none such – I do now, and always did, protest against it...'

39. J.W.S. (Vol.2, p.378.)
40. J.W.S. (Vol.1, pp.394-5.)

A few lines further, he gave an unsatisfying answer to the question, 'But is there not sin in those that are perfect?':

> 'I believe not; but be that as it may, they feel none, no temper, but pure love, while they rejoice, pray and give thanks continually. And whether sin is *suspended* or *extinguished*. I will not dispute, it is enough that they feel nothing but love...'[41]

'Therefore,' he wrote in the *Plain Account*, '*Sinless Perfection*[42] is a phrase I never use, lest I should seem to contradict myself.' However, he reiterated what he had already said in his sermon on *Christian Perfection*, namely that perfection did not exclude involuntary transgression as infirmities, ignorance and mistakes. Others may call these sins, but he did not. Little wonder that Sidney in his biography of Rowland Hill[43] said of such a perfection that 'It is a singular kind of *perfection* that lacks all these requisites; and is much the same as though a man were to call a thing infinite or eternal, but at the same time premise it was not so infinite as infinity, or eternal as eternity.'

A second fault lay in Wesley's adoption of the very term *Perfection*. It was an unfortunate choice. *Perfection* was quite naturally associated with 'sinless' or 'moral' and those who made this association amongst his critics would not entirely be to blame. G.C.B. Davies makes the excellent suggestion that Wesley should have used the term *Perfect Love* which would have been self-explanatory of the doctrine Wesley taught.[44] It would also have helped to clear up the ambiguity about his notion of sin, namely that sin was a failure in 'perfect love'. There would have been less controversy over whether or not sin was eradicated completely

---

41. J.W.L. (Vol.4, pp.212-3.) Cf. his statement in *Brief Thoughts on Christian Perfection* contained in the Plain Account etc. (London, 1960, p.112): 'And I do not contend for the term *sinless*, though I do not object against it...'
42. *Plain Account of Christian Perfection* (London, 1960, p.45.)
43. Sidney, E. *The Life of the Revd Rowland Hill, AM* (London, 1834, p.435.)
44. Davies, G.C.B. *The Early Cornish Evangelicals. 1735-1760. A Study of Walker of Truro and others* (London, 1951, p.157.)

in the believer, but rather sin could exist less and less as love increased –
it would literally 'crowd out sin'.

The Evangelicals were no less at fault for not bearing with Wesley in
his modifications and for taking his earlier statements as final. He
believed that sanctification could be entire before death; they believed
that perfection could never be attained before death and in many cases it
was after death. To them it was a gradual process; to Wesley, whilst it
could be gradual, it could also be instantaneous. To the Evangelicals, sin
was always present; Wesley believed it could be overcome. He admitted
infirmities, mistakes, ignorance or error remained but were not sins. To
this the Evangelicals could never agree.

There was one other cause of criticism which Wesley received from
his Evangelical opponents. It was indeed a lesser point than those just
discussed, but nevertheless relevant. What of those who actually professed
to have received entire sanctification or perfection?

It will be recalled that Venn based part of his objection to Wesley's
teaching on the effect it was having on some of his members in
Huddersfield. Grimshaw was equally perturbed by similar effects in his
'Round', especially in the town of Otley.[45] But the main instances were in
London and their importance was not so much the criticism they incurred
for Wesley – rather the havoc they created in Methodism. Yet they
became an added basis of understandable criticism by the Evangelicals.

Thomas Maxfield was one of Wesley's earliest lay-preachers, for
whom, it will be remembered, ordination had been procured from the
Bishop of Londonderry. Because of this he was the object of envy and the
recipient of no small amount of criticism from other preachers. In 1760,

---

45. Otley was the place where the perfection movement had its northern origin.
    'Here,' said Wesley, 'began that glorious work of sanctification which had been
    nearly at a stand for twenty years; but which now, from time to time, spread
    through various parts of Yorkshire, afterward in London, then through most parts
    of England; next through Dublin, Limerick, and all the south and west of Ireland.
    And wherever the work of sanctification increased, the whole work of God
    increased in all its branches. Tyerman, L. *The Life and Times of John Wesley*
    (London, 1871-2, Vol.2, pp.416-7.)

Wesley had placed him in charge of a small group in London, each member of which had professed entire sanctification. They claimed to have seen visions, had dreams and impressions, which, they alleged, came from God. Instead of censuring them, he encouraged them. Soon, this little band held all others in contempt and would hear no other preacher except Maxfield. He confirmed that they should not be willing to be taught except by those with at least as much 'grace' as they themselves possessed. By the time Wesley returned to London in October, 1762, the society there had split and those who followed Maxfield, now greatly grown in number, had become almost a separate community. Naturally Wesley rebuked them, but two of them, a man and his wife, returned their membership tickets to Wesley.

On 2 November 1762, Wesley wrote Maxfield a long letter telling him of all he had heard about his activities:

> 'I like your doctrine of Perfection, of pure love; love excluding sin, your insisting that it is merely by faith; that consequently it is instantaneous (though preceded and followed by a gradual work), and that it may be now, at this instant...But I dislike your supposing man may be as perfect as an angel; that he can be absolutely perfect...'[46]

Maxfield protested that he had no thought of separation. He felt that Wesley and his brother had contradicted the highest truths in their teaching and what was more, almost all the ministers of Christ believed sin would remain in the heart of man as long as he lived.

George Bell was another of the 'sanctified'. Converted in 1758, he claimed sanctification in March 1761. Soon afterwards he wrote to Wesley and the latter's suspicions were aroused by this 'enthusiasm'. Bell began to hold meetings of his own, saying that God had done away with all preaching and sacraments and was to be found nowhere except in his own meetings. Both he and his followers professed a sanctification

---

46. J.W.L. (Vol.4, pp.192ff.)

which could never fall. They claimed to have the gift of healing and believed they would never die. Wesley determined to hear Bell for himself but without being seen. Having done so, he remonstrated with Bell for his outlandish claims and practices. In vain Wesley preached especially on sanctification – in what sense it was gradual and in what sense it was instantaneous; on humility and simplicity and a willingness to be taught. Bell became worse and crowned his follies by prophesying that the end of the world would take place on 28 February 1763. The outcome of this was that Bell was arrested on the very day the end was predicted to take place! This was also the end of his association with the Wesleys. Maxfield later left on 28 April 1763, taking with him more than two hundred of Wesley's London society and founded his own chapel.[47]

That was not all. The matter was aired in the Press. A writer using the pseudonym 'Philodemas' complained of Methodist extravagances in *Lloyd's Evening Post* making special reference to Bell's prediction. Damage to Methodism was great and nothing could have served Wesley's critics better than these events. However, two good results came from this trouble. The first was that Wesley wrote in 1763 his sermon on *Sin in Believers* which greatly modified his perfection teaching. The second was the publication of his *Cautions and Directions given to the greatest professors in the Methodist Societies*. In it he bade believers to watch and pray continually against pride; to beware of enthusiasm; to beware of antinomianism; to beware of sins of omission; to beware of desiring anything but God; to beware of schism and be exemplary in all things.[48]

Maybe it was somewhat late, but all Whitefield and his fellow Calvinists had feared and warned him about had taken place and now Wesley learnt from his mistake in not stating fully and clearly what he meant by Christian Perfection, leaving no loopholes for enemies to misinterpret it.

The doctrine of Perseverance belongs to Augustinian and Calvinistic theology. It affirmed quite simply that those, once truly regenerate or

---

47. J.W.L. (Vol.4, pp.192ff.)
48. It must be remembered that Wesley, the purveyor of this doctrine never claimed entire sanctification for himself.

united to Christ by genuine faith, could neither totally nor finally fall away from the state of grace; but would certainly persevere to the end and be eternally saved. It flowed quite naturally from the central concept of the Sovereignty of God who saved sinners by unconditional election and irresistible grace. The Arminians and the Lutherans on the other hand taught that the justified and regenerate by neglecting grace and falling into many sins could finally fall into perdition.

This doctrine which John Fletcher described as 'the first card which the devil played against man "Ye shall not surely die..."[49] was held and taught by the Calvinistic Evangelicals as a necessary corollary to the doctrine of Election. Yet it will be seen from their writings[50] that the emphasis they made was not so much on the fact that the justified Christian *would* persevere but rather that he *must* do so. If this did not happen, then the Christian's profession of religion '...will be utterly vain, for they only that endure to the end shall be saved.'[51]

It was a promise of God to his people, made possible from the Unchangeableness of God, the intercession of Christ, the union which subsisted between Him and his people and from the principle of spiritual life he had implanted in their hearts, which in its own nature was connected with everlasting life for '...grace was the seed of glory.'

Three facts of importance were to be noted, according to Berridge.[52] The first was that Perseverance was promised to the saints but it was only possible by the effect of persevering grace which must be prayed for. Perseverance did 'not make us in Christ', but showed we were so. A persevering walk was an evidence that we were blessed with persevering grace. Secondly the *persevering* had to be done by the Christian. If

49. Fletcher, John *The Whole Works of* (London, 1836, p.268.) *The Last Check to Antinomianism*
50. The writings are actually very few, e.g. Whitefield did not preach one sermon on the subject, but only made brief references to it.
51. Omicron (Newton, John *nom de plume*) *Twenty-Six Letters on Religious Subjects* (London, 1775, p.91.)
52. Berridge, John *The Christian World Unmasked: Pray come and Peep* (London, 1850, pp.136-7.)

perseverance was promised to the saints, then they must be found persevering in the path of duty and the means of grace, otherwise they were condemned by the very doctrine and the evidence was destroyed. The first fact was that the doctrine yielded no real shelter to licentiousness or laziness. It lent no wanton cloak to corrupt hearts.

The value of the doctrine of perseverance, according to 'Omicron' was the same as that of Election – it was a 'comfortable' one and it cut off all pretence of boasting and self-dependence and exalted the Saviour. It stained the pride of all human glory and left us nothing to glory in but the Lord.[53]

Thus Whitefield, in a farewell sermon confessed to being amazed that there were people who could fight against this doctrine of Perseverance. Of course, he admitted that there were abuses of this teaching:

> 'What?' he asked. 'Because some people spoil good food, are we never to eat it?'[54]

When the dispute between the Arminian and Calvinistic principles had caused the rift between Whitefield and the Wesleys, it was proposed to Wesley by John Cennick,[55] one of his preachers, that a conference be called to reconcile the opposing parties. To this, the Moravians were also invited. The attempt, made in 1743, proved abortive. Wesley, in preparation, drew up a list of the disputed points in which he stated how far he could make doctrinal concessions. It will be seen that he was prepared to go a good way – a determination he was soon to withdraw:

> 'With regard to...Final Perseverance, I incline to believe (I believe),[56]

---

53. 'Omicron' (i.e. Newton, John) *op.cit.* (p.94.)
54. Whitefield, George *Select Sermons of* (Edited by J.C. Ryle and R. Elliot) (London, 1960, p.196.)
55. He was soon to leave Wesley owing to his developing Calvinistic views. He became a Moravian.
56. The words in brackets are insertions in the first edition.

That there is a state attainable in this life, from which a man cannot finally fall; and
That he has attained this who (is, according to St Paul's account, "a new creature"; that is, who) can say, "Old things are passed away; all things in me 'are become new.'" (And I do not deny that all those eminently styled The Elect will infallibly persevere to the end.)'[57]

Henry Moore gives an important note on this paragraph. He says:

'Mr Wesley told me, that, *at the time he wrote this*, he believed (with Macarius, a writer of the fourth century) that all who are perfected in love, 1.John.iv, were thus elect. But he afterwards doubted of this. I believe all that can be safely held on the doctrine of the Divine Predestination, is contained in these propositions; so rare a talent had Mr Wesley of speaking much in few words...'[58]

However, by 1751, Wesley had a firmer view on the subject which amounted to complete rejection. This was set forth in his *Serious Thoughts upon the Perseverance of the Saints* which he published that year.

Many books, he admitted, had already been written on the subject, but because of their length they were not easily understood. By the saints, he understood them to be those who were holy or righteous in the judgement of God Himself. 'Those who are endued with the faith that purifies the heart, that produces a good conscience; those who are grafted into the good olive tree, the spiritual, invisible church; those who are branches of the true vine, of whom Christ says: "I am the vine, ye are the branches"; those who so effectually know Christ as by that knowledge to have escaped the pollutions of the world; those who see the light of the glory of

---

57. J.W.J. (Vol.3, p.86.)
58. Moore, Henry *The Life of the Revd John Wesley, MA* (London, 1824, Vol.1, p.508.)

God in the face of Jesus Christ, and who have been made partakers of the Holy Ghost, of the witness and fruits of the Spirit; those who live by faith in the Son of God; those who are sanctified by the blood of the covenant; those to whom all, or any of these characters belong, I mean by the term SAINTS.'

Could any of these fall away? he asked. By falling away he meant not 'Barely falling into sin', but totally. Quoting from Ezekiel, chapters 18 and 23 and also Psalm 89, he affirmed that they could perish everlastingly. In fairness, Wesley quoted Scripture which may have seemed to deny this assertion, but pointed out that even though God has 'loved them with an everlasting love', this did not prevent their falling away permanently. There was no inconsistency between Scriptures. Jeremiah also said: 'I have loved thee with everlasting love; therefore with loving kindness have I drawn thee.' Did these words assert that no righteous man ever turned from his righteousness? No such thing, answered Wesley.[59]

He proceeded:

> 'One who is endued with the faith that purifies the heart, that produces a good conscience, may nevertheless so fall from God, as to perish everlastingly. For thus saith the inspired apostle, "War a good warfare, holding faith and a good conscience, which some having put away, concerning faith have made shipwreck!" (1.Tim.Ch.1, verses 18 & 19.)
> Observe 1. These men (such as Hymenus and Alexander) had once the faith that purifies the heart, that produces a good conscience; this they once had, or they could not have put it away.
> Observe 2. They made shipwreck of the faith which necessarily implies the total and final loss of it. For a vessel once wrecked can never be recovered. It is totally and finally lost.'

Furthermore he declared:

---

59. J.W.W. (Vol.14, pp.418-428.)

'How can this be reconciled with the words of Our Lord, "He that believeth shall be saved"?' This text implies that he that believeth, if he continue in faith, shall be saved; he that believeth not. If he continue in unbelief, shall be damned.'

'Those who "see the light of the glory of God in the face of Jesus Christ" and (who have been made partakers of the Holy Ghost) of the witness and the fruits of the Spirit; may nevertheless so fall from God, as to perish everlastingly. Those who live by faith, may yet fall from God and so perish. Those who are sanctified by the blood of the covenant, may so fall from God as to perish.'

Lastly, Wesley asked, Could a child of God then go to Hell? Or could a man be a child of God today, and a child of the devil tomorrow? If God was our Father once, was he not our Father always? He answered that a child of God, that is, a true believer (for *he* that believeth is born of God) whilst he continued a true believer cannot go to hell, but, if a believer makes shipwreck of the faith, he was no longer a child of God. Then he could go to hell, yes, and certainly will, if he continued in unbelief. If the Scriptures were true, he argued, finally, it was quite possible for those who were at the moment, followers of Christ, to fall away and perish everlastingly, therefore, he concluded: 'Let him who standeth, take heed, lest he fall.'

Perseverance of the Saints was as much the goal of the Calvinist believer as was Perfection to the Methodist. It will have been seen from an earlier part of this chapter, that the evangelical opposition to much that Wesley taught about Christian Perfection was based on misunderstanding. The same could justifiably be said of Wesley's rejection of Perseverance.

If by Perseverance, moral endeavour was meant, there was little doubt that Wesley could have accepted it; but his obvious fear was that the Calvinists implied an automatic perseverance – that once regenerate, the believer could not possibly fall. As it was God's will to save him, it was also His will to keep him so to the end and 'none shall pluck them out of

His hand'. To this, Wesley quite rightly could never assent. He had, in his experience seen too many who had later fallen after they had begun with a genuine conversion. Inevitably looming close and large behind this reason – was the bogey of Antinomianism. Just as the doctrine of Predestination and Election gave rise to the possible setting aside of the moral law, so Perseverance could make a man morally careless – for would he not gain his eternal destiny, come what may? It will be noted again, how Wesley was constantly on the watch for any notion that would encourage an Antinomian stand. If there was one emphasis more important than any other in the Evangelical's presentation of Perseverance, it was that Perseverance was no cover for laziness, carelessness or wickedness. Furthermore there must be endeavour on the part of the believer to fulfil all the duties of the Christian life. This, Wesley seemed to have overlooked in his obsession with Antinomianism. He should have realized that all doctrines were open to abuse and none more than his Christian Perfection, as in the cases mentioned earlier of extravagant claims. An abuse of Perfection was just as liable to lead to an Antinomian attitude as Perseverance. In his earlier writings on Perfection, one gleans the idea that Wesley thought Perfection to be a state from which a man could not fall. This was borne out in his early statement in 1743[60] that he did not deny that '...all those eminently styled The Elect will infallibly persevere to the end.' If Moore's statement about Wesley is to be accepted, then the Elect are the 'perfected' and thus they would persevere.[61] It will be seen how near Wesley came in those early days to the doctrine of Final Perseverance. No doubt his experience of so many who did fall from grace, together with his fear of encouraging Antinomianism changed his views.

Finally, could there not have been any reconciliation between the two views? An Arminian such as Wesley would see in the doctrine of Final Perseverance what he saw in Predestination and Election – a threat to the

---

60.   J.W.J. (Vol.3, p.86.)
61.   Moore, Henry *The Life of the Revd John Wesley, MA* (London, 1824, Vol.1, p.508.)

freedom of the will. It may be thought that a man's will is always uncertain and unstable in its choices. Nevertheless, if a man's will was, after conversion, grounded in goodness, yet still free, his choices would probably be the right ones and his 'Final Perseverance' be assured. Thus 'perseverance' would not be in conflict with the idea of the freedom of the human will. There was, of course, no indication that Wesley ever considered this alternative. He taught a Perfection which a man could attain in this life, but which, on the other hand, he might never attain. The Calvinists held out for every believer, the surety of finally gaining his eternal destiny.

CHAPTER ELEVEN

THE 'MINUTE CONTROVERSY'

JUSTIFICATION BY FAITH

(THE THIRD CALVINISTIC CONTROVERSY)

Before the Hervey–Wesley conflict had ceased, that is, if this could ever be said to have been effected, Wesley began to realize that his relationships with the Evangelicals were worsening. It became a matter of deep concern to him. Men who previously had been on good terms with him were now either cool or openly hostile. A typical example was that of Dr Richard Conyers, LL D, incumbent of Helmsley in North Yorkshire who had previously received Wesley with great warmth. On Tuesday 17 April 1764, John complained that when he called at Conyers' home, the latter was out and the housekeeper 'faintly' asked him in. Wesley noted from books lying open on his table that Conyers was immersed in Calvinism. When Conyers came in, the coolness was obvious and John, to his surprise was not even asked to preach in his church.[1]

In a letter to Lady Huntingdon dated 20 March 1763[2] he complained bitterly that his previous Evangelical friends were crying 'Down with him, down with him, even to the ground'. Only Romaine, he believed, had shown a truly understanding spirit. How wrong Wesley was! Lady

---

1.   J.W.J. (Vol.5, pp.58-9.)
2.   J.W.L. (Vol.4, pp.205-6.)

Huntingdon sent John's letter to Romaine for his comments only to receive a reply stating that Wesley was to be pitied – he was deluded; his societies were in great confusion. Romaine blamed it all on Wesley's preaching 'Perfection'.[3]

Why Wesley should have been surprised at the attitude of many of the Evangelicals is hard to understand. Had he not broken church rules whilst they (or, at least, the greater part of them) confined themselves to their parishes? Had he not employed lay-preachers – a step which most of them had shunned? Had he not preached 'Perfection' whilst they maintained 'Final Perseverance of the Saints'? Did they not hold to Election and Predestination (even if they did cautiously avoid mentioning Reprobation) instead of joining him in proclaiming Universal Redemption? What then, was the cause of Wesley's surprise, hurt and disappointment? His open breach with Whitefield, behind whom was the considerable support, financial and influential, of Lady Huntingdon; his conflict with Hervey which was carried on posthumously after the latter's death; all militated against any possibility of friendship and cooperation.

However, his unfruitful visit to Conyers of Helmsley and a further rebuff from a clergyman at Snainton, a village not far from Helmsley, constrained Wesley only two days later (19 April 1764)[4] to compose a letter to as many Evangelical clergy (regardless of theological allegiance) and others as he expected to be on friendly terms with him. He pleaded for unity even though, maybe, they disagreed about opinions. They could be regular or irregular or partly both. Did they not remember the great work of revival when it began in the country and yet first one and then another broke away, thus hindering its progress. Thus, their common enemies had seen a wonderful opportunity to rejoice. Moreover there were many sincere Christians who were perplexed at the lack of cooperation between the clergy who all preached the gospel and worked

---

3. Houses of Shirley and Hastings, A Member of *The Life and Times of Selina, Countess of Huntingdon* (London, 1830, Vol.1, p.330.)
4. J.W.L. (Vol.4, pp.235-239.) The letter is given in full in Appendix Two at the end of this study.

for the salvation of men's souls. Why should it be that when labourers increased, disunion also increased? A union of opinions was not looked for but each must respect the outlook of the other. Remove all the hindrances to a united usefulness, he begged – cease from envy, unkindness and emphasizing another's faults. Rather, the aim should be to speak respectfully of each other and promote brotherly love. All this would be better for the people. It would put a stop to their enemies' criticism that they could not agree amongst themselves. Some have thought such a union an impossibility like Dr Conyers but surely, with God, all things were possible?

The letter was sent to 'forty or fifty clergyman' but only three replies were received. Wesley mentioned in this letter that it was a copy of one composed and sent out some two and a half years previous to this date but there is no trace of this in the *Letters*. There was a similar letter addressed on 11 March 1745 to 'A Clerical friend'[5] though this was rather too early to be connected with this circular epistle. There was also a letter sent to the Earl of Dartmouth[6] written on 10 April 1761 from Liverpool. The contents of this letter were more or less the same as the 'Eirenicon' letter, but was it intended to be sent to the clergy as well? Of the replies received in respect of the 'Eirenicon' was one from Wesley's friend and colleague, Vincent Perronet,[7] who was one with John in doctrine but did not indulge in irregular practices. Another received was from W.S. who could have been Walter Sellon, an even closer friend and colleague of Wesley and one who was in the very near future to afford much literary help in the 'Minute Controversy' as he had already done during the Hervey–Wesley dispute. On the other hand, but less likely, it could have been from the Revd Walter Shirley, a relative of Lady Huntingdon who was a decided Calvinist. However, the letter was short and whilst such a proposed union would cause the writer to rejoice, he

---

5.   J.W.L. (Vol.3, pp.29-33.)
6.   *ibid.* (Vol.4, pp.146-152.)
7.   J.W.J. (Vol.5, pp.65-6.) Perronet, as would be expected, agreed wholeheartedly with Wesley's effort.

was an 'infidel' regarding it![8] Richard Hart, Vicar of St George's, Bristol was the third colleague to reply. His was a hopeful letter suggesting a meeting of these ministers somewhere between Bristol and London, but, before they met, they should all decide what they were to discuss and leave off contentious ideas, agreeing to differ on certain points of doctrine. They must meet in the spirit of love and humility. Nevertheless, his three replies brought Wesley no nearer to his admirable goal. His 'Eirenicon' was a decided failure. At least, he had tried, though it is disappointing to see his neglect to take some measure of the blame for all this.

A minute taken at the 1770[9] Conference began what must be termed the Third Calvinistic Controversy. Soon after the Conference, the minute appeared in print, primarily for all Wesley's preachers, yet for all to see. It declared:

> 'We said in 1744, "We have leaned too much toward Calvinism". Wherein?
>
> 1. With regard to man's *faithfulness*. Our Lord himself taught us to use the expression. And we ought never to be ashamed of it. We ought steadily to assert, on his authority, that if a man is not "faithful in the unrighteous mammon", God will not give him true riches.
> 2. With regard to *working for life*. This also our Lord has expressly commanded us. Labour (Εργαζεσθη), literally "work for the meat that endureth to everlasting life". And in fact every believer, till he comes to glory, works for, as well as *from* life.
> 3. We have received it as a maxim, that "a man is to do nothing in order to receive justification". Nothing can be more false. Whoever desires to find favour with God should "cease from evil, and learn to do well". Whoever repents,

---

8. J.W.J. (Vol.5, pp.64-5.)
9. *Minutes of the Methodist Conferences from the First Held in London by the late Revd John Wesley, MA In the year 1744* (London, 1862, pp.95-6.)

should do "works meet for repentance". And if this is not in order to find favour, what does he do them for?
Review the whole affair.

1. Who of us is *now* accepted of God? He that now believes in Christ, with a loving, obedient heart.
2. But who among those who never heard of Christ? He that feareth God, and worketh righteousness according to the light he had.
3. Is this the same with "he that is sincere"? Nearly, if not quite.
4. Is not this "salvation by works"? Not by the *merit* of works, but by works as a *condition*.
5. What have we then been disputing about for these thirty years? I am afraid, about words.
6. As to merit itself, of which we have been so dreadfully afraid; we are rewarded *"according to our works!"* yes, *"because of our works"*. How does this differ from, *secundum merita operum*, as our works *deserve*? Can you split this hair? I doubt, I cannot.
7. The grand objection to one of the preceding propositions is drawn from matter of fact, God does in fact justify those who, by their own confession, neither feared God nor wrought righteousness. Is this an exception to the general rule? It is a doubt whether God makes any exception at all. But how are we sure that the person in question never did fear God and work righteousness? His own saying so is not proof; for we know how all that are convinced of sin undervalue themselves in every respect.
8. Does not talking of a justified or a sanctified state tend to mislead me, almost naturally leading them to trust in what was done in one moment? Whereas we are every hour and every moment pleasing or displeasing to God, according to our works; according to the whole of our inward tempers

and our outward behaviour.'

No one could have doubted Wesley's fidelity to the great Reformation doctrine of Justification by Faith after thirty years of public preaching. What was more, quite recently he had propounded this doctrine very forcefully in the funeral sermon for Whitefield at the latter's Tabernacle in Tottenham Court Road, near Moorfields on Sunday 18 November 1770.[10] It may seem that one is now digressing somewhat from the controversy under discussion, but here, chronologically in order, was an event which added a little of the necessary fuel to a fire already being kindled. He had declared on this occasion:

> '...there is *no power* (by nature) and no merit in man...no, we are all *dead* in trespasses and sins...He [Christ] was delivered for our offences, and was raised again for our justification...But by what means do we become interested in what Christ has done and suffered? Not by works, lest any man should boast, but by faith alone...'[11]

A close examination of the sermon reveals that there was nothing contained in it to give offence to the Calvinistic multitudes who heard it. However, some of the latter had different thoughts on the matter. Wesley had expressed in the *Journal*,[12] but in vain, the hope that:

> 'Here, likewise, I trust God has given a blow to that bigotry which had prevailed for many years.'

The very fact that Wesley preached this funeral sermon was by Whitefield's own request. This fact did not prevent his Calvinistic

---

10. Whitefield died in the Presbyterian manse at Newburyport, Massachusetts on 30 September 1770 and was buried under the pulpit of the church there.
11. J.W.S. (Vol.2, pp.506-527.)
12. J.W.J.(Vol.5, p.393.)

antagonists taking advantage of the occasion to further the controversy which was already beginning. Nor did the knowledge that whilst Wesley and Whitefield had openly disagreed over doctrine to the very last, they had at least been reconciled and that there was a friendly spirit between them, seem to make any difference. Wesley preached this sermon on at least two more occasions and then published it in Dublin the same year. There came a quick attack on it in the *Gospel Magazine* to the effect that Wesley had uttered a great falsehood in saying that the 'grand fundamental doctrines which Mr Whitefield everywhere preached' were those John had specified.[13] The Editor of the Standard *Sermons* of John Wesley (The Revd Edward H. Sugden) thinks the author of the assault was Romaine.[14] It was also said:

> 'How improper to apply the words of a mad prophet to so holy a man as Mr Whitefield.'

John quietly replied:

> 'I join issue on this head. Whether the doctrines of eternal covenant, and of absolute Predestination are the grand fundamental doctrines of Christianity or not, I affirm again, 1. That Mr Whitefield did not everywhere preach these. 2. That he did everywhere preach the New Birth and Justification by faith.

again:

> 1. He did not everywhere preach the eternal covenant, and absolute predestination. In all the times I myself heard him

---

13. Tyerman, Luke *The Life of George Whitefield* (London, 1890, Vol.2, p.619.)
14. J.W.S. (Vol.2, p.507.) The text was Numbers xxiii.verse 10: 'Let me die the death of the righteous and let my last end be like his.' The sermons included Charles Wesley's tribute hymn.

preach, I never heard him utter a sentence, either on one or the other...Yes, all the times he preached in West Street Chapel, and in our other chapels throughout England, he did not preach these doctrines at all – no, not in a single paragraph; which, by the bye, is a demonstration that he did not think them the fundamental doctrines of Christianity.

2. Both in West Street Chapel, and all our other chapels throughout England, he did preach the necessity of the new birth, and justification by faith, as clearly as he has done in his two volumes of printed sermons. Therefore all that I have asserted is true, and provable by ten thousand witnesses.'[15]

Returning now to the debatable 'Minute', it might be mentioned that Wesley had always been loyal to the great Reformation theme of Justification by Faith when expounding in Lady Huntingdon's chapels. Nevertheless, once brought to the attention of that same lady, Wesley's minute about Justification was to begin a dispute which was to last at least six years. She '...apprehended that the fundamental truths of the Gospel were struck at.'[16]

Wesley then took the tactless step of writing to her and telling her his inmost thoughts about her faults! He defended the minute and reaffirmed his previous statement that he preached no other gospel than that which he preached thirty years ago.[17] Naturally, Lady Huntingdon resented this

---

15. Tyerman, Luke *The Life of George Whitefield* (London, 1890, Vol.2, p.619.)
16. Houses of Shirley and Hastings, A Member of *The Life and Times of Selina, Countess of Huntingdon* (London, 1839, Vol.2, p.230.)
17. There is no trace of this letter in the Standard *Letters*, but it is referred to in a letter by Wesley to Joseph Benson written in London, dated 30 November 1770 (J.W.J. Vol.5, p.211-212): 'For several years I had been convinced that I had not done my duty with regard to that valuable woman; that I had not told her what I was thoroughly assured no one else would dare do, and what I knew she would bear from no other person, but possibly might bear from me...' Wesley had certainly thought incorrectly on that occasion.' Cf. Letter of Wesley's to Lady Huntingdon dated 19 June 1771. (J.W.L. Vol.5, pp.258-260.)

and opposed the minute with even greater fervour. The Hon. and Revd Walter Shirley, her first cousin, also joined in the fray and proved to be Selina's greatest supporter in the affair. Lady Huntingdon decreed that all at Trevecca College who did not join her in opposing the minute should leave. Immediately Joseph Benson, an Arminian and a helper of Wesley's who was headmaster at the College, resigned. John Fletcher, in defence of Benson, followed suit and resigned as President of the Institution.

Wesley now sent Her Ladyship a letter defending his minute and referring her to his sermons on *Salvation by Faith* and *The Lord Our Righteousness* and protested his orthodoxy.[18] However, the Countess was not satisfied and issued a circular to which Shirley, with other Evangelical clergy and laymen appended their signatures. It ran as follows:

'Sir,

Whereas Mr Wesley's Conference is to be held at Bristol on Tuesday 6th of August next, it is proposed by Lady Huntingdon and many other Christian Friends (real Protestants) to have a meeting at Bristol at the same time, of such principal Persons both Clergy and Laity who disapprove of the underwritten Minutes; and as the same are thought injurious to the very fundamental Principles of Christianity, it is proposed that they go in a body to the said Conference and insist upon a formal Recantation, of the said Minutes; and in the case of a refusal, that they sign and publish their protest against them. Your presence, Sir, on this occasion is particularly requested; but if it should not suit your convenience to be there, it is desired that you will transmit your sentiments on the subject to such persons as you think proper to produce them. It is submitted to you, whether it would not be right, in the opposition to be made to such a dreadful heresy, to recommend

18. J.W.L. (Vol.5, pp.258-260.)

it to as many of your Christian Friends, as well of the Dissenters as one of the established Church, as you can prevail on to be there, the case being of so public a nature.

> I am, Sir,
>
> Your obedient Servant,
>
> Walter Shirley.[19]

A postscript was added giving a list of names to whom a reply could be made together with a copy of the offending minute. Lodgings were to be provided for those who required them.

Wesley did not appear unduly worried by this, but printed on 10 July 1771 a defence of the minute for use of his preachers. He did, however, regard the impending visit of the Calvinists to his Conference as an unjustifiable imposition and remonstrated with Lady Huntingdon. She too saw the point of this, but it was too late for her to withdraw. She wrote to Wesley on the eve of the 1771 Conference trying to soften the proceedings.[20] Shirley, too, on arrival, realized he was in an embarrassing position and he also wrote a letter to John. Wesley replied orally, stating that the protest group would be received on Thursday, the third day of the Conference. The protesting party comprised Shirley with two of the Countess's preachers and three laymen.[21] The Conference was well attended, a fact due, no doubt, to the prevailing controversy.

The reconciliatory letters of the Countess and Shirley were read and it was proposed that these should be published just as their 'Circular' letter had been. Wesley defended himself against the accusation that he had not preached the doctrine of Justification by Faith. What was more, he declared that he felt that there was some personal hostility against him but at this statement, Shirley affirmed his regards and goodwill towards Wesley. Shirley submitted a Declaration which he had drawn up. After a

---

19. Fletcher, John *The Whole Works of* (London, 1836, p.3.)
20. J.W.L. (Vol.5, pp.274-5.)
21. i.e. Revd Glascot and Revd Owen; Messrs John Lloyd of Bath; Mr James Ireland of Bristol, and Mr Winter.

few but not inconsiderable amendations made by Wesley, it was signed by fifty-three of his preachers, though two objected. These were Thomas Olivers, who was to feature prominently in the controversy in due course, and John Nelson, the former stonemason-preacher from Birstall in Yorkshire. It must be noted, too, that Charles Wesley's signature was also omitted. The Declaration ran as follows:

> 'Whereas the doctrinal points in the Minutes of a conference held in London, 7 August 1770, have been understood to favour justification by works; now the Revd John Wesley and others assembled in Conference do declare that we had no such meaning, and that we abhor the doctrine of Justification by Works as a most perilous and abominable doctrine, and, as the said *Minutes* are not sufficiently guarded in the way they are expressed, we hereby solemnly declare, in the sight of God, that we have no trust or confidence but in the alone merits of Our Lord and Saviour Jesus Christ, for Justification or Salvation, either in life, death, or the day of judgement; and though no one is a real Christian believer (and consequently cannot be saved) who doth not good works, where there is time and opportunity, yet our works have no part in meriting our purchasing our salvation from first to last, either in whole or in part.'[22]

Wesley then demanded a public statement from Shirley to the effect that he had misconstrued Wesley's minute. Shirley hesitated but after being prompted by one of the laymen, reluctantly agreed.

It might be thought that the affair was now over, but actually the worst was yet to come.

The very reason why the minute of the 1770 Conference had been made was to stay the incoming tide of Antinomianism from which, according to Fletcher, Methodists needed a reformation as much as their ancestors did from Popery.

---

22. J.W.J. (Vol.5, p.427.)

Fletcher had written a pamphlet defending the minute some time before the reconciliation at the Conference. However, he heard of the agreement there and offered, in a letter to James Ireland, to stop publication for it included personal references to Shirley. Unfortunately Wesley, who by now had resumed his itinerant work, had left instructions with Thomas Olivers for its publication and distribution. With the aid of Benson, this pamphlet, which was entitled Fletcher's *First Check to Antinomianism*,[23] was published. It contained nothing offensive and breathed the very spirit of Christian charity, as did all Fletcher's writings. Space permits only a very brief summary of the work but it consisted of five letters to Shirley in which he described Wesley's doctrine. He defended the 'Minute' and vindicated the 1770 Conference's propositions. Naturally, as the title suggested, he warned against the dangers and prevalence of Antinomianism; but he also commended some of Shirley's sermons, which, he maintained, agreed with Wesley's teaching. Above all, he made an impassioned appeal for peace.[24]

Whilst this *Check* was being prepared, Wesley wrote to the Countess of Huntingdon[25] openly declaring that the publication of Fletcher's work was no afterthought and had been intended before the 'reconciling' Conference began.

When Shirley saw the *Check* he was naturally disturbed. He immediately intimated to Fletcher his intention of publishing a *Narrative*[26] of the controversy which would include Fletcher's letter to James Ireland offering to stop the publication of the *Check*. Fletcher immediately said that he

---

23. Fletcher, *The Whole Works of* (London, 1836, pp.3-35.)
24. Fletcher, John *The Whole Works of* (London, 1836, pp.3-37.) The full title was *Vindication of the Revd Mr Wesley's last Minutes; occasioned by a circular letter, inviting persons both clergy and laity as well of the Dissenters as of the Established Church, who disapprove of those Minutes to oppose them in a body, as a dreadful heresy; in Five Letters to the Hon. and Revd Author of the circular letter. Published by Wm. Pine.*
25. J.W.L. (Vol.5, pp.274-5.)
26. The full title was: *Narrative of the Principal Circumstances relative to the Revd Mr Wesley's late Conference held in Bristol, 6 August 1771.*

would give him permission to publish his letter to Ireland and moreover would buy copies of it, bind it with his own document and distribute the combined MSS free of charge.

However, when Shirley's *Narrative* was available, it was soon seen that his publication of Fletcher's letter to Ireland was given prominence, making out that Fletcher was reluctant to publish his *Check* because of the *latter's doubts about the 1770 minutes!* Shirley gave an extract of Fletcher's epistle to Ireland which was written on 15 August:

> 'I feel for poor dear Mr Shirley, whom I have (considering the present circumstances) treated too severely in my vindication of the minutes. My dear sir, what must be done? I am ready to defray, by selling to my last shirt, the expense of the printing of my Vindication, and suppress it.'

Furthermore, a phrase in the last line of the *Declaration* which was printed with the *Narrative* contained the words 'our salvation' instead of 'our justification' – a not unimportant error!

The upshot of this was that Fletcher felt compelled to issue a *Second Check to Antinomianism.*[27] In this he published the letter he had written to Shirley which showed that his letter to Ireland simply offered to call off publication of his first *Check* purely for personal reasons and not because he had any doubts about the veracity of the minute. He admitted in his *Second Check* that he had written to Mr Ireland not only offering to stop publication of the *First Check* but pointing out that in some way those Minutes '*must* be vindicated' – that 'Mr Wesley owed this to the Church, to the 'real Protestants', to all his societies, and to his own aspersed character.' Fletcher reminded Shirley that he had 'begged' Wesley to keep out of his letter anything 'unkind or sharp' and he had been given

---

27. Fletcher, John *The Whole Works of* (London, 1836, pp.37-74.) The full title was: *A Second Check to Antinomianism occasioned by a late narrative, in three letters to the Hon. and Revd Author. By the Vindicator of the Revd Mr Wesley's Minutes.* (12mo.109.pp.)

this assurance by John. Shirley had not to forget that the task of publishing was in the hands of Thomas Olivers who was one of the preachers who had declined to sign the *Declaration*. Therefore Olivers had possibly used this opportunity for producing his own arguments since 'both parties refused' to listen to him at Conference, by including Fletcher's points with which he was in entire agreement.[28] Doctrinally, the *Second Check* set out to emphasize the necessity of good works after justification which, contrary to what had been said, the Wesleys and their preachers had never given up expounding.

Shirley did not reply but publicly recanted some of his own sermons which Fletcher had commended as supporting Wesley's 'minute'. However, acrimony was now at its height and even Lady Huntingdon saw fit to describe Wesley as a 'Papist unmasked, a heretic and an apostate'.[29]

It was in 1772 that there appeared another antagonist to enter the lists against Methodism – Sir Richard Hill. Hill had received great spiritual help from both Fletcher and John Berridge during his youth. He was never ordained but itinerated as a lay-preacher, and was sometimes found preaching to the Kingswood colliers as the Wesleys and Whitefield had. Like his brother Rowland who was shortly to enter this present controversy, he suffered many persecutions during his early days. He wrote five letters to Fletcher who by now appeared to have lost his timidity and reluctance to engage in controversy and he quickly replied to Richard in a *Third Check to Antinomianism*.[30] Hill's polemical contribution was threefold. His first piece was: *A Conversation between Richard Hill Esq., the Revd Mr Madan*[31] *and Father Walsh, superior of a convent of English*

28. Fletcher, John *The Whole Works of* (London, 1836, pp.35-37.)
29. Jackson, Thomas *The Life of the Revd Charles Wesley MA* (London, 1841, Vol.2, pp.255-6.) Cf. article in the *Gospel Magazine* (August 1771) where Wesley was described as a 'dictator and employer'.
30. Fletcher, John *The Whole Works of* (London, 1836, pp.74-114.)
31. Martin Madan was minister of the Lock Hospital in London and was also a hymn and tune writer. He caused great offence to many, especially his evangelical colleagues – and Wesley, because of his *Defence of Polygamy*. Many tried to dissuade him from publishing this. It arose from his experiences of ministering to sufferers from venereal diseases at the Lock Hospital.

Benedictine monks at Paris held at the said convent, July 13 1771. relative to some doctrinal Minutes. advanced by the Revd Mr John Wesley and others, at a Conference in London August 7 1770. To which are added some remarks by the Editor; as also Mr Wesley's own Declaration concerning his Minutes, verified by another hand.[32] This really appears to be an unnecessarily long title for its rather foolish contents. Its main purpose was to show that Wesley's views were worse than Popery – that 'Popery is about midway between Protestantism and Mr J. Wesley'. The 'versification' referred to was a piece of doggerel the last line of which ran:

'Whene'er we *say* one thing, we mean quite another.'

However, this was not enough, for Hill then quickly followed this by issuing a penny 12mo.12pp. tract entitled: *An Answer to some capital errors contained in the Minutes.* The substance of this publication differed little from Hill's previous tract and the doggerel was for some reason repeated. Then came his third work – a pamphlet of forty pages:. *Five Letters to the Reverend Mr Fletcher, relative to his Vindication of the Minutes of the Revd Mr John Wesley.* In this piece, Hill seemed to change his attitude. The work was not only indicative of real scholarship but there was evidenced a more charitable spirit, although again, its contents were similar to his previous attempts. Tyerman regards it as characteristic of the work 'of a scholar and a Christian gentleman'.[33]

Hill was then joined by his brother Rowland[34] who wrote: *Friendly*

---

32. A sixpenny tract, 8vo. and 31 pages.
33. Tyerman, Luke *The Life and Times of John Wesley* (London, 1871-2, Vol.3, p.107.)
34. Rowland Hill became ordained as deacon only. He, like his brother was friendly with Berridge. Berridge wrote to Lady Huntingdon about him as follows: 'I find you have got honest Rowland Hill down to Bath; he is a pretty young spaniel, fit for land or water, and has a wonderful yelp. He forsakes father and mother and brethren and gives up all for Jesus; and I believe will prove a useful labourer, if he keeps clear of petticoat snares. The Lord has owned him more abundantly in the West.' Houses of Shirley and Hastings, A Member of *The Life and Times of Selina,*

Remarks occasioned by the spirit and doctrines contained in the Revd Mr Fletcher's Vindication and more particularly in his 'Second Check to Antinomianism'. 8vo.71.pp.1772. Defending his work in a letter written to Captain Joss from London on 16 November 1772, he declared:

> 'Mr W— said last night, election was the most horrid monster upon earth; no name said he, is bad enough for it...Indeed he seems almost [in a] frenzy...'[35]

On a contemporary occasion after being attacked by Wesley both in writings and from the pulpit, Hill protested:

> 'Yet with the greatest injustice is Mr Wesley ever branding us with the detested name of *antinomians*, while he *must* be convinced, that in our inmost souls we entirely disown both the principles and practices of those revolters from obedience...'

There was, he continued, as much astonishment at what folk have heard in favour of holiness '...as if they had been sitting on enchanted ground.'[36] However, Berridge gave the young Hill some useful advice, even though what moral grounds he had for doing so were hard to understand when one realizes that Berridge himself just could not keep out of the controversy:

> 'The latest contest at Bristol seems to turn upon this hinge, whether it shall be *Pope John* or *Pope Joan*. My dear friend, keep out of all controversy, and wage no war but with the devil.'[37]

Countess of Huntingdon (1839, Vol.2, p.49.) After years as an itinerant preacher and also chaplain to Lady Huntingdon, he unwittingly offended her by making a humorous remark but she never overlooked the offence. He had the Surry Chapel built for him in London where he ministered to the end of his days.

35. Sidney, Edwin *The Life of the Revd Rowland Hill, MA* (London, 1834, p.75.)
36. *ibid.* (p.76.)

It was now the turn of two other Methodist apologists, both preachers of Wesley's, to defend his position. They were not from the cultured, educated or literary field. Thomas Olivers had been a shoemaker with an admitted gift of logic and for hymn writing. Walter Sellon had been a baker and it will be recalled that he had already written in defence of Wesley in the controversy over the *Eleven Letters*.[38] To some extent it was unfortunate that they undertook this task of polemical writing, not so much because of their background, but because it did give Richard Hill the opportunity of adopting a superior and decidedly snobbish attitude to them, likening Olivers, for example, to a yapping puppy – a reference which the latter naturally resented; but Olivers had not yet received the worst of his treatment. He was to receive this from the composer of the famous hymn: *Rock of Ages* – Augustus Montague Toplady.[39] Toplady referred to him as the 'Methodist Cobbler' and of both of them he wrote:

'Of all my ragged regiment,
This cobbler gives me most content:
My forgeries and faith's defender,
My barber, champion, and shoe-mender.'

As Toplady's biographer, Thomas Wright says, Augustus did not shine as a writer of burlesque.[40]

A *Fourth Check to Antinomianism* now came from Fletcher with the additional title of *Logica Genevensis* replying to both the Hills.[41] In this work, Fletcher pointed out with regret in his Letter 1 of his new work,

---

37. *ibid.* (p.428.)
38. See page 261 of this study.
39. Toplady was educated at Westminster School and Trinity College, Dublin. Ordained in 1763 he held livings at Hapford and Broad Hembury (Devon). Later Minister of Orange Street Chapel, London. Died 14 August 1778. Came under Methodist influence which effected his conversion whilst a student at Dublin. See Chapter One of this study, page 21.
40. Wright, Thomas *The Life of Augustus Montague Toplady* (London, 1911, p.118.)
41. Fletcher, John *The Whole Works of* (London, 1836, pp.116-189.)

that his opponent's attitude had worsened.[42] After Hill's previous Five Letters were answered by Fletcher's *Third Check*,[43] Fletcher was described as '...a shower of rain gently descending from the placid heaven. But the six which have followed resemble a storm of hail, pouring down from the lowering sky, ushered by some harmless flashes of lightning, and accompanied by the rumbling of distant thunder.'[44] Part of the work consisted of letters to Richard Hill but some are addressed to his brother Rowland and some to both. The subjects under discussion were Justification by Faith (the misunderstanding of which had caused the controversy to begin), the necessity of works in the justified and the fact that the believer would be justified but that justification had to be evidenced in good works and on these a man would be judged. As the full title implied,[45] it was not only a defence of Arminian Methodism – it went deeper and a thorough exposition of St James's definition of true and pure religion was expounded, reconciled as it should be, with the idea of Justification by faith as found in the Pauline Epistles. Naturally Fletcher does not lose the opportunity again of proving Calvinism unscriptural and cites notable Puritan writers to support his case.[46] What is noteworthy is that before he began the *Fourth Check*, a special page was devoted to *An Address to All Candid Calvinists in the Church of England*. Although not intended to do so, it acted admirably as an introduction to his *Fourth*

---

42. *ibid.* (p.116.)
43. The *Third Check* had been a gracious and courteous reply to Hill's *Five Letters*. Fletcher felt that Hill in the first *Letter* had agreed with Wesley's definition of faithfulness 'in the gospel sense'; To the second *Letter*, Fletcher opposed Election and maintained Universal Redemption; The third is answered by the affirmation that good works are demanded of the believer who will be judged by them. The Fourth Letter is answered by a plea for humility especially in respect of learning and admitting mistakes.
44. Fletcher, J. *The Whole Works of* (p.116.)
45. i.e. *Logica Genevansis or a Fourth Check to Antinomianism: in which St James's pure religion is defended against the charges, and established upon the concessions of Mr Richard and Mr Rowland Hill, In a Series of Letters to those Gentlemen* (12mo.237.pp.)
46. e.g. Dr Owen (1616-1683.)

Check.[47] If ever a writer came near to reconciling Calvinistic and Arminian thought, it was Fletcher in this page of two paragraphs. If the charge of bitterness did not set the readers from using this book, then some would try to frighten them off doing so by saying that he (Fletcher) was throwing down the foundation of Christianity and helping Wesley to place works and merit on the Redeemer's throne and God forbid he should be guilty of this.

Fletcher continued his line of argument in a second part of *Logica Genevensis* or a *Fifth Check to Antinomianism*,[48] primarily as an answer to Richard Hill's *The Finishing* stroke. Fletcher charged Hill with giving a false view of the whole controversy. He refuted Hill's assertion that in the *Fourth Check*. Fletcher had undermined both 'Law and Gospel'. Article Nine of the Established Church quoted by Hill in support of Calvinism was ably refuted. In a commendably delicate manner, he showed that Hill had exhausted his ammunition by way of finding accusations and false misrepresentations. Hill had 'apologised' on behalf of Fletcher to his fellow-Calvinists! Fletcher took this opportunity of taking friendly leave of Hill. It was obvious that Hill had really felt that he had met his theological match in Fletcher and wrote a letter to Fletcher suggesting that the dispute might now finish. Strange to relate, Fletcher rather uncharacteristically would not hear of it.

It was at this juncture that Berridge came on to the scene, much as he had advised others to keep out of controversy. His sole published work was the outcome: *The Christian World Unmasked: Pray Come and Peep.*[49] The first edition of this work included a defence of the doctrine of Baptismal Regeneration but this was omitted in later editions. Berridge's work was not of a high literary standard but whilst it was full of coarse humour, displaying fully all the tenets of Calvinism, it could not be regarded as dull reading. There were certainly no virulent, acrimonious

---

47. Fletcher, John *The Whole Works of* (London, 1836, p.115.)
48. Fletcher, John *The Whole Works of* (London, 1836, pp.190-220.)
49. There was of course, his edition of the 'mended hymns' of the Wesleys referred to on pages 68-9 of this study.

attacks on anyone. There was, however, a slanderous poem which appeared about this time in the *Gospel Magazine* under the signature of 'Old Everton', calling himself 'a riding pedlar' which seemed to be aimed at Wesley and entitled: *The Serpent and the Fox: or an Interview between Old Nick and Old John.* As the author also admitted to have been of Clare Hall, Cambridge, there is little wonder that Berridge received the blame for it.

A reconciliation between the opposing parties was now attempted by (it must be noted) two evangelical laymen – James Ireland and John Thornton of London. A meeting took place between Fletcher and Lady Huntingdon but another *Check* was already on its way (1774). It was entitled *An Equal Check to Pharisaism and Antinomianism.* It contained *An Essay on Truth, or a Rational Vindication of the Doctrine of Salvation by Faith*,[50] which he dedicated to Her Ladyship. This work was obviously not intended to be controversial. Rather it indicated the possibility of a safe middle ground between Antinomianism and Pelagianism which any considerate man could accept. Fletcher began by briefly going over once again his definition of Justification by Faith and the necessity of resultant good works. A 'plain definition' of Saving faith followed stating that the believing itself was a gift of God and how far it was in the power of man to believe. 'Truth cordially embraced faith and saved under every dispensation of divine Grace, though in different degrees'. That saving faith was more particularly described by its rise and operations was shown by distinguishing that faith from the one held by Antinomians, 'trembling devils and modish professors'. Fletcher went on to argue the reasonableness of the doctrine of Salvation by Faith and that they were under a debt to the Solifidians who stood up firmly in defence of faith; but therein lay the danger – the Solifidians had so enforced Article VI which guarded salvation by faith that they made void the XIIth Article which guarded morality. In the remainder of the essay, Fletcher dealt with the inferences of this cardinal doctrine; issued a series of addresses to 'Baptized heathens, Christianized Jews, Antichristian

---

50. Fletcher, John *The Whole Works of* (London, 1836, pp.396-423.)

moralists, penitent mourners and Christian believers.' Finally in an Appendix he answered possible objections to the premiss that all men universally, in 'the day of their visitation' had SOME gracious power to believe SOME saving Truth.

Once again one might be excused for thinking that the last word had been spoken, or rather – written, but not so. Late in 1774, Walter Sellon, a gifted preacher of Wesley's but not possessed of great tactfulness, published a treatise on *The Church of England Vindicated from the charge of Absolute Predestination*,[51] together with two others: *Arguments against the Doctrine of General Redemption considered.* Toplady was quick to the Calvinist defence with his *Historic Proof of the Doctrinal Calvinism of the Church of England*, as an answer to Sellon's first work.[52] Toplady developed his argument from the writings of the Apostolic Fathers and traced the essentiality of the Calvinistic interpretation of the Christian faith down to his own day. He ended with an appeal to the clergy for a Calvinistic interpretation of the Articles, quoting Dr Gilbert Burnet in support of his own view.[53] He accused certain men 'ordained in the Church of England'[54] of disbelieving the Articles to which they had subscribed. They were 'free-willers' and therefore 'free-livers', for Arminianism 'was nothing more than Atheism in masquerade'. Moreover Methodism was Arminianism in a 'Pandoraean Box'.[55] Toplady followed this tract by a sermon on *Free Will and Merit* and other works, including his *Scheme of Christian and Philosophical Necessity Asserted.* The *Scheme* was an answer to a tract of Wesley's but a counter-reply was provided by Fletcher in his *Remarks on Mr Toplady's Scheme*[56] and *An*

---

51. I am indebted to the Ryland's Library, Manchester for permission to peruse and summarize Toplady's works in their original form – mostly in pamphlets.
52. Fletcher, J. *Whole Works of* (London, 1836, p.109) commended Sellon's work as a 'masterful mixture of the skill belonging to the sensible scholar, the good Logician etc.'
53. Burnet did not take sides on this matter – see pp.157-160 of this study.
54. Toplady *op.cit.* (Vol.2, p.727.)
55. Toplady *op.cit.* (Vol.2, p.731.)
56. Fletcher, John *The Whole Works of* (London, 1836, pp.317-344.)

Answer to Mr Toplady's Vindication of the Decrees.[57] The latter work
was simply a refutation of Calvinistic claims and their relation to holiness.
The 'right leg of Calvinism', or the Calvinian doctrine of Election and
necessary Holiness was compared with the 'left leg of Calvinism, or the
Calvinian doctrine of reprobation and necessary wickedness'. Fletcher
quite effectively demolished Toplady's appeal to Scripture for support
and also the latter's assertion that holiness was more likely to be found in
adopting the Calvinistic system than Arminianism. As for the first of
Toplady's works quoted here, Fletcher again scored well in demolishing
Toplady's use of the Scriptures and averred that Augustus had made God
the author of sin!

Then came Fletcher's *Last Check to Antinomianism* which was mostly
a defence of the Methodist teaching on Christian Perfection.[58]

As far as the relationship between Wesley and Toplady is concerned,
it was indeed a literary affair. Toplady wrote much,[59] especially against
Wesley; Wesley wrote little against Augustus Montague for he relied
upon others to write in his defence.

Toplady had become a decided Calvinist at the age of eighteen years[60]
after reading Manton's *Discourses on the Seventeenth of John*. The rest
of his short life was spent defending these doctrines often with great
vehemence and vindictiveness, yet pursuing a gracious ministry amongst
his flock.

From London, on 30 December 1769 (a year before the Minute
Controversy), Wesley wrote to Walter Sellon, one of his literary helpers,
bidding him to:

---

57. Fletcher *op.cit.* (pp.275-316.)
58. Fletcher *op.cit.* (Part 2, pp.161-274.)
59. So much, in fact, that space permits only the most important and relevant works to
     be mentioned here, namely: those directly bearing upon the Calvinistic Controversy.
60. Wright, Thomas *The Life of Augustus Montague Toplady* (London, 1911, p.11.)
     This conversion took place in 1758. Thomas Manton was a Presbyterian Divine
     (1620-1677). He discussed 'accommodation' with Tillotson and Stillingfleet in
     1674.

'...add a word to that lively coxcomb, Mr Toplady, not only with regard to Zanchius, but his slander on the Church of England. You would do well to give a reading to both his tracts. He does certainly believe himself to be the greatest genius in England. Pray, take care, or *notus sit pro suis virtutibus*.'[61]

This epistle arose from two tracts of Toplady's, namely: *The Church of England Vindicated from the Charge*[62] *of Arminianism* and *The Doctrine of Absolute Predestination Stated and Asserted*,[63] the latter being largely a translation from the Latin of Jerome Zanchius. Both tracts were published in 1769.

The first of these (an attack, as the title suggests, on the Arminian interpretation of the Church of England's doctrines) was, in effect, a letter to Revd Dr Nowell and *Occasioned by some Passages in that Gentleman's answer to Pietus Oxoniensis By a Presbyter of the Church of England*.[64] Wesley published an abridgement of the *Doctrine of Absolute Predestination Stated and Asserted* with the following closing paragraph:

'The sum of all this is: One in twenty (suppose) of mankind is elected; nineteen in twenty are reprobated. The elect shall be saved, do what they will; the reprobate shall be damned. Reader, believe this or be damned. Witness my hand. A— T—.'[65]

---

61. J.W.L. (Vol.5, p.167.) 'Let him be known in proportion as he deserves.'
62. The full title adds: *In a Letter to Revd Dr Nowell: occasioned by some passages in that gentleman's answer to the Author of Pietas Oxoniensis*. (8vo.136pp.1769.)
63. 8vo.,134pp.,1769.
64. The Presbyter, of course, was Toplady. The writer of *Pietas Oxoniensis* was Sir Richard Hill (1768). In the year 1768 Hill attacked the University of Oxford for the expulsion of some evangelical students from St Edmund's Hall.
65. J.W.L. (Vol.5, p.167.)

John Wesley

Toplady had asked for this reply by publishing his literary efforts. Not only had he stated that Arminianism was the 'greatest religious evil',[66] but the Arminian pulpits and the press, he asserted, were both being used to promote the Romish doctrine of merit and freewill and such preachers were 'Antichrist'! He dealt fully with Predestination and Election and declared:

> 'Did I not believe a Predestination, I could not believe in a Providence. For, it would be most absurd to suppose that a Being of Infinite Wisdom would act without a plan, for which plan, Predestination is only another name.'[67]

However, Toplady attacked Wesley in the form of *A Letter to the Revd Mr John Wesley*[68] in which he charged John with summarizing his pamphlet on Zanchius untruthfully and unfairly. He also described him as displaying a '...dictatorial authority of a Pope and the sophistry of a Jesuit'. Moreover, Wesley's fear of Antinomianism was only 'pretended' and, in any case, what led more to Antinomianism than Wesley's teaching on Christian Perfection? His last statement was not, of course, without foundation.[69]

A further treatise by Toplady appeared in 1770: *A Caveat against Unsound Doctrines. A Sermon preached in St Ann's Blackfriars. Sunday 29 April 1770.*[70] The texts were twofold: 2 Cor.3.v.12.: 'Seeing then that we have such hope' and 1.Tim.1.v.10: 'And if there be any other thing that is contrary to sound doctrine...' This was a bait to which Wesley did not rise. Fletcher answered it in the first part of his *Fifth* and *Last Check to Antonomianism*,[71] Section XIV. According to a letter dated 22 March

---

66. *op.cit.* (pp.ix and x.)
67. Toplady *op.cit.* (p.xiii.)
68. The full title was: *Letter to the Revd Mr John Wesley relative to his published Abridgement of Zanchius on Predestination* (Holborn, London, 1770.)
69. This fact has been dealt with on page 298 of this study.
70. The third edition has been used here. 1778.
71. Fletcher, John *The Whole Works of* (Part 1, pp.201-206 and Part 2, pp.161-274.)

1775[72] from Wesley to Fletcher, the former did not seem too sure that the latter's methods were the right ones but humbly admitted that folk were more likely to take notice of Fletcher than they would of himself! However, he told Fletcher: 'It is well you have bestowed a little time on Mr Toplady. He might have been angry with you if you had taken no notice of him.' It seems strange that this letter about Fletcher's reply in the first part of his Last Check [1773] was not written until 1775 and both concerned a sermon preached in 1770.

The Caveat, however, was nothing more than a wearisome repetition of Toplady's previous themes plus an attack on Christian Perfection. He dealt with Arminianism, Conditional Election, Uneffectual [sic] Grace,[73] Justification by Faith and Antinomianism.[74] As for 'Sinless Perfection',[75] a perfect saint would only be seen in heaven and a final stress was placed on the final perseverance of God's chosen ones.

In the last section of this chapter only the works of Toplady which were written against Methodists other than Wesley were dealt with. In this section, it will be seen how little Wesley was brought out into open literary conflict with Toplady and even then, as in the last instance, Wesley simply noted Toplady's remarks and was quite happy to ask Fletcher to deal with them. Apart from Wesley's 'offending' abridgement of Zanchius, only two works of Wesley appeared due to Toplady's opposition, namely: '*The Question, What is an Arminian? Answered By a Lover of Free Grace (John Wesley. 8.pp.12mo. Bristol. Pine. 1770)*[76] and *The Consequences Proved* (1773), the latter being answered by Toplady the following year by his *More Work for John Wesley. 1774.* In 1775 Toplady published his *Historical Proof of the Doctrinal Calvinism of the Church of England.* Of a work so controversial one would have been justified in expecting a lengthy reasoned treatise from Wesley

---

72. J.W.L. (Vol.6, p.146.)
73. *op.cit.* (p.43.)
74. *op.cit.* (p.53.)
75. *op.cit.* (pp.53-56.)
76. See page 150 for details of this work.

opposing it but he made no reference to it, obviously regarding silence as golden. There was, however, one final brush with Augustus in 1776. The Conference of that year had pronounced that:

(i)   The preachers were requested to read with carefulness the tracts published by Wesley, Fletcher and Sellon

(ii) They were to preach Universal Redemption frequently, explicitly and lovingly.

(iii) They were not to imitate the Calvinist preachers in screaming, allegorizing, and boasting; but to visit as diligently as they did, to answer all their objections, to advise the Methodists not to hear them, to pray constantly and earnestly that God would stop the plague.

Whether or not this was a wise step to publish those instruction is a matter of opinion but Toplady seized the opportunity to reply in the *Gospel Magazine* (of which he had been appointed the Editor), by re-publishing these Conference instructions without note or comment – and presumably without permission. He gave them the heading: *Authentic Extract of what passed at a certain Confabulation held at London, 6 August 1776.* Wesley must have known about this but again kept his silence. Wright, the biographer of Toplady, omits this publication in the bibliography of his subject.[77]

The *Gospel Magazine* was noted for its scurrilous articles and because many of them were anonymous, suspicion must rest on Toplady for some of them. The Hills too, were guilty of publishing similar articles in that magazine, their literary efforts making strange reading for those in search of 'evangelical' writings.[78]

Apart from polemical discourse on the part of both Toplady and

77. Wright, Thomas *The Life of Augustus Montague Toplady* (London, 1911, pp.289-292.)

78. For further disgusting examples of this kind of writing see Tyerman, Luke *The Life and Times of John Wesley* (Vol.3, pp.255-266.)

Wesley – or more correctly, those written on behalf of Wesley – what was the real attitude of the one to the other? Against Toplady, the charge of virulence and scurrility cannot be denied. As distinct, of course, from today, one would have thought that in those days, especially in religious circles, there would have been some respect shown to age. Toplady's first occasion of dipping his pen in vitriol rather than ink when writing against Wesley was when he was but twenty-nine years of age; Wesley was then sixty-six years of age. What was more, Augustus very soon showed a disinclination to discuss and argue rationally and soon lost his temper. It was then he used to employ an endless string of uncharitable and decidedly unchristian expressions, some of which bordered on the obscene. No words were strong enough to portray the venerable Wesley, but on the other hand, Wesley could not be absolved from the blame of inviting much that he received on account of his utterances and controversial writings.

> 'Mr Wesley,' declared Toplady in an unpublished manuscript,
> 'is singularly infamous for the grossest misrepresentations of
> men he does not like, and of doctrines he opposes. He first
> dresses up hideous figures, and then pretends to be frightened
> at them, like the insane man who employed himself in drawing
> monstrous images upon the walls of his cell, and then battered
> his knuckles in fighting them.'[79]

Because of the great difference in age between the two men, Wesley treated Toplady as many a man of that age would a youthful opponent by either ignoring him or dismissing him with a humorous comment. Writing to George Merryweather in 1770, Wesley simply declared that as far as Mr Toplady was concerned, Wesley didn't 'fight with chimney-sweepers' – Toplady was too dirty a writer for John to meddle with as he would only

---

79. Wright, Thomas *The Life of Augustus Montague Toplady* (London, 1911, p.115.)
    Cf. too, Toplady's description of Wesley in the title of a pamphlet dated 1775, as
    An Old Fox tarr'd and feathered.

foul his fingers![80]

Yet there is a hint of another side of Toplady's character. His biographer, Thomas Wright,[81] speaks of an unpublished letter to the Revd Erasmus Middleton dated 5 February 1775 in which, whilst he opposed Wesley's doctrines zealously, he showed himself sympathetic with Wesley on account of John's troubles with his wife. Another letter, quoted by Abbey and Overton showed Toplady writing of Wesley in this manner:

> 'O, that He, in whose hand the hearts of all men are, may make even this opposer of grace a monument of almighty power to save! God is witness how earnestly I wish it may consist with the divine will to touch the heart and open the eyes of that unhappy man. I hold it as much my duty to pray for his conversion as to expose the futility of his writings against the truths of the Gospel.'[82]

These then can be taken as the most charitable example of Toplady's attitude to Wesley, which is not, of course, saying a great deal!

One might doubt the wisdom of allowing and encouraging his friends, Fletcher and Sellon to reply to Toplady's invectives instead of conducting his own defence. There is no doubt that Wesley adopted the better attitude of the two. Wesley was not above giving credit where it was due. In a letter to Thomas Cahill written from London and dated 23 January 1778[83] Wesley admitted that Toplady was consistent in his contention about the Absolute Decrees. Comparing Toplady with Hervey, Wesley declared Toplady consistent, whereas Hervey was not.

---

80. J.W.L. (Vol.6, p.192.)
81. *op.cit.* (p.161.)
82. Abbey, C.J. and Overton, J.H. *The English Church in the Eighteenth Century* (London, 1878.) They say Toplady said absolutely nothing new about Calvinism but gave just a wearisome repetition of what had already been said.
83. J.W.L. (Vol.6, p.296.)

Charles Wesley told James Hutton on 17 October 1773[84] he had never yet heard his brother speak one unkind word on Mr Hill or Mr Toplady. When one reads the past few pages, it may be felt that this statement may not be the whole truth but at least Wesley showed a little more charity than ever he received.

One final matter must be mentioned before leaving the subject of Wesley's relationship with this youthful clergyman. Toplady died in 1778 when only thirty-eight years of age. Just before his death he was greatly perturbed to hear 'a wicked and scandalous' report which was supposed to have been spread by Wesley's supporters to the effect that he had changed some of his religious sentiments, especially relating to the doctrines of grace. Moreover it had been said that he had withdrawn some of his personal remarks about Wesley and that before he died he had a strong desire to see John. Toplady's reaction was, against his physician's orders, to insist on being conveyed to his chapel in Orange Street, London where he was minister and publicly to deny these statements. This he did to the amazement of the large congregation present.[85] Another report was also circulated that Wesley had stated that Toplady died in despair uttering blasphemy. Actually Wesley had heard the rumour from others and there was no evidence that he propagated it. Sir Richard Hill who quickly wrote a *Letter to the Revd Mr John Wesley* found to his embarrassment that the rumour was no less than fourth-hand. Wesley ignored the controversy, treating it with the contempt it deserved.

It was the year 1779 before this last Calvinistic Controversy could be said to have ceased and all parties returned to their more useful labours, regular or otherwise. The Minute Controversy makes sorry reading like the previous one involving Hervey and Wesley. So much time and energy had been dissipated in dispute – and to what end? To apportion blame is not an easy task and hardly a useful exercise. One cannot avoid coming to

84. *ibid.* (Vol.8, p.267.)
85. Wright, Thomas *The Life of Augustus Montague Toplady* (London, 1911, pp.215-217.)

the opinion that Toplady[86] had much to answer for, for had he not attacked Wesley the very year before the Conference at which the offending 'Minute' had been passed? Fertile ground had certainly been prepared. Wright[87] gives a whole chapter to Toplady's friendship with Lady Huntingdon. Was he one of the clergy invited by her to the 1771 Conference? One will never know, but had he been there, one wonders what the results might have been!

Perhaps one useful outcome of the Minute Controversy was that through it and the subsequent literary arguments, Methodism had brought Arminianism to a permanent place in Protestantism – an Arminianism that was reasonably pure, simply explained and practical but, as the previous pages had shown, also open to unfortunate misunderstandings. It allied itself to no political party, its chief sin being purely evangelistic. It may well have been the means too, of moderating Calvinistic thought in the days which followed.

Regrets were soon voiced by a number of participants in the struggle and reconciliation was effected between some of them – such as Fletcher, Richard Hill, Berridge and Shirley. Toplady alone remained unrepentant and in any case his time on earth had run its course before the debate had finished. Too little place has been given by historians to the two evangelical laymen who showed by far the most Christian spirit in the whole controversy – James Ireland and John Thornton. They strove more than once during the heat of the battle to effect a reconciliation between the opposing parties – but to no avail. Yet it was in the hospitable home of the former that a few reconciliations were finally made, once the truce was called.

---

86. It should be noted that one of Toplady's greatest friends was the Baptist minister, Revd John C. Ryland, who was also one of Hervey's main literary helpers. Although there is no written evidence, one cannot help wondering – was Toplady not one of the other literary assistants to whom Hervey often referred? If so, Toplady's opposition to Wesley may well have taken an indirect, but nevertheless damaging form a few years previously.
87. Wright, Thomas *The Life of Augustus Montague Toplady* (London, 1911, Chapter 14, pp.194-204.)

However, to assess the cost of the struggle: the two parties were now irreconcilable as far as doctrine was concerned and the price paid was the end of what co-operation there had been between them, save an external venture to which reference will be made later in this chapter. Even then only a few personalities were involved.

Wesley himself did not emerge blameless from the dispute. His 'Minute' was justified. As Fletcher said, the Methodist people needed a reformation from Antinomianism for excesses had certainly crept into the societies. Also it must be admitted that some of these were due just as much to an abuse of the doctrine of Christian Perfection as they were to Calvinistic influences.[88] Nevertheless a careful study of Wesley's 'Minute' would show how easily it gave offence to the Calvinists who, in any case, had misunderstood it.

No amount of explanation could dilute such a statement as the very first one in the 'Minute': 'We have leaned too much towards Calvinism.' The 'Minute' implied that Calvinists placed no emphasis on the necessity of good works after conversion. This was neither fair nor true, and provided grounds for objection. Of course, it was obvious that the Calvinist party took offence at the opening sentence and paid less attention to Wesley's explanation of it. Once the Calvinist delegation attended the Conference of 1771, the members realized what Wesley had meant and it was then that an agreement was drawn up.

Wesley's excuse after the 1771 Conference that he must hasten away on business was a flimsy one. It *was* his business to see that the agreement so carefully made during that Conference became the end of the matter. Before leaving, it is abundantly clear that Wesley should have cancelled his instructions to Olivers to publish Fletcher's First *Check*, which, after all, contained personal references to Shirley. Was Wesley's neglect to do this an oversight or was it deliberate?

Another opportunity for cutting short the struggle was Hill's written suggestion to Fletcher that both sides should call a halt. It will be remembered that this followed Fletcher's publication of his *Fourth*

88. See previous Chapter of this study.

Check – Logica Genevensis. It is hard to understand why such an erudite, courteous scholar and writer of undisputed saintliness should refuse this request. Disputes in the church there have always been and still will be, but the distinction must be made between a dispute and the tone in which it is pursued. In Fletcher, the eighteenth century had one of its few examples of one who could express disagreement on a decent, Christian, gentlemanly level.

Again, a further mistake Wesley made, was in delegating Methodist apologetics to others. None can dispute the fact that in Fletcher of Madeley, Wesley and his movement had an apologist second to none. However, again, apart from his three works inspired by Toplady's opposition there was only one polemical piece deserving of mention from Wesley,[89] in respect of the 'Minute Controversy'. Ought he to have been 'too busy' to find time to pen statements which were to become doctrinal foundations for Methodism? In Olivers and Sellon, his choice was unfortunate, not only because of their background but because one was a lay-preacher and the other had been.[90]

To sum up, as Wesley said, the actual 'Minute' was 'disputing about words'. There was a victory – and an unfortunate one. Firmly held ideas, important as they may have seemed, won the day over Christian Love and mutual respect. It advertised in no favourable light either the teaching of Perfect Love or the behaviour of the Lord's Elect.

From the year 1778 when the final Calvinistic Controversy could be said to have died down, any real cooperation between Wesley and the Evangelicals had, to all intents and purposes, ceased. Wesley's bitterest opponents, Hervey and Toplady had passed on but so had some of his best supporters including Grimshaw of Haworth. Grimshaw's successor, John Richardson, whilst an Evangelical soon differed from Wesley and refused him the use of his church.

---

89. i.e. *Some Remarks on Mr Hill's 'Review of all the Doctrines taught by John Wesley*, (12mo. Bristol, 1772.)

90. Sellon had obtained Anglican ordination through the influence of Lady Huntingdon, but apparently his previous career as a baker and Methodist lay-preacher was not to be forgotten.

According to the Standard *Letters*, not a word passed between Lady Huntingdon and John. Looking down the list of Anglican churches in which Wesley was invited to preach, one is quite impressed with the number but they did not include those belonging to the remaining Evangelicals with whom Wesley had had so much to do. There were, of course, others such as the Revd David Simpson, of Macclesfield,[91] in whose church he officiated nine times after 1778. With clergy such as Simpson, Wesley had always been on friendly terms. In any case, Simpson was an Arminian but had never indulged in any form of irregularity. Whilst the Calvinistic Evangelicals for the most part declined to cooperate with Wesley after the 'Minute' dispute, there was one exception – Hicks of Wrestlingworth who asked Wesley to preach in his church, which he did on three occasions. Berridge, in the neighbouring parish outlived Wesley but not once (or at least, according to available evidence) did Wesley ever visit him or officiate for him. It was very obvious that the separation was now complete. John Newton who owed no small spiritual debt to Wesley and the Methodists, once wrote to Wesley stating he knew no one to whom his heart was more united in affection, nor to whom he owed more as an instrument of grace than John. However, such indebtedness did not move him sufficiently to offer his pulpit at any time, either at Olney or London.[92]

The one exception of real cooperation between 1778 and Wesley's

---

91. David Simpson had been curate at St Michael's Parish Church but owing to opposition to his 'Methodist' sympathies, a church (Now Christ Church – still Conservative Evangelical) was built for him by Mr Charles Roe. Simpson was usually referred to as a 'Methodist' clergyman for he was no Calvinist. On one occasion he experienced great trouble from some preachers of Lady Huntingdon's Connexion but he bade them find some other sphere of labour. In his *A Plea for Religion and the Sacred Writings* (London, 1836, p.317) he announced his intention of leaving the Established Church because of the difficulties he had experienced. However, he died as the result of a stroke before he could carry out his resolve. He often joined in the worship at Wesley's Chapel in Sunderland Street (recently closed). See Smith, Benjamin *The History of Methodism in Macclesfield* (Chapters 8,10,14 & 17.) Simpson's tomb is situated just outside the main entrance of the church in which he was minister.

92. *Arminian Magazine* (1780, p.441.)

death in 1791 was that which took place between John and an evangelical layman – William Wilberforce of Hull. The subject was, as is well known, that of slavery and the slave trade.

Of course, a whole chapter could be written on this subject alone. The early Evangelicals could never be given the credit for opposing the practice of slave-owning or trading, but rather be accused of encouraging it. In this, Whitefield must take a large share of the blame, considering his influence over Lady Huntingdon and her clerical circle.

Whitefield approved of slave-owning. As early as 1740, he wrote an open letter to 'The Inhabitants of Maryland, Virginia, and North and South Carolina' dated 23 January.[93] In it he had made no protest about slave-owning – only about inflicting cruelty upon them. 'Whether it be lawful for Christians to buy slaves, I shall not take upon me to determine...' He obviously regarded them as necessary in hot countries to cultivate the land. They should be well fed and housed and receive a 'share of their labours'. For his trouble in writing this epistle, he was soon in conflict with slave-owners. One can only guess what the results would have been, had he written *against slave owning*! Soon after, Whitefield became a slave-owner and in 1752 received £30 from James Hervey for the purpose of purchasing a slave, so it appears George could have had no objections to the slave trade as distinct from slave-owning.

When Whitefield died, in his will, he bequeathed fifty slaves to Lady Huntingdon who bought still more and complained bitterly that her Georgian overseer had driven forty-one of them to Boston and sold them.

She remained discreetly silent about her ideas on slavery as did her clerical coadjutors – and for obvious reasons. Such acquiescence seems strange to twentieth-century readers, but it must be remembered that Whitefield had seen sufficient scriptural warrant, especially in the Old Testament (to say nothing of the inference of Paul's letter to Philemon in respect of the runaway slave Onesimus) for his actions. What was sufficient for him in Scripture was also sufficient for his fellow-Calvinists. When one considers the tenets of Calvinism, it was a system that did not

93.   Tyerman, Luke *The Life of George Whitefield*, (Vol.1, pp.354-355.)

seem to be incongruous with slave-owning. If men were predestined before birth to be saved or damned, it would not be beyond the Calvinist's mind to believe too, that a man could be predestined to his earthly station, be it bond or free. Mrs Alexander's verse written in the following century (now discreetly omitted from modern hymnbooks) would have fitted in well with the Calvinists' outlook:

> 'The Rich man in his castle,
> The poor man at his gate,
> God made them high and lowly;
> Each in his own estate.'[94]

Wesley appeared to have decided against slavery in 1772 after reading Anthony Benezet's book on the subject which led him to describe the practice as 'that execrable sum of all villainies'.[95] In 1774, he published his *Thoughts on Slavery*[96] which denounced the master's unquestioned and absolute rights over his slaves and the cruelty which they inflicted. He traced how the negroes were brought in the first instance to America. They were procured by fraud and the whole business was an affront to justice. Self-selling was illogical because to whom belonged what he received for himself? There was no such person as a born slave. Slave-holding was utterly inconsistent with mercy. The argument that slavery was necessary for the wealth of a nation was one which did not hold water for such wealth was just not necessary: wisdom, virtue, justice and mercy were. Why were they cruelly treated? To prevent their escaping, of course. Had one tried gentleness? Did one know what mildness could effect? Wesley concluded with an attack not only on slave-owners but

---

94. From the hymn: 'All things bright and beautiful...'
95. J.W.J. (Vol.5, p.445.) He had, of course already seen something of this cruelty when on a visit to South Carolina. General Oglethorpe, the Governor of Georgia, to his credit would not allow slavery there but there was the custom of 'self-selling' or 'self-hiring'.
96. J.W.W. (Vol.6, pp.442-466.)

slave-*traders*. There was a God; He was a God of retribution. The whole business had to be stopped. There was no excuse – not even that of having been 'left' slaves by one's father. He prayed that all the slaves might burst their chains asunder and with them the chains of all the sins of those associated with the practice.

It will be quickly noticed that Wesley began his opposition to the slave-trade long before it aroused the attention of Wilberforce and his contemporaries but nowhere do historians give him credit for this. Wesley was fifty-six years older than Wilberforce but it was the latter who dealt with it. He did this through the very necessary channels of Parliamentary procedure. Wesley's last recorded letter in the Standard Edition[97] was addressed to Wilberforce from Balam [*sic*], urging him in the name of God to oppose that 'execrable villainy' which was the scandal of religion of England and of human nature.

Wilberforce, it must be noted in passing, was an Evangelical whose conversion was due to the Calvinists. Among these were Isaac Milner, John Newton, Thomas Scott, the famous Bible expositor and, later, John Venn, son of Henry Venn, late of Huddersfield. However, it could not be said that his Calvinism was very marked,[98] certainly not as much as that of his spiritual guides. One major work, to say nothing of a number of smaller ones, stands out as his classic contribution to religious thought: *A Practical View of the Prevailing Religious System of Professed Christians in the Higher and Middle Classes in this country contrasted with Real Christianity*.[99] Nowhere in this work was there a hint of any characteristic doctrine of Calvinism. It was indeed a 'practical view'. It breathed the very spirit of true Christian living and belief. Wilberforce as a layman, deeply committed to a very practical task, made no claims to being a theologian. He stressed the corrupt nature of man and answered the usual

---

97. Vol.8, pp.264-5. Dated 24 February 1791.
98. Scott, John AM *The Life of the Revd Thomas Scott* (London, 1836, p.225.) He said that Wilberforce was afraid of Calvinism.
99. The edition used here is that printed in Glasgow in 1841. There was a lengthy introductory essay by Dr Daniel Wilson, Bishop of Calcutta.

objections to this view.[100] For two chapters he warned his readers of the inadequate conceptions of Christ and the Holy Spirit[101] and was dissatisfied with the prevailing religious systems of the day. There was not enough emphasis being placed on the true practice of Christianity. (What greater relevance it would have had, if the publication had been in the early 1770s!) Too many professing Christians were seeking praise, position and esteem when there were ample opportunities awaiting exploitation by them in the realms of community and politics.[102] He ended with a plea for full commitment to Christ and Christian principles.[103] How true was Thomas Scott[104] when he said of Wilberforce's treatise: 'It is a most noble and manly stand for the Gospel, full of good sense, and most useful observations on subjects quite out of our line.' No doubt Scott, like others of his Calvinist friends would be more used to reading polemical discourses of which there had been no shortage for many years. It would indeed be on subjects 'out of their line'!

Apart from the isolated incident described above, cooperation between Wesley and the Evangelicals had now ceased.[105] A glance, however, at the list of preaching appointments in Anglican churches by invitation of the incumbents, taken by Wesley from 1778 to the end of his lifetime, showed that the clergy who owed allegiance neither to the Calvinists nor himself, had become quite friendly. Many of the clergy made him welcome in their churches. Approximately 168 invitations were accepted during this period, most of them to preach and some, in addition, to assist in Divine worship and concelebrate the Holy Communion. In the *Journal* (Standard edition)[106] Wesley felt that the tide had turned so that he had more invitations offered him by the clergy than he could accept. It has already been mentioned that apart from Hicks of Wrestlingworth, the

---

100. *op.cit.* (pp.105-131.)
101. *op.cit.* (pp.190-394.)
102. Wilberforce *op.cit.* (pp.394-443.)
103. *op.cit.* (pp.439-444.)
104. Scott, John AM *The Life of Revd Thomas Scott* (London, 1836, pp.225ff.)
105. See pages 332-3 where this matter has previously been mentioned.
106. Vol.6, p.387.

Calvinistic Evangelicals with whom Wesley had previously associated
were not among those who offered their pulpits to Wesley. One of the
invitatory clergy in the list was the Revd Thomas Pentycross,[107] Vicar of
St Mary's Wallingford, who *had* been a Calvinist but had relinquished
his views and had quarrelled with Lady Huntingdon on the subject.
Pentycross it should be mentioned had attempted, though unsuccessfully,
to make peace between Wesley and Richard Hill in 1773. As for the
remaining names amongst these clergy listed in the *Journal*, it would be
useful to know their doctrinal allegiance or whether they were 'Evangelical'
in the ordinary sense of the term without either 'Calvinistic' or 'Methodist'
overtones, or maybe men who, like many today, refused to have any label
attached to them.

Two spheres of opportunity which could have been exploited jointly
by both sides were pursued separately. The first was in the formation of
Sunday Schools. Long before Robert Raikes and Hannah More, whose
names will always be linked with this movement, it must be said that
Wesley was no stranger to the idea. He had held his own Sunday Schools
when in Georgia. His interest in education, both secular and spiritual, is
well known, even though his methods would horrify the modern
educationists.

His love and concern for children, though, were genuine enough.
Robert Raikes received scanty attention in Wesley's writings. Though
not one of the Evangelicals, he was an Anglican and worked within the
parish system. On the other hand, Hannah More was a convinced
Evangelical and in some respects resembled Lady Huntingdon in her
attempts to influence the affluent section of the community. Nevertheless,
Wesley, when writing to his niece on 31 July 1790[108] said he would like to
meet the More sisters but he doubted whether his conversation would suit
them. He had little relish for anything which did not 'concern the upper

---

107. Pentycross was educated at Christ's Hospital and Pembroke College, Cambridge
and distinguished himself as a Grecian. He was friendly with Calvinists and
Arminians alike, always endeavouring to make peace.
108. J.W.L. (Vol.8, p.230) (See also p.69.)

world'. Such was his opinion of one of the pioneers of the Sunday School movement. Rather he encouraged his preachers to set up their own. He spoke in the *Letters* and *Journal* of their beginning and success, for example at Bolton, Chester and Newcastle.[109] In each case he praised the system and often addressed the schools. Yet on one occasion only did he record addressing an Anglican Sunday School and that was at Bingley where he was friendly with the incumbent who appeared to be neither labelled an 'Evangelical' or a 'Calvinist'.[110] The Evangelicals used the Sunday School movement to great effect to build up their parish work, but nowhere did Wesley appear on the scene.

The second sphere of usefulness and even of more importance was that of the work overseas. Of course, Wesley again could be said to have taken the lead but in a very irregular way. His 'ordination' in 1786 when he 'ordained' two preachers for work overseas indicated his serious concern to exploit this opportunity. Two more 'ordinations' followed the next year. Later Thomas Coke was to superintend the work in America and give a great impetus to missionary endeavour.[111] At the Conference of 1790 a committee of nine preachers, of which Coke was the chairman, was appointed to take charge of this work. Strange to relate, the subscribers included the names of evangelical laymen such as Wilberforce, John Thornton and his brother, the Earl of Dartmouth; and, hard to believe though it might be, Berridge of Everton! Whether or not this was merely a written act of sympathy with Wesley's views on the slave-trade, it is difficult to say. Berridge never revealed his views on that subject but, being the individualist he was, there was no reason to suppose that he necessarily shared the usual evangelical views on slavery. The Wesleyan

---

109. See J.W.L. (Vol.7, p.265, Letter to John Fletcher; Vol.7, p.364 to Richard Rodda at Chester; Vol.8, p.23 to Alexander Suter at Bolton; Vol. 8, pp.207-8 to Charles Atmore at Newcastle.)

110. J.W.J. (Vol.7, p.3.) Although the Sunday School was held at the Parish Church and run by the Curate, the Editor of the *Journal* has a curious note to the effect that the school was interdenominational. It was founded in 1784. Wesley visited it on 18 July 1784.

111. For the full story see Moister, *William History of Wesleyan Missions in all parts of the world* (London, 1871.)

Missionary Society, however, was not formally founded until 1817. By that time, the Calvinistic Evangelicals had gone their own way. J.H. Overton gives a brief outline of the founding of the London Missionary Society and mentions that, at first, it was interdenominational, including representatives from Churchmen, Dissenters and Methodists.[112] The Society, however, soon became exclusively Dissenting and eventually formed the Missionary Society of the Congregational Church. The Calvinistic Evangelicals formed their own missionary enterprise – The Church Missionary Society (which exists today) in 1799. Henry Venn, his son John, and especially Simeon were among the greatest leaders. The movement was first originated by the 'Eclectic Society' formed by these men in 1783, receiving its present title in 1799. However, this society was later to suffer division and a splinter society was brought into being – The Bible Churchman's Missionary Society. This took place in 1922 because some members felt that the traditional evangelical emphasis on the inerrancy of Scripture was being played down. It was also a revolt against the Liberal Evangelicals who had separated from the more Conservative members on the subject of the necessity of restating Biblical doctrines and theology in a form more consistent with modern thinking. Nevertheless, it is encouraging to see that the work overseas is the one sphere where real and effective church unity and union are taking place today.

Before leaving the subject of cooperation, or rather, the lack of it, between the Calvinistic Evangelicals and Wesley, it is necessary, briefly, to state what the term would imply to him. Of course, he wrote not one treatise about it, the only deliberate mention of it, apart from passing comments or complaints, was the 'Scarborough Eirenicon'.[113] However, looking over the previous pages of this study it will be seen that cooperation had for him a much deeper meaning than preaching in the churches of friendly clergy or even receiving expressions of encouragement and sympathy with his work. In fact its meaning for him was a very strong

---

112. Overton, J.H. *The Evangelical Revival in the Eighteenth Century* (London, 1886.)
113. See Appendix Two of this study.

one and threefold.

Firstly it involved not only agreement by the clergy with his own irregular itinerancy but the insistence that a really effective evangelical witness by them would necessitate their own itinerating.

Secondly, his fellow clergy had to accept his practice of employing lay-preachers. Whilst he never insisted on other clergy using laymen, he did expect each incumbent to welcome Wesley's lay-preachers and approve their work within that clergyman's parish.

Thirdly, and, of course, later in his career, Wesley sought for recognition by the clergy of his own 'ordinations' as being valid.

In respect of the first requirement only four Calvinistic Evangelicals had been prepared to cooperate in this way, apart from Whitefield and the Welsh Evangelicals. The same applied to his second ideal with the same exceptions.[114] Whilst the Countess of Huntingdon remained within the Established Church, she could not be included amongst those who agreed for she had found a convenient loophole in the law to do the same herself and yet commit no illegality. As for the third point, he found no support or agreement from the Evangelicals, though by the time Wesley had decided to 'ordain', the friendliest of the Evangelicals had died; but it is doubtful whether they would have agreed with him. As for the Countess of Huntingdon and a few of her clergy, they had done the same the previous year and were by this time, Dissenters.

What of Wesley's views of the parish system? It does seem that Wesley never appreciated the good that was done, even in the smallest Anglican parishes. Had he not, years ago, declared, quite unfairly that, apart from Walker of Truro, he knew of no clergyman who had converted one soul if he had not become 'irregular'.[115] Of course parish work, by its very nature, was limited and Wesley had experienced only a very short time in it when he was his father's curate at Wroote. To a man of Wesley's limitless energy and undoubted evangelistic concern, parish

---

114. Added to this number could be Joseph Easterbrook, a Non-Calvinistic minister of the Temple Church, Bristol who sent his own converts to the local Methodist societies.

115. See pp. 75-6 of this study.

work afforded him too small a sphere. Comparing the list of evangelical clergy given in such works as Balleine's *History of the Evangelical Party in The Church of England* or Elliot Binns': *The Early Evangelicals: A Religious and Social Study* with the Standard *Letters* or *Journal* of Wesley, it seems that Wesley knew very few of them, or of them.[116] Take for example the tiny parish of Ashford near Barnstaple in North Devon (now amalgamated with the parish of Pilton in Barnstaple). In Wesley's day, there was an incumbent resident there – an Evangelical by the name of Thomas Bliss. Ashford is still only a hamlet but who can assess the good that was done in that small sphere in the eighteenth century? Wesley certainly could not for nowhere did he ever mention the place or the man.[117] Another fact that seems to have evaded Wesley's thinking is that the Evangelicals were not only working for the salvation of men's souls but for the reformation of their church from *within*. This was something Wesley was not in a position to do. Furthermore, the clergy who remained parish-bound no doubt had an eye to their security of tenure and even those who were acting as curates for absentee incumbents had a reasonable security provided that the absenteeism of their superiors was long-lasting. In the parish, one's duties were more clearly and precisely defined and organization was simpler. What is more, there was a security in itself in the fact of tradition, i.e. in doing things as they had always been done. Such was the outlook of those who saw value in the Established parish system.

Nevertheless, what would have happened to religion in England if

---

116. Cf. Wesley's sparse references to William Cowper, the Calvinistic layman and hymnwriter. He was the protégé of Newton when the latter was curate of Olney. See *Journal* of Wesley (Vol.6, p.400) where he had read Cowper's poems but had given no comment. Note too, that Wesley never made reference to Thomas Scott, the evangelical Bible expositor.
117. I am grateful to Mr D.V. Cannon of Ashford for the information that Bliss was minister there from 20 March 1770 to 9 June 1803, but that there are no other facts available about him. In Wesley's day, Ashford, says Mr Cannon, had a population of about 70 living in 18 houses. There is no memorial to Bliss in the church or yard.

Wesley had heeded the advice of Hervey[118] and 'settled in a cure' or, for example, had accepted the teaching post at Skipton Grammar School?[119] Wesley's concern and the need he felt called to meet meant for him, the setting aside, reluctantly at first maybe, of the rules and traditions of the Church for which he professed a loyalty and love to his dying day and which he swore he would not leave.

The other point in respect of Church order which caused so much dissension was his employment of lay-preachers. The Evangelicals could be excused for their opposition to the system. Laymen had little to do in their own movement within the church except spread their influence in the work-a-day world. Their group was predominantly a clerical one. Their laymen did not preach or assist in worship. Wesley, on the other hand involved himself in an immense and widespread work which he could not control alone. Few were the clergy who cast in their lot with him. Too many saw in the new Methodist movement a potential new sect of Dissenters. Therefore, the alternative was lay-help which Wesley had to organize. At organizing he was a genius, but in the controlling of the ever-growing band of lay-preachers, he found a group which in the end tended to organize him. What is more, they, together with the people they served, were the driving force behind his 'ordinations', strengthened by the fact that the Methodist people were all too often deprived of the Sacrament at Anglican tables. The bishops (with an odd exception) refused to ordain Methodist lay-preachers merely to remain itinerant preachers and who could really blame them? There was, indeed, a peculiar naivety about Wesley which will never be understood. These 'ordinations' of 1784 onwards were but another death-blow to cooperation between the two parties. It simply indicated the contemporary deadness in ecclesiastical circles that Wesley was allowed to remain an Anglican priest with so many of his irregular activities ignored.

---

118. See page 70 ff. of this study.
119. J.W.L. (Vol.1, pp.42-43.) I am indebted to my friend, Mrs J. Mansergh, BA, AMA, of Settle, former Curator of Skipton Museum for information about the offer made to Wesley and about the letter, a copy of which is kept at the Museum. It was dated Lincoln College 19 March 1727.

The doctrinal differences were even more pronounced. It may be hard for some to judge whether Church order or theological considerations did the most to lead to separation between the two evangelizing sections of the Church. Of the two, however, the doctrinal disagreements caused longer controversies and far more literary activity. First of all, was there a *social* basis as well as a theological one for the initial difference between the Wesleys and Whitefield?[120] Lady Huntingdon as well as Whitefield must take her share of the blame for some of the controversies which raged during this period. The Countess, it has been said, became a Calvinist for two reasons, namely: the defence paid to her by Whitefield and because Calvinism appealed to her as 'it was a doctrine which makes a privileged order of souls'.[121] Such servility makes sickening reading today but one has to remember that such an attitude was common enough in those days. Even so there seemed to be little need in his correspondence for the flowery language used and the subservient manner in which he addressed her. Some of the other Evangelicals were not absolved from the same fault. Standing out in stark contrast in this matter was John Berridge of Everton. He stood his ground with Her Ladyship. On one occasion he wrote to her when she had made a too-pressing request upon him: 'You threaten me, Madam, like a Pope, not like a mother in Israel...My instructions, you know just come from the Lamb, not from the Lamb's wife, though she is a tight woman.'[122]

Wesley, on the other hand, with a background distinct from that of Whitefield, spoke and wrote to her just in the way a gentleman would to a lady of that period, but on one occasion had no hesitation in pointing out her faults.[123] Her influence amongst the nobility and also her considerable

---

120. See Preface to this study.
121. Southey, Robert *The Life of Wesley and the Rise and Progress of Methodism* (London, 1881, p.467.) Southey said that the Countess was a Supralapsarian whereas Selina's biographer declared she was a Sublapsarian.
122. Houses of Shirley and Hastings, A Member of *The Life and Times of Selina, Countess of Huntingdon* (London, 1839, Vol.1, p.324 and Vol.2, p.20.) Also Tytler, Sarah *The Countess of Huntingdon and Her Circle* (London, 1907, p.32.)
123. See pp. 308-9 of this study.

wealth placed her in a privileged position. Whitefield obviously felt he was far more successful among the coronet-wearers than he really was. True, members of the nobility like Bolingbroke and Chesterfield were deeply impressed by his oratory but this did not seem to have had a salutary effect on their lives. In turn, the Evangelicals fell under Her Ladyship's influence, embraced her doctrinal outlook, were appointed as her chaplains and officiated in her proprietary chapels until this remarkable system came to a disastrous end in 1783. After Wesley and Whitefield had made their peace following the first controversy over such Calvinistic tenets as Election, Predestination, and the Perseverance of the Saints, the other Evangelicals took every opportunity to cavil at John henceforth,

By far the greatest damage done on account of doctrinal controversy was that resulting from the dispute between Wesley and Hervey regarding the notion of the Imputed Righteousness of Christ. After a thorough reading of the three fair-sized volumes of *Theron and Aspasio*, it is difficult for a twentieth-century mind to understand the reason for the wide popularity of the work. Poor sensitive Hervey, hyper-sensitive in fact, made worse by his terminal illness, unscrupulously influenced by some of Wesley's worst enemies, received all the sympathy whilst Wesley took all the blame for criticizing *Theron and Aspasio*,[124] a task which James had insisted on John performing. Of course, Wesley's dealing with the gentle, secluded Hervey was as rough as one would expect of a man who was leading a full and exacting life, exposed to all winds and weathers; but Hervey struck at John from the grave. One may be sure of the blame that can be apportioned to Hervey's brother William, but the names of Ryland, Cudworth, Toplady and even Whitefield, will never be cleared of suspicion.

It was the lasting damage that was done, the effects of which can be seen today, which is perturbing. Hervey's *Eleven Letters* although published (supposedly against his wishes) and used so unscrupulously by Glass, Sandeman and the Erskines, all of Scotland (the latter being friends of Whitefield), hindered Wesley's work in that country and hence

---

124. See Appendix One of this study.

the smallness of Methodism in Scotland today.

Just as Whitefield was one of the first influences on Hervey (at least doctrinally), it was he who also took the initiative with the Calvinistic layman, Howell Harris, in Wales, and when the Calvinistic Methodist Church was formed, Whitefield became its first Moderator. So again, little wonder then there need be that Wesley's Methodism (either Welsh- or English-speaking) was never strong and prosperous in the Principality.

Yet, for all his irregularity, in exercising his influence over the Countess of Huntingdon, and she, in turn of the evangelical clergy, Whitefield could be said to have laid the foundation for the only evangelical movement which remained loyal to the Established Church.

The doctrinal dispute which took place between Wesley and Hervey (involving numerous other controversialists, of course), was but a prelude to the 'Minute' Controversy which followed soon after, arising out of the minute taken at Wesley's 1770 Conference. The scurrilous writing of Toplady the previous year was produced at an opportune time. The Hervey business was dying down but there can be no doubt that Toplady provided the link between the two controversies by keeping alive the already engendered acrimonious spirit.

A final summing up of the doctrinal differences all of which have been dealt with in turn, must mention that if Wesley had ignored many of the expressions of Calvinism and had not, as he did on so many occasions, taken the initiative in writing controversially about them, the Evangelicals might well have never troubled to fight against him as they did. To begin with, why did Wesley do this in respect of Whitefield in the first place? If only Wesley could have foreseen the future extent of George's theological influence. Secondly, Wesley saw in Calvinism[125] a system, logical though it claimed to be, which limited the salvation he felt called upon to preach to all, because it was *for* all. Calvinism, to him, made God an Almighty tyrant. To be a Calvinist and preach salvation was to him illogical. The

125. Coomer, Duncan *English Dissent under the Hanoverians* (London, 1946, p.109) says Wesley was a 'sound Calvinist' when he spoke of himself as a 'brand plucked from the burning' referring to the fire at Epworth Rectory when he was six years of age.

Elect would finally be saved, regardless of their conduct and the reprobates damned.

It is obvious too, that another factor overlooked by Wesley was the declaration made by many of his critics that whilst they were decided Calvinists, they were but *moderate* ones. Such was the written admission of Venn,[126] Hervey, Whitefield and Berridge whilst indirect hints were afforded by Newton,[127] Scott and Simeon. Moderate or not, to John, this was no excuse. They were still Calvinists; they held the notion of Election, Predestination and the Perseverance of the Saints, against which he wrote with vehemence. What these Calvinists meant by being moderate was that they held these doctrines without admitting the logical conclusion that if God elected those who were to be saved, then he must also reprobate the remainder to be damned. This conclusion they were not prepared to admit but Wesley with commendable logic, insisted that Election presupposed Reprobation. Furthermore, if the Calvinists held that the saved would infallibly persevere to the end and gain their eternal destiny, then the way was open to Antinomianism, the 'Calvinistic tendency' which he opposed more strongly than the other tenets. Therein lay the irreconcilable difference.

However, pursuing the matter of Antinomianism a little further, it is possible that Wesley had allowed his fear of this tendency to become an obsession. He was worried over its effect on morality. It was, to him, tantamount to blasphemy to believe that one could attain heaven and yet, if one wished, the requirements of the moral law could be set aside. Yet, in actual fact, there was not a great deal of evidence that many Calvinists took advantage of this view.

Conversely, it can be seen that there were some – albeit, only a few –

---

126. Henry Venn, when asked if a certain young minister was an Arminian or a Calvinist, he replied: 'I really do not know; he is a sincere disciple of the Lord Jesus Christ, and that is of infinitely more importance than his being a disciple of Calvin or Arminius.' Venn, J. *The Life and Letters of Revd Henry Venn, MA* (London, 1837, pp.32-3.)
127. Newton in his *Cardiphonis etc.* (London, 1780, p.290) said he had no time for Arminianism – or for dispute.

who were equally Antinomian by becoming fanatically persuaded that they had attained Christian Perfection in all its fullness, i.e. Entire Sanctification. This was Wesley's doctrine but he accepted no responsibility for the extravagances of this minority. Again, the Calvinists were not blameless here. Whitefield, in the early days set the tone for the wrong interpretation of Christian Perfection, i.e. not as Perfect Love of God and Man, but as Sinless Perfection – or Moral Perfection. It is true that Wesley had not been altogether consistent in his exposition of his favourite theme.

Had Wesley not been obsessed about the effects of Calvinism and Whitefield not been so ready to reply so hotly and thus light a fire which was to burn for many years, there might well have been less acrimony, more friendliness and, as far as principles of Church order were concerned, more united service in the one increasing purpose of the Revival.

In contrast with much of the prevailing bitterness during this period is an account of a conversation which took place between Wesley and Charles Simeon:[128]

> 'Sir,' said young Simeon, 'Sir, I understand you are called an Arminian; now I am sometimes called a Calvinist, and therefore, I suppose we are to draw daggers. But, before I begin to combat, with your permission, I will ask you a few questions, not from impertinent curiosity, but for real instruction. Pray, Sir, do you feel yourself a depraved creature, so depraved that you would never have thought of turning to God, if God had not put it into your heart?'
>
> 'Yes,' said the veteran, 'I do indeed.'

---

128. Tyerman, Luke *The Life and Times of Revd John Wesley, MA* (London, 1872, Vol.2, pp.510-511.) Tyerman says the conversation was obtained from Dr Dobbin. Why it was not recorded in the *Journal* is difficult to understand.

'And do you utterly despair of recommending yourself to God by anything that you can do; and look for salvation solely through the blood and righteousness of Christ?'

'Yes, solely through Christ.'

'But, Sir, supposing you were *first* saved by Christ, are you not somehow or other to save yourself afterwards by your good works?'

'No; I must be saved by Christ, from first to last.'

'Allowing then, that you were first turned by the grace of God, are you not in some way or other, to keep yourself by your own power?'

'No.'

'What, then? Are you to be upheld every hour and every moment, by God, as much as an infant in its mother's arms?'

'Yes, altogether.'

'And is all your hope in the grace and mercy of God, to preserve you unto His heavenly kingdom?'

'Yes, I have no hope but in Him.'

'Then, Sir, with your leave, I will put up my dagger again; for this is all my Calvinism; this is my election, my justification, my final perseverance. It is in substance all that I hold, and as I hold it; and, therefore, if you please, instead of searching out terms and phrases to be a ground of contention between us, we will cordially unite in those things wherein we agree.'

There is little doubt that in an atmosphere such as this, the other Evangelicals would have united themselves with these sentiments. Oh! that such conversations had been possible some forty years before!

One other difference between the two groups, to which passing reference must be made, is that put forward by Elliott Binns.[129] This is that they appealed to different classes. This surely, is rather an exaggeration. Whitefield appealed just as much to the colliers of Kingswood as he did to the nobility in the drawing-rooms and chapels of Lady Huntingdon; and possibly with a more lasting effect. It is true that whilst Wesley also had his aristocratic friends, he did spend most of his time with the common folk, but what Evangelicals, faithful as most of them were to their own parishes, would appeal only to the upper classes? In many places, especially in the country, the upper class would be represented purely by the local squire or noble and his family. Whether in town or country the greater part of the congregation might well have consisted mainly of the working classes to whom the evangelical clergy would have a relevant word, week by week.

No historical subject such as this study would be complete without a word about its contemporary relevance. The effects of these eighteenth-century controversies can be seen today. The limited Methodist presence in Scotland and Wales has already been cited, and is not the sole effect. In recent times, the schemes for Anglican–Methodist Reunion have broken down – mainly due to the irreconcilable differences on the Church, Ministry,[130] and Sacraments. It was not only the extreme Anglo-Catholic element who opposed the terms of this union, but the Conservative Evangelicals, who opposed with equal force but for what appeared to be the opposite reason. Whilst the latter have maintained faithfully the parish system, they have never laid the same stress on Church order as

129. From his *The Early Evangelicals: A Religious and Social Study* (London, 1953, Chapter 12.) He believes the lay-preachers would appeal to the lower classes.
130. See my book: *John Wesley and the Christian Ministry etc.* (London, 1963) where I have given the historical reasons for the Methodist ministry and the sources and development of Wesley's views.

have the Anglo-Catholics. The main reason given for their objection was that the proposed Service of Reconciliation of the Ministries in which there was to be the mutual 'laying on of hands' was unessential and irrelevant. Some of the Evangelicals like a considerable number of Methodists interpreted this as 're-ordination'.

Furthermore, whilst many of the eighteenth-century Calvinistic-Arminian differences may have been forgotten, the differences thus caused, still remain. The Conservative Evangelicals of the Church of England of today are the successors of the eighteenth-century group discussed in this study and they exist today as small, yet strong vocal section of the Establishment.[131] They work still with the same zeal and faithfulness as did their predecessors in their respective parishes; but it is easily noticed that so often they find a more natural and congenial sphere of unity and cooperation with their Calvinistically-based Strict Baptist and Brethren colleagues, than with local Methodism. It is also a fact that the Keswick Movement, largely supported by the Anglican Conservatives, rarely has a Methodist, and therefore an Arminian speaker on its platform. W.E. Sangster[132] quoting the Revd Prebendary Webb-Peploe, speaking at a Keswick Convention in 1895 records that the latter saw the Methodist teaching on Christian Perfection as a stumbling-block:

> 'When I read such words as dear John Wesley's, "The evil root, the carnal mind, is destroyed in me; sin subsists no longer," I can only marvel that any human being, with the teaching of the Holy Ghost upon the Word of God, can thus deceive himself, or attempt to deceive others. It is, I think, a miracle of blindness that we can study God's word, and imagine that any man can be free from sin experimentally while here in the mortal body.'

---

131. This is not intended to include the *Liberal* Evangelicals.
132. Path to Perfection. *An Examination and Restatement of John Wesley's Doctrine of Christian Perfection* (London, 1943, page 81.)

Mr M.J. Micklewright[133] of the Evangelical Library, London, furnishes the following explanation and whilst agreeing about the differences between Methodist and Keswick teaching, does not think that the Calvinism of the founders of Keswick was very pronounced:

'The difference between the Wesley and Keswick teaching on Perfection is stated by Samuel Chadwick as "Wesleyan perfection is eradication of sin; Keswick – suppression of sin" [Page 148 *Life of Samuel Chadwick* by Norman Dunning].[134]

'As to the Calvinistic background of the Evangelicals who formed the Keswick Movement, their Calvinism does not seem to have been very pronounced. The original meetings would hardly have got very far had there been any real grasp of Calvinistic theology. Brethrenism no doubt influenced the Church of England and other Evangelicals a great deal because of the Brethren stress on the imminent return of Our Lord Jesus Christ and no doubt had its influence on Keswick. The fact of the closeness to Brethren and Strict Baptists by the Church of England Evangelicals is due to the close adhesion of these bodies to the authority of the Scriptures, which authority has been challenged so greatly in the nineteenth and

---

133. I am greatly indebted to Mr Micklewright for his kindness in providing me with this information which he has done in a recent letter. The Library and the Keswick Movement are closely associated and the doctrinal outlook of the former, both its founders and committee are Calvinistically inclined.

134. Mr Micklewright quotes from Benjamin B. Warfield *Studies in Perfection*, (Oxford University Press, New York 1931, Vol.2, pp.368-395.) In it Dr W. H. Griffith Thomas asserts that in his view, Perfection is that 'Deliverance from the guilt of sin, deliverance from the penalty of sin, deliverance from the bondage of sin and deliverance hereafter from the very presence of sin'. Warfield says that the insertion of the word 'hereafter' into the last clause tells the story. We must wait for the 'hereafter' to be delivered from the 'presence of sin' – that is to say from the corruption of our hearts – but meanwhile we may very well live as if sin were not present; its presence in us need not in any way effect our life-manifestation.'

twentieth centuries. There are novel ideas in the Brethren views because they have no theological, doctrinal or credal statements in their teaching. The Strict Baptists' emphasis on Calvinism also gives support to the position of Conservative Evangelicals, but this would be less noticeable than the influence of Brethrenism and hardly at all on Keswick.'

Finally, time brings its changes and amongst them changes of methods. The Anglican Church today finds a place for lay-preaching and, not least, the evangelical wing. It is even following Methodism by receiving women into the ranks of its ministry. Pronounced Calvinism is rarely, if ever, heard from Anglican pulpits, whether or not the theological differences of the eighteenth century are still with us, though silently.

Three lessons can be learnt from such a study as this. Briefly they are these. Firstly, there is the paradoxically divisive nature of Revival for one would normally look to Revival as a unifying factor. However, new truth (or rather old truth re-discovered) finds itself in opposition to set tradition in which so many are content to rest. Secondly, it is true that as the work of God prospers, so the work of the Devil seems also to increase correspondingly. Thirdly, when one looks carefully at the two opposing doctrinal systems, the consideration of which has taken up approximately half of this present study, they do at least agree on the basic element of the Christian Religion – the assumption of the Sovereignty of God. It is what develops from this basis which seems irreconcilable; but need the difficulties have been made out to be so great when one looks at the charitable and loving conversation which took place between Wesley and Simeon quoted above?

Unfortunately, one principle precious to the Arminians was omitted by the Calvinists, namely, freewill. Therefore Wesley could not agree even with 'moderate' Calvinism if it meant that God had favourites – has elected some to be saved and the rest to be damned. Yet if Calvinism could recognize freewill, man's right of choice, and temper its views so that Election and Predestination simply implied that God *foreknew* who would or would not respond to the offer of salvation, then the two could agree. However unjust the tenets of Calvinism may have seemed (and still do seem), one cannot help observing in modern society those who appear to be congenitally impervious to the Gospel claims. There is certainly no shortage of those who apparently find it impossible to listen or be convinced and are, to all intents and purposes, unconvertible. Pragmatically, Calvinism seems to have practical experience on its side in the twentieth century!

If, however, one must return to the irreconcilable position as seen in the eighteenth century, it may well be that both sides should, in all Christian humility, admit that they are looking into a glass darkly and, with prayerful patience, await the day when they will see face to face and know even as they are already known.

APPENDIX ONE

Letter from John Wesley to James Hervey

Re – Theron and Aspasio

15 October, 1756.

Dear Sir,

A considerable time since, I sent you a few hasty thoughts which occurred to me on reading the *Dialogues between Theron and Aspasio.* I have not been favoured with any answer. Yet upon another and a more careful perusal of them, I could not but set down some obvious reflections, which I would rather have communicated before these Dialogues were published.

In the First Dialogue there are several just and strong observations which may be of use to every serious reader. In the Second, is not the description often too laboured, the language too stiff and affected? Yet the reflections on the creation, in the thirty-first and following pages, make abundant amends for this. (I cite the pages according to the Dublin edition, having wrote the rough draught of what follows in Ireland.)

Is justification more or less than God's pardoning and accepting a sinner through the merits of Christ? That God herein 'reckons the righteousness and obedience which Christ performed as our own' (page 39) I allow; if by that ambiguous expression you mean only, as you here explain it yourself, 'They are as effectual for obtaining our salvation as if they were our own personal qualifications' (page 41).

'We are not solicitous as to any particular set of phrases. Only let me

355

be humbled, as repenting criminals at Christ's feet, let them rely as devoted pensioners on His merits, and they are undoubtedly in the way to a blissful immortality' (page 43). Then for Christ's sake, and for the sake of the immortal souls which He has purchased with His blood, do not dispute for that *particular* phrase, 'the imputed righteousness of Christ'. It is not scriptural; it is not necessary. Men who scruple to use, men who never heard, the expression, may yet 'be humbled, as repenting criminals at His feet, and rely as devoted pensioners on His merits'. But it has done immense hurt. I have had abundant proof that the frequent use of this unnecessary phrase, instead of 'furthering men's progress in vital holiness', has made them satisfied without any holiness at all – yea, and encouraged them to work all uncleanness with greediness.

'To ascribe pardon to Christ's passive, eternal life to His active, righteousness, is fanciful rather than judicious. His universal obedience from his birth to His death is the one foundation of my hope.' (Page 45.)

This is unquestionably right. But if it be, there is no manner of need to make the imputation of His active righteousness a separate and laboured head of discourse. Oh that you had been content with this plain scriptural account, and spared some of the dialogues and letters that follow!

The Third and Fourth Dialogues contain an admirable illustration and confirmation of the great doctrine of Christ's satisfaction. Yet even here I observe a few passages which are liable to some exception:-

'Satisfaction was made to the divine law' (page 54). I do not remember any such expression in Scripture. This way of speaking of the law, as a person injured and to be satisfied, seems hardly defensible.

'The death of Christ procured the pardon and acceptance of believers even before He came in the flesh' (page 74). Yes, and ever since. In this we all agree. And why should we contend for anything more?

'All the benefits of the new covenant are the purchase of His blood' (page 120). Surely they are. And after this has been fully proved, where is the need, where is the use of contending so strenuously for the imputation of His righteousness as is done in the Fifth and Sixth Dialogues?

'If He was our substitute as to penal sufferings, why not as to justifying obedience?' (page 135). The former is expressly asserted in

Scripture; the latter is not expressly asserted there.

'As sin and misery have abounded through the first Adam, mercy and grace have much more abounded through the Second: so that none can have any reason to complain' (page 145). No, not if the second Adam died for all: otherwise all for whom He did not die have great reason to complain; for they inevitably fall by the first Adam, without any help from the Second.

'The whole world of believers' (page 148) is an expression which never occurs in Scripture, nor has it any countenance there: the world in the inspired writings being constantly taken either in the universal or in a bad sense; either for the whole of mankind or for that part of them who know God.

'In the Lord shall all the house of Israel be justified' (page 149). It ought unquestionably to be rendered '*By* or *through* the Lord': the argument therefore proves nothing.

'Ye are complete in Him'. The words literally rendered are 'Ye are filled with Him'; and the whole passage (as any unprejudiced reader may observe) relates to sanctification, not justification.

'They are accepted for Christ's sake; this is justification through imputed righteousness' (page 150). That remains to be proved. Many allow the former who cannot allow the latter.

'The righteousness which justified us is already wrought out' (page 151). A crude, unscriptural expression! 'It was set on foot, carried on, completed.' Oh vain philosophy! The plain truth is, Christ lived and 'tasted death for every man'; and through the merits of His life and death every believer is justified.

'Whoever perverts so glorious a doctrine shows he never believed' (page 152). Not so. They who 'turn back as a dog to the vomit' had once 'escaped the pollutions of the world by the knowledge of Christ.'

'The goodness of God leadeth to repentance' (page 153). This is unquestionably true; but the nice, metaphysical doctrine of Imputed Righteousness leads not to repentance but to licentiousness.

'The believer cannot but add to his faith works of righteousness' (page 154). During his first love, this is often true; but it is not true afterwards, as we know and feel by melancholy experience.

'We no longer obey in order to lay the foundation of our final acceptance' (page 155). No; that foundation is already laid in the merits of Christ. Yet we obey in order to our final acceptance through his merits; and in this sense by obeying we 'lay a good foundation that we may attain eternal life'.

'"We establish the law"; we provide for its honour by the perfect obedience of Christ' (page 156). Can you possibly think St Paul means this? that such a thought ever entered into his mind? The plain meaning is, We establish both the true sense and the effectual practice of it; we provide for its being both understood and practised in its full extent.

'On those who reject the atonement, just severity' (page 157). Was it ever possible for them not to reject it? If not, how is it just to cast them into a lake of fire for not doing what it was impossible they should do? Would it be just (make it your own case) to cast *you* into hell for not touching heaven with your hand?

'Justification is complete the first moment we believe, and is incapable of augmentation' (page 159). Not so: there may be as many degrees in the favour as in the image of God.

'St Paul often mentions *a righteousness imputed*.' Not a *righteousness*, never once; but simply righteousness. 'What can this be but the righteousness of Christ?' (page 190). He tells you himself – 'To him that believeth on Him that justifieth the ungodly, faith is imputed for righteousness' (Rom.iv.5.) 'Why is Christ styled *Jehovah our Righteousness*?' Because we are both justified and sanctified through Him.

'My death, the cause of their forgiveness. My righteousness, the ground of their acceptance' (page 191). How does this agree with page 45? – 'To ascribe pardon to Christ's passive, eternal life to His active, righteousness, is fanciful rather than judicious.'

'He commends such kind of beneficence only as were exercised to a disciple as such (page 195). Is this not a slip of the pen? Will not our Lord then command, and reward eternally, all kinds of loving faith – yea, that which was exercised to a Samaritan, a Jew, a Turk, or an heathen?

Even these I would not term 'transient bubbles', though they do not procure our justification.

'How must our righteousness exceed that of the Scribe and Pharisees? No only in being sincere, but in possessing a complete righteousness, even that of Christ' (page 197). Did our Lord mean this? Nothing less. He specifies in the following parts of His sermon the very instances wherein the righteousness of a Christian exceeds that of the Scribes and Pharisees.

'He brings this specious hypocrite to the test' (page 198). How does it appear that he was an hypocrite? Our Lord gives not the least intimation of it. Surely He 'loved him' not for his hypocrisy, but his sincerity.' Yet he loved the world, and therefore could not keep any of the commandments in their spiritual meaning. And the keeping of these is undoubtedly the way to, though not the cause of, eternal life.

'"By works his faith was made perfect"; appeared to be true' (page 200). No; the natural sense of the words is, 'By' the grace superadded while he wrought those 'works his faith was' literally 'made perfect'.

'"He that doeth righteousness is righteous"; manifests the truth of his conversion' (ibid). Nay; the plain meaning is, He alone is truly righteous whose faith worketh by love.

'St James speaks of the justification of our faith' (page 201). Not unless you mean by that odd expression our faith being made perfect; for so the Apostle explains his own meaning. Perhaps the word 'justified' is once used by St Paul for *manifested*; but that does not prove it is to be so understood here.

'"Whoso doeth these things shall never fall" into total apostasy' (page 202). How pleasing is this to flesh and blood! But David says no such thing. His meaning is, 'Whoso doeth these things' to the end 'shall never fall' into hell.

The Seventh Dialogue is full of important truths. Yet some expressions in it I cannot commend.

'"One thing thou lackest" – the imputed righteousness of Christ' (page 216). You cannot think it is the meaning of the text. Certainly the 'one thing' our Lord meant was the love of God. This was the thing he lacked.

'Is the obedience of Christ insufficient to accomplish our justification?' (page 222). Rather I would ask, Is the death of Christ insufficient to purchase it?

'The saints in glory ascribe the whole of their salvation to the blood of the Lamb' (page 226). So do I; and yet I believe 'He obtained for all a possibility of salvation'.

'The terms of acceptance for fallen men were a full satisfaction to the divine justice and a complete conformity to the divine law' (page 227). This you take for granted; but I cannot allow it. The terms of acceptance for fallen men are repentance and faith. 'Repent ye, and believe the gospel'.

'There are but two methods whereby any can be justified either by a perfect obedience to the law, or because Christ hath kept the law in our stead' (*ibid.*) You should say, 'Or by faith in Christ.' I then answer, This is true; and fallen man is justified, not by perfect obedience, but by faith. What Christ has done is the foundation of our justification, not the term or condition of it.

In the Eighth Dialogue likewise there are many great truths, and yet some things liable to exception.

David 'God Himself dignifies with the most exalted of all characters' (page 253). Far, very far from it. We have more exalted characters than David's, both in the Old Testament and the New. Such are those of Samuel, Daniel, yea and Job, in the former; of St Paul and St John in the latter.

'But God styles him "a man after His own heart".' This is the text which has caused many to mistake, for want of considering (1) that this is said of David in a particular respect, not with regard to his whole character; (2) the time at which it was spoken. When was David 'a man after God's own heart'? When God found him 'following the ewes great with young,' when He 'took him from the sheepfolds' (Ps.lxxviii.70-1). It was in the second or third year of Saul's reign that Samuel said to him, 'The Lord hath sought Him a man after His own heart, and hath commanded him to be captain over His people' (I.Sam.xiii.14). But was he 'a man after God's own heart' all his life? or in all particulars? So far from it, that we have few more exceptionable characters among all the men of God recorded in Scripture.

'There is not a just man upon earth that sinneth not'. Solomon might truly say so before Christ came. And St John might, after He came, say as truly. 'Whosoever is born of God sinneth not' (page 261). But 'in many things we offend all'. That St James does not speak this of himself or of real Christians will clearly appear to all who impartially consider the context.

The Ninth Dialogue proves excellently well that we cannot be justified by our works.

But have you thoroughly considered the words which occur in the 270th page? -

'O children of Adam, you are no longer obliged to love God with all your strength, nor your neighbours as yourselves. Once, indeed, I insisted on absolute purity of heart; now I can dispense with some degree of evil desire. Since Christ has fulfilled the law for you, you need not fulfil it. I will connive at, yes accommodate my demands to, your weakness.'

I agree with you that 'this doctrine makes the Holy One of God a minister of sin'. And is it not your own? Is not this the very doctrine which you espouse throughout your book?

I cannot but except to several passages also in the Tenth Dialogue.

I ask first, 'Does the righteousness of God ever mean,' as you affirm, 'the merits of Christ'? (page 291). I believe not once in all the Scripture. It often means, and particularly in the Epistle to the Romans, God's method of justifying sinners. When, therefore, you say, 'The righteousness of God means such a righteousness as may justly challenge His acceptance' (page 292), I cannot allow it at all; and this capital mistake must needs lead you into many others. But I follow you step by step.

'In order to entitle us to a reward, there must be an imputation of righteousness' (*ibid.*) There must be an interest in Christ, and then 'every man shall receive his own reward according to his own labour.'

'A rebel may be forgiven without being restored to the dignity of a son' (page 293). A rebel against an earthly king may, but not a rebel against God. In the very same moment that God forgives we are the sons of God. Therefore this is an idle dispute. For pardon and acceptance, though they may be distinguished, cannot be divided. The words of Job which you cite are wide of the question. Those of Solomon prove no more than this (and who denies it?), that justification implies both pardon and acceptance.

'Grace reigneth through righteousness unto eternal life' (page 295) – that is, the free love of God brings us through justification and sanctification to glory. 'That they may receive forgiveness, and a lot among the sanctified' (*ibid.*) – that is, that they may receive pardon, holiness, heaven.

'Is not the satisfaction made by the death of Christ sufficient to obtain both our full pardon and final happiness?' (*ibid.*) Unquestionably it is, and neither of the texts you cite proves the contrary.

'If it was requisite for Christ to be baptized, much more to fulfil the moral law' (page 296). I cannot prove that either one or the other was requisite in order to His purchasing redemption for us.

'By Christ's sufferings alone the law was not satisfied' (page 297). Yes, it was; for it required only the alternative, Obey or die. It required no man to obey and die too. If any man had perfectly obeyed, He would not have died. 'Where the Scripture ascribes the whole of our salvation to the death of Christ a part of His humiliation is put for the whole' (*ibid.*) I cannot allow this without some proof. 'He was obedient unto death' is no proof at all, as it does not necessarily imply any more than that He died in obedience to the Father. In some texts there is a necessity of taking a part for the whole; but in these there is no such necessity.

'Christ undertook to do everything necessary for our redemption' (page 300) – namely, in a covenant made with the Father. It is sure He did everything necessary; but how does it appear that He undertook this before the foundation of the world, and that by a positive covenant between Him and the Father?

You think this appears from four texts: (1) From that, 'Thou gavest them to Me'. Nay; when any believe, 'the Father gives them to Christ.' But this proves no such previous contract. (2) 'God hath laid upon Him the iniquities of us all.' Neither does this prove any such thing. (3) That expression, 'The counsel of peace shall be between them,' does not necessarily imply any more than that both the Father and the Son would concur in the redemption of man. (4) 'According to the counsel of His will' – that is, in the way or method He had chosen. Therefore neither any of these texts, nor all of them, prove what they were brought to prove. They do by no means prove that there ever was any such covenant made between the Father and the Son.

'The conditions of the covenant are recorded: "Lo, I come to do Thy will"' (page 301). Nay; here is no mention of any covenant, nor anything from which it can be inferred. 'The recompense stipulated in this glorious treaty.' But I see not one word of the treaty itself; not can I possibly allow the existence of it without far other proof than this. 'Another copy of this grand treaty is recorded, Isa.xlix., from the 1st to the 6th verse' (*ibid.*) I have read them, but cannot find a word about it in all those verses. They contain neither more nor less than a prediction of the salvation of the Gentiles.

'By the covenant of works man was bound to obey in his own person' (page 302). And so he is under the covenant of grace; though not in order to his justification. 'The obedience of our Surety is accepted instead of our own.' This is neither a safe nor a scriptural way of speaking. I would simply say, 'We are accepted through the Beloved. We have redemption through His blood.'

'The second covenant was not made with Adam or any of his posterity, but with Christ, in those words, "The seed of the woman shall bruise the serpent's head"' (page 303). For any authority you have from these words, you might as well have said it was made with the Holy Ghost. These words were not spoken *to* Christ but *of* Him, and give not the least intimation of any such covenant as you plead for. They manifestly contain, if not a covenant made with, a promise made to Adam and all his posterity.

'Christ, we see, undertook to execute the conditions' (*ibid.*) We see no such thing in this text. We see here only a promise of a Saviour made by God to man.

'It is true I cannot fulfil the conditions' (*ibid.*) It is not true. The conditions of the new covenant are, 'Repent and believe'; and these you can fulfil through Christ strengthening you. 'It is equally true this is not required at my hands.' It is *equally* true – that is, absolutely false; and most dangerously false. If we allow this, Antinomianism comes in with a full tide. 'Christ has performed all that was conditionary for me.' Has He repeated and believed for you? You endeavour to evade this by saying, 'He performed all that was conditionary in the covenant of works.' This is nothing to the purpose; for we are not talking of that, but of the covenant of grace. Now, He did not perform all that was conditionary in this covenant unless He repented and believed. 'But he did unspeakably more'. It may be me; but He did not do this.

'But if Christ's perfect obedience be ours, we have no more need of pardon than Christ Himself' (page 308). The consequence is good. You have started an objection which you cannot answer. You say indeed, 'Yes, we do need pardon; for in many things we offend all.' What then? If His obedience be sure, we still perfectly obey in Him.

'Both the branches of the law, the perceptive and the penal, in the case of guilt contracted must be satisfied' (page 309). Not so. 'Christ by His death alone' (so our Church teaches) 'fully satisfied for the sins of the whole world.' The same great truth is manifestly taught in the Thirty-First Article. Is it therefore fair, is it honest, for any one to plead the Articles of our Church in defence of Absolute Predestination, seeing the Seventeenth Article barely defines the term without either affirming or denying the thing, whereas the Thirty-first totally overthrows and razes it from the foundation?

'Believers who are notorious transgressors in themselves have a sinless obedience in Christ' (*ibid.*) Oh syren song! Pleasing sound to James Wheatley, Thomas Williams, James Relly!

I know not one sentence in the Eleventh Dialogue which is liable to exception; but that grand doctrine of Christianity. Original Sin, is therein proved by irrefragable arguments.

The Twelfth likewise is unexceptionable, and contains such an illustration of the wisdom of God in the structure of the human body as I believe cannot be paralleled in either ancient or modern writers.

The former part of the Thirteenth Dialogue is admirable: to the latter I have some objection.

'Elijah failed in his resignation, and even Moses spoke unadvisedly with his lips' (vol.ii.p.44). It is true; but if you could likewise fix some blot upon venerable Samuel and beloved Daniel, it would prove nothing. For no Scripture teaches that the holiness of Christians is to be measured by that of any Jew.

'Do not the best of men frequently feel disorder in their affections? Do not they often complain, "When I would do good, evil is present with me"?' (page 46). I believe not. You and I are only able to answer for ourselves. 'Do not they say "We groan, being burthened with the workings of inbred corruption"?' You know this is not the meaning of the text. The whole context shows the cause of that groaning was their longing 'to be with Christ'.

'The cure' of sin 'will be perfected in heaven' (page 47). Nay; surely in paradise, if no sooner. 'This is a noble prerogative of the beatific vision.' No; it will then come too late. If sin remains in us till the day of judgement, it will remain for ever. 'Our present blessedness does not consist in being free from sin.' I really think it does; but whether it does or no, if we are not free from sin, we are not Christian believers; for to all these the Apostle declares, 'Being made free from sin, ye are become the servants of righteousness' (Rom.vi.18).

'If we were perfect in piety' (St John's word is 'perfect in love'), 'Christ's priestly office would be superseded.' No; we should still need His Spirit, and consequently His intercession, for the continuance of that love from moment to moment. Beside, we should still be encompassed with infirmities and liable to mistakes, from which words or actions might follow, even though the heart was all love, which were not exactly right. Therefore in all these respects we should still have need of Christ's priestly office; and therefore, as long as he remains in the body, the greatest saint may say,

'Every moment, Lord, I need
The merit of Thy death'

The text cited from Exodus asserts nothing less than that iniquity 'cleaves to all our holy things till death'.

'Sin remains, that the righteousness of faith may have its due honour' (page 48). And will righteousness of faith have its due honour no longer than sin remains in us? Then it must remain not only on earth and in paradise but in heaven also. 'And the sanctification of the Spirit its proper esteem.' Would it not have more esteem if it were a perfect work?

'It' (sin) 'will make us lowly in our own eyes' (*ibid.*) What! will pride make us lowly? Surely the utter destruction of pride would do this more effectually. 'It will make us compassionate.' Would not an entire renewal in the image of God make us much more so? 'It will teach us to admire the riches of grace.' Yea; but a fuller experience of it, by a thorough sanctification of spirit, soul, and body, will make us admire it more. 'It will reconcile us to death.' Indeed it will not; nor will anything do this like perfect love.

'It will endear the blood and intercession of Christ' (page 49). Nay; these can never be so dear to any as to those who experience their full virtue, who are 'filled with the fullness' of God. Nor can any 'feel their continual need' of Christ or 'rely on Him' in the manner which these do.

'The claims of the law are all answered' (Dialogue 14, p.57). If so, Count Einzendorf is absolutely in the right: neither God nor man can claim any obedience to it. Is not this Antinomianism without a mask?

'Your sins are expiated through the death of Christ, and a righteousness given you by which you have free access to God' (page 59). This is not scriptural language. I would simply say, 'By Him we have access to the Father'.

There are many other expressions in this Dialogue to which I have the same objection – namely (1) that they are unscriptural; (2) that they directly lead to Antinomianism.

The First Letter contains some very useful heads of self-examination. In the Second I read, 'There is a righteousness which supplies all that the creature needs. To prove this momentous point is the design of the following sheets.' (Page 91.)

I have seen such terrible effects of this unscriptural way of speaking, even on those 'who had once clean escaped from the pollutions of the world,' that I cannot but earnestly wish you would speak no otherwise than do the oracles of God. Certainly this *mode of expression* is not *momentous*. It is always dangerous, often fatal.

'Where sin abounded, grace did much more abound; that as sin had reigned unto death, so might grace,' the free love of God, 'reign through righteousness,' through our justification and sanctification, 'unto eternal life' (Rom.v.20-1). This is the plain, natural meaning of the words. It does not appear that one word is spoken here about imputed righteousness; neither in the passages cited in the next page from the Common Prayer and the Articles. In the Homily likewise that phrase is not found at all, and the main stress is laid on Christ's shedding His blood. Nor is the *phrase* (concerning the *thing* there is no question) found in any part of the Homilies. (Letter 3, p.93.)

'If the Fathers are not explicit with regard to the imputation of active righteousness, they abound in passages which evince the substitution of Christ in our stead – passages which disclaim all dependence on any duties of our own and fix our hopes wholly on the merits of our Saviour. When this is the case, I am very little solicitous about any particular forms of expression' (page 101), O lay aside, then, those questionable, dangerous forms, and keep closely to the scriptural!

'The authority of our Church and of those eminent divines' (Letter 4, p.105) does not touch those 'particular forms of expression'; neither do any of the texts which you afterwards cite. As to the doctrine we are agreed.

'The righteousness of God signifies the righteousness which God-Man wrought out' (*ibid.*) No; it signifies God's method of justifying sinners.

'The victims figured the expiation by Christ's death; the clothing with skins, the imputation of His righteousness' (page 107). That does not appear. Did not the one rather figure our justification, the other our sanctification?

Almost every text quoted in this and the following letter in support of that particular form of expression is distorted above measure from the plain, obvious meaning which is pointed out by the context. I shall instance in a few, and just set down their true meaning without any farther remarks (page 109).

To 'show unto man His uprightness,' to convince him of God's justice in so punishing him.

'He shall receive the blessing,' pardon, 'from the Lord, and righteousness,' holiness, 'from the God of his salvation'; the God who saveth him both from the guilt and from the power of sin (page 110).

I will 'make mention of Thy righteousness only.' Of Thy mercy; so the word frequently means in the Old Testament. So it unquestionably means in that text, 'In' or by 'Thy righteousness shall they be exalted' (page 111).

'Sion shall be redeemed with judgement,' after severe punishment, 'and her converts with righteousness,' with the tender mercy of God following that punishment (page 112).

'In,' or through, 'the Lord I have righteousness and strength,' justification and sanctification; 'He hath clothed me with the garments of salvation,' saved me from the guilt and power of sin: both of which are again expressed by, 'He hath covered me with the robe of righteousness' (page 113).

'My righteousness,' My mercy, 'shall not be abolished' (page 114).

'To make reconciliation for iniquity,' to atone for all our sins, 'and to bring in everlasting righteousness,' spotless holiness into our souls. And this righteousness is not human, but divine. It is the gift and the work of God (page 116).

'The Lord our Righteousness,' the author both of our justification and sanctification (page 117).

'What righteousness shall give us peace at the last day, inherent or imputed? (page 127). Both. Christ died for us and lives in us, 'that we may have boldness in the day of judgement.'

'That have obtained like precious faith through the righteousness,' the mercy, 'of our Lord.' 'Seek ye the kingdom of God and His righteousness,' the holiness which springs from God reigning in you (Letter 5, p.131).

'Therein is revealed the righteousness of God,' God's method of justifying sinners (page 132).

'We establish the law, as we expect no salvation without a perfect conformity to it – namely, by Christ' (page 135).

Is not this a mere quibble? and a quibble which, after all the laboured evasions of Witsius[1] and a thousand more, does totally 'make void the law'? But not so does St Paul teach. According to him, 'without holiness,' personal holiness, 'so man shall see the Lord'; none who is not himself conformed to the law of God here 'shall see the Lord' in glory.

This is the grand, palpable objection to that whole scheme. It directly 'makes void the law.' It makes thousands content to live and die 'transgressors of the law,' because Christ fulfilled it 'for them.' Therefore, though I believe He hath lived and died for me, yet I would speak very tenderly and sparingly of the former (and never separately from the latter) even as sparingly as do the Scriptures, for fear of this dreadful consequence.

'"The gift of righteousness" must signify a righteousness not their own' (page 138). Yes; it signifies the righteousness or holiness which God gives to and works in them.

'"The obedience of one" is Christ's actual performance of the whole law' (page 139). So here His passion is fairly left out! Whereas His 'becoming obedient unto death' – that is, dying for man – is certainly the chief part, if not the whole, which is meant by that expression.

'"That the righteousness of the law might be fulfilled" in us – that is, by our representative in our nature' (*ibid.*) Amazing! But this, you say, 'agrees with the tenor of the Apostle's arguing. For he is demonstrating we cannot be justified by our own conformity to the law.' No; not here. He is not speaking here of the cause of our justification, but the fruits of it. Therefore that unnatural sense of his words does not at all 'agree with the tenor of his arguing.'

I totally deny the criticism on δικαιοσυνη and δικαιωμα cannot conceive on what authority it is founded. Oh how deep an aversion to inward holiness does this scheme naturally create! (Page 140).

'The righteousness they attained could not be any personal

---

1.   Hermann Witsius (1636-1708), Professor at Utrecht and then at Leyden. His principal work, *De Oeconomia Foederum Deicum Hominibus* 1677, sought unsuccessfully to mediate between the Orthodox and the Federalists.

righteousness' (page 142). Certainly it was: it was implanted as well as imputed.

'For "instruction in righteousness," in the righteousness of Christ' (page 145). Was there ever such a comment before? The plain meaning is, 'for training up in holiness' of heart and of life.

'He shall convince the world of righteousness'; that I am not a sinner, but innocent and holy (page 146).

'"That we might be made the righteousness of God in Him." Not intrinsically, but imputatively' (page 148). Both the one and the other. God through Him first accounts and then makes us righteous. Accordingly, '"the righteousness which is of God by faith" is both imputed and inherent' (page 152).

'My faith fixes on both the meritorious life and atoning death of Christ' (page 153). Here we clearly agree. Hold, then, to this, and never talk of the former without the latter. If you do, you cannot say, 'Here we are exposed to no hazard.'

Yes, you are to an exceeding great one, even the hazard of living and dying without holiness. And then we are lost for ever.

The Sixth Letter contains an admirable account of the earth and atmosphere, and comprises abundance of sense in a narrow compass, expressed in beautiful language.

Gems have 'a seat on the virtuous fair one's breast' (page 177). I cannot reconcile this with St Paul. He says, 'Not with pearls'; by a parity of reason, not with diamonds. But in all things I perceive you are too favourable, both to 'the desire of the flesh and the desire of the eye.' You are a gentle casuist as to every self-indulgence which a plentiful fortune can furnish.

'Our Saviour's obedience' (page 182). Oh say, with the good old Puritans, 'Our Saviour's death or merits'! We swarm with Antinomians on every side. Why are you at such pains to increase their number?

'My mouth shall show forth Thy righteousness and Thy salvation'; Thy mercy, which brings my salvation (page 194).

The Eighth Letter is an excellent description of the supreme greatness of Christ. I do not observe one sentence in it which I cannot cheerfully subscribe to.

The Ninth Letter, containing a description of the sea, with various inferences deduced therefrom, is likewise a masterpiece for justness of sentiment as well as beauty of language. But I doubt whether 'mere shrimps' (page 241) be not too low an expression; and whether you might not as well have said nothing of 'God, the standing repast of Lent,' or concerning 'the exquisite relish of turbot or the deliciousness of sturgeon.' Are not such observations beneath the dignity of a minister of Christ? I have the same doubt concerning what is said of 'delicately flavoured tea, finely scented coffee, the friendly bowl, the pyramid of Italian figs, and the pastacia nut of Aleppo' (page 264). Beside that, the mentioning these in such a manner is a strong encouragement of luxury and sensuality. And does the world need this? The English in particular! *si non insaniunt satis suasponte, instiga.*[2]

'Those treasures which spring from the imputation of Christ's righteousness' (Letter 10, p.271). Not a word of His atoning blood! Why do so many men love to speak of His righteousness rather than His atonement? I fear because it affords a fairer excuse for their own unrighteousness. To cut off this, is it not better to mention both together – at least, never to name the former without the latter?

'Faith is a persuasion that Christ has shed His blood for me and fulfilled all righteousness in my stead' (page 285). I can by no means subscribe to this definition. There are hundreds, yes thousands, of true believers who never once thought one way or the other of Christ's fulfilling all righteousness in their stead. I personally know many who to this very hour have no idea of it, and yet have each of them a divine evidence and conviction. 'Christ loved me, and gave Himself for me.' This is St Paul's account of faith; and it is sufficient. He that thus believes is justified.

'It is a sure means of purifying the heart, and never fails to work by love' (page 287). It surely purifies the heart – if we abide in it; but not if

---

2.   Terence's *Andria*. iv.ii.9: 'If they do not rave enough of their own accord, stir them up.'

we 'draw back to perdition'. It never fails to work by love while it continues; but if itself fail, farewell both love and good works.

'Faith is the hand which receives all that is laid up in Christ.' Consequently, if we make 'shipwreck of the faith,' how much soever is laid up in Christ, from that hour we receive nothing.

'Faith in the imputed righteousness of Christ is a fundamental principle in the gospel' (Letter 11, p.288). If so, what becomes of all those who think nothing about imputed righteousness? How many who are full of faith and love, if this be true, must perish everlastingly!

'Thy hands must urge the way of the deadly weapon through the shivering flesh till it be plunged in the throbbing heart' (page 297). Are not these descriptions far too strong? May they not occasion unprofitable reasonings in many readers? *Ne pueros coram populo Medea trucidet.*[3]

'How can he justify it to the world?' (page 298). Not at all. Can this, then, justify his faith to the world?

'You take the certain way to obtain comfort – the righteousness of Jesus Christ' (page 304). What, without the atonement? Strange fondness for an unscriptural, dangerous mode of expression!

'So the merits of Christ are derived to all the faithful' (page 306). Rather the fruits of the Spirit, which are likewise plainly typified by the oil in Zechariah's vision.

'Has the law any demand? It must go to Him for satisfaction' (page 310). Suppose, 'Thou shalt love thy neighbour as thyself'; then I am not obliged to love my neighbour: Christ has satisfied the demand of the law for me. Is not this the very quintessence of Antinomianism?

'The righteousness wrought out by Jesus Christ is wrought out for all His people, to be the cause of their justification and the purchase of their salvation. The righteousness is the cause and the purchase' (page 311). So the death of Christ is not so much as named! 'For all His people.' But what becomes of all other people? They must inevitably perish for ever. The die was cast or ever they were in being. The doctrine to pass them by

---

3. Horace's *Ars Poetica*.1. 185: 'Medea must not slay her children in the presence of the people.'

has

> Consigned their unborn souls to hell,
> And damned them from their mother's womb![4]

I could sooner be a Turk, a Deist, yes an Atheist, than I could believe this. It is less absurd to deny the very being of God than to make Him an almighty tyrant.

'The whole world and all its seasons are rich with our Creator's goodness. His tender mercies are over all His works' (page 318). Are they over the bulk of mankind? Where is His goodness to the non-elect? How are His tender mercies over them? 'His temporal blessings are given to them.' But are they to them blessings at all? Are they not all curses? Does not God know they are? that they will only increase their damnation? Does not He design they should? And this you call goodness; this is tender mercy!

'May we not discern pregnant proofs of goodness in each individual object?' (page 321). No; on your scheme, not a spark of it, in this world or the next, to the far greater part of the work of His own hands.

'Is God a generous benefactor to the meanest animals, to the lowest reptiles? And will He deny my friend what is necessary to his present comfort and his final acceptance?' (page 334). Yea, will He deny it to any soul that He has made? Would you deny it to any, if it were in your power?

> But if you loved whom God abhorred,
> The servant were above his Lord.[5]

'The "wedding garment" here means holiness' (page 337).

'This is His tender complaint, "They will not come unto Me!"' (page 340). Nay, that is not the case; they cannot. He Himself has decreed not to give them that grace without which their coming is impossible.

'The grand end which God proposes in all His favourable dispensations to fallen man is to demonstrate the sovereignty of His grace.' Not so: to impart happiness to His creatures is His grand end herein. Barely to

---

4. *Poetical Works of J. and C. Wesley. (Hymns on God's Everlasting Love) iii.33.*
5. *Ibid.* (iii, 39.)

demonstrate his sovereignty is a principle of action fit for the great Turk, not the Most High God.

'God hath pleasure in the prosperity of His servants. He is a boundless ocean of good' (page 341). Nay, that ocean is far from boundless, if it wholly passes by nine-tenths of mankind.

'You cannot suppose God would enter into a fresh covenant with a rebel' (page 342). I both suppose and know He did. 'God made the new covenant with Christ, and charged Him with the performance of the conditions.' I deny both these assertions, which are the central point wherein Calvinism and Antinomianism meet. '"I have made a covenant with My chosen"' namely, with 'David My servant.' So God Himself explains it.

'He will wash you in the blood which atones and invest you with the righteousness which justified' (page 362). Why should you thus continually put asunder what God has joined?

'God Himself at the last day pronounces them righteous because they are interested in the obedience of the Redeemer' (page 440). Rather because they are washed in His blood and renewed by His Spirit.

Upon the whole, I cannot but wish that the plan of those Dialogues had been executed in a different manner. Most of the grand truths of Christianity are herein both explained and proved with great strength and clearness. Why was anything intermixed which could prevent any serious Christian's recommending them to all mankind? Anything which must necessarily render them exceptionable to so many thousands of the children of God? In practical writings I studiously abstain from the very shadow of controversy; nay, even in controversial I do not knowingly write one line to which any but my opponent would object. For opinions, shall I destroy the work of God? Then am I a bigot indeed. Much more, if I would not drop any mode of expression rather than offend either Jew or Gentile or the Church of God – I am, with great sincerity, dear sir,

Your affectionate brother and servant.

APPENDIX TWO

THE SCARBOROUGH EIRENICON[1]

Scarborough, 19 April 1764.

REVEREND SIR,

Near two years and a half ago, I wrote the following letter. You will please to observe (1) that I propose no more therein than is the bounden duty of every Christian: (2) that *you* may comply with this proposal, whether any other does or not. I myself have endeavoured so to do for many years, though I have been almost alone therein, and although many, the more earnestly I talk of peace, the more zealously make themselves ready for the battle. -

I am, reverend sir,

Yours affectionate brother,

DEAR SIR,

It has pleased God to give you both the will and the power to do many things for His glory; although you are often ashamed you have done so little, and wish you could do a thousand times more. This induces me to mention to you what has been upon my mind for many years, and what I

---

1. Wesley J. *Letters* (Standard ed., Vol.4, pp.235-39.)

am persuaded would be much for the glory of God if it could once be effected: and I am in great hopes it will be, if you heartily undertake it, trusting in Him alone.

Some years since, God began a great work in England: but the labourers were few. At first those few were of one heart; but it was not so long. First one fell off, then another and another, till two of us were left together in the work besides my brother and me. This prevented much good, and occasioned much evil. It grieved our spirits and weakened our hands; it gave our common enemies huge occasion to blaspheme. It perplexed and puzzled many sincere Christians; it caused many to draw back to perdition; it grieved the Holy Spirit of God.

As labourers increased, disunion increased. Offences were multiplied; and, instead of coming nearer to, they stood farther off from each other till at length those who were not only brethren in Christ but fellow labourers in His Gospel had no more connexion or fellowship with each other than Protestants and Papists.

But ought this to be? Ought not those who are united to one common Head and employed by Him in one common work to be united to each other? I speak now of those labourers who are ministers of the Church of England. These are chiefly:

Mr Perronet, Romaine, Newton, Shirley;
Mr Downing, Jesse, Adam;
Mr Talbot, Riland, Stillingfleet, Fletcher;
Mr Johnson, Baddiley, Andrews, Jane;
Mr Hart, Symes, Brown, Rouguet;
Mr Sellon, (Cooper, Harmer, Owen);
Mr Venn, Richardson, Burnett, Furly;
Mr Conyers, Bentley, King;
Mr Berridge, Hicks, John Wesley, Charles Wesley, John Richardson, Benjamin Colley:[2] not excluding any other clergyman who agrees in these

---

2.   The Editor of the *Standard Letters* (Vol.4, p.237) mentions Mr Crook, Mr Eastwood and "G.W." Edward Perronet adds, 'Cooper, Harmer, Owen.'

essentials -
 I.   Original Sin.
 II. Justification by Faith.
 III. Holiness of Heart and Life, provided their life be answerable to
their doctrine.

'But what union would you desire among these?' Not an union in
opinions: they might agree or disagree touching absolute decrees on the
one hand and perfection on the other. Not an union in expressions: these
may still speak of the imputed righteousness and those of the merits of
Christ. Not an union with regard to outward order; some may still remain
quite regular, some quite irregular, and some partly regular and partly
irregular. But, these things being as they are, as each is persuaded in his
own mind, is it not a most desirable thing that we should –

> 1. Remove hindrances out of the way? not judge one another,
>   not despise one another, not envy one another? not be
>   displeased at one another's gifts or success, even though
>   greater than our own? not wait for one another's halting,
>   much less wish for it or rejoice therein?
>   Never speak disrespectfully, slightly, coldly, or unkindly
>   of each other? never respect each other's faults, mistakes,
>   or infirmities, much less listen for and gather them up?
>   never say or do anything to hinder each other's usefulness
>   either directly or indirectly?
>   Is it not a most desirable thing that we should –
> 2. Love as brethren? think well of and honour one another?
>   wish all good, all grace, all gifts, all success, yea greater
>   than our own, to each other? expect God will answer our
>   wish, rejoice in every appearance thereof, and praise Him
>   for it? readily believe good of each other, as readily as we
>   once believed evil?
>   Speak respectfully, honourably, kindly of each other?
>   defend each other's character? speak all the good we can of
>   each other? recommend one another where we have

influence? each help the other in his work, and enlarge his
influence by all the honest means he can?

This is the union which I have long sought after; and is it not the duty
of every one of us to do so? Would it not be far better for ourselves? a
means of promoting both our holiness and happiness? Would it not
remove such guilt from those who have been faulty in any of these
instances? and much pain from those who have kept themselves pure?
Would it not be far better for the people, who suffer severely from the
clashings and contentions of their leaders, which seldom fail to occasion
many unprofitable, yea hurtful, disputes among them? Would it not be
better even for the poor, blind world, robbing them of their sport, 'Oh
they cannot agree among themselves'? Would it not be better for the
whole work of God which would then deepen and widen on every side?

'But it will never be; it is utterly impossible.' Certainly it is with men.
Who imagines we can do this? that it can be effected by any human
power? All nature is against it, every infirmity, every wrong temper and
passion; love of honour and praise, of power, of pre-eminence; anger,
resentment, pride; long-contracted habit, and prejudice lurking in ten
thousand forms. The devil and his angels are against it. For if this takes
place, how shall his kingdom stand? All the world, all that know not God,
are against it, though they may seem to favour it for a season. Let us
settle this in our hearts, that we may be utterly cut off from all dependence
on our own strength or wisdom.

But surely 'with God all things are possible'; therefore 'all things are
possible to him that believeth': and this union is proposed only to them
that believe, that show their faith by their works.

When Mr Conyers was objecting the impossibility of ever effecting
such an union, I went upstairs, and after a little prayer, opened Kempis
on these words: *Expecta Dominum: Viriliter age; Noli diffidere: Noli
discedere; sed corpus et animam expone constanter pro gloria Dei.*[3]

Your affectionate servant.

---

3.   Imitation III.xxxv.3. 'Wait for the Lord. Quit thyself like a man. Yield not to
     distrust. Be unwilling to depart (desert); but constantly expose body and soul for
     the glory of God.'

APPENDIX THREE

THE ATTENDANCE AT WESLEY'S CONFERENCES OF CALVINISTIC EVANGELICALS: 1744-1758[1]

Year	Place	Name	Position
1744	London	John Hodges	Vicar of Wenvoe[2]
1745	Bristol	John Hodges	" " "
1746	Bristol	John Hodges	" " "
1747	London	Howell Harris (layman)	-----
1748	London	Nil (Beginning)	-----
		Howell Harris (added)	-----
		Friday, June 3.	
1749	London	Nil	-----
1750	Bristol	No Record	
1751	Bristol	No Record	
1752	Limerick	Nil	
1753	Leeds	William Grimshaw	Vicar of Haworth

---

1. No record is given for Conferences after this date of members attending. An exception is 1762 when William Romaine attended (Leeds).
2. It is a matter of conjecture as to whether or not Hodges became a Calvinist. His friendship with Wesley waned later on, though Hodges had become a Mystic.
   For Calvinistic Evangelicals attending the 1771 Conference, see the list of these who were self-invited given in Chapter Eleven during the 'Minute Controversy'.

1754	London	No Record	
1755	Leeds	William Grimshaw	Vicar of Haworth
1756	Bristol	No Record	
1757	London	No Record	
1758	Bristol	Nil	

BIBLIOGRAPHY

(i) *Primary Sources*

The Works of the Reverend John Wesley (Edited by Joseph Benson), 16 Volumes. (London, 1809.) [Abbreviated: J.W.W.]

The Journal of John Wesley (Standard Edition. Edited by Nehemiah Curnock), 8 Volumes. (London, 1938.) [Abbreviated: J.W.J.]

The Letters of John Wesley (Standard Edition. Edited by John Telford), 8 Volumes. (London, 1931.) [Abbreviated: J.W.L.]

The Standard Sermons of John Wesley (Edited by E.H. Sugden), 2 Volumes. (London, 1933.) [Abbreviated J.W.S.]

Notes on the New Testament by John Wesley, MA (London.)

A Plain Account of Christian Perfection by John Wesley. (Modern Edition.) (London, 1960.)

The Journal of Charles Wesley (1736-9) (Edited by John Telford.) (London, 1909.) [Abbreviated C.W.J. 1736-9.]

Minutes of the Methodist Conference from the First held in London by the late Revd John Wesley, MA in the year 1744 (Vol.1, London, 1862.) [Abbreviated: 'Minutes'.]

Handbook and Index to the Minutes of the Conference, 1744-1890. (London, 1890.)

The Bennet Minutes of the Conferences of 1744, 1745, 1747 and 1748 with those of Wesley for 1746 (Wesley Historical Society, London, 1896.) [Abbreviated: Bennet Minutes.]

The Poetical Works of John and Charles Wesley (Edited by George Osborn), 13 Volumes. (London, 1868-72.)

* * * * * * *

Adam, Thomas:　*Private Thoughts on Religion* (Glasgow, 1824.)

Berridge, John:　*The Christian World Unmasked; Pray, Come and Peep* (London, 1850.)

Burnet, Gilbert:　*History of His own Time,* 4 Volumes (London, 1766.)
Burnet, Gilbert:　*An Exposition of the XXXIX Articles of the Church of England* (Oxford, 1796.)

Calvin, John:　*Institutes of the Christian Religion* (Translated by Henry Beveridge), 2 Volumes (London, 1949.)

Doddridge, Philip: *Rise and Progress of Religion in the Soul* (London, 1745.)

Fletcher, John:　*The Whole Works of* (London, 1836.)

Furly, Samuel:　*Original Hymns* (edited) (London, 1776.)

Goodwin, John:　*A Treatise on Justification* (London.)

Hervey, James:　*The Works of,* 7 Volumes (London, 1787.)

Hervey, James: *Theron and Aspasio, Or a Series of Dialogues and Letters upon the Most Important and Interesting Subjects. In Three Volumes* (First Edition) (London, 1755.)

Hervey, James: *Meditations and Contemplations. With the Life of the Author, and a Sermon on His Death by the Revd Wm. Romaine, MA* (London, 1812, also 1803.)

Hervey James: *The Works of, containing Aspasio Vindicated. In Eleven Letters from Mr Hervey to Mr John Wesley, in answer to that Gentleman's Remarks on Theron and Aspasio. With Mr Wesley's Letter prefixed. To Which is Annexed: A Defence of Theron and Aspasio against the Objections contained in Mr Sandeman's Letters to the Author prefixed* (London, 1771.) [Abbreviated: *Aspasio Vindicated, 1771.*]

Hill, Richard: *A Conversation between Richard Hill, Esq., The Revd Mr Madan and Father Walsh, Superior of a convent of English Benedictine monks at Paris, held at the said convent, July 13, 1771, relative to some doctrinal Minutes advanced by the Revd Mr John Wesley and others at a Conference in London, August 7, 1770. To which are added some Remarks by the Editor, and also Mr Wesley's own Declaration concerning his Minutes, versified by another hand* (London, 1771.)

Hill, Richard: *An Answer to some capital errors contained in the Minutes* (London, 1771.)

Hill, Richard: *Five Letters to the Revd Mr Fletcher relative to his Vindication of the Minutes of the Revd Mr John Wesley* (London, 1771.)

Hill, Rowland: *Friendly Remarks occasioned by the spirit and doctrine contained in the Revd Mr Fletcher's*

Vindication and more particularly in his 'Second Check to Antinomianism' (London, 1772.)

Law, William: *A Practical Treatise upon Christian Perfection* 2nd Edition (London, 1728.)

Law, William: *A Serious Call to a Devout and Holy Life* 5th Edition (London, 1750.)

Marshall, W.:   *The Gospel Mystery of Sanctification* (London, 1692.)

Newton, John: *Out of the Depths: Autobiography of the Revd John Newton* (London, 1916.)

Newton, John: *Twenty-Six Letters on Religious Subjects by 'Omicron'* (London, 1775.)

Newton, John: *Memoirs of the Life of the late Revd William Grimshaw, AB with occasional reflections; inSix Letters to the Revd Henry Foster* (London, 1799.)

Newton, John: *Cardiphonia, or the Utterances of the Heart, in the Course of a Real Correspondence* (London, 1780.)

'Palaemon':   *Letters on Theron and Aspasio: To the author of that Work* (Edinburgh, 1757.)

'Philolethes':   *Aspasio Vindicated, and the Scripture Doctrine of Imputed Righteousness Defended against the Objections and Animadversions of the Revd Mr John Wesley. In Eleven Letters and prepared for the Press by the late Mr J– H– AB* (London, 1760.)

Romaine, William: *Treatise on the Life, Walk and Triumph of Faith* (Glasgow, 1838.)

Sellon, Walter: *An Answer to Aspasio Vindicated In Eleven Letters* said to be wrote (sic) by the late Revd Mr James Hervey (London, 1767.)

Sellon, Walter: *The Church of England Vindicated from the Charge of Absolute Predestination* (London, 1774.)

Sellon, Walter: *Arguments against the Doctrines of Predestination* (London, 1774.)

Sellon, Waler: *Defence of God's Sovereignty* (London, 1774.)

Shirley, Rt.Hon. Revd Walter: *Narrative of the Principal Circumstances relative to the Revd Mr Wesley's late Conference held in Bristol, August, 1771* (London, 1772.)

Simpson, David: *A Plea for Religion and The Sacred Writings addressed to The Disciples of Thomas Paine and Wavering Christians of every persuasion. With an Appendix etc.* (London, 1837.)

Toplady, A.M: *The Church of England Vindicated from the charge of Arminianism; and the case of Arminian subscription particularly considered; in a letter to Revd Dr Nowell. Occasioned by some Passages in that Gentleman's answer to Pietas Oxoniensis. By a Presbyter of the Church of England* (London, 1769.)

Toplady, A.M: *The Doctrine of Absolute Predestination stated and asserted; with a preliminary Discourse on the Divine Attributes, translated in great measure from the Latin of Jerome Zanchius* (London, 1769.)

Toplady, A.M: *A Letter to Revd Mr John Wesley relative to his pretended Abridgement of Zanchius on Predestination* (London, 1770.)

Toplady, A.M: *A Caveat against Unsound Doctrines: Being the Substance of a Sermon preached in the Parish Church of St Ann, Blackfriars, on Sunday, April 29, 1770.*

Toplady, A.M: *More Work for John Wesley: or a Vindication of the Decrees and Providence of God from the Defamations of a late printed paper, entitled, 'The Consequence Proved'* (London, 1772.)

Toplady, A.M: *Historical Proof of the Doctrinal Calvinism of the Church of England,* 2 Volumes (London, 1774.)

Toplady, A.M: *The Scheme of Christians and Philosophical Necessity asserted, in answer to Mr John Wesley's tract on that subject* (London, 1775.)

Toplady, A.M: *An Old Fox tarr'd and feathered* (London, 1775.)

Venn, Henry: *The Complete Duty of Man* (London, 1799.)

Walker, Samuel: *Christ The Purifier* (London, 1824.)

Walker, Samuel: *Fifty-Two Sermons on the baptismal Covenant,* 2 Volumes (London, 1763.)

Watts, Isaac: *The Works of* (Edited by G. Burder), 6 Volumes (London, 1810.)

Whitefield, George: *Journals* (Edited by Ian Murray) (London, 1960.) [Abbreviated G.W.J.]

Whitefield, George: *Sermons on Important Subjects* (Edited by S. Drew) (London, 1833.)

Whitefield, George: *Selected Sermons of George Whitefield* (Edited by J.C. Ryle and R. Elliot) (London, 1958 and London, 1960.)

Wilberforce, Wm: *A Practical View of the Prevailing Religious System contrasted with Real Christianity. With an introductory essay by Daniel Watson, DD* (Glasgow, 1841.)

(ii) *Secondary Sources*

Abbey, G.C. and
Overton, J.H: *The English Church in the Eighteenth Century* 2
                 Volumes (London, 1878.)

Ahier, Philip: *The Story of the Three Parish Churches of St Peter
                 The Apostle, Huddersfield* (Huddersfield, 1948.)

Andrews, J.R: *George Whitefield – A Light Rising in Obscurity*
                 (Kilmarnock, 1930.)

Baker, Eric W: *A Herald of the Evangelical Revival: A Critical
                 Enquiry into the Relation of William Law to John
                 Wesley and the Beginning of Methodism* (London,
                 1948.)

Baker, F.H: *William Grimshaw, 1708-1763* (London, 1963.)
Baker, F.H: *John Wesley and the Church of England* (London,
                 1970.)

Balleine, G.R: *A History of the Evangelical Party in the Church of
                 England* (London, 1951.)

Belden, A.E: *Whitefield, The Awakener* (London, 1950.)

Bennet, R: *The Early Life of Howell Harris* (translated from the
                 Welsh by Gomer M. Roberts) (London, 1962.)

Binns, L. Elliott: *The Early Evangelicals: A Religious and Social
                 Study* (London, 1953.)

Bretherton, F.F: *The Countess of Huntingdon* (Wesley Historical
                 Society Lecture No.6, London, 1940.)

Brown, Abner A: *Recollections of the Conversation Parties of the Revd Charles Simeon, MA* (London, 1863.)

Bull, Josiah: *John Newton* (2nd Edition, London, 1868.)

Carter, G.S: *The English Church in the Eighteenth Century* (Anglican Church Handbooks, London, 1910.)

Carus, W.:   *Memoirs of the Life of the Revd Charles Simeon, MA* (London, 1847.)

Cecil, Lord David: *The Stricken Deer, or the Life of Cowper* (London, 1933.)

Clarke, Adam: *Memoirs of the Wesley Family* (London, 1823.)

Collins, A. (Ed.):   *Typical English Churchmen* (London, 1902.)

Coomer, Duncan: *English Dissent under the Hanoverians* (London, 1946.)

Cox, Leo G: *John Wesley's Concept of Perfection* (Kansas City, 1964.)

Cragg, George C: *Grimshaw of Haworth* (Canterbury, 1948.)

Cragg, C.R: *From Puritanism to the Age of Reason* (London, 1959.)

Cragg, C.R: *The Church and the Age of Reason* (London, 1960.)

Dakin, A: *Calvinism* (Duckworth Theology Series, London, 1949.)

Davies, G.C.B: *The Early Cornish Evangelicals, 1735-60* (London, 1951.)

Davies, Rupert E: *Methodism* (Pelican Series, London, 1963.)

Davies, R.E. and
Rupp, E.G. (Eds.): *The History of the Methodist Church in Great Britain* (London, 1965.)

Dimond, S.G: *The Psychology of the Methodist Revival* (Oxford, 1926.)

Dimond, S.G: *The Psychology of Methodism* (London, 1932.)

Doughty, W.L: *John Wesley, His Conferences and His Preachers* (Wesley Historical Society Lecture No.10, London, 1944.)

Eayrs, George: *John Wesley, Christian Philosopher and Church Founder* (London, 1926.)

Edwards, Maldwyn:*Family Circle: A Study of the Epworth Household in Relation to John and Charles Wesley* (London, 1949.

Flew, R. Newton: *The Idea of Perfection in Christian Theology. An Historical Study of the Christian Ideal for the Present Life* (Oxford, 1934.)

Gill, F.C: *In the Steps of John Wesley* (London, 1962.)

Gillies, John: *Memoirs of the Life of the Reverend George Whitefield, MA* (London, 1772.)

Gledstone, J.P: *George Whitefield; Field Preacher* (London, 1901.)

Green, J. Brazier: *John Wesley and William Law* (London, 1945.)

Green, V.H: *The Young Mr Wesley; A Study of John Wesley and Oxford* (London, 1961.)

Greenwood, D.&A: *A History of Elland Church* (Huddersfield, 1954.)

Griffiths, E: *The Presbyterian Church of Wales* (Calvinistic Methodists. Historical Handbook, 1735-1905, Wrexham)

Guthrie, J: *Life of Arminius* (London, 1854.)

Hardy, R. Spence: *William Grimshaw: Incumbent of Haworth. 1742-1763* (London, 1860.)

Harrison, A.W: *Arminianism* (Duckworth Theology Series, London, 1937.)

Haweis, Thomas: *The Life of William Romaine, MA* (London, 1797.)

Hennell, M: *John Venn and The Clapham Sect* (London, 1958.)

Henson, H. Hensley: *Sibbes and Simeon: An Essay on Patronage* (London, 1932.)

Hockin, F: *John Wesley and Modern Methodism* (London, 1887.)

Hopkins, Mary A: *Hannah More and Her Circle* (New York, 1947.)

Houses of Shirley
and Hastings. A
Member of: *The Life and Times of Selina, Countess of Huntingdon,* 2 Volumes (London, 1841.)

Jackson, Thomas: *The Life of the Reverend Charles Wesley MA,* 2 Volumes (London, 1841.)

Jackson, Thomas: *Centenary of Wesleyan Methodism* (London, 1839.)

Jenkins, D.E: *Calvinistic Methodist Holy Orders* (Caernarvon, 1911.)

Kempis, Thomas À: *Imitation of Christ* (Challenor, London.)

Knox, R.A: *Enthusiasm* (Oxford, 1950.)

Lawson, A.B: *John Wesley and The Christian Ministry: The Sources and Development of His Opinions and Practice* (London, 1963.)

Lawton, George: *Shropshire Saint: A Study in the Ministry and Spirituality of Fletcher of Madeley* (Wesley Historical Society Lecture, London, 1960.)

Laycock, J.W: *Methodist Heroes in the Great Haworth Round, 1734-1784* (Keighley, 1909.)

Lindstrom, H: *Wesley and Sanctification: A Study in the Doctrine of Salvation* (London, 1956.)

Loane, Marcus L: *Oxford and the Evangelical Succession* (London, 1950.)

Loane, Marcus L: *Cambridge and the Evangelical Succession* (London, 1952.)

Monk, Robert C: *John Wesley; His Puritan Heritage. A Study of the Christian Life* (London, 1966.)

Moore, Henry: *The Life of the Revd John Wesley, AM,* 2 Volumes

(London, 1824.)

Moorman, J.H: *A History of the Church in England* (London, 1953.)

Moule, H.G.C: *Charles Simeon: Biography of a Sane Saint* (London, 1892. Modern edition: London, 1965.)
Moule, H.G.C: *The Evangelical School in the Church of England* (London, 1901.)

Myles, W: *A Chronological History of the People called Methodists* (London, 1813.)

Nicholas, James: *Calvinism and Arminianism Compared*, 2 Volumes (London, 1824.)

Nightingale, J: *Portraiture of Methodism* (London, 1807.)

Nuttall, G.E: *The Puritan Spirit* (London, 1967.)
Nuttall, G.E: *Howell Harris, 1714-1773. The Last Enthusiast* (Cardiff, 1965.)

Overton, J.H: *John Wesley* (London, 1891.)
Overton, J.H: *The Evangelical Revival in the Eighteenth Century* (London, 1885.)

Overton, J.H. &
Relton, F: *The English Church from the Accession of George I to the End of the Eighteenth Century. (1714-1800)* (London, 1906.)

Piette, M: *John Wesley in the Evolution of Protestantism* (London, 1937.)

Roberts, Q.R: *Howell Harris* (Wesley Historical Society Lecture

No.17, London, 1951.)

Ryle, J.G: *The Christian Leaders of England in the Eighteenth Century* (London, 1868.)

Ryle, J.G: *Five Christian Leaders of the 18th Century* (Popular abridgement of above, London, 1960.)

Sangster, W.E: *Path to Perfection: An Examination and Restatement of John Wesley's Doctrine of Christian Perfection.* (London, 1943.)

Schmidt, M: *The Young Wesley* (translated by Fletcher) (London, 1958.)

Schmidt, M: *John Wesley: A Theological Biography* (Volume 1 [translated by Goldhawk], London, 1962.)

Scott, John: *Life of the Revd T. Scott* (9th Edition [revised] London, 1836)

Sidney, Edwin: *The Life of the Revd Rowland Hill, AM* (London, 1834.)

Sidney, Edwin: *The Life and Ministry of the Revd Samuel Walker, BA of Truro* (2nd edition, London, 1838.)

Simon, J.S: *The Revival of Religion in England in The Eighteenth Century* (London)

Simon, J.S: *Studies of John Wesley,* 5 Volumes:
Vol.1. John Wesley and the Religious Societies (London, 1921.)
Vol.2. John Wesley and The Methodist Societies (2nd.edition, London, 1937.)
Vol.3. John Wesley and the Advance of Methodism (London, 1925.)

Vol.4. John Wesley: The Master Builder (London, 1927.)
Vol.5. John Wesley: The Last Phase (London, 1934.)

Simpson-Spurrow,
J.W: *John Wesley and The Church of England* (London, 1934.)

Smith, B: *Methodism in Macclesfield* (London, 1875.)

Smith, G: *History of Wesleyan Methodism,* 3 Volumes (London, 1858-1861)

Smyth, Charles: *Simeon and Church Order* (London, 1940.)

Snell, F.J: *Wesley and Methodism* (London, 1900.)

Southey, Robert: *The Life of Wesley and the Rise and Progress of Methodism* (Bohn, London, 1881.)

Stephen, James: *Essays in Ecclesiastical Biography* (London, 1875.)

Stevens, Abel: *The History of the Religious Movement of the Eighteenth Century called Methodism, to the Death of Wesley* (London, 1862.)

Sykes, Norman: *The English Religious Tradition* (London, 1953.)

Taylor, Isaac: *Wesley and Methodism* (London, 1851.)

Telford, John: *The Life of John Wesley* (London, 1953.)
Telford, John: *The Life of Charles Wesley, MA* (London, 1900.)
Toon, Peter: *Hyper-Calvinism, The Emergence of, in English Nonconformity, 1689-1765* (London, 1967.)

Towlson, C.W: *Moravian and Methodist: Relationships and Influences in the Eighteenth Century* (London, 1957.)

Townsend, W.J.,
Eayrs, G. &
Workman, H.B: *A New History of Methodism,* 2 Volumes (London, 1909.)

Tyerman, Luke: *The Life and Times of the Revd John Wesley, MA Founder of the Methodists* 3 Volumes (London, 1871-2.)
Tyerman, Luke: *Wesley's Designated Successor* (London, 1882.)
Tyerman, Luke: *The Life of George Whitefield of Pembroke College,* 2 Volumes (London, 1890.)
Tyerman: Luke: *The Oxford Methodists* (London, 1873.)

Tytler, Sarah: *The Countess of Huntingdon and Her Circle* (London, 1907.)

Urlin, R. Denny: *John Wesley's Place in Church History* (London. 1870.)
Urlin, R. Denny: *The Churchman's Life of Wesley* (London, 1880.)

Venn, John: *The Life and a Selection of Letters of Henry Venn, MA* (London, 1837.)

Vulliamy, C.E: *John Wesley* (London, 1931.)

Wakeman, Henry O: *An Introduction to the History of the Church of England: From the Earliest Times to the Present Day (Revised by S.L. Ollard with an additional chapter)* (London, 1920.)

Warren, M.A.C: *Charles Simeon* (Great Churchman Series, No.vi,

London, 1950.)

Watson, R: *The Life of the Revd John Wesley, MA* (London, 1839.)

Wedgewood, Julia: *John Wesley and the Evangelical Revival of the Eighteenth Century* (London, 1870.)

Whitehead, J: *The Life of Wesley,* 2 Volumes (London, 1793-6.)

Williams, Colin W: *John Wesley's Theology To-day* (London, 1960.)

Wood, A. Skevington: *Thomas Haweis, 1734-1820* (London, 1957.)

Woodward, Dr. J: *Account of the Religious Societies in the City of London*

Wright, Thomas: *The Life of Augustus Montague Toplady* (London, 1911.)

Yates, Arthur S: *The Doctrine of Assurance, with Special reference to John Wesley* (London, 1952.)

* * * * * * *

Unpublished Secondary Source

Pask, A.H.S: *The Influence of Arminius on the Theology of John Wesley.*
(Unpublished Ph.D. Thesis for Edinburgh University, 1937.)

* * * * * * *

(iii) *Reference Works*

The Clergyman's Assistant, Or a Collection of Acts of Parliament, Forms and Ordinances, Relative to Certain Duties and Rights of the Parochial Clergy etc. (Oxford, 1808.)
Dictionary of English Church History Edited by Ollard, S.L. and Cross, G. (London, 1912.)

Encyclopaedia of Religion and Ethics Edited by Hastings, J. (14 Volumes, Edinburgh, 1908-1920.)

The Oxford Dictionary of National Biography
Concise Edition (1903.)

The Oxford Dictionary of the Christian Church.
Edited by Cross, F.L. (1958.)

Sermons or Homilies Appointed to be read in Churches in the Time of Queen Elizabeth of Famous Memory (London, 1824.)

* * * * * * *

(iv) *Periodicals*

The Methodist (or *Arminian Magazine*) (First Published 1778.)

The Gospel Magazine (First published 1770.)

Proceedings of the Wesley Historical Society (First published 1893) [Abbreviated W.H.S. Proc.]

The Bulletin of the Evangelical Library, London.

INDEX

399

John Wesley